Introduction to Computer Data Processing

Introduction to Computer

Harcourt Brace Jovanovich, Inc.

New York   Chicago   San Francisco   Atlanta

Margaret S. Wu

University of Iowa

Data Processing

Introduction to Computer Data Processing
Margaret S. Wu

COVER picture © Jean Michel Folon, John Locke Studio and Société de Traitement Automatique des Données

ISBN: 0-15-541631-6

Library of Congress Catalog Card Number: 75-855

Printed in the United States of America

Picture Credits appear on p. 453.

To Shih Yen, Jennifer, and Gregory

Preface

Today computers touch the lives of nearly everyone. Thus, it is essential that we alert ourselves to the possibilities and implications of this basic tool, which has extended our ability to cope with vast amounts of data and perform repetitive and extensive calculations. Although predictions of the computer's role in our future may, at times, strain our credibility, it is often astonishing to realize even the present degree of involvement of computers in our everyday world.

Introduction to Computer Data Processing is designed for an introductory course in data processing. The book presents an overall view of the computer and its applications, focusing on fundamental concepts of computer hardware and software rather than on detailed descriptions of a particular computer or programming language.

Chapters 1 and 2 place the computer in historical perspective and give its current role in a variety of applications; Chapter 22 discusses the computer's place in our society. Chapter 3 explains the binary, octal, and hexadecimal number systems; Chapter 4 introduces punched card equipment. (Because many small data processing installations are turning to the use of minicomputers rather than punched card equipment, some instructors may wish to omit Chapter 4.) Chapters 5, 6, 7, and 9 introduce the hardware and software of the computer; data input, output, and storage devices are discussed and compared. Chapter 8 presents data entry devices while Chapter 10 discusses minicomputers. Chapters 11 through 18 consider the use of the computer from the start to the finish of a problem: problem design, choice of a language, testing of the programming system, and other elements that must be combined to make a successful computer system. Features of FORTRAN AND COBOL—the two most popular programming languages—are discussed; PL/I is also treated in some detail. COBOL and PL/I are compared with FORTRAN. This wide range of material is not designed to teach the student how to program but to give an appreciation of the role of high-level languages and the merits of each. Chapters 19, 20, and 21 present information on the management of computer centers and computer personnel. In addition, BASIC and RPG II programming languages are discussed in appendixes. A glossary of data processing terms is also provided for easy reference.

I wish to acknowledge the many people who assisted in the preparation of this book. I wish to thank Captain Grace M. Hopper and Dr. John Atanasoff for supplying information; Professor Thomas G. De Lutis, Ohio State University, and Professor Edwin Towster, University of Southwestern Louisiana, for their careful reading of the initial manuscript; and the representatives of various computer manufacturers, particularly Mr. Howard Soroos of IBM, and Mr. David R. Paul of UNIVAC, for their assistance. I wish to thank Professor Harold Shipton, University of Iowa, for his encouragement in the initial undertaking. This text was begun while the author was employed at the Bioengineering Resource Facility, University of Iowa.

Margaret S. Wu

Contents

CONTENTS

Introduction to Computer Data Processing

The Evolution of Computers

Today we live in a highly developed, sophisticated world where men travel to the moon and bring back samples of moon rock, television pictures are transmitted by satellite to distant locations around the earth, and nuclear plants supply a portion of our electricity. Although we marvel at these human achievements, we ignore the complexity and wonder of our everyday existence. At the click of a switch, we turn on the lights in a room. Our houses are comfortably heated by fuel and the internal temperature regulated by a thermostat. The cars most of us drive were manufactured on assembly lines many miles from where we live. The gasoline for their engines was refined at a distant location and transported to a gas station near our home. These are among the numerous instances of services and goods supplied to us by others. The outstanding attribute of modern society consists in such interdependence.

These technological accomplishments would be for naught without the modern miracle of marketing and the distribution of goods and services. And this massive handling of products would not be economically possible without the use of modern data-processing techniques. To function successfully, a modern business firm must record, process, and analyze large amounts of information. For example, an electric company must bill its customers for their use of electricity; a bank must maintain accurate records of all customer accounts and issue monthly statements for checking accounts. All levels of government — local, state, and federal — are similarly involved with the retention of data and its manipulation. The federal government, for example, must process income-tax returns, verify the accuracy of calculations, check the truth of statements made by taxpayers, and issue any refunds due. Data processing encompasses all these activities. We can define *data processing* as the manipulation of data, the retention of data, and its subsequent retrieval. The term *data* means any meaningful facts or figures. A list of data pertinent to an individual, for example, may include:

name,
Social Security number,
birthdate,
place of birth,
street address, city, and state of residence,
citizenship,
marital status,
height, and
weight.

For some purposes, of course, certain data, such as a person's place of birth, may not be relevant.

COMPUTER DATA PROCESSING

Data processing may be accomplished in any one of four ways: manually, mechanically, electronically, or by a synthesis of these methods. For example, a clerk may manually record the sale of an item to a charge-account customer; but the store's sales records may later be recorded on punched cards, and the customer's monthly bill may be issued by an electronic computer. We can categorize *manual methods* of data processing as those performed without the use of a machine apart from a desk calculator. Data processing by *mechanical* or *electromechanical* facilities generally means the use of punched-card equipment. At one time, the term *automatic data processing (ADP)* indicated the use of this type of equipment. Now this term is also used to indicate the use of computers. By *electronic data processing (EDP),* we mean the processing of data by electronic computers. The introduction of computers into data processing in the late 1950s made it possible to process a voluminous number of records quickly and efficiently. Today the developments in computer technology have far exceeded the original expectations of the businessman. Computers are used to control project activities, to provide current inventory information, and to give management immediate access to up-to-date information for decision making, as well as for routine activities such as record keeping and billing.

BUSINESS AND SCIENTIFIC DATA PROCESSING There are two major areas of data processing: business and scientific. *Business data processing* includes all the routine handling of data such as payroll, sales, and billing information as well as highly sophisticated management-information systems. *Scientific data processing* requires the collection and analysis of data produced by scientific activities. It includes, for example, the collection of data from the manned spaceflights and its subsequent analysis by a computer. It also includes the development of files containing data from scientific experiments and their processing for experimental analysis. On the other hand, the basic aims of business data processing are the retention of information, the updating of information, and the summarization of this data. For example, a college or university must maintain records of all students currently enrolled at the school. The names and addresses of the current student population, the courses they have taken, the courses they are currently taking, and other data must be retained in files. In addition, records must be permanently retained for all the students who have ever enrolled in the school. The data file for the current student population is constantly changing. The cumulative file of all students— past and present—increases each year. The purpose of these data files is to retain this information accurately. This information may be used in many ways: to report on student enrollment over the past ten years, to analyze the geographic areas from which students are drawn, and so on.

Another illustration of business data processing is the recording of insurance policies issued by an insurance company. Each policy must be identified by the name of the policyholder, his current address, the provisions of the policy, the cost of the policy, the date of the policy, and so on. This information is recorded in a file. It is important that this file be kept, for it is, in effect, the company's recording of its relationship with a policyholder. In an automated system, such files may be used for statistical analyses of the policyholders or of the type and number of claims paid for the policies. The files may also serve as input for a computerized billing system.

WHY AUTOMATE DATA PROCESSING?

The volume of data generated and processed in one day in the 1970s exceeds the quantity produced in an entire year in the nineteenth century. A major New York bank issues over 25,000 checking-account statements daily. The U.S. government annually processes income-tax returns for a population of more than 200 million. (There were only 62 million persons in the country in 1890.) A utility company in a large city must issue over 100,000 bills monthly. All this processing could be accomplished manually, but it is not. What are the reasons for the popularity of computers in data processing?

Accuracy The repetitive nature of data-processing activities make them ideally suited for computer processing. A computer can tirelessly perform a task over and over again with complete accuracy and without complaint. The human worker in the same situation becomes bored and tired. He finds constant repetition of

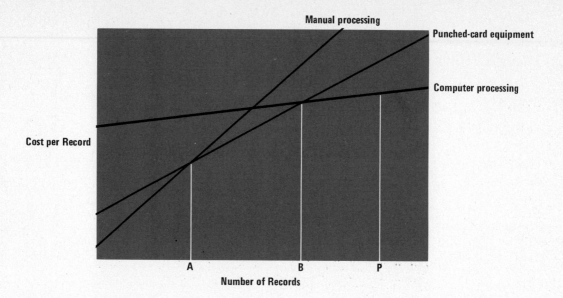

Manual processing

Punched-card equipment

Computer processing

Cost per Record

A   B   P

Number of Records

the same task tedious and begins to make errors. He records information incorrectly; he begins to write illegibly; he transposes letters or numbers; in short, he ceases to function efficiently. Yet the keeping of accurate records and the calculation of correct billing information are essential to the successful operation of a business.

Economies of Scale The cost of processing records manually can be calculated at a fixed cost per record. After the number of records surpasses a certain volume the cost per record will increase slightly, for two reasons. First, the manual worker will begin to make more errors and additional checking of the processing will be necessary. Second, the sheer volume of data will make the handling and storing of records more and more difficult.

When a computer is employed to process records, the cost per record decreases as the volume of records increases. The initial expenses for the establishment of a computer data-processing system are high and are usually justified by the problem of processing vast quantities of information manually or with punched-card equipment. For a visual comparison of manual and automated processing costs, see Figure 1–1.

Ease of Handling This factor is directly related to the volume of data. The retrieval of information recorded on paper and stored in ordinary files can be a time-consuming task. The misfiling of one item may mean that it is irrevocably lost unless it is accidentally discovered. The physical problems of adding information to the file and correcting existing data multiply as the file increases in size. This fact is directly related to the next reason for computer processing, its speed.

Speed Retrieving a particular item of data from a file is an everyday task in business. A policyholder wishes to increase the coverage of his insurance policy, and, therefore, the policy information must be retrieved. A prospective customer of an airline desires to know what flights are available to a certain destination. A manager wishes to know the current status of inventory. In all these cases, accurate information must be supplied quickly.

WHAT IS A COMPUTER?

Computers are divided into two types: digital and analog. *Digital computers* are machines

Figure 1–1
Processing Costs

As the number of records to be processed increases, the cost of processing them manually eventually (in this instance, at point A) will exceed the cost of processing the same number of records using punched-card equipment. As the number of records continues to increase, the cost per record of processing with punched-card equipment will exceed the cost of processing by a computer (at point B). At a further point (P), the cost per record of processing with a particular type of computer may become excessive, or the computer itself may reach the limit of its capabilities, and a computer with greater processing capabilities may have to be introduced.

that perform calculations by operating on numbers; *analog computers,* on the other hand, calculate by measuring physical quantities. An example of a digital computer is an adding machine or a desk calculator. Figure 1–2 is a photograph of a modern electronic digital computer. An example of an analog computer is the slide rule. In Figure 1–3, the number 2 is multiplied by 3 and the product of the multiplication is given on the lower portion of the rule, beneath the digit 3. Numbers are physically represented by a length on the slide rule. The accuracy of the slide rule is limited by the user's ability to handle it correctly and judge the result and the physical limitations of the device itself. An electronic analog computer can be used to solve complex mathematical problems such as differential equations. The accuracy of all analog computers is limited by the representation of numbers by physical quantities.

In the area of electronic computers, digital computers are more versatile than analog machines and provide greater accuracy in arithmetic calculations. A desk calculator is a tool that is operated manually under the control of a human. A person keys in a number, depresses a switch, keys in another number, then pushes a lever that triggers the addition of the two numbers. All arithmetic operations are performed by the direct intervention of a human being. A modern electronic digital computer performs calculations automatically under the control of a program, and no manual intervention is required. A *program* is a logical set of commands expressed according to certain rules and symbols. The computer can perform arithmetic calculations and compare numerical values. The power of the modern computer derives from its ability to make a logical choice among alternative paths. It does this by examining a value and, based on that value, choosing a path.

Computers are particularly useful for the performance of repetitive tasks. For example, the calculation of a paycheck for each employee in a large company requires the repeated computation of a simple formula. The computer will not tire of this repetition, but will gladly compute and print each check. But what about the computer that issues a weekly paycheck for one million dollars to a night watchman? Isn't the computer an idiot? No. Unfortunately the idiot is the person who created the program for the computer. The computer is directed by its master, the program, and can do only what the program tells it to do. An

Figure 1–2
IBM System/370 Model 165

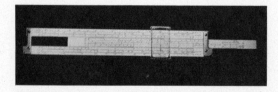

Figure 1–3
Multiplication with a Slide Rule

error by a computer is almost always caused by an error in the program; that is, the program was not constructed correctly by its creator, the *programmer.* A second possible source of error is the input of erroneous data. A third is a malfunction of the computer equipment. The reliability of modern computers is extremely high, and the most likely source of error is the human element, the programmer. Nevertheless, computers are affectionately "cussed" at and treated as animate beings instead of cold boxes of wires and circuitry.

THE HISTORY OF COMPUTERS

Computers today are so much a part of our lives that it is astonishing to realize that the history of modern computer systems began less than thirty years ago. In 1946, it was anticipated that the "enormous" quantity of 100 computers would be sufficient computing power for the United States for decades to come. Today there are approximately 90,000 computers in operation, and it is forecast that this number will increase to 500,000 by 1980 in the United States alone. The era of electronic digital computers began with the successful completion of the ENIAC by the Moore School of Electrical Engineering of the University of Pennsylvania in 1946. Though the history of the modern digital computer covers a short period of time, there has been a constant search for better ways to compute and process data. Table 1–1 summarizes these efforts to create devices to aid in handling data and performing calculations.

Early in our history, we learned to count, formulated a number system, and developed the rules for arithmetic computations. The tremendously important concept of zero as a place holder began under the Egyptians. The scribe would leave a space for a position; later he marked a dot; and, at last, the Phoenicians expanded this dot to something resembling our modern-day zero. Our number system is decimal (it is generally agreed) because we have ten

Table 1–1

LANDMARKS IN THE HISTORY OF COMPUTERS

450 B.C.	Abacus in use in Asia and Greece.
1617 A.D.	Invention of logarithms by Napier, and Napier's bones.
1642	Pascal's adding machine.
1662	Invention of slide rule by William Oughtred.
1671	Leibnitz's calculator.
1801	Jacquard's loom—the first use of punched cards.
1823	Babbage's Analytical Engine.
1890	The 80-column punched card of Herman Hollerith.
1900	The 90-column punched card of James Powers.
1925	First large-scale analog computer designed by Vannevar Bush and associates.
1939	The electromechanical computer MARK I (completed in 1944) proposed by Aiken.
1939	Prototype of electronic digital computer completed by Atanasoff, with the assistance of Berry; final version completed in 1942.
1943-46	Eckert and Mauchly design an all-electronic digital computer, the ENIAC.
1944-46	Von Neumann, Goldstine, and Burks design the EDVAC (with Eckert and Mauchly) and the IAS computer. The stored-program concept is born and binary number representation used.
1948	Transistors developed.
1951	The UNIVAC I, the first commercially available computer, delivered to the Bureau of the Census.
1954	First business application of computers—UNIVAC I at General Electric.
1960	The UNIVAC 490 Real-Time System—the first commercial real-time data processing system—is introduced.
1967	The IBM System/360 series begins the third generation of computers.

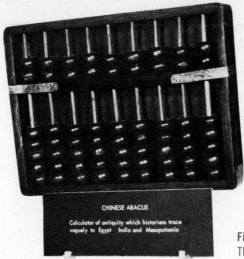

CHINESE ABACUS

Calculator of antiquity which historians trace
vaguely to Egypt India and Mesopotamia

Figure 1–4
The Abacus

fingers. Our notation for a number indicates the powers of ten. For example, 35,679 means 3 ten thousands, 5 thousands, 6 hundreds, and 7 tens, plus 9. This amount can also be expressed another way as $3 \times 10^4 + 5 \times 10^3 + 6 \times 10^2 + 7 \times 10 + 9 \times 10^0$. (Remember that any number to the zero power is one; that is, $10^0 = 1$.)

THE ABACUS (ca. 450 B.C.) The position of a digit within a number indicates its relationship to the power of ten. The abacus (Figure 1–4) is a device for computing and was in use around 450 B.C. It is considered to be the first digital computer. It consists of a rectangular frame with wires strung across the frame. Each wire is divided by the frame into two sections with two beads on the top and five beads on the bottom. Each bead on top represents the quantity "five" while each of the five bottom beads represents the quantity "one." Each wire represents a place: units, tens, hundreds, and so on. The computations are performed by moving the correct number of beads up against the top of the frame. The abacus is attributed to the Chinese but was also developed independently by the Greeks. The Japanese version of the abacus is called the

soroban. The abacus is still widely used in Asia, and adept abacus operators have been known to outrace clerks using high-speed desk calculators.

NAPIER'S BONES (1617) The invention of logarithms by John Napier, a Scottish mathematician, is a landmark in the history of mathematics. Using logarithms, it is easy to multiply or divide large numbers quickly and accurately. A human computer, Henry Briggs, devoted his life to computing a table of the logarithms that Napier had invented. Many forgotten mathematicians also spent years in the calculation of tables of logarithms or trigonometric functions such as the sine and cosine.

As a by-product of logarithms, Napier devised a tool for multiplication and division that was nicknamed *Napier's bones*. The bones were actually rods. Each rod was divided into nine squares; each square was divided diagonally, and numbers were given in each half of the square. To multiply two numbers, it was only necessary to manipulate the rods and then add the numbers in the adjacent squares. This invention was popular in Europe for multiplication, division, and the extraction of square and cube roots.

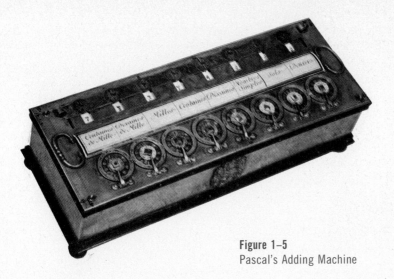

Figure 1–5
Pascal's Adding Machine

PASCAL'S ADDING MACHINE (1642) The first adding machine was built by Blaise Pascal, a well-known French philosopher and mathematician who devised it to assist his father, a customs officer in Rouen. The gear-driven machine was designed to add eight columns of numbers. Each wheel was divided by ten teeth numbered from zero to nine. Whenever a wheel moved from nine to zero, an automatic carry was accomplished by rotating the adjacent wheel by one digit. Addition was accomplished by stepping the gears through the number of intervals equivalent to the numbers being added. This principle is similar to that of the mechanical adding machines developed in the nineteenth century. Although Pascal's device is termed the first mechanical calculator, it never worked reliably enough for wide-scale adoption. Mechanical calculators did not come into widespread use until the twentieth century.

LEIBNITZ'S CALCULATOR (1671) Leibnitz, a famous German mathematician and philosopher, using the same principle as Pascal, built a machine for multiplication, division, and extraction of square roots. These operations were accomplished by successive additions, subtrac-

tions, or tallies. Leibnitz's machine, like Pascal's, never performed satisfactorily, and Leibnitz is best remembered for his independent development of calculus that paralleled Newton's work.

THE HUMAN COMPUTERS (1790) The difficulties involved in the computation of tables without mechanical devices were considerable. Nevertheless, a computing project organized and executed by human beings was attempted. The French First Republic began an elaborate scheme for the computation of mathematical tables, using human computers, in 1790. Professor M. V. Wilkes describes this project in *Automatic Digital Computers* (1956) as follows:

This project was organized on what we should now call production lines, and the staff were divided into three grades. First, there were some five or six mathematicians who decided the best mathematical methods and formulae to be used. Secondly, there were eight or ten computers who were competent to handle these formulae and to compute numerical values from them; their role was to compute "pivotal values," that is, selected values of the function spaced at five or ten times the interval required in the final table. Thirdly, there were computers of lower grade, nearly 100 in number, who understood only the elements of arithmetic, but who were able, by following rules laid down, to perform the final stage of the tabulation.

The step-by-step details of this computing activity could be termed a program, albeit one for humans. Unfortunately the project was never finished.

JACQUARD'S LOOM (1801)   In the late eighteenth century and early nineteenth century, weaving was an important industry in Europe. When a pattern was woven into cloth, it was necessary to lift the threads of the warp in the proper sequence while simultaneously controlling the throw of the shuttles that carried the weft. Joseph Marie Jacquard, a French weaver, devised a method of weaving using punched cards. All the threads were fastened to a single rod. Cards were punched with holes and rods were lifted in the order indicated by the cards, which pushed against them. Those rods that did not pass through a set of holes were lifted. A repetitive pattern was woven by using the same cards in succession. Quite intricate designs could be achieved in this manner. As a demonstration of his method, a portrait of Jacquard was woven using over 20,000 punched cards. This portrait was once to be seen at the home of Charles Babbage, another famous name in the history of computing.

CHARLES   BABBAGE   (1792–1871)
Charles Babbage, an English mathematician and frustrated genius, is one of the most interesting figures in the history of computers. He had the vision to design a computer that could perform arithmetic calculations, read input data, write results, and also contain data within a storage device. The technological limitations of his era made it impossible for him to realize his dream. Ironically, the later development of the modern computer was accomplished without any knowledge of Babbage's work. He is a modern-day discovery who belatedly has been given the acclaim he wished for in his lifetime.

Babbage was born in 1792 in Devonshire, the son of a wealthy banker. Upon his father's death, he inherited a considerable fortune, which was useful in the development of his scientific inventions. After a haphazard early education, he went to Cambridge to study but found to his dismay that he knew more mathematics than his tutor. At that time, English mathematicians were still using the dot notation of Newton's calculus while the continent had adopted the *dy/dx* notation of Leibnitz. Babbage and several of his friends, including John Hershel (the discoverer of the planet Uranus) and George Peacock, banded together to found the Analytical Society for the promotion of mathematical analysis. The first volume of proceedings was titled with a pun suggested by Babbage: "The Principles of Pure-D-ism in opposition to the Dot-age of the University." In 1828 Babbage was named to the Lucasian Chair of Mathematics (the chair of Newton), even though he had never taken an honors degree. He held the Chair for eleven years without giving a single lecture.

In 1812, Babbage conceived the idea of building a calculating machine to compute mathematical tables, which were then laboriously computed by hand and filled with errors. The machine would be based on the mathematical principle of differences, which states that the level differences between values computed for a formula remain the same. For example, the computation of cubes of numbers can be done very simply by the use of differences, as shown in Table 1–2. The first column contains the numbers 0 to 6. The second column shows the cubes of the numbers 0 through 6. The third column gives the differences between successive numbers in the second column; for example, 8 minus 1 is 7. These are called first-order differences. The fourth column gives differences between successive numbers in the third column; for example, 19 minus 7 is 12. These are second-order differences. The fifth column gives the differences between successive members of the fourth column; these third-order differences are equal to the same number, 6. Once the differences are constant, there is no need to calculate any further differences. To compute the cube of the next number (7^3), we simply add the last numbers in columns 5 through 2; that is

$$7^3 = 6 + 30 + 91 + 216$$
$$= 343$$

Table 1–2

CALCULATING MATHEMATICAL DIFFERENCES

N	N^3	FIRST DIFFERENCE (D_1)	SECOND DIFFERENCE (D_2)	THIRD DIFFERENCE (D_3)
0	0			
1	1	1		
2	8	7	6	
3	27	19	12	6
4	64	37	18	6
5	125	61	24	6
6	216	91	30	6

Figure 1-6
Babbage's Difference Engine

Because the third difference is constant, it is a simple matter to compute successive values for the first and second differences and thus compute the cubes of numbers ad infinitum. For example,

$$8^3 = 6 + 36 + 127 + 343$$
$$= 512$$

With this method, it is always necessary to compute successive differences until a difference is found for which all values are the same.

In 1822, Babbage constructed a small working model of his machine, known as the Difference Engine. He then proposed to build a large machine which would work to twenty decimal digits and compute sixth-order differences, which he believed were necessary for calculating certain formulas. The British government provided financial support for the project, but Babbage never completed the design. Instead he conceived the idea of the *Analytical Engine*, a machine that embodied the principles of the modern automatic computer. The Analytical Engine was designed to have 1,000 fifty-digit numbers in its *store* (similar to the computer memory). It could compare numbers, make judgments, and act on its judgments. Data would be fed into the machine on punched cards similar to those used by Jacquard's loom, and output would be engraved on metal plates ready for printing. It would also be possible to have output on punched cards that could be fed back into the Analytical Engine for use in further computations. Arithmetic operations would be performed automatically without the intervention of a human operator. A program would be prepared on punched cards. The Analytical Engine was designed to read one card at a time, execute the instruction it contained, then read the next card, and so on. A branch in the program was made possible by instructing the machine to examine the results of a calculation; if the results were negative, the program cards could then be moved either forward or backward a specified number of cards. The limitations of machine tooling in Babbage's day prevented the implementation of this fantastic design. There were no standardized machine parts, and all the bolts, nuts, claws, ratchets, cams, links, shafts, and wheels for the Engine required hand-fitting. Nevertheless, though never built, the Analytical Engine was a great achievement. But the Chancellor of the Exchequer was not impressed with an unfinished Difference Engine or the design for an unrequested Analytical Engine. After spending

Figure 1–7
Early Card-Punch Equipment

£17,000 on the project, the British government withdrew its support.

Interested in many fields, including what would now be called operations research, Babbage wrote a treatise on manufacturing pins, analyzed factories and processes, and detailed ways of finding the proper size and location of factories. He also greatly influenced machine tooling and made substantial contributions in other areas. He went on to design a second Difference Engine. Yet his genius was unrecognized by his contemporaries. Only now do we marvel at this remarkable man who attempted to build an automatic computer in an age that lacked the necessary scientific tools. We can only speculate about what Babbage might have accomplished had he been alive in 1937.

PUNCHED CARDS (1890) The U.S. Bureau of the Census took seven and a half years to compile the census figures for the 1880 census. Herman Hollerith, a special agent for the Bureau, saw the need for mechanical tabulating equipment while working with this data. During the 1880s, he devised a 3 by 5 inch card to contain data represented by holes punched in the card. He also built machines for tabulating and

sorting the punched cards. With a projected 25-percent increase in population by 1890, the Census Bureau recognized the need for machines to assist in the compilation of the next census. It selected the Hollerith machines for use in the 1890 census after comparing them with two other sets of tabulating machines in a preliminary test. This time, the census was completed in two and a half years. Realizing the potential business applications of his punched-card equipment, Hollerith organized the Tabulating Machine Company in 1896. In 1924, the company merged with the Time Recording Company and the Dayton Scale Company to form the International Business Machines Corporation (IBM). The IBM 80-column card, although differing from Hollerith's original punched card, is known as the *Hollerith card*.

For the 1910 census, James Powers, a statistical engineer at the Census Bureau, designed a set of punched-card equipment with slightly different features. His keypunch machine allowed an operator to key an entire card without actually punching holes in it. The subsequent depression of a release key caused the punching of the entire card at one time. This "simultaneous punching" feature allowed an operator to correct a punching error without destroying the card. In

Figure 1–8
MARK I

1911, Powers founded the Powers Accounting Machines Company, which later merged with other office-supply companies to form the Remington Rand Corporation. The Powers card was originally 45 columns long but was later modified to contain 90 columns of data. Unlike the 80-column IBM card, which has rectangular holes, the Powers card has round holes.

THE MARK I COMPUTER (1937–1944)
In 1925, the first large-scale analog computer was designed by Vannevar Bush and his associates at Harvard University. It had electrical motors but otherwise was completely mechanical. In 1942, an improved model of this computer was used to calculate artillery firing tables. World War II created a demand for computing power that could not be satisfied by the existing analog computers or by hundreds of persons sitting at desks with mechanical calculators. The need for accuracy and speed in computing was overwhelming. In 1937, Howard Aiken was engaged at Harvard in writing his Ph.D. dissertation in physics involving the solution of nonlinear differential equations. Because of the lengthy computations necessary to solve these equations by numerical approximations, he invented a machine

to evaluate simple polynomial functions. He then formulated the idea of a general-purpose computer and, in 1939, with the support of IBM, began work on the machine. It became known as the MARK I and was completed at Harvard in 1944. The basic operations of the MARK I computer were performed mechanically under the control of electrical relays. The computer was directed to perform its operations according to a program punched on paper tape that resembled a player-piano roll. Two numbers could be added together in one third of a second. Despite its imperfections, the MARK I was successfully used for many years at Harvard University. Babbage's dream of an automatic digital computer was realized by the completion of the MARK I computer.

JOHN ATANASOFF (1939 to 1942) In 1937 Dr. John Atanasoff was a professor of physics at Iowa State College (now Iowa State University). He was interested in finding faster ways of performing computations for the problems confronting him and his students in physics. In 1934 he modified an IBM punched-card machine to perform computations mechanically. Dissatisfied with this device, he formulated plans for an electronic digital computer. He built the prototype of the machine in 1939. With the help of an assistant, Clifford Berry, the ABC (Atanasoff-Berry computer) was assembled by May 1942. In 1942 Atanasoff left Iowa State for government service and ceased his activities in the computer field. He later formed his own research and development firm, which he later sold to North American Rockwell.

THE ENIAC (1943–1946)   During World War II, the Moore School of Electrical Engineering at the University of Pennsylvania and the Ballistics Research Laboratories in Aberdeen, Maryland, were jointly engaged in the calculation of artillery firing tables for the Army. The resources available for this computing task were a Bush analog computer and a hundred women who supplemented the computer output with hand calculations. Not surprisingly, the results were less than satisfactory. Because of the urgent need for an accurate and fast computational device, John Mauchly and J. Presper Eckert, both at the Moore School, proposed the building of an all-electronic computer. Mauchly was familiar with Atanasoff's work and had visited him in his home in 1940.* The Army liaison officer to the Moore School was Herbert Goldstine, formerly an assistant professor of mathematics at the University of Michigan. He supported Eckert and Mauchly's idea and arranged a meeting of scientists and Army personnel in April of 1943. The Army agreed to sponsor the project, and work on the ENIAC (Electronic Numerical Integrator and Computer) was begun. The ENIAC had 18,000 vacuum tubes, all of which had to function simultaneously without failure and for a reasonable period of time. Programs were wired on boards, a task that might take several days, and finding a program error or

---

* Because of the work of Eckert and Mauchly, UNIVAC was granted the basic patent on electronic digital computers, but only after much litigation. UNIVAC then sued Honeywell for royalties, claiming an infringement of its patent rights. After a long court battle, the court ruled that Atanasoff's work was the genesis for the development of the automatic electronic digital computer.

Figure 1–9
Clifford Berry Holding Vacuum Tube Memory of ABC Computer

MACHINE REMEMBERS

The giant computing machine under construction at Iowa State college has a "memory" consisting of 45 vacuum tubes. Holding the unit (above) is Clifford Berry, assistant to Dr. John V. Atanasoff, the inventor.

Figure 1–10
ENIAC

an incorrect wiring connection was very difficult. The ENIAC was completed in 1946 and was immediately obsolete. However, it was used to solve ballistic problems at the Aberdeen Proving Grounds until 1955.

THE EDVAC AND THE EDSAC (1946– 1952)   The EDVAC (Electronic Discrete Variable Automatic Computer) was begun in 1946 at the Moore School of Engineering. Unlike the ENIAC, it had mercury delay lines for memory and the stored-program feature. The term *stored program* means that the program instructions which control the operation of the computer are placed in its storage unit (called its *memory*) and then executed. Mathematician John von Neumann is generally credited with the concept of the stored program, but Eckert and Mauchly also share this fame. The EDVAC itself was the result of a joint effort by several persons — Eckert, Mauchly, von Neumann, Goldstine, and A. W. Burks. It used the binary number system for computations. Due to changes in engineering and personnel, the EDVAC was not actually completed until April 1952. Meanwhile, Professor Maurice Wilkes, who had spent the summer of 1946 at the Moore School, started work on the

EDSAC (Electronic Delay Storage Automatic Calculator) early in 1947 at Cambridge, England. Ready for use in 1949, EDSAC was the first active computer to have the stored-program feature.

OTHER EARLY COMPUTERS   In addition to working on the EDVAC, von Neumann, Burks, and Goldstine designed a second computer at the Institute for Advanced Studies at Princeton University. Completed in January 1952, the IAS computer was a popular model for later computers because of its superior speed and straightforward circuitry. The Korean War stimulated the production of several computers: the ILLIAC, ORACLE, ORDVAC, JOHNNIAC (named in honor of von Neumann), and MANIAC, based on the IAS model; and the SEAC and SWAC, which resembled the EDVAC.

The WHIRLWIND I, begun in 1947 at M.I.T., was conceived by J. W. Forrester, Norman Taylor, R. R. Everett, and W. N. Papian. An adaptation of a machine originally designed as an aircraft simulator, its features included electrostatic storage and magnetic core. The core memories designed for this machine at M.I.T. were the basis for memories later built by IBM and others.

In 1947, the University of Manchester in

COMPUTING THE WEATHER

In 1922 Lewis Fry Richardson wrote a book called *Weather Prediction by Numerical Process*, in which he described a numerical model for forecasting the weather. The model required the performance of a great number of computations within a brief, fixed period if a forecast were to be ready before the weather arrived. Such a feat was beyond the reach of the then-current technology and remained so for nearly thirty years.

Richardson, working in 1922, did not envision the development of the electronic computers of today. Instead, he imagined a gigantic computing laboratory with 64,000 mathematicians serving as human computers. The "computers" worked together, each with a single equation, or part of one, to calculate. On an elevated platform was the director of this whirlwind of activity, the conductor, who coordinated the human computers, busy at their slide rules and calculating machines. Richardson knew, of course, that this type of computing laboratory was impossible to achieve in fact. He had no way to know that a machine one day would perform within minutes all the required computations, or that his work would be the basis for the weather-prediction model in use a half-century later.

Adapted from Charles and Ray Eames,
A Computer Perspective (Cambridge, Mass.:
Harvard University Press, 1973).

England began the development of a computer that led to the design of the Atlas computer, a commercial success in Europe. It featured the first practical electrostatic memory, magnetic drum for auxiliary storage, and index registers. Several other computers also were built under the auspices of universities or the U.S. government before commercial computers became available.

GENERATIONS OF COMPUTERS

We can divide the growth of computers into three generations. The first generation was marked by the use of vacuum tubes. However, with the development of the transistor in 1948, it was obvious that vacuum tubes soon would be obsolete. In 1954, the Philco Corporation developed a surface-barrier transistor which was suitable for the highest-speed computers. Second-generation computers were all-transistorized and had greatly improved reliability and large high-speed memories. We can designate the era of the second generation as roughly the period from 1959 to 1964.

The demarcation between second- and third-generation computers is somewhat blurred by the manufacturers' eagerness to call any computer marketed after 1965 a third-generation computer. In April 1964, IBM introduced the System/360 series of computers featuring integrated circuits, a manufacturing advance that substantially decreased the cost of the machines. The System/360 line ranges from a small computer, the Model 20, at the bottom of the line to a supercomputer, the Model 91. All the models in the series, with a few exceptions, are upward compatible, which means a company can gradu-

Table 1–3

A REPRESENTATIVE LIST
OF COMPUTERS BY GENERATION

MANUFACTURER	FIRST	SECOND	THIRD
Burroughs	E101, Burroughs 220	B5000, 200 series	1700, 5700, 6700, 7700
Control Data		CDC 1604, 3600, 160A	3300, 6600, 7600
General Electric[a] (purchased by Honeywell)		GE 635, 645, GE 200	GE 600 series, GE 235
Honeywell	DATAMATIC 1000	800, 400 series	200 series, Honeywell 100 to 1200 (large), 60 series
IBM	604 Electronic Calculating Punch, CPC, 650 (drum memory), 702, 704, 705, 709	7070, 7080, 7090, 1400 series, 1600 series	System/360 series, System/3, System/7 System/370 series
National Cash Register	CRC 102A, 102D	NCR 300 series	Century series
Philco[a]		Philco 2000	
RCA[a] (purchased by UNIVAC)	BICMAC (variable word length)	501	Spectra 70 series
UNIVAC	UNIVAC I, UNIVAC II; 1101, 1102, 1103; UNIVAC 1103A, 1105; File computer Models 0 and 1	1107, UNIVAC III, SS80 and SS90, 490	1100 series, 9000 series

[a] No longer manufactures computers.

Table 1–4

COMPUTERS CLASSIFIED BY PRICE

CLASSIFICATION	SELLING PRICE	AVERAGE MONTHLY RENTAL
Minicomputer	$5,000–$100,000	$550–$2,000
Small-scale computer	$100,000–$500,000	$2,000–$10,000
Medium-scale computer	$500,000–$1,000,000	$10,000–$25,000
Large-scale computer	Over $1,000,000	$25,000–$75,000
Supercomputer	Over $3,500,000	Over $75,000

ate upwards to a larger computer as the volume of work increases and use the programs already written for the smaller computer. Other characteristics often found in third-generation computers are microprogramming, multiprocessing, multiprogramming, and the use of remote terminals for real-time processing.

As yet, there is no fourth generation of computers. The next major breakthroughs are expected to include a fast, cheap device for storing vast amounts of information, better facilities for time-sharing, and still lower costs. The fourth generation may be marked by giant strides in programming for the user, by the use of the human voice for direct input of data, or by some feature yet undreamed of.

SMALL, MEDIUM, AND LARGE-SCALE COMPUTERS

The terms *small-, medium-,* and *large-scale* as applied to computers are not well defined. The large-scale computer of the first generation may be characterized by a memory of 8,192 numbers, a "fantastic" access time of 16 milliseconds, and input-output equipment of high-speed magnetic tapes. Even a small-scale computer of the third generation has features far surpassing these marvels of the 1950s. Consequently, the gauge for determining the "scale" of computers has been their cost. Today we designate computers as mini, small, medium, large, or super according to their selling price. Table 1–4 presents a classification of machines by price.

THE DEVELOPMENT OF THE COMPUTER INDUSTRY

UNIVAC DIVISION, SPERRY-RAND CORPORATION One reason for the delay of the EDVAC project was the departure of Eckert and Mauchly to form their own company. Their first effort, the BINAC computer, built in 1947, was never successful. In 1951, however, they produced the UNIVAC I, the first commercially available computer, which was purchased by the Bureau of the Census. For several years, the UNIVAC I (*Uni*versal *A*utomatic *C*omputer) was the best large-scale computer for data processing. It was completely self-checking and had a magnetic-tape system with a read-forward and -backward capability comparable in speed to

Figure 1–11
UNIVAC I

that of some recent equipment. The first computer used for business data processing was a UNIVAC I delivered to General Electric in 1954.

A leader in scientific computers, Engineering Research Associates, located in St. Paul, Minnesota, produced the 1101, 1102, and 1103 computers. This firm and the Eckert-Mauchly Computer Corporation eventually were incorporated as the UNIVAC division of Remington Rand (later the Sperry-Rand Corporation). Two distinct lines of computers continued for a time, as UNIVAC produced the UNIVAC II and UNIVAC III for business users and the UNIVAC 1103A for scientific users. However, the UNIVAC 1105 was built as a modified version of the 1103A, and several were used by the Bureau of the Census for processing the 1960 census returns. The late 1950s marked the turning point for the strict labeling of certain computers as for scientific calculations only. Two small second-generation business computers with drum memories were the UNIVAC SS80 and SS90. The UNIVAC 1107, with a thin-film memory, was introduced in 1961. The successful large-scale UNIVAC 1100 series and medium-scale UNIVAC 9000 series were produced as third-generation computers.

IBM   In the 1940s, IBM was a major supplier of punched-card equipment. From 1939 to 1944, the firm cooperated with Howard Aiken in building the MARK I at Harvard University. The MARK II, MARK III, and MARK IV—all one-of-a-kind computers—were also constructed. In 1948, IBM manufactured the 604 Electronic Calculating Punch to handle punched cards at electronic speeds. It also produced the CPC (Card Programmed Calculator). The CPC was not a stored-program calculator, but executed a program read from cards. It served as an interim computer until larger and better machines could be manufactured.

IBM manufactured several computers in a 700 series. The 702 was designed for commercial data processing and was first delivered in 1955. However, it was never sufficiently reliable and was too slow in comparison to the UNIVAC I. Consequently, it was withdrawn from the market and the 705, an improved model, was introduced. The IBM 704, delivered in 1956, was a popular scientific computer. The later 709 was based on the 704. Other IBM computers of the first generation are listed in Table 1–3.

In 1953, the workhorse of the computing field

Figure 1–12
UNIVAC 1110

Figure 1–13
Burroughs 6700

was the IBM 650. Fifty were originally scheduled for production, and over 1,000 were sold. The IBM 1401 was a second-generation computer widely used in business.

IBM announced the System/360 series of computers in April 1964. This marked the beginning of the third generation of computers. The line included the small System/360 Model 20 (also called the 360/20) and the super System/360 Model 91 (or 360/91). A special time-sharing computer, the 360/67, was unsuccessful and was withdrawn from the market after only a few were delivered. The System/360 provided microprogramming, which enabled IBM System/360 models to execute programs formerly executed on an IBM 7094 or 1401 computer.

The System/370 series of computers, compatible with the System/360 series, is considered to be a late third-generation computer. It is faster than earlier machines, has improved input-output devices, and has variable micrology. This latter feature permits the duplication of any previous computer logic directly by the System/370 hardware, making the transition from one computer system to another considerably easier.

OTHER COMPUTER FIRMS   The major commercial computer manufacturers are listed in Table 1–3. Although a number of private firms initially were active in the computer field, the tremendous initial investment required for the development of a computer and the need for a large marketing and technical support staff eventually caused the departure of such companies as RCA, Philco, and General Electric from the computer business. However, with the advent of low-cost components, the minicomputer field has expanded substantially in the past ten years. There are now dozens of manufacturers in this area. Many minicomputers are used as terminals for large-scale computers. Chapter 10 discusses the minicomputer field in some detail.

Control Data Corporation was founded in 1957 by a group of former UNIVAC employees. It is now a leader in the supercomputer field with the CDC 7600. Other current CDC computers are the

6600 and the 3300 series. Burroughs, Honeywell, and National Cash Register are also leading contenders in the computer field. In 1963, Burroughs was very successful with the B5000 computer, which has an interesting internal logical structure strongly influenced by the ALGOL language. The 5700, 6700, and 7700 computers are Burroughs computers of the third generation. Honeywell now has a popular line of computers ranging from the small 58 to the large 1200 computer. Honeywell, after purchasing the computer division of General Electric, developed several new computers, including its series 60 computers.

National Cash Register, long involved in the manufacture of business computers, is marketing the Century series of computers. Digital Equipment Corporation, active since 1959 in the manufacture of small computers, recently entered the medium-scale field with the DECsystem-10. Its earlier PDP-10 was a successful time-sharing computer.

Figure 1–14
Honeywell 68/80

REFERENCES

Babbage, Charles. *Passages from the Life of a Philosopher.* London: Dawson of Pall Mall, 1968.

Bernstein, Jeremy. *The Analytical Engine.* New York: Random House, 1964.

Bowden, B. V., ed. *Faster than Thought.* London: Sir Isaac Pitman & Sons, 1953.

Chapin, Ned. *An Introduction to Automatic Computers.* Princeton, N.J.: Van Nostrand, 1955.

Denning, Peter. "Third Generation Computer Systems." *Computing Surveys* December 1971, pp. 175–216.

Eames, Charles and Ray. *A Computer Perspective.* Cambridge, Mass.: Harvard University Press, 1973.

Morrison, Phillip and Emily. "Charles Babbage." *Scientific American,* April 1952, pp. 66–71.

Pantages, Angeline. "Computing's Early Years." *Datamation,* October 1967, pp. 60–65.

Pylyshun, Zenon W., ed. *Perspectives on the Computer Revolution.* Englewood Cliffs, N.J.: Prentice-Hall, 1970.

Rosen, Saul. "Electronic Computers: A Historical Survey." *Computing Surveys,* March 1969, pp. 7–36.

Wilkes, M. V. *Automatic Digital Computers.* New York: John Wiley & Sons, 1957.

Withington, Frederic. "The Next (and Last?) Generation." *Datamation,* May 1972, pp. 71–75.

"Herman Hollerith." *Systems and Procedures Journal,* November-December 1963, pp. 18–24.

"News in Perspective." *Datamation,* February 1974, pp. 84–90.

QUESTIONS

1. Outline the historical development of computers.
2. Compare the characteristics of Babbage's Difference Engine with the Analytical Engine. How did the Analytical Engine resemble today's computers?
3. Who were the principal contributors to the design and building of the first electronic digital computers?
4. Describe the contributions of Herman Hollerith and James Powers to punched-card data processing.
5. Define the term *analog computer.* Give some examples of this type of computer.
6. What is a stored-program computer? What are the advantages of the stored-program feature?
7. What is meant by the term *generations of computers?* Give examples of each generation.

CHAPTER TWO

The Information-Processing Revolution

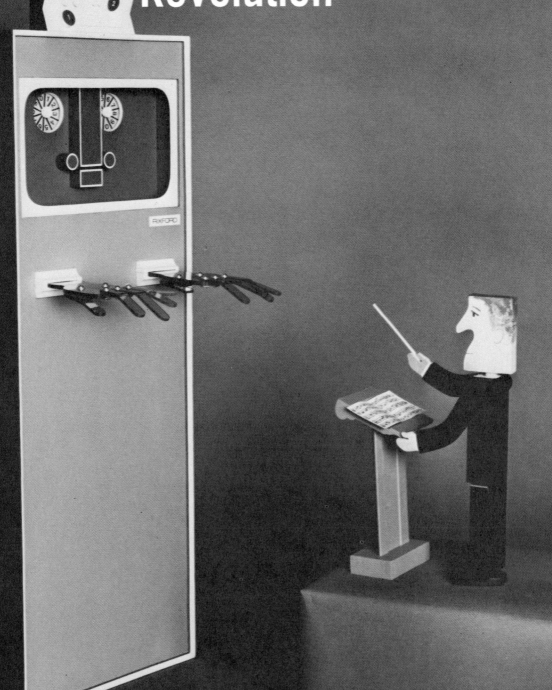

oday we truly are witnessing a revolution in information-handling techniques. Computers are at work nearly everywhere, processing data, digesting information, sending out bills, inventory slips, paychecks, and a multitude of other forms. Each day more computers are being installed and utilized around the world, performing services of extraordinary number and variety. Already, some of the pipe dreams of yesterday have been realized. Now that this revolution is here, we must begin to understand the power and limitations of the computer and its effect on society.

Once, handling data was a relatively simple matter. Business information was recorded in ledgers. Whenever an inquiry was made regarding the financial state of an enterprise, the answer was furnished by a quick perusal of the ledgers. If the matter demanded a faster response, the cash drawer was pulled out and the money counted by hand. As businesses grew, the amount of data used in each business expanded rapidly. The ledgers grew more complex, and billing and inventory control became more difficult. With the advent of sophisticated and efficient computers, there at last were tools adequate for the control and management of the burgeoning amount of business data. Although computers were originally conceived as tools for scientific calculations, they rapidly gained a foothold in the business world. The computer not only provided fast and accurate answers to numerical problems, but had the capacity to store data and to perform repetitive acts with unfailing efficiency. Businessmen were not slow to recognize these values, and soon computers used for business data processing outnumbered those employed in scientific work.

Computer technology, no longer the province of scientists and engineers alone, affects almost every aspect of our daily life. And if the predictions of increased computer usage are any guide, we should be able to delete the word "almost" in the preceding sentence within the next ten years. First, let us consider how the computer is being used today. Our gas, electricity, and telephone bills are prepared by computer, as are bills for credit-card purchases; most paychecks are now prepared by computer; in schools, class schedules may be arranged on the computer; and so on. Often without our conscious recognition of the fact, the computer is being used to process data directly affecting us. We turn on the electric lights in our home, casually accepting the presence of electricity and the proper functioning of our electric lights. In a similar fashion, the computer functions behind the scenes, doing many jobs without our being actively aware of its role.

The computer is a tool — perhaps our most powerful tool. It extends our ability to calculate and process data. The computer is directed by a program stored within it. The program is the means by which the computer performs its task and makes decisions. The program instructs the computer to act upon data stored in the computer's memory. Since the program itself is stored within the computer, it can modify itself. The capability of self-modification gives the stored program the power to do complex logical tasks.

The processing of business data usually requires a set of actions to be repeated for various sets of data. For example, the actions required to produce a weekly paycheck are repeated using a set of data on each employee of a firm. The calculations required to determine the amount of each paycheck, the amount of withholding tax, and so on are basically the same and can be incorporated into a program. The production of inventory reports and billings also entails repetitive calculations.

The computer is often viewed with awe and surrounded by an aura of mystery. The cult of the computer professional and computer jargon encourage this aura. And while it is true that the computer cannot do anything that we ourselves cannot do, it is also true that it would have taken innumerable years for us to perform all the tasks the computer has accomplished in the last quarter-century. Yet the computer is, in the last analysis, only a machine, and the mystique that surrounds it is bound to fade as the number of computers in use increases.

Computers are proliferating because their cost has decreased greatly over the last five years. Mass production and the introduction of solid-logic technology in third-generation computers have made their use by small businesses economically feasible. The introduction of the minicomputer may well lead to a computer in every laboratory and small workshop that needs computing power. At the same time, the development of computer languages that make programming a relatively simple task has enabled everyone to jump on the programming bandwagon, although the design and execution of large, complex computer systems remain a task for the professional. Given computers at a price within the reach of all, and computer languages designed for all, a computer in every home is not a wild dream. Fifteen years ago, computer networks were a pipe dream; today they are a fact. Will the computer in every living room also become a fact? The computer prophets think so.

THE COMPUTER TODAY

Computers have a great variety of applications. Examples in the business data processing area include: the control of inventories, the automated mailing of magazines to subscribers, the production of payroll checks, the conduct of banking transactions, and the scheduling of classes for high schools and colleges. Less obvious com-

puter applications include highway design, computer-aided typesetting, the design of dress patterns, the statistical analysis of election returns, and the diagnosis of physical ailments. Computers even are used to design new computers. Some of these applications are discussed below.

INVENTORY CONTROL Companies producing goods must maintain inventories to supply orders from purchasers. Inventory carrying costs are estimated to be 25 percent of the total value of inventory. Consequently, it is economically desirable to maintain optimum inventory levels. There must be sufficient goods to fill orders quickly, but having too many goods on hand ties up financial assets that could be utilized elsewhere. Furthermore, shifts in buying

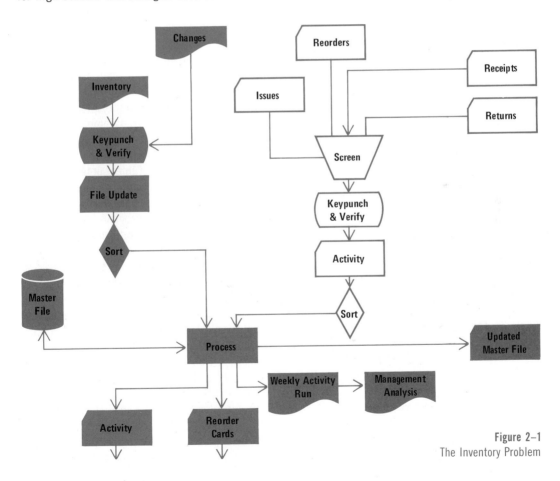

Figure 2–1
The Inventory Problem

patterns may cause some items in stock to become obsolete. A large inventory of such goods could mean a considerable loss for the firm. In the past, the complex matter of what and how much of each item to stock was left in the hands of personnel who relied on their own experience and judgment for sound inventory control. Sales were lost and capital was tied up if their guesses were wrong.

The advent of the computer has enabled firms to base their inventory levels on accurate data. The computer maintains records on all stock on the shelf, on stock in the warehouse, and on sales. It can project buying trends based on previous sales, and it can automatically reorder items when stocks reach a low point. The reorder point can be constantly reevaluated and raised or lowered, as appropriate. If an item is selling rapidly in one area and not in another, the computer can request a shift in the stock of goods from one warehouse to another. Computerized control reduces excess inventory and maintains warehouse supplies at an optimum level. Thus, both small and large companies have profited from computerized inventory control.

LINEAR PROGRAMMING *Linear programming* is a mathematical technique used to solve a set of linear equations in order to find the optimum values for variables. It is used in business to learn which allocation of resources will achieve a desired result, such as minimizing costs or maximizing profits. However, because of the large number of calculations necessary to find a solution in a linear-programming problem, this mathematical technique is not practical without the use of the computer.

An example of the use of linear programming in business is in the selection of a new site for a factory within a given region. It is desirable to minimize the cost of transporting goods to the firm's markets and also the time needed for the journey. A set of equations describing various possible sites and incorporating the distances to the markets is written. The optimum solution to these equations will indicate the most desirable location. In some cases, there may be no single optimum solution, and the firm may have to base its decision on factors other than market distances and transportation costs.

Another application of linear programming, in the oil industry, is in the selection of the most profitable blend of a gasoline, which may have some thirty to fifty ingredients. Automobile fuel must be adjusted to take into account the climate in different markets. The precise composition of aviation fuel, jet fuel, kerosine, and other refinery products must also be determined. The constraints of the problem are storage, the formula used for each product of the refinery, and the composition of the oil available for refining. This problem can also be expressed as a set of linear equations whose solution is an everyday task for the oil companies' computers.

BANKING   In later chapters we will discuss in greater detail the use of computers in banking. It is common for bank tellers to have access to a computer via a keyboard device. Entries in savings-account books are typically made by inserting the books in the machine and keying the necessary information. At the same time figures are recorded in the book, they are transmitted to the central computer, which updates the record of the account. Branch banks find computer terminals especially useful, since they provide immediate access to records at other locations. Thus the status of an account can be checked while the customer waits for approval of his transaction. Since the computer can respond to a request for information within four to eight seconds, the customer does not become impatient. The transaction is completed quickly, and the necessary safeguards are provided.

SUBSCRIPTION SERVICES   All magazines with a large list of subscribers utilize computers for storing customer records and for addressing mailing labels. Each subscriber is given a composite code that incorporates selected alphanumeric characters of his name, address, and zip code. The computer provides billing information to customers, tabulates the payments received, and prints the mailing labels for each issue. It can also sort the mail for various geographic areas for faster handling by the post office. A typical mailing label is shown in Figure 2–3. All changes of address are entered in the computerized master file. There are special devices for the high-speed printing of the mailing labels. One type of label printer produces 130,000 labels per hour.

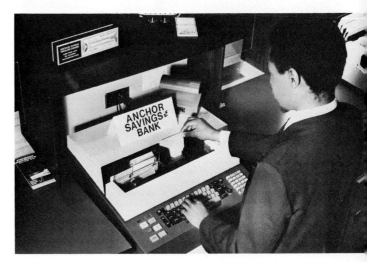

Figure 2–2
A Banking Terminal

```
10017harczz75rx 39pbw06065
Library 4th Floor
Harcourt Brace Jovanovich
757 Third Ave.
New York, NY  10017
```

Figure 2–3
A Mailing Label for a Computerized Mailing

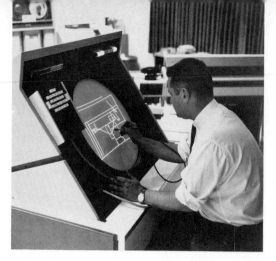

Figure 2–4
Engineering Design by Use of a Computer

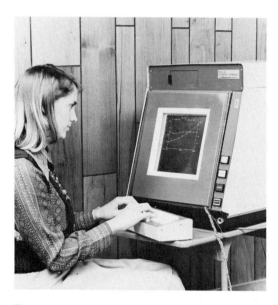

Figure 2–5
A Student at a CAI Terminal

Figure 2–6
A Child Interacting with a CAI Program

ENGINEERING DESIGN BY COMPUTERS One of the more recent uses of computers has been in the completion of engineering designs. Graphic-display devices and the availability of computers capable of generating and changing the display image quickly have made this type of human-computer interaction practical. As the engineer draws a design, it is projected on a device that resembles a TV tube. The technical feasibility of the drawing can be assessed by the computer in seconds. The engineer can alter his design freely and, each time he does so, determine the technical merits of his change in short order. The computer thus acts as an aid to the drafting of technical designs. Once a design is finalized, the computer can produce the technical specifications and a hard copy of the line drawings can be made.

THE COMPUTER IN THE CLASSROOM
The use of the computer in the classroom is still a controversial topic. Some believe it is of little value, while others claim it can replace the classroom teacher. Undoubtedly the truth lies somewhere between these two extremes; it is much too early for a final statement on the subject. The use of the computer as a teaching device is called *computer-assisted instruction* (CAI). The student sits at a terminal that resembles an electric typewriter or a TV set with a typewriter keyboard. He "signs on" for a lesson by giving his name and selecting a unit to study. The computer may "teach" either by posing questions and presenting information or by drilling the student on various materials, recording his scores for review by a human teacher.

Computer terminals that can display both alphanumeric data and pictures, plus slide materials projected on the screen, provide more flexibility in the type of material that can be presented to the student. Although such units have, in the past, been too expensive for widespread use in the public schools, new technical developments may bring costs down. The design of CAI programs, and the expense of terminals, are other obstacles in the path of CAI. A program

must be sufficiently sophisticated to hold the student's interest and must enable the computer to interpret the responses indicated by the student. Despite the many drawbacks, the appearance of terminals in elementary-school classrooms seems imminent. Students coming to maturity in a world where typing skills, TV, and computers are assumed as part of their environment should adapt rather easily to interaction with the computer. However, human teachers surely will still be required, to provide supplemental materials and give individual attention.

TRAFFIC CONTROL   Computer control of the traffic lights in certain major cities is now a reality. Data on automobile traffic are obtained from sensing devices on major street arteries and transmitted to the computer. The computer controls the action of the traffic lights on such streets to maintain a smooth flow of traffic. This type of computer operation is called a *real-time* operation because the system must respond to a situation within a matter of seconds and decide upon an appropriate course of action.

MACHINE TOOLING   It is now possible to machine-tool a part without special dies or hand-work. To do this, a computer is programmed to produce a set of specially coded instructions punched on a paper tape. The tape is fed to a machine which sculpts the part by lifting and moving a cutter and the toolbed. Either the cutter or the toolbed can be rotated in any direction. The production of a machine part in this fashion saves time and ensures accurate dimensions for the machine part.

COMPUTERS IN MEDICINE   The computer is used in a variety of medical applications. It is very useful for scheduling medical appointments. It can cancel appointments, make new ones, and provide an accurate listing of the day's appointments each morning. The computer is also used in many hospitals for the maintenance of medical records. While this sounds like a routine task, it is full of difficulties. Numerous medical records must be retained for many years; recording, filing, and retrieving all this information accurately and efficiently, and within a minimum amount of time, is an extraordinarily difficult job, even for a computer. Another medical application of the computer is the continuous monitoring of patients to detect changes in their physical con-

COMPUTER: THIS IS A COMPUTER TALKING TO YOU. I CAN ASK YOU QUESTIONS BUT I CAN ONLY UNDERSTAND SIMPLE ANSWERS, SO YOU CAN ONLY TALK TO ME BY PUSHING EITHER THE 'YES', 'NO' OR '?' BUTTON. YOU SHOULD ONLY PRESS THE '?' BUTTON IF YOU DON'T UNDERSTAND THE QUESTION I AM ASKING YOU. NOW, DO YOU UNDERSTAND EVERYTHING I'VE SAID UP TO NOW? PUSH ONE OF THE BUTTONS?

OPERATOR: YES

COMPUTER: THANKS. NOW I WANT TO ASK YOU ONE OR TWO QUESTIONS ABOUT WHY YOU ARE HERE. PLEASE REMEMBER THAT THIS IS ALL IN COMPLETE CONFIDENCE JUST AS WITH DOCTORS. ONLY DOCTORS AND NURSES WILL SEE YOUR ANSWERS. ARE YOU QUITE HAPPY ABOUT THIS? PUSH ONE OF THE BUTTONS?

OPERATOR: YES

COMPUTER: GOOD. BY THE WAY, DON'T FEEL THAT YOU HAVE TO PRESS THE BUTTON THE VERY INSTANT THAT I HAVE FINISHED TYPING. IF YOU FEEL YOU NEED TO THINK A BIT BEFORE YOU ANSWER, OR NEED TO READ THE QUESTION OVER AGAIN THEN GO AHEAD AND DO SO. TAKE YOUR TIME IF YOU WANT TO. REMEMBER, HOWEVER, THAT I CAN'T TALK TO YOU AGAIN UNTIL YOU HAVE PUSHED ONE OF THE BUTTONS. WELL, FIRST OF ALL THEN, IS ONE OF THE REASONS YOU VISITED YOUR DOCTOR BECAUSE YOU WERE SUFFERING FROM DISCOMFORT OR PAINS IN THE STOMACH?

OPERATOR: YES

COMPUTER: COULD YOU TELL ME HAS THE PAIN OR DISCOMFORT BEEN CONTINUOUS SINCE IT STARTED? PRESS ONE OF THE BUTTONS?

OPERATOR: NO

COMPUTER: I'D JUST LIKE TO BE QUITE CERTAIN OF THIS POINT. HAVE YOU HAD TIMES, DAYS OR WEEKS WHEN YOU'VE BEEN COMPLETELY FREE OF THE PAIN?

OPERATOR: YES

COMPUTER: I SEE. TELL ME IS THE DISCOMFORT RELATED TO TAKING FOOD— DOES EATING HAVE SOMETHING TO DO WITH IT? PUSH 'YES' OR 'NO'?

OPERATOR: ?

COMPUTER: I AM TRYING TO FIND OUT WHETHER THIS PAIN OR DISCOMFORT OF YOURS IS IN SOME WAY AFFECTED BY THE THINGS THAT YOU EAT OR WHEN YOU EAT. IF IT DOES SEEM TO HAVE SOMETHING TO DO WITH EATING PRESS 'YES', IF NOT PRESS 'NO'?

OPERATOR: YES

COMPUTER: WHEN YOU HAVE THE PAIN OR DISCOMFORT DO YOU GET RELIEF FROM INDIGESTION TABLETS OR LIQUID MEDICINES? PRESS 'YES' OR 'NO'?

OPERATOR: YES

COMPUTER: TELL ME DOES THE PAIN EVER WAKE YOU IN THE EARLY HOURS OF THE MORNING? PLEASE PUSH 'YES' OR 'NO'?

OPERATOR: NO

dition. Any abnormal signals by a patient cause the computer to alert a nurse or physician.

Another popular medical application still under development is the use of the computer as a diagnostic device. The computer interrogates the patient via a remote terminal, asking question after question without tiring, while the patient responds by typing on the keyboard. Surprisingly, many patients prefer this computer interrogation to a question-and-answer session with a human doctor, believing the computer to be more thorough. The computer saves physicians time, provides a summary of the patient's replies, and suggests possible diagnoses and tests. Given a substantial reduction in costs of computers and terminals, the use of the computer by hospitals is bound to expand enormously.

THE COMPUTER TOMORROW

The predictions of the computer's role in the future would appear fantastic were it not for the essential role it plays in today's society. In order to envision the computer's role in the world of tomorrow, let us look at a hypothetical day in the life of an American family, the Joneses, some-

time in the future. Mr. Jones gets up and reaches out for the family's computer. He requests the current weather forecast for his area and the time of day. He receives a visual response (data is flashed on a screen) or, if he chooses, there is a vocal summary. Mr. Jones then dresses, eats, and goes off to work on the city transit system, which is controlled by computer. (San Francisco already has such a subway system.) He arrives at his office and reviews the daily sales summary prepared by the company's computer. A few items particularly interest him, so he turns to his computer terminal and requests further information. He then prepares for a meeting on a new product line. He uses the computer freely in planning his remarks. At the meeting, he knows that any questions raised can be directed to the computer, which will draw on its massive files for an immediate response. Meanwhile, at home, Mrs. Jones sends the two children off to school, where they promptly begin a review of yesterday's lessons using computer terminals. The human teacher is preparing new material while the children review what they have learned. The computer teacher will be busy throughout the day assisting with the learning of new material and giving drills. Mrs. Jones now plans her week's menu with the

NEWS BY COMPUTER

. . . Of all commercial activities, few have seemed more immune to technological progress than the production of daily papers. But the pace of change is now accelerating. In a small but growing number of offices, reporters are writing stories, and editors are correcting them, without touching pencil, typewriter or paper. . . . Technology's beachheads have been made at the two major U.S. wire services, the Associated Press and United Press International. The major innovation . . . is the use of a modified cathode-ray-tube device (CRT), which combines a television screen and a keyboard linked to a central computer.

CRTs glow early at U.P.I. headquarters in New York and at ten A.P. regional "hubs" across the U.S. When correspondents' stories reach these central offices, they are now fed directly into computers. Seated next to their CRTs, wire-service editors can order the computer to display on-screen a list of all stories filed during the previous 24 hours. Another command can call up the text of a story, which is then seen on the screen in segments of up to 31 lines at a time. As the editor electronically rolls the story forward, he can maneuver a lighted blip called a "cursor" to make changes in the copy. If he wants to revise a paragraph, he presses buttons that tell the cursor to remove that block of text. Then he types in his own version on the screen. The edited story is returned to the computer and sent to subscribing papers. . . . Without special receiving equipment, wire-service stories still creep in over Teletype machines at the maximum rate of 66 words a minute. Papers that have invested in new machines are a long leg up on competitors; high-speed printers can receive wire stories at 1,050 words a minute. . . .

One paper prepared to take full advantage of wire-service advances is the Detroit *News* (circ. 683,452), the nation's largest evening paper. . . . Once stories are edited in the newsroom, computers transmit them to the printing plant, set type photographically at 300 lines a minute and partially control the operation of six new three-story-high presses. The changes mean that late-breaking stories can get into the paper 15 minutes before press time, as compared with the hour required previously.

From "News by Computer," *Time*, December 17, 1973. Reprinted by permission from TIME, The Weekly Newsmagazine; © TIME Inc.

computer as an aid. She has previously entered the family's likes and dislikes in food into the computer memory, and the machine now presents a selection of menus for her to choose from. She makes her selection and receives a list of the foods she must buy to prepare the menus she has chosen. The computer, which keeps an inventory of other household items, also tells her when to buy laundry soap, cleaning materials, and so on. She then telephones the supermarket to provide a link from her computer to the supermarket's computer. Her order is then automatically transmitted. When she arrives at the supermarket, her groceries will be waiting for her. She will pay for her purchases with a computer credit card. No money or check will change hands, but the Jones' bank account will be debited for the correct amount. After her shopping has been completed, Mrs. Jones goes to her part-time job at a department store. As she sells goods, the sales are entered directly into the store's computer, which updates the inventory list and the company's assets. Once again, no money changes hands. The customers' bills are charged directly to their bank accounts. Only very small amounts require the handling of cash. Mrs. Jones goes home at 5 P.M. to prepare the family's meal. Mr. Jones also returns home and reads his mail. There are no bills, since all payments are authorized by the home computer. He interrogates his computer to find out which payments have been issued that day, authorizes any new payments, and checks on the amount of cash in the family account. After dinner, the Joneses decide to watch a TV show they missed the previous evening. The computer had been asked to record it during their absence, and now the show is replayed for their enjoyment.

This description of a typical day shows only a few of the future applications of the computer. The computer is an accepted part of the Jones'

"If this machine isn't out of whack, reading is going to be even harder than I expected."

family life in the same way that the automobile, electric lights, television, and the telephone are an accepted part of life today. A computer is present in every home, business office, physician's office, library, and hospital, in every place where information is recorded or exchanged. Is this picture of life in the future unrealistic? The use of the computer in the home, in the store, in every business, may become a reality before we even are aware of its far-reaching effects on our lives.

REFERENCES

Martin, James, and Adrian, R. D. *The Computerized Society.* Englewood Cliffs, N.J.: Prentice-Hall, 1970.

Orr, William D. *Conversational Computers.* New York: John Wiley & Sons, 1968.

Taviss, Irene, ed. *The Computer Impact.* Englewood Cliffs, N.J.: Prentice-Hall, 1970.

Weiss, Eric A., ed. *Computer Usage/Applications.* New York: McGraw-Hill Book Co., 1970.

Withington, Frederic. *The Real Computer: Its Influences, Uses, and Effects.* Reading, Mass.: Addison-Wesley Publishing Co., 1967.

QUESTIONS

1. What types of problems are most suitable for solution by a computer? Why?
2. What is a "tool"? Why is the computer called a tool?
3. List five computer applications that affect you directly.
4. List five computer applications that may be implemented in the future.
5. Investigate and report on one of the following computer applications: weather forecasting, the translation of material from one language to another, the retrieval of information on legal codes and precedents, the construction of management-forecasting models, the retrieval of information from libraries, or the playing of chess games.

CHAPTER THREE

Number Systems for Computers

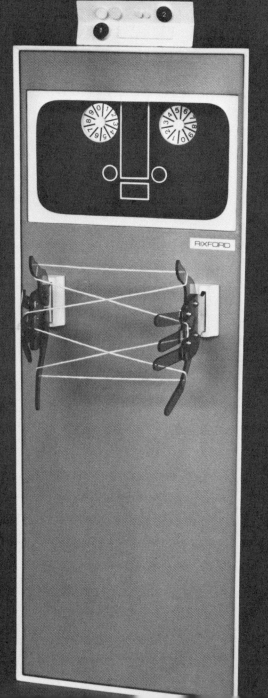

When we examine a problem in either mathematics or business, we invariably propose certain calculations to be performed on numbers. The type of numbers we use in solving problems in the business world, and in all our everyday transactions, are known as *decimal numbers.* When electronic computers were first developed, they too used decimal numbers. Today, almost all computers use *binary numbers* in computations. Problems are stated, and numeric results are given, in decimal numbers; but the computer itself adds, subtracts, multiplies, and divides binary numbers.

WHY BINARY NUMBERS?

Decimal numbers may consist of any combination of ten digits from zero to nine. To represent a decimal number electronically, it is necessary to have a way of representing each of these ten digits. Binary numbers require the representation of only two digits: zero and one. This makes them simpler to use and makes the building of computers less expensive.

DECIMAL NUMBERS

Though we all use decimal numbers, we seldom consider how they are formed. Each digit in a number has a special meaning that depends on its *position.* For example, the number 9876 equals

$$9 \times 10^3 + 8 \times 10^2 + 7 \times 10^1 + 6 \times 10^0$$
$$(\text{where } 10^0 = 1)$$

We read 9876 as nine thousand (9×10^3), eight hundred (8×10^2), and seventy-six ($7 \times 10^1 + 6 \times 10^0$). Each digit in the number is multiplied by a different power of ten. To take another example, the number 51030 equals

$$5 \times 10^4 + 1 \times 10^3 + 0 \times 10^2 + 3 \times 10^1 + 0 \times 10^0$$

The number 10 is the *base* of the decimal number system. If we are writing numbers in different systems, we indicate the base of each system by a subscript. For example, 4250_{12} means 4250 to the base 12, or $4 \times 12^3 + 2 \times 12^2 + 5 \times 12^1 + 0 \times 12^0$.

BINARY NUMBERS

Binary numbers, we have said, are composed of only two digits: zero and one. An example of a binary number is any string of zeros and ones, such as 1011101. Binary numbers are numbers to the base 2; to interpret them, we multiply each binary dig*it* (called a *bit*) by a power of 2. We count powers of 2 from the right. Often, the simplest way to do this is to line up the digits, as follows:

1 0 1 1 1 0 1 ⟵ binary number

6 5 4 3 2 1 0 ⟵ powers of 2 for each position

The decimal value of 1011101 is

$$1 \times 2^6 + 0 \times 2^5 + 1 \times 2^4 + 1 \times 2^3$$
$$+ 1 \times 2^2 + 0 \times 2^1 + 1 \times 2^0$$

which is the same as

$$64 + 0 + 16 + 8 + 4 + 0 + 1$$

or 93. All binary numbers have an equivalent decimal form, and all decimal numbers have an equivalent binary form.

The rules for adding numbers in the binary system are

$$0 + 0 = 0$$

$$0 + 1 = 1$$

$$1 + 0 = 1$$

$$1 + 1 = 0 \text{ and carry } 1$$

Although $1 + 1 = 10_2$, we do not read 10_2 as "ten," but simply as "one, zero."

OCTAL NUMBERS

Binary numbers are clumsy to handle, difficult to remember, and tedious to write. Consequently, the octal number system serves as a bridge between the computer's binary numbers and the humans who sometimes must look at the internal workings of the machine. *Octal numbers* are numbers to the base 8; they have a direct relationship to binary numbers since $8 = 2^3$. They are represented by digits from zero to seven. Each digit in an octal number is multiplied by a power of 8. For example,

$$17_8 = 1 \times 8^1 + 7 \times 8^0$$

and

$$205_8 = 2 \times 8^2 + 0 \times 8^1 + 5 \times 8^0$$

Division can also be performed using the same format as in the decimal system:

$$\begin{array}{r} 62 \\ 25\overline{)2032} \\ \underline{176} \\ 52 \\ \underline{52} \end{array}$$

CONVERTING OCTAL NUMBERS TO DECIMAL NUMBERS   While octal numbers are somewhat more comprehensible than binary numbers, to really understand the value of a number we must generally convert it to decimal form. The position of a digit in a number indicates the power of the base by which that digit is multiplied. Thus:

$$275_{10} = 2 \times 10^2 + 7 \times 10^1 + 5 \times 10^0$$
$$275_8 = 2 \times 8^2 + 7 \times 8^1 + 5 \times 8^0$$
$$101_2 = 1 \times 2^2 + 0 \times 2^1 + 1 \times 2^0$$

The octal number 275 is equal to the decimal number 189. An easier way to compute the decimal value of 275_8 is to consider it as

$$[(2 \times 8) + 7] \times 8 + 5$$

That is, we take the leftmost digit and multiply it by 8. We then add the next digit, and again multiply by 8. We continue until the last digit has been added, but *do not multiply* after the addition of the rightmost digit. The decimal equivalent of any octal number can be computed in this way. The number 6754_8 is converted to decimal form as follows:

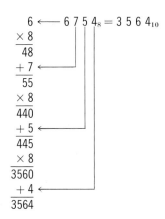

CONVERTING DECIMAL NUMBERS TO OCTAL NUMBERS   To convert numbers from decimal to octal form, we must find how many powers of 8 they contain. This is accomplished

Thus $17_8 = 15_{10}$ and $205_8 = 133_{10}$.

Since $8 = 2^3$, all octal digits can be represented by exactly three binary digits:

OCTAL	BINARY
1	001
2	010
3	011
4	100
5	101
6	110
7	111

This table can be easily memorized. To translate from binary to octal or octal to binary numbers, we simply substitute the appropriate representation. For example, to convert the octal number 675431 to binary form, we write

OCTAL	6	7	5	4	3	1
BINARY	110	111	101	100	011	001

Thus 675431 equals 110111101100011001. To convert the binary number 10110111001101000 to an octal number, we group the binary digits in threes, starting with the rightmost digit:

BINARY	10	110	111	001	101	000
OCTAL	2	6	7	1	5	0

ADDITION   Octal numbers are added in the same way as decimal numbers, except that 7 plus 1 gives us 10_8. We "carry one" after 9 in the decimal system, after 1 in the binary system, and after 7 in the octal system:

DECIMAL	BINARY	OCTAL
$9 + 1 = 10$	$1 + 1 = 10_2$	$7 + 1 = 10_8$

For example, in the octal system,

$$\begin{array}{r} 175 \\ 672 \\ \hline 1067 \end{array}$$

The octal expression $7 + 7$ is equivalent to $7 + 1 + 6$ or $10 + 6$, which is 16.

MULTIPLICATION AND DIVISION   Multiplication and division of octal numbers is not usually done. However, both operations can easily be accomplished by consulting or memorizing the octal multiplication table shown below.

	0	1	2	3	4	5	6	7
0	0	0	0	0	0	0	0	0
1	0	1	2	3	4	5	6	7
2	0	2	4	6	10	12	14	16
3	0	3	6	11	14	17	22	25
4	0	4	10	14	20	24	30	34
5	0	5	12	17	24	31	36	43
6	0	6	14	22	30	36	44	52
7	0	7	16	25	34	43	52	61

For example, we can multiply 47_8 by 52_8 as follows:

$$\begin{array}{r} 47 \\ 52 \\ \hline 116 \quad (47 \times 2 = 116) \\ 303 \quad (47 \times 5 = 303) \\ \hline 3146 \end{array}$$

by repeatedly dividing the decimal number by 8 until a remainder less than 8 is obtained. The octal number is then constructed by reading the remainders, beginning with the last. For example:

REMAINDER

```
8|4986
  8|623      2
    8|77      7
      8|9      5
        8|1      1
          0      1
```

The octal equivalent of 4986_{10} is 11572_8.

OCTAL FRACTIONS   An octal fraction is represented in the same fashion as a decimal fraction. In the decimal system, each position after the decimal point represents a negative power of 10. Any number raised to a negative power is defined as 1 divided by that number raised to the indicated power. For example, $10^{-3} = 1/10^3$, or .001. Since the base of the octal system is 8, positions to the right of the base

point in that system indicate a negative power of 8. For example,

$$0.2356_8 = \ 2 \times 8^{-1}$$
$$+\ 3 \times 8^{-2}$$
$$+\ 5 \times 8^{-3}$$
$$+\ 6 \times 8^{-4}$$

To convert a decimal fraction to an equivalent octal fraction we multiply the number by 8. The integral portion of the result is the first digit of the octal fraction. To find the second digit, we take the remaining fractional portion of the product and multiply it by 8. The process is repeated until the fraction becomes zero or sufficient digits are obtained for the octal fraction. For example, we can convert $.1875_{10}$ to an equivalent octal fraction as follows:

```
    .1875
        8
  1|.5000
        8
  4|.0
```

The octal equivalent of $.1875_{10}$ is $.14_8$.

The process of converting an octal fraction to a decimal fraction is similar, but slightly more difficult because of the use of octal arithmetic. The octal fraction is multiplied by 12_8 (10_{10}); the integral portion of the result is the first digit of the decimal fraction. If necessary, the decimal digits 8 and 9 are substituted for 10_8 and 11_8. The fractional portion of the product is saved and multiplied by 12_8. This process is repeated until a fraction of zero or sufficient digits have been obtained. For example, to convert $.44_8$ to its decimal equivalent we must multiply by 12_8 four times:

$$
\begin{array}{r}
.44 \\
12 \\
\hline
110 \\
44 \\
\hline
5\,|.50 \\
12 \\
\hline
6\,|.2 \\
12 \\
\hline
2\,|.4 \\
12 \\
\hline
5\,|.0
\end{array}
$$

The decimal equivalent of $.44_8$ is $.5625_{10}$.

THE HEXADECIMAL SYSTEM

The *hexadecimal system* is used by some computers, including those in the IBM System/360 and System/370 series. In this number system, the number 16 serves as the base. Positional values are given by powers of 16. The hexadecimal system requires a way of representing numbers up to 15. To represent the numbers from 10 to 15, the capital letters A through F are used. Since the largest hexadecimal character can be expressed in binary form as 1111, it is a simple matter to convert a binary number to a hexadecimal number. We divide the binary number into groups of four bits, starting with the rightmost digit. We then substitute the corresponding hexadecimal character. For ease of conversion, the four-bit groups are first interpreted as octal numbers, then written as decimal numbers and, lastly, as hexadecimal characters.

BINARY	1011	1111	0111	1001
OCTAL	13	17	07	11
DECIMAL	11	15	7	9
HEXADECIMAL	B	F	7	9

To convert hexadecimal numbers to binary form, we simply reverse the process.

The conversion of hexadecimal notation to decimal form or decimal notations to hexadecimal form is more complex. It is generally performed with the use of tables.

COMPUTER ARITHMETIC

Computers perform arithmetic in a somewhat different manner than we have explained here. Some computers perform all arithmetic operations by additive methods. In these machines, subtraction is performed by taking the negative of the number to be subtracted and then adding the two numbers [that is, $a - b = a + (-b)$]. Still other computers perform all arithmetic operations by subtracting numbers. Here the addition of two numbers is accomplished by forming the negative of the number to be added and subtracting it from the first number [that is, $a + b = a - (-b)$]. These machines are known as *subtractive machines.* Computers typically perform multiplication by repeated addition and division by repeated subtraction.

The negative of a binary number within a computer memory is ordinarily represented by its complement. There are two types of binary complements: the ones complement and the twos complement. The *ones complement* of a binary number is the number obtained by replacing each 1 with a 0 and each 0 with a 1. A binary number and its ones complement added together yield a number containing all 1's. The *twos complement* of a number is the ones complement plus 1; the sum of a number and its twos complement is a power of 2; hence the name "twos complement." A particular computer uses either the ones or twos complement for negative numbers. An example of a binary number and its complements is shown below:

Binary number	010110100000
Ones complement	101001011111
Twos complement	101001100000

When subtraction is performed by taking the ones complement of the number to be subtracted and adding the two numbers, the resulting sum may cause an overflow of a one-bit in the leftmost digit. This overflow bit is brought around to the rightmost position and added to the initial result to obtain the correct sum. This addition of

RIDE ME, I'M CLEAN

Some of the more unusual applications of computers range from watching TV to controlling the transit systems in large cities. Before compiling ratings will Neilsen ever consult computers for their opinions on TV shows? Probably not, but the Canadian Radio-Television Commission (CRTC) is programming a computer to watch, analyze, and classify shows. The basic assumption of this research is that different types of programs have distinctive patterns of action. For instance, a talk show has relatively little action, whereas a western usually has a lot of movement on the screen. The computer will store a digitized image of 65,000 points on a television screen. Every few seconds a new television image will be compared with the stored image to see how much change has occurred.

Computers have helped Americans launch spaceships, build buildings, look for dates or prospective marriage partners, make airline reservations, and provided other time-saving services. Now computers even can help find people something to do with the time they save by using them. A computerized approach to the problem of coordinating leisure time with avocational activities was unveiled recently by Lawrence Hartlage of the American Psychological Association. Psychologist Hartlage used a computer to match general interest patterns of employees of a press-clipping service and a large bank with appropriate leisure activities.

Computer-controlled people movers are used at the new Dallas–Fort Worth airport, and they work very well most of the time. But there are the normal petty malfunctions that are to be expected with any automated system. And several weeks ago one of the cars was missing. Although the computer indicated that the car was en route, carrying passengers, the vehicle was nowhere to be found. As it turned out, the car had apparently decided it needed a washing. Maintenance personnel finally located the wayward vehicle after it had run itself through the wash cycle five times. Looking on the bright side, one technician remarked, "At least there were no passengers on board."

Adapted from *Computerworld* — " 'What Shall We Do Tonight?' Let's Ask the Computer," p. 9, and " 'Boob Tube' Welcomes Another Watcher," p. 26, December 26, 1973; "Ride Me, I'm Clean," p. 6, April 17, 1974. © Computerworld, Newton, Mass. 02160 the overflow bit is called an *end-around carry*. For example, we subtract 01010 from 01101 as follows:

$$
\begin{array}{r}
01101 \\
+ \ \underline{10101} \text{ (ones complement of 01010)} \\
00010 \\
\underline{+ \ 1} \text{ end-around carry} \\
00011
\end{array}
$$

If the overflow bit does not exist, no end-around carry takes place. For example, we subtract 01111 from 00101 as follows:

$$
\begin{array}{r}
00101 \\
+ \ \underline{10000} \text{ (ones complement of 01111)} \\
10101 \\
\underline{+ \ 0} \\
10101
\end{array}
$$

The result, 10101, represents the negative of 01010.

For subtraction using the twos complement in an additive machine, no end-around carry is necessary. If an overflow occurs, the overflow bit is ignored. For example, we subtract 00110 from 01110 as follows:

$$
\begin{array}{r}
01110 \\
+ \ \underline{11010} \text{ (twos complement of 00110)} \\
01000
\end{array}
$$

Thus far, we have discussed computer arithmetic using only binary integers. However, many problems, especially in scientific areas, require the use of decimal numbers with fractional portions with or without a decimal exponent. Examples of such numbers are 1.5672, 2.865×10^{-5}, and -8.9234×10^{8}. Computations with such numbers can be performed using integer arithmetic with the numbers expressed as binary numbers with a fractional portion. This way of expressing numbers with fractional portions within the computer is called *scaling*. When computing with *scaled numbers*, it is necessary to keep track of the position of the binary (or decimal) point after each arithmetic operation. A simpler method is to use *floating-point numbers*. Arithmetic performed with floating-point numbers is called *floating-point arithmetic*. A floating-point number consists of a fraction (or mantissa) and an exponent (or characteristic) that combine to form one number within the computer. The binary exponent is frequently expressed with a *bias,* that is, as the exponent plus an additional amount (the bias). For example, a binary exponent may be biased by 200_8. (Octal numbers rather than their binary equivalents are used here for convenience.) Thus a binary exponent of 15_8 would be given as 215_8 within the computer. This notation provides for the expression of negative exponents as positive numbers. A zero exponent is given as 200_8, while a negative exponent of -2 is expressed as 176_8. The use of a biased exponent permits the negative of a floating-point number to be given by its binary complement within the computer.

CODING SYSTEMS

Computers deal only with numbers. They can perform arithmetic operations on numbers, compare two numbers, and manipulate numbers in other ways. As we have seen, these numbers are represented in the binary number system. But many problems include both alphabetic and numeric data. The production of payroll checks requires the manipulation of names and company codes (which may include alphabetic characters, or *alphabetics*) in addition to the calculation of numerical values for the dollar amount of the checks; part numbers used in inventory control generally include alphabetics; and so on. In many cases symbols such as $+$, $-$, or $ also appear in computer data. Data containing any combination of letters, numbers (that is, *numerics*), or symbols is called *alphanumeric* data or *alphameric* data.

Since the computer can only handle numbers, alphabetic and symbolic characters must be represented by numeric codes. When numbers are included in data to be coded, these numbers are also represented by a special code. Data which is

Medical Tribune

"I do hope they get along.
Fred is binary and Eric is digital."

Table 3–1

THE STANDARD BCD CODES

CHARACTER	6-BIT BCD CODE
0	001010
1	000001
2	000010
3	000011
4	000100
5	000101
6	000110
7	000111
8	001000
9	001001
A	110001
B	110010
C	110011
D	110100
E	110101
F	110110
G	110111
H	111000
I	111001
J	100001
K	100010
L	100011
M	100100
N	100101
O	100110
P	100111
Q	101000
R	101001
S	010010
T	010011
U	010100
V	010101
W	010110
X	010111
Y	011000
Z	011001

coded may never be used in arithmetic computations. In some instances, data which contains only numbers may be given in the computer in a coded form. For example, Social Security numbers are never used in any arithmetic computation; they are ordinarily handled in the same way as alphanumeric data.

Different computers use different codes. Data is typically prepared on an input device, such as a keypunch, and then read by the computer. The computer itself or the device reading the data translates the data on the punched cards into the code required for internal manipulation. Output is similarly decoded by the computer or an associated device.

THE BINARY CODED DECIMAL SYSTEM (BCD) The computer manufacturer determines the code to be used for a particular computer. A popular code in the past was the *Binary Coded Decimal System* (BCD). Table 3–1 illustrates the standard BCD codes. Each alphanumeric character is represented by six bits. The two leftmost bits are called *zone bits;* the remaining bits are known as *numeric bits.* The code for the numeric digits 1 to 9 is simply the six-bit expression for each digit in binary form. For example, 9 is coded as 001001. The

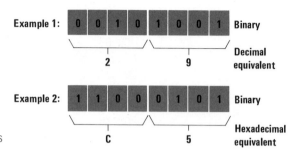

Figure 3–1
The Division of a Byte into Two Hexadecimal Digits

code 001010 (which has the decimal value 10) represents the numeric digit 0. The letter A is coded as 110001. Thus, the code for A91 in BCD is 110001001001000001. The octal code for the same data is 611101. The BCD codes for symbols are non-standard because of the (later) introduction of additional symbols to the keypunch device and the change of Hollerith codes for some symbols. Thus, the BCD code for a symbol may have varying representations, depending on the computer.

THE EXTENDED BINARY CODED DECIMAL INTERCHANGE CODE (EBCDIC) A six-bit code such as BCD permits the representation of sixty-four characters. To represent more than sixty-four characters directly, it is necessary to increase the number of bits in the code. The *Extended Binary Coded Decimal Interchange Code* (EBCDIC) uses an eight-bit pattern, thus permitting 256 characters to be represented. Both upper-case and lower-case letters are represented, plus many special characters. Some bit patterns have not yet been assigned a meaning. The EBCDIC code for alphabetics and other characters are shown in Table 3–2. This code is frequently encountered since many computers (including those in the IBM

System/360 and 370 series, the UNIVAC 90/60, and the Burroughs 2500 and 3500) have an eight-bit unit known as a *byte*.

By dividing the byte into two parts of four bits each, two decimal digits can be coded in each byte. The representation of decimal digits in this manner is called the *packed-decimal method*. Certain computers provide for arithmetic operations using packed-decimal numbers. The division of the byte into two four-bit units also allows an interpretation of the byte as two hexadecimal digits. Four bits may contain any binary number from 0000 up to 1111; 1111 is equivalent to 17_8 or 15_{10} and thus can be expressed as F in the hexadecimal system. Therefore, any four-bit number has an equivalent hexadecimal representation.

THE AMERICAN STANDARD CODE FOR INFORMATION INTERCHANGE (ASCII) The *American Standard Code for Information Interchange* is a seven-bit code developed for use in the transmission and processing of data. Because many computers are designed to process eight-bit codes most efficiently, an eight-bit version of the seven-bit ASCII has been developed. ASCII and EBCDIC are the two most common codes for data transmission.

Table 3–2

EBCDIC (EXTENDED BINARY CODED DECIMAL
INTERCHANGE CODE)

CHARACTER	BINARY CODE	CHARACTER	BINARY CODE	CHARACTER	BINARY CODE
Blank	01000000	d	10000100	G	11000111
¢	01001010	e	10000101	H	11001000
.	01001011	f	10000110	I	11001001
<	01001100	g	10000111	J	11010001
(	01001101	h	10001000	K	11010010
+	01001110	i	10001001	L	11010011
|	01001111	j	10010001	M	11010100
&	01010000	k	10010010	N	11010101
!	01011010	l	10010011	O	11010110
$	01011011	m	10010100	P	11010111
*	01011100	n	10010101	Q	11011000
)	01011101	o	10010110	R	11011001
;	01011110	p	10010111	S	11100010
¬	01011111	q	10011000	T	11100011
—	01100000	r	10011001	U	11100100
/	01100001	s	10100010	V	11100101
,	01101011	t	10100011	W	11100110
%	01101100	u	10100100	X	11100111
_	01101101	v	10100101	Y	11101000
>	01101110	w	10100110	Z	11101001
?	01101111	x	10100111	0	11110000
:	01111010	y	10101000	1	11110001
#	01111011	z	10101001	2	11110010
@	01111100			3	11110011
'	01111101	A	11000001	4	11110100
=	01111110	B	11000010	5	11110101
"	01111111	C	11000011	6	11110110
a	10000001	D	11000100	7	11110111
b	10000010	E	11000101	8	11111000
c	10000011	F	11000110	9	11111001

REFERENCES

Awad, Elias M. *Business Data Processing.* Englewood Cliffs, N.J.: Prentice-Hall, 1971.

Davis, Gordon B. *Computer Data Processing.* New York: McGraw-Hill Book Co., 1969.

Sanders, Donald H. *Computers in Society.* New York: McGraw-Hill Book Co., 1973.

QUESTIONS

1. Convert the binary number 101111001 to its octal and decimal equivalents.
2. Add the following binary values. Check your answers by converting the numbers to decimal form.

a. 100	b. 111	c. 001	d. 101	e. 101	f. 110
011	101	010	100	011	110

3. Convert the octal number 765 to its decimal equivalent.
4. Add the following octal numbers:

a. 123	b. 705	c. 215	d. 634	e. 520	f. 376
345	102	111	165	777	462

5. Multiply the following octal numbers:

a. 23	b. 17	c. 65	d. 37	e. 45	f. 67
35	54	21	72	16	12

6. Convert the following decimal numbers to octal equivalents: 219, 7934, 678.
7. Convert the hexadecimal number 4FA to its decimal equivalent.
8. Give both the ones and the twos complement of the following binary numbers:

   a. 0101111   b. 101101001   c. 01101101

9. Code the following message in EBCDIC: PAYROLL NO. A-2861. Include the spaces in your coded message.
10. Define the term *byte*.
11. Design a coding system for the 26 alphabetic characters, using only five bits to represent each character. Is it possible to represent the numeric digits and other characters in your coding system also? Why or why not?

CHAPTER FOUR

Punched-Card Systems

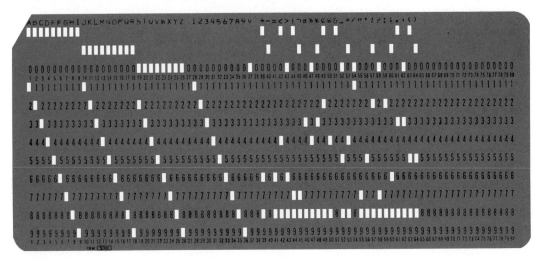

Figure 4–1
The 80-Column Card

Cards are the most popular medium for entering data into the computer. There are two types of punched cards currently in use. The industry-wide standard is the *80-column IBM card,* also called the *Hollerith card.* IBM recently introduced a 96-column card for use with its System/3 computer. UNIVAC, which based its card design on the Powers card, developed a 90-column card punched with round holes. However, this card is no longer in use; the line of equipment for the 90-column card was discontinued in 1966, and UNIVAC now manufactures a complete set of punched-card equipment for the 80-column card.

THE 80-COLUMN CARD

PHYSICAL CHARACTERISTICS   The 80-column card is a rectangular card measuring 7⅜ by 3¼ inches and .007 inches thick. Usually one corner is cut to provide a way of visually checking that all the cards in a deck have been inserted correctly. Generally machines for reading cards ignore the corner cut, but some machines are designed to recognize it and stop upon encountering a card in the wrong position.

The card is divided into 80 columns numbered horizontally from 1 to 80. It is also divided vertically into 12 rows. The first row from the top is designated as row 12. The row immediately below row 12 is row 11. The remaining rows are numbered from 0 to 9. Row 0 is immediately below row 11. Printing on the card indicating the columns and rows is a visual aid for those preparing or examining the card; it is not read by the machine.

Digits, alphabetics, and symbols are represented on the card by the punching of one, two, or three rectangular holes in the appropriate columns. A digit is indicated by punching a hole in a particular row: row 0 for the digit 0, row 1 for the digit 1, row 2 for the digit 2, and so forth. Alphabetics are represented by a combination of two holes punched in a column. For example, the letter A is indicated by a punch in row 12 and a punch in row 1; the letter Z is represented by punches in rows 0 and 9. Certain symbols can be coded directly into the card. The code used for 80-column cards is known as the *Hollerith code.* (A card punched with alphabetics, numerics, and symbols is shown in Figure 4–1.) A list of the Hollerith code for symbols produced on the IBM 129 keypunch is given in Table 4–1.

Table 4–1

THE HOLLERITH CODE

CHARACTER	HOLLERITH CODE	CHARACTER	HOLLERITH CODE
0	0	W	0-6
1	1	X	0-7
2	2	Y	0-8
3	3	Z	0-9
4	4		
5	5	&	12
6	6	¢	12-2-8
7	7	.	12-3-8
8	8	<	12-4-8
9	9	(	12-5-8
A	12-1	+	12-6-8
B	12-2	|	12-7-8
C	12-3	–	11
D	12-4	!	11-2-8
E	12-5	$	11-3-8
F	12-6	*	11-4-8
G	12-7	)	11-5-8
H	12-8	;	11-6-8
I	12-9	¬	11-7-8
J	11-1	/	0-1
K	11-2	,	0-3-8
L	11-3	%	0-4-8
M	11-4	—	0-5-8
N	11-5	>	0-6-8
O	11-6	?	0-7-8
P	11-7	:	2-8
Q	11-8	#	3-8
R	11-9	@	4-8
S	0-2	'	5-8
T	0-3	=	6-8
U	0-4	"	7-8
V	0-5	Blank	

Figure 4–2
The IBM 129 Keypunch

The top edge of the punched card is called the *twelve-edge;* the bottom edge is known as the *nine-edge,* since it is nearest to row 9. When the printed side of the card faces up, the card is said to be *face up. Face down* means the printed side of the card is turned down. This terminology is used to indicate how card decks are placed in the machine. Requirements differ for various machines. One machine may process cards "twelve-edge, face up." This means that the deck of cards is inserted in the machine with the printed side up and in such a way that the twelve-edge is encountered first.

PREPARING PUNCHED CARDS   Data is placed on punched cards by means of a *keypunch.* The keypunch has a keyboard similar to a typewriter keyboard but with some differences to facilitate the punching of numerics and special characters. One card at a time is fed from a deck of cards to the position for punching. By pressing a key, the keypunch operator causes the proper holes to be punched in a column. A *master-control card* lets the keypunch operator skip columns quickly, in the same way that a typist tabs across a page. The control card makes it possible to specify the automatic dupli-cation of specified columns from one card to the next. A printed line on the card denoting the punched data is optional.

VERIFYING DATA   After the cards have been punched, it is necessary to verify that the correct data has been entered. If only a few cards have been punched, it is simple to scan them visually and compare them with the original data. For a larger volume of cards, a device called a *verifier* can be used. The verifier resembles the keypunch. A person, preferably someone other than the operator who punched the data, enters each card in the verifier and depresses the keys that he believes would recreate the data card. The machine checks that the keys depressed match the codes punched on the card. Cards that match the keyed-in data are notched on the right edge by the verifier. If a particular column does not match, the verifier operator is notified by a light and the locking of the keyboard. The verifier then permits the operator two more attempts to key in the data as given on the card. If the third attempt fails, each incorrect column is notched on the top edge of the card. Errors may still exist in a card deck that has been verified, but the chance of such errors is substantially reduced.

Figure 4–3
Recording Invoice Data on Punched Cards

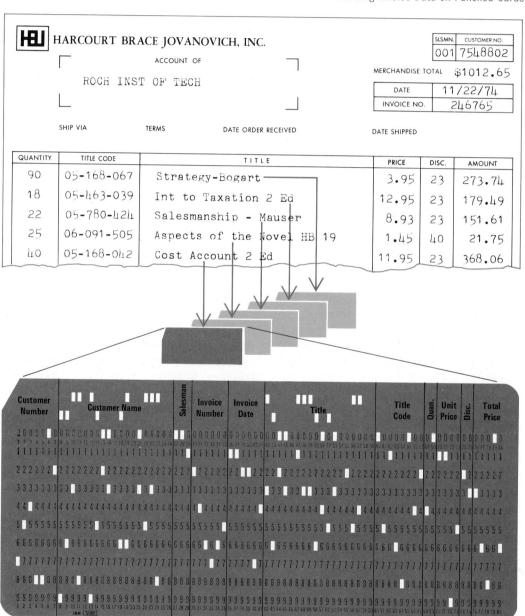

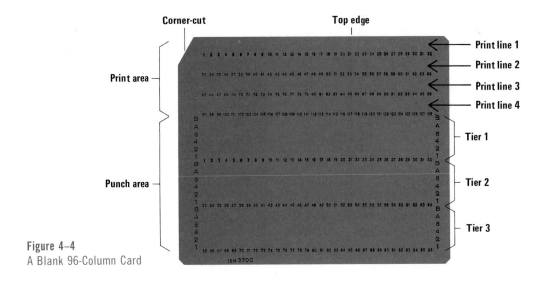

Figure 4–4
A Blank 96-Column Card

THE UNIT-RECORD CONCEPT

A punched card is also known as a *unit record,* because it is customary for a card to contain all the data for one "unit" of information. This unit of information is called a *logical record.* However, the size of a punched card is limited, and a logical record may extend over two or more cards. Alternatively, the contents of the logical record may be abbreviated to fit on one card. Figure 4–3 illustrates the recording of various items of data from an invoice onto punched cards. Each item is recorded on a single card.

After a deck of cards has been punched, it is easy to correct any errors by punching new cards and substituting them for the erroneous cards in the deck. The limited physical capacity of each card (80 columns of data) and the possibility of keypunch errors are the main disadvantages of cards. Other methods of preparing data for entry into the computer are discussed in Chapter 8.

THE 96-COLUMN CARD

In July 1969 IBM announced the System/3 computer, designed for use by small business firms. With this computer system, IBM departed from the standard 80-column card and introduced the 96-column card. This new card measures 2.63 by 3.25 inches and holds 20 percent more information than the 80-column card.

PHYSICAL CHARACTERISTICS Figure 4–4 illustrates a blank 96-column card. The card is divided into two sections: a top section for printing and a lower section for punching. The first three print lines correspond to the data punched in the card; each *print position* is numbered from 1 to 96 to indicate the *punching position.* The fourth print line does not correspond to any punches and may be used for identifying characters.

The punch area is divided into three vertical sections called *tiers.* Each tier has 32 positions,

THE ARTIST AND THE COMPUTER COOPERATE

Watching a musical tune become two-dimensional art; translating the Mona Lisa into an arrangement of digits– breaking the shackles of conventional thinking in the creative arts is what these activities are all about. William Larson, chairman of photography at the Temple University Tyler School of Art, hopes to open unlimited creative possibilities in the visual arts by establishing a Communications Research Laboratory in the school. He is assembling computers, transmitters, video systems, sound equipment, and holographic apparatus to produce new kinds of art.

"This equipment will help us look into the ways in which machines handle imagery," explains Larson. "They enable us to extend our sensory capabilities way beyond our powers as individual artists." Using telefacsimile equipment, a complete picture can be transmitted by phone anywhere in the world in six minutes. The process begins when a simple telephone is placed into a holder and exposed to a beeping signal. The signal is determined by a scanner, which assigns an audible tone to areas of lightness and darkness on the artwork. The tones are transmitted by phone and activate a stylus at the receiving end, where the pattern is recorded on paper. The tonal message is then translated into numbers or second-generation artwork. A musical tune is translated into a signal that produces a printed image.

The laboratory, with its experiments in blending light and sound, is expected to be a "hub of concern for inter-disciplinary-minded people." Much creative activity has involved searches backward in time. The emphasis in this laboratory will be on the future—on combining new technology to produce second- and third-generation art. To those who ask whether a computer or a videotape camera is really a fine-arts tool, Larson has this to say: "When you think about it, a brush is a machine to a painter. It's the creative idea that makes it art."

Adapted from *Computer*, "Hardware Technology Can Extend Artist's Percention," January 1974, p. 55. Reprinted from *Computer* Magazine, a publication of the IEEE Computer Society.

or columns, where data can be recorded. The columns are numbered consecutively from 1 to 96.

A character is represented by a combination of round hole-punches in a column. Each column has six vertical punch positions, which are labeled B, A, 8, 4, 2, and 1. The topmost punch positions, B and A, are called the *zone punches;* the remaining four positions are known as the *digit portion.* There are 64 possible characters. A digit is represented by its binary equivalent. Each punch is considered a one-bit. An unpunched position indicates a zero-bit. For example, the number 8 (001000_2) is indicated by a hole in position 8, while the digit 3 (000011_2) is represented by punches in positions 2 and 1. Alphabetics and special characters are represented by a specified combination of punches. (See Figure 4–5.)

RECORDING DATA To punch a 96-column card, the *IBM data recorder* is utilized. This device punches, prints, and verifies cards. The keyed-in data for a card is collected in a storage area and is not punched until the card has been completed. This permits the operator to erase and rekey any data. One character, one area, or the entire card can be erased and rekeyed.

TYPES OF CARDS

Cards are further classified according to what they are used for. Some common types of cards are master cards, detail cards, summary cards, mark-sensed cards, stub cards, and price-tag cards.

MASTER CARDS Master cards contain permanent or semipermanent information. An example of a master card is a stock card containing a part's code number, the quantity in stock, and its cost.

DETAIL CARDS Detail cards contain detailed information regarding a specific account or transaction. A detail card is also called a

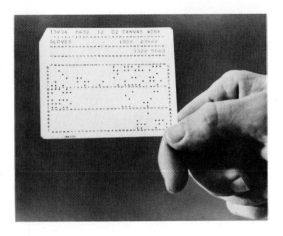

Figure 4–5
A Punched 96-Column Card

Figure 4–6
The IBM 5496 Data Recorder

transaction card. An example of a detail card would be one containing a part number, the amount shipped that day, and the name of the customer.

SUMMARY CARDS   These cards contain totals or accumulated results of data given on detail cards. Summary cards are generally produced automatically by card-processing equipment.

MARK-SENSED CARDS   Mark-sensed cards are specially printed cards, usually 80 columns in length, that are used for directly recording information from pencil marks. The marked cards are punched with appropriate holes by a device called a *reproducer* when it senses the marks made by an electrographic pencil. This type of card is useful for recording low-volume data such as the individual electric-meter readings taken by a utility company's meter reader.

STUB CARDS   Another type of card that is popular for billing customers is the stub card. The "bill" is an 80-column card perforated into two sections, one with 51 columns and one with 29 columns. One section is retained by the customer, while the other is returned with the bill payment. The returned portion is generally the 51-column section. These cards are processed by a special attachment to the standard card equipment. In some cases, the stub card is a 22-column card to be returned intact for processing.

PRICE-TAG CARDS   A type of card found primarily in the retail industry is a small, perforated card used for price tags. After an item has been sold, the section of the card punched with information on the size, color, and so on is torn off and retained. These sections are processed by a special card reader which transfers the data to a standard computer input medium, such as 80-column punched cards or magnetic tape, for processing by the computer.

PUNCHED-CARD EQUIPMENT

In addition to the keypunch and verifier for preparing punched cards, there are several card machines that together provide data-processing capabilities without the use of a computer. To-

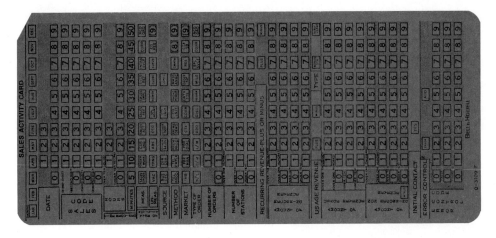

Figure 4–7
A Mark-Sensed Card

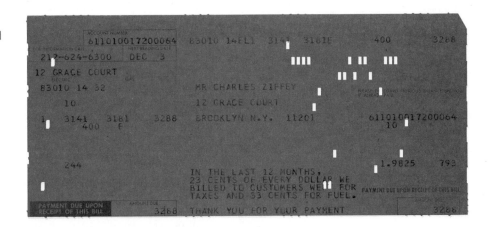

Figure 4–8
A Stub Card

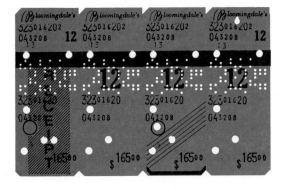

Figure 4–9
A Price-Tag Card

Figure 4–10
The IBM 083 Card Sorter

Figure 4–11
A Sorting Pass

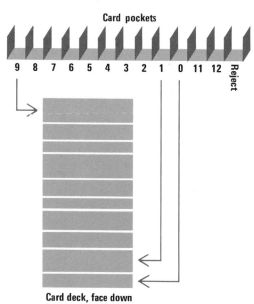

Card pockets

9 8 7 6 5 4 3 2 1 0 11 12 Reject

Card deck, face down

day, due to the availability of low-cost, small-scale computer systems, it is more common to see card equipment used in conjunction with a computer. There are four types of card equipment: sorters, collators, interpreters, and calculator-printers.

SORTERS   *Sorting* is a process by which data are arranged in a prescribed order. For example, a card file of names, payroll numbers, and dates of employment could be ordered by payroll numbers. The data by which a file is ordered are called *keys*. A *sorter* is a machine that sorts punched cards automatically.

The IBM 083 sorter is a typical sorting machine. The basic elements of the machine are an *input hopper,* a mechanism to detect the contents of a column, and thirteen *pockets* for output. Twelve of the pockets are for the twelve punch positions on the card, and the thirteenth pocket is used for rejects or blanks. The mechanisms for detecting a punch are *wire brushes* or *photoelectric cells.*

To sort a card deck, it is necessary to pass the cards through the sorter once for each numeric column sorted. Two passes are required for any column containing alphanumeric data. For example, to sort a card deck on keys in columns 10, 11, and 12 would require three passes through the sorter. If each column contained alphabetic data, three additional passes would be required, to make a total of six passes. Sorting is begun at the rightmost position of the last key in a sequence of keys. In our example, we would begin with column 12. The cards would be placed in the input hopper and the sorting procedure initiated. Each card would drop into an appropriate pocket according to the contents of column 12. Then the cards would be retrieved from the pockets, beginning with pocket 0, and stacked face down to form a new deck. This deck would then be sorted according to the keys in column 11, the cards would be retrieved, and the process would be repeated, this time using the keys in column 10. The final deck would be correctly ordered in an ascending sequence according to the data in columns 10, 11, and 12. An additional sorting pass would be necessary for each column containing alphabetic data.

After each pass, the operator can check the accuracy of the sort by sighting through the cards taken from each pocket. Since all the cards in a pocket should have a punch in the same position, it is easy to check them by seeing if the light passes through that position in the deck. Sometimes a small *sort needle* is pushed through the deck at that position to check the sort. Because sorters are not 100-percent reliable, it is advisable to perform either a visual or a needle check of the cards in each sort pocket to ensure a properly sorted deck.

COLLATORS   *Collating* is a process by which data records are combined according to specified keys; this process is also known as *merging.* For example, consider two card decks ordered by a salesman's number given in columns 21 and 22. Figure 4–13 shows how the two decks are combined to form one deck ordered by the key in columns 21 and 22 and a secondary key in column 80.

A sorting machine may be utilized for collating decks if the keys for merging are in the same location for each card. A collator is designed to merge two card decks when the location of the merge key may differ for each card deck. It can merge two decks much faster than a sorter. It can also be used to perform matching, a combination of matching and merging, sequence checking, and selecting. These functions are discussed later in this section.

An example of a collator is the IBM 88 collator. It has two input hoppers, known as the primary and secondary hoppers, to hold the two decks to be merged. There are five pockets to hold the cards after they have been read by the collator. The machine carries out a given operation, such as merging, by comparing a card from the primary hopper with a card from the secondary hopper. Based on the result of the comparison, each card is ejected into one of the five pockets in a sequence dependent on the operation called for.

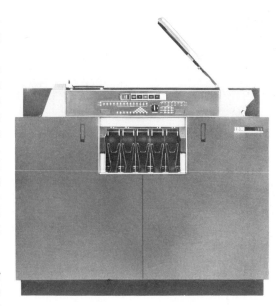

Figure 4–12
A Collator

Figure 4–13
The Merging of Two Decks

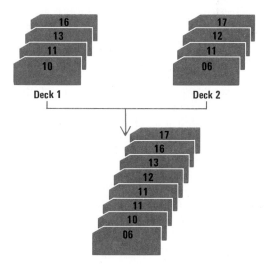

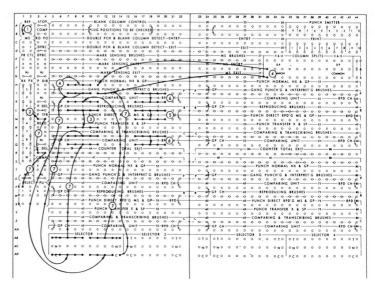

Figure 4–14
A Wiring Diagram

Matching Matching means checking whether a specific field is the same in each card of two given card decks. Matching cards drop into pockets 2 and 4. The cards that do not match fall into pockets 1 and 5.

Match-Merging In match-merging, the matching process is performed and, in addition, cards that match are merged into one deck placed in pocket 3.

Sequence Checking In sequence checking, the card deck is examined to ensure that the values for a specified field are in a sequential order.

Selecting Particular cards may be selected from a file according to the values in a specified field. The selection can be based on a specified value or values, or on a range of values.

WIRED CONTROL PANELS The operation of a collator is controlled by a wired control panel. Reproducers, interpreters, and calculator-processors, all of which will be described later, are similarly controlled. To change the operation of the machine, a different control panel is in-serted. The wiring of machine operations and the removability of the panel give these machines a great degree of flexibility.

The control panel consists of a board with rows of holes. The board is wired by inserting one end of a connecting wire into one hole and the other end in another hole called a *hub*. After the wiring for a particular job has been completed, the panel is inserted in the machine, causing each socket to be connected to the internal wiring of the machine. Thus, each wiring connection on the board causes the joining of two hubs to complete a circuit within the machine, and a machine operation to be performed.

A card-machine job is designed by showing the connections desired on a diagram of the hubs in the control panel. Figure 4–14 shows such a wiring diagram. After the wiring diagram has been drawn, the board is wired from this document. Complex wiring jobs are left on a control panel for use whenever necessary. Jobs seldom performed are wired when they are needed, and the board is disassembled after the jobs have been completed. The wiring diagram serves as a record of the control panel for a job and is useful both in wiring the board and in restoring any wires that come loose.

REPRODUCERS A *reproducer* is used for reproducing cards, gang punching, and summary punching. A card deck can be reproduced exactly, or part of each card can be punched to form a new deck. The sequence of data can also be altered. About 100 cards can be reproduced in one minute, using a wired control panel to direct the job.

Gang punching is the copying of information from a master card onto the cards that follow it. For example, the date on which detail cards were updated may have not been punched on the last run. This information can easily be inserted by gang punching the cards on the reproducer.

Summary punching is the punching of a card containing the total sum of a particular data item from a set of cards. For example, a set of detail cards containing the record of cash transactions for a day can be summed to give the cash

receipts for the day. Summary punching may be accomplished by a special summary machine or a reproducer connected by cable to an accounting machine.

INTERPRETERS Cards produced by the computer do not have any printing showing which characters have been punched. Similarly, cards prepared on a reproducer or summary punch do not have any printing to identify the punched data. The keypunch also permits the punching of data without an accompanying print line. The *interpreter* is a machine that prints on a card all or part of the data punched on it. An interpreter usually prints information on the top of a card, but some models print on any of 25 lines on the card. It is possible to arrange the printing on the card to suit a particular purpose. Data do not have to be printed in the

Albert © Punch, London

"And if you get stuck, give me a shout."

Figure 4–15
An Interpreter

Figure 4–16
The UNIVAC 1005 Calculator-Printer

same order as they are punched. The interpreter functions at speeds of up to 100 cards per minute. A combination keypunch-interpreter is also available, but it functions at much lower speeds.

CALCULATOR-PRINTERS   Calculator-printers are also known as *accounting machines.* They read data from cards, perform arithmetic operations, and print the results of their calculations. These machines can also select a path for calculation depending on whether a number is positive or negative. A calculator-printer can be used, in conjunction with the other card equipment—a card punch, a sorter, a collator, and so on—to produce management reports, invoices, and checks, and for other data-processing activities. It is controlled by a wired panel.

Calculator-printers are slow compared to most computer systems. A typical machine processes 100 to 150 cards per minute. The IBM 609 Calculator and the IBM 407 Accounting Machine are two of the many machines of this type in use today.

The UNIVAC 1005 card processor is an electronic card processor that combines the features of a calculator-printer with some features of a computer. It is programmed by means of a wired control panel but has a memory of 961 characters. Because of its memory, this unit has a variety of data-processing applications. It reads cards at a rate of 600 cards per minute and prints up to 600 lines per minute. Because it is versatile, it has been a popular machine for small businesses. Since relatively inexpensive minicomputers are now available, UNIVAC has discontinued the 1005 card processor.

UNIVAC 80-COLUMN CARD EQUIP-MENT   UNIVAC produces a complete line of 80-column card equipment called the 1701-4 series. It offers an improved keypunch that is a combination keypunch-verifier. The operator keys the entire card, corrects any errors, then initiates the punching of the card. While one card is being punched, the next card can be keyed in. A second

machine provides automatic interpreting with punching and verifying. The card sorter works at a speed of up to 1,000 cards per minute and is controlled by a program.

IBM 96-COLUMN CARD EQUIPMENT
IBM offers a keypunch and card sorter for use with the 96-column card. The keypunch, called a *data recorder,* is similar to the UNIVAC keypunch in that it permits the keying and correction of an entire card prior to punching. The next card can be keyed in while the previous card is being punched. Verification is provided by the same unit. The card sorter arranges cards in alphabetic or numeric order. It can operate at speeds of 1,000 or 1,500 cards per minute.

Figure 4–17
The IBM 5486 Card Sorter (96-Column)

REFERENCES

Awad, Elias, and Data Processing Management Association. *Automatic Data Processing.* Englewood Cliffs, N.J.: Prentice-Hall, 1966.

Levy, Joseph. *Punched Card Data Processing.* New York: McGraw-Hill Book Co., 1967.

Thierauf, Robert J. *Data Processing for Business and Management.* Edited by Daniel W. Geeding. New York: John Wiley & Sons, 1973.

QUESTIONS

1. Describe the physical characteristics of the 80-column punched card. Contrast this card with the 96-column card.
2. Describe the function of the verifier. When is a verifier necessary in the preparation of punched-card data?
3. What is a unit record?
4. List four common types of cards. Give examples of how they may be used.
5. What are the functions of the sorter, collator, interpreter, and calculator-printer?
6. What are the advantages and disadvantages of a wired panel for controlling machine operations?
7. What advantages does the 96-column card offer? What disadvantages does it have?

CHAPTER FIVE

Computer Hardware

This chapter is a general introduction to computer hardware—that is, to the computer and its associated equipment. Later chapters will present details of input/output equipment.

To understand the structure of a computer, we must know what operations it must perform in order to solve a problem. Consider the simple problem of computing the arithmetic mean of five numbers. To accomplish this task manually, we would perform the following steps:

1. Write the five numbers on a sheet of paper.
2. Add the five numbers together to obtain their sum.
3. Divide the sum by 5.
4. Record the answer.

Steps 1 and 4 are usually taken for granted. Generally, we must put numbers on paper to perform calculations; and, just as obviously, we must record the results so that we can remember them and communicate them to others.

Now let us speculate about how a machine might accomplish the task described above without any outside assistance during the calculations. First, the five numbers would have to be made available to the machine in a form it could comprehend. Then it would have to read these

numbers and store them temporarily. Next, it would need instructions directing it to perform each step in the computation. A set of such instructions is called a *program*. The program must be in a language that the machine will understand. For our purposes, we can write the program in English, as follows:

[Prepare the input data of five numbers.]
[Create the computer program.]
1. Read the five numbers.
2. Compute the sum.
3. Divide the sum by 5.   } COMPUTER PROGRAM
4. Write the result.

Before any problem can be solved on the computer, it is necessary to perform two preliminary steps. A program must be designed and created for the computer, and the input data must be prepared in a form suitable for entry into the computer. These two steps will be discussed in later chapters. A computer "reads" data and "writes" results in computer terminology; or, we also say, it inputs data and outputs results or data. From this outline, we can see that the computer must have a means of inputting data and outputting answers. It must also have a place to retain data while it works with it. A

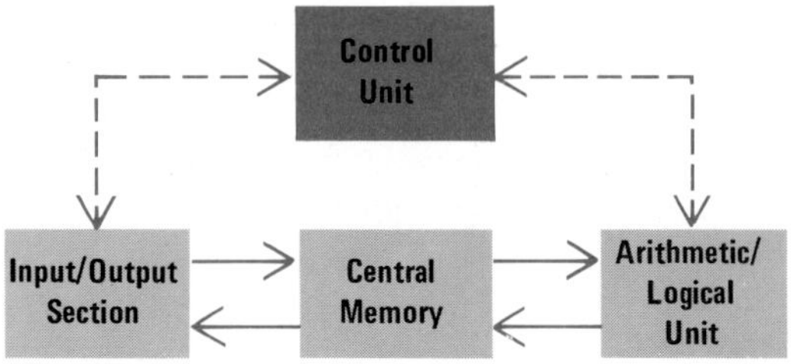

Figure 5–1
The Structure of the Computer

human may store information in his mind or on paper. The place where a computer stores data is called its *memory.* Since the computer is directed by a program, it must have a means of interpreting the program instructions. This interpretation is performed by a *control unit.* The arithmetic computations required by a program are executed by a separate *arithmetic unit.*

The basic structure of a computer is shown in Figure 5–1. The control unit is the unifying portion of the computer and directs all its functions. Now that we have an idea of the basic form of the computer, let us examine each section of the computer in detail.

THE STRUCTURE OF THE COMPUTER

An electronic computer is composed of four basic sections: (1) a control unit, (2) an arithmetic/logical unit, (3) a central memory, and (4) input/output devices. The term *central processing unit* (CPU) is used to denote two units: the control unit and the arithmetic/logical unit. Some authors also consider the central memory as part of the central processing unit.

THE CONTROL UNIT The *control unit* determines which instruction is to be executed, fetches the instruction from the central memory, and interprets the instruction. The instruction is then executed with the aid of other machine units. The entire operation of the computer and its input/output devices are under the direction of the control unit.

THE ARITHMETIC/LOGICAL UNIT The *arithmetic/logical unit* is the section of the computer that performs arithmetic operations as directed by the control unit. For example, an instruction to add two numbers causes the transfer of the numbers to this unit. The addition is performed, and the resulting sum returned to the memory unit. Subtraction, multiplication, and division are also performed within the arithmetic/logical unit.

THE CENTRAL MEMORY Program instructions and data are stored as binary numbers in the *central memory unit,* also known as the *primary memory.* The memory consists of storage locations, each of which has a numerical designation called its *address.* (See Figure 5–2.) The content of each location is a binary number representing either an instruction or data. A computer memory is analogous to a set of mailboxes where each box is labeled with a number that is its address. (See Figure 5–3.) Within each mailbox is exactly one sheet of paper with a number written on it. All the numbers are the same length. The contents of any mailbox may be removed and a sheet of paper with a different number placed in the box. The address of the box remains unchanged, but its contents may be constantly changing. Just as each box has only one sheet of paper in it, so each storage location in a computer memory contains exactly one number. To retrieve the contents of a location, it is necessary to specify its address. Though the contents of a location may change, its address is never altered.

Computer Words   Each storage location, we have said, contains the same number of bits. Storage locations that contain exactly eight bits are called *bytes*. Each byte can be used to represent one alphanumeric character in an eight-bit code. The term *byte* is frequently used also to designate any storage location that can contain only one alphanumeric character, regardless of the number of bits used.

In some computers, a storage location may contain several coded alphanumeric characters. For example, the PDP-8 has storage locations that contain sixteen bits; the UNIVAC 1110 has locations that contain thirty-six bits, and Control Data 6600 computers have locations that contain forty-eight bits. If a computer has forty-eight bits in each storage location and uses a six-bit character code, each location may contain eight characters of alphanumeric data. In this case, the storage locations are called *words*. The number of bits in the storage locations determines the length of the words. If the computer memory contains bytes, several consecutive bytes must be grouped together to form one word. Commonly, four bytes are used to form a computer word thirty-two bits long. The computer word is the smallest unit used in arithmetic computations. For more precision, some computers provide arithmetic operations on double words; that

Address	Contents of Location (in binary form)
00100	001011000100110100100101101010100110
00101	110000000000000000000000000000000000
00102	000011111111111110000000011111111111111
00103	001101101100000000001101111000000000
00104	000000000000000000000000000000000001

Figure 5–2
An Example of Computer Addresses

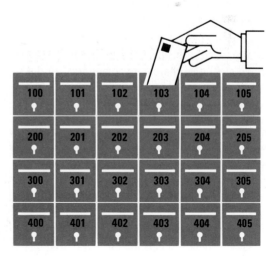

Figure 5–3
Mailboxes in an Apartment Building

is, the contents of two consecutive words are used to represent a numerical quantity. This is known as *double-precision arithmetic.*

Variable Field Lengths   In a computer with a fixed word length, each storage location is defined to be a word. Each word has a unique address, which is specified in an instruction. The PDP-8, UNIVAC 1110, and CDC 6600 are examples of computers with a fixed word length.

A *variable-field-length computer* permits a variable number of characters to be retrieved at a given time. In this case, a *field* indicates a group of bits or characters. There are two methods of specifying the number of characters to be retrieved by an instruction. One is to use a *word-mark bit* that signals the end of the field to be retrieved. In this case, the instruction specifies the starting location of the word. When the word-mark bit is encountered, the field is complete. The second method is to give both the starting location and the number of locations to be fetched in the instruction. In this case, no special control mark is required.

Some computers can handle both fixed word lengths and variable field lengths. Some of the instructions automatically assume either a fixed word length of four bytes or a double word length of eight bytes. Other instructions indicate the starting byte for a field and the number of bytes in the field. Business data processing requires the manipulation of both individual characters and strings of characters in addition to arithmetic computations, and this type of computer provides maximum flexibility.

Memory Sizes   The number of storage locations in a central memory defines the size of the memory. The size of a computer memory containing bytes is expressed in terms of the number of bytes available, whereas other computer memories are described in terms of the number of computer words available. Because of the way computer memories are built, the number of words or characters available is always some multiple of 1,024. The size of a memory is quoted as 8K, 16K, 32K, 64K, and so on, where K represents 1,024. Thus 64K means 64 times 1,024, or 65,536. The number 65K is sometimes used rather than 64K to give the memory size to the nearest decimal thousand.

Any comparison of a character-oriented computer with a word-structured computer must be done with several factors in mind. First, the num-

AFTER TALKS OF GREMLINS, THEY FLOODED THE CPU

In the early days of computers with vacuum tubes, the hardware's performance was not always as reliable as it is today. There are many amusing stories about those "good old days." Reiner E. Baer contributed the following story to *DP Dialog*, published by IBM:

"Way back in the dark ages of computers with tubes, say 1956 or 1957, our computer developed some hard-to-identify intermittent hardware problems. After considerable searching, headscratching, and talks of gremlins, it occurred to one maintenance engineer that the intermittent bugs happened most frequently during periods of dry weather. Without understanding the complete relationship between humidity and error-free computer operation, we determined that higher humidity levels inside the computer did alleviate the problem.

"We then ran a copper tube from the water system into the bottom of the CPU. Afterwards, whenever the computer stopped because of a malfunction, the first thing the operator or maintenance engineer did was *not* to try to isolate and identify the problem, but to turn on the water tap and flood the bottom of the CPU.

"The consternation of existing dignitaries at this apparently irrational behavior was priceless and led to much suppressed hilarity. Just try to imagine the computer with this marvelous console and dozens of lights and switches (they just don't make operator consoles impressive enough any more) humming along and suddenly stopping. Everybody leans forward to see the chief operator flip switches, read lights, get printouts, dial the scope, select the proper cycle time, step forward in memory (what a magician a good operator could be in those days) and then call to his assistant to turn on the water — all of which was done in front of everyone present.

"Unfortunately, the periodic flooding of the CPU created such a hothouse atmosphere that the contacts behind the boards or chassis began to separate. Eventually, the chassis had to be pulled out so all the contacts could be polished and goldplated. But while it lasted, we had great fun confounding visiting brass by giving the impression that this computer truly ran on water."

Adapted from *DP Dialog* advertisement published by IBM Corporation 1974 ber of characters possible in each memory should be calculated. Second, the total quantity of numbers that can be stored for arithmetic computations should be compared. Lastly, the number of instructions possible if the entire memory were devoted to program instructions should be determined. Using these three figures, a rough evaluation of different computer memories can be made.

TYPES OF MEMORIES

The speed of the primary memory is the key factor in determining the speed of a computer. The use of binary numbers within the computer means that a two-state device is needed to represent the two binary digits, 0 and 1. An example of a two-state device is a light bulb, which is either on or off. Another example is a gate, which is either open or shut. The contents of a memory location are altered by switching the two-state device from one state to another. The speed of switching from one state to another determines the speed at which new strings of bits can be written in the memory. Thus the speed of computation is limited by the device used for the primary memory. The speed of a memory device is often quoted in terms of its *access time,* which is defined as the interval from the instant the CPU initiates the retrieval of the contents of a memory location until the time the operation has been completed.

In the early days of computers, vacuum tubes served as the basic two-state device for memory storage. Today there are various devices in use, and research is underway to produce more reliable and faster memories. In this section, the

INTERNAL STORAGE

devices currently in use and the research now in progress are discussed.

CORES   The central memory section of a computer is also commonly known as its *core* because, in many units, each bit is physically represented by a doughnut-shaped core, or ring, of ferrite, a ferromagnetic ceramic. Each core is about the size of a pinhead. A core memory is composed of hundreds of individual cores strung like beads on wires to form a three-dimensional array. Even computer memories that do not use ferrite cores are often called cores.

Each tiny core in a memory represents a one- or zero-bit, depending on its magnetic state. The direction of the magnetic current in a core is called its *polarity.* A core with a counterclockwise polarity can represent a zero-bit while a core with a clockwise polarity represents a one-bit, or vice-versa. The selection of the type of polarity used to represent one- and zero-bits is a task of the computer designer.

To form the three-dimensional core array, cores are strung on wires in a two-dimensional array called a *core plane.* Several core planes are then stacked and connected by wires to form a *core stack.* The wires provide the means of changing the magnetic polarity of the cores. The third dimension of the core determines the number of bits in a computer word. The number of core planes in a stack is dependent on the structure of the individual computer.

There are several possible designs for reading and writing cores. We will discuss the most common one, which requires the passing of four wires through each core. Two wires known as the *x* and *y* wires are used for applying the magnetic current to change the polarity; the function of the other two wires, called the *inhibit* and *sense wires,* is discussed below.

Writing Cores   Although cores are strung on common wires, it is possible to select a particular core to represent a one- or zero-bit by sending current along the *x* and *y* wires that intersect it. (See Figure 5–6.) Half the current re-

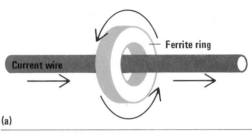

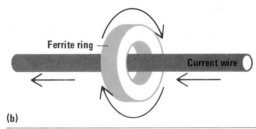

(a)

(b)

Figure 5–4
Magnetic Cores

Figure 5–5
A Portion of a Magnetic Core Memory

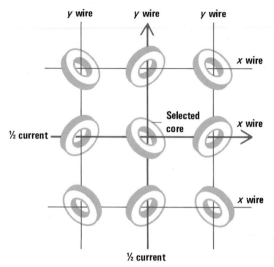

y wire   y wire   y wire

x wire

Selected core   x wire

½ current

x wire

½ current

Figure 5–6
Selecting a Core

quired to give the core a specific polarity is carried by each wire. Thus the full load of current reaches only the core containing the intersection of those wires, and only that core is affected.

Reading Cores   Reading a core is similar in many respects to writing a core. Current is sent through the x and y wires intersecting the core so that the writing of a zero-bit will occur. If the core already "contains" a 0, no change will occur. Because the polarity of the core is not altered, no current will flow in the sense wire. If the core contains a 1, the current will cause the polarity to *flip* (or reverse); this flipping will cause current to flow in the sense wire, signifying a 1 in the core position. However, the reading of a 1 will have caused the core to reverse its polarity and left the core position with a 0. This method of reading, which destroys the initial contents of a storage location, is called a *destructive read-out*. Because the reading of information should not change it, the core must be restored to its former state. This is done by sending current through the x and y wires to attempt to write a 1 in the core. If the core initially contained a 0, the attempt to write a 1 simultaneously will cause current to flow in the inhibit wire. The current

flowing in the inhibit wire will prevent the reversal of the core's polarity and the content of the core will remain a 0. In the case of the core initially containing a 1, the current in the sense wire will prevent any current from being sent through the inhibit wire; thus the core will be flipped to its former state of 1.

Figure 5–7
Core with Inhibit and Sense Wires

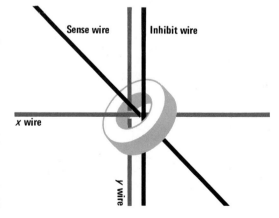

Sense wire   Inhibit wire

x wire

y wire

Case A. The core represents a one-bit.
1. Half the current needed to cause the writing of a zero-bit is sent through the x wire and half through the y wire.
2. The polarity of the core is reversed, that is, flipped, so that it contains a 0.
3. The detection of the reversal of the core's polarity causes current to flow in the sense wire, signifying a one-bit in the core's initial state.
4. The core's former state is restored by sending current through the x and y wires to write a one-bit.
5. Since the sense wire has current flowing in it, no current flows in the inhibit wire. The restoration is performed and the core contains a one-bit once again.

Case B. The core represents a zero-bit.
1. Half the current needed to cause the writing of a zero-bit is sent through the x wire and half through the y wire.
2. No current flows in the sense wire since the core is not flipped.
3. An attempt is made to restore the core's initial state by sending the current needed to write a one-bit through the x and y wires.
4. Simultaneously with the current in the x and y wires, current flows through the inhibit wire. The current in the inhibit wire prevents the flipping of the core to a one-bit. The core's polarity is unchanged.

Figure 5–8
Steps in Reading a Core

Extended Core Storage   Extended core storage (ECS) provides large-capacity core storage in which each location can be specified by its address. As in the use of primary storage, the access time for each location is the same, and considerably faster than the access time for any other data-storage medium except the central memory itself. For example, the extended core storage for the CDC Cyber 70 series of computers has an access time of 3.2 microseconds for 61 bytes of storage. It has a maximum capacity of 20 million characters, compared to a capacity of the main storage unit of less than 132,000 bytes. ECS is particularly advantageous when rapid access to a large volume of data is important.

THIN-FILM MEMORIES   Although the core memory has been highly successful as the primary storage unit for computers, the expense of manufacturing core memories is high. One alternative is the *thin-film memory,* first produced by UNIVAC and used for supplementary high-speed storage in its 1107 computer.

A *thin-film memory plane* consists of a small ceramic or metal plate with deposits of metallic alloys forming a rectangular array. Each spot representing a bit is connected by two

Figure 5–9
An Extended Core Storage Unit

Figure 5–10
A Segment of a Thin-Film Memory

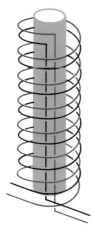

Figure 5–11
A Plated Wire Memory

etched copper wires. No sense or inhibit wires are necessary because the polarity of a particular spot is rotated but not flipped by the passage of a current. A *digit pulse* restores the original polarity of the spot. A typical thin-film memory plane measures 0.025 by 0.050 inches and has a thickness of about 1,000 angstroms (0.0000004 inches). Despite automatic manufacturing techniques, the thin-film memory is still too costly for widespread use.

PLATED WIRE MEMORIES   Plated wire primary memories have been developed by UNIVAC and NCR. The NCR type of plated wire memory is composed of fine copper wires with a coating of thin metallic film. Each wire is cut into tiny lengths (or rods) used to represent a bit. A storage plane consists of rods inserted into coiled wires, which serve as both the activating and sensing elements. Several planes are assembled to form a stack similar to the core stack. The reading of a bit is nondestructive; that is, the reading process does not destroy the original contents and no rewrite is necessary, as with core memories. Because of automatic manufacturing techniques, the rod memories are competitive from a cost standpoint with core memories.

SEMICONDUCTOR MEMORIES   A semiconductor memory uses silicon chips with interconnecting on-off switches (called *flip-flops*). The direction of the electric current passing through each cell determines whether the position of the switch is on or off; that is, whether the bit is 1 or 0. Each silicon chip is about one-eighth of an inch square. There are two types of chips: bipolar and metal oxide semiconductor (MOS) chips. A single MOS chip contains 1,024 bits. A bipolar chip holds fewer bits but offers faster speeds than the MOS chip. Because of the difference in manufacturing processes, the MOS chips are less expensive to produce. Semiconductor memories are also known as *integrated circuits*.

For many years, the most common type of main

Figure 5–12
A Semiconductor Memory

memory has been core storage. However, semi-conductor memories are both faster and more compact. Because their manufacturing costs have dropped, it is estimated that 50 percent of all computers will have semiconductor memories within the next few years. Computers that already utilize semiconductor storage for their main memory include the IBM System/370 Model 145, the UNIVAC 90/60, and the NCR Century 151.

FUTURE DEVELOPMENTS Research is constantly underway to develop faster and cheaper high-speed data-storage methods, and a substantial reduction in the cost of computer memories is expected in the next few years. Since the primary storage unit is the most expensive part of the computer, the cost of computer hardware will be substantially reduced. Techniques now being studied are based on research on cryogenics, photodigital storage, and laser beams.

Cryogenics The study of physical phenomena at very low temperatures is called *cryogenics*. Because metals that are very cold are super-conductive, cryogenic techniques can be used to produce very fast, though small, memories. But the problems in creating a refrigeration system to maintain the temperature of −450°F needed for this type of computer memory have impeded its development.

Photodigital Storage A photodigital storage device uses an electron beam to record binary data on small pieces of film. The film is read by a flying spot scanner. After development of the film chips internally by an automated laboratory, the data are permanently recorded. The film chips cannot be reused. More than a trillion bits of storage can be provided by this device. This type of storage is currently too expensive for commercial use.

Laser Beams The use of laser beams for recording bits on a film chip is another technique under study. It is estimated that 1 million bits could be recorded on 1 square inch of film. Another type of laser-based memory uses magnetic-coated mylar tape wrapped about a drum and gives a density of 13 million bits per square inch. This is 1,000 times greater than the density of magnetic tape now in use. A trillion-bit laser-beam memory was developed for the ILLIAC IV computer by the Precision Instrument Company.

COMPUTER PROGRAMS

Now that the structure of the computer has been defined, it is appropriate to take a closer look at the term *computer program.* A *program* is composed of an ordered set of instructions that are designed to achieve the performance of a certain task. If the instructions are not properly formulated and ordered, the program will be incorrect and the task will not be correctly executed. Each instruction consists of two parts: an operation code and one or more operands. The *operation code* denotes a particular operation such as the addition, multiplication, or comparison of two numbers. The *operands* specify the addresses of the locations in the memory which contain the data to be used in the operations. Since a computer memory contains only binary numbers, the instructions are stored within the computer in this form. For example, an instruction to "add the contents of location 2 and the contents of location 1000_8 and place the result in location 2" might be represented, using octal digits, by the number 110000201000. In the binary system, this would be

001001000000000000010000001000000000.

In this case, 11_8 would be the operation code, and the operands would be the addresses 000002 and 001000. The numerical representation of a program is called a *machine-language program.*

Instructions are typically executed in sequence until an instruction to the contrary is given. For example, a program that began at location 05000_8 would execute the instructions stored at 05000_8, 05001_8, 05002_8, and so on until an instruction was executed that altered this sequence. An operation that may change the sequence in which instructions are executed is called a *branching operation,* and the instruction, a *branch.* An example is a logical operation such as the comparison of the contents of one location with the contents of another location. If the two locations contained the same number, the path of the program might be altered to execute instructions sequentially beginning at another storage location instead of the next instruction in the sequence.

MACHINE CYCLES

The amount of time required by a computer to perform one individual machine operation is called a *machine cycle.* The speed of the computer is related to its machine cycle. The time required to execute a program instruction is often quoted in terms of machine cycles. An instruction may cause several machine operations to take place and thus require several machine cycles.

A machine cycle is measured by the pulses of an electronic clock that emits millions of regularly spaced pulses each second. The time required to fetch and interpret an instruction is called *instruction time,* or *I-time.* The first machine cycle in I-time is called an *instruction cycle.* During I-time, an instruction is selected by the control unit and the operation code is interpreted. The CPU performs all the steps necessary prior to the execution of the instruction. The location of the next instruction is also determined during I-time. *Execution time,* or *E-time,* follows I-time and is the time required for the execution of the instruction. It varies for each instruction; an instruction may require several machine cycles for E-time, although I-time remains constant for all instructions.

REFERENCES

Bohl, Marilyn. *Information Processing.* Chicago: Science Research Associates, 1971.

Brown, John A. *Computers and Automation.* New York: ARCO Publishing Co., 1968.

Bylinsky, Gene. "Little Chips Invade the Memory Market." *Fortune,* April 1971, pp. 100–4.

Greenblatt, Stanley. "360/370 Compatible Peripherals—Part I—Tape, Disk, and Main Memory." *Modern Data,* July 1973, pp. 46–49.

Rosen, Saul. "Electronic Computers: A Historical Survey." *Computing Surveys,* March 1969, pp. 7–36.

Sanders, Donald G. *Computers in Society.* New York: McGraw-Hill Book Co., 1973.

"IBM Goes All Out for IC Memory." *Electronics,* October 1970, pp. 125–26.

QUESTIONS

1. Define the basic sections of a computer.
2. Write step-by-step directions for adding three numbers and placing the result in a mailbox with the address 80. There are 100 mailboxes with addresses from 1 to 100. The three numbers are located on slips of paper in boxes with the addresses 15, 28, and 69. Do not disturb the contents of these mailboxes. What does the mailbox with address 80 contain after the person has followed your directions? What does the mailbox with address 53 contain?

3. Define the term computer address. What is a computer word?
4. In what terms is the capacity of a computer memory described? What is the capacity of the PDP-8, the IBM System/3, and the UNIVAC 90/60 computers?
5. Describe a central memory section made up of cores. What is a core? What is a core plane?
6. How are data read by a computer with a core memory?
7. What types of primary memory storage are currently in use? What types of primary storage do the computers mentioned in question 4 have?

CHAPTER SIX

Secondary Storage Devices

The computer executes instructions and acts upon data stored in the central memory. Data is transferred to the central memory by means of input devices. After the computer has processed part or all of the information, the results must be transmitted to the outside world. This transmission is performed by output devices. *Input/ output devices* are external equipment linked directly to the computer. This type of equipment is also known as *peripheral equipment.* Some devices function as both input and output devices. When the program requests data from an input device, it "inputs" or "reads" data. When the program transfers data to an output device, it "outputs" or "writes" data.

The peripheral equipment available on a computer depends on the particular installation. A computer must have at least one input device and one output device to function efficiently. The configuration of a particular computer comprises the peripheral equipment plus the central memory. Examples of peripheral devices are magnetic-tape units, magnetic disks, magnetic drums, card readers, card punches, paper-tape readers, paper-tape punches, character-recognition devices, line printers, console printers, and cathode-ray-tube (CRT) devices.

In this chapter, we will focus on three devices: magnetic-tape units, magnetic drums, and magnetic disks. These devices supplement the primary storage unit and are called *secondary storage* devices. They are necessary for the storage and manipulation of large data files. The channels that control the operation of input/ output devices, together with the physical characteristics, advantages, and disadvantages of secondary storage devices, will be discussed in the following sections.

CHANNELS

Channels are the portholes from the computer to its peripheral devices. The input/output devices attached to a channel are controlled by the channel unit. There are two basic types of channels: selector and multiplexer.

SELECTOR CHANNELS   A selector channel is capable of transferring data to or from one input/output device at a time. For example, a selector channel may have six tape units assigned to it. The computer signals the channel to transfer data to a particular unit. The channel

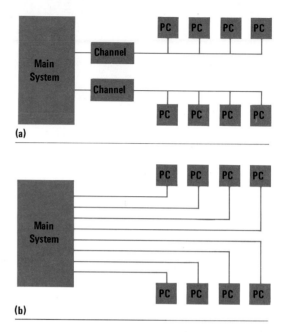

(a)

(b)

controls the transfer of the data and signals the computer when the transfer has been completed. This signal is called an *interrupt.* (Other types of interrupts are discussed in Chapter 18.) Data can be transferred to or from only *one* tape unit at a given time.

MULTIPLEXER CHANNELS When several devices are attached to a multiplexer channel, more than one device may operate at a time. Data transferred to or from one input/output device are interleaved with data being transmitted to or from another device. For example, a multiplexer channel may control a card reader, a card punch, and a line printer. If all three devices are activated, a byte from the card reader sent to the computer may be followed by a byte from the computer sent to the card punch, and then by bytes sent by the computer to the line printer, and so on until the data transfers are completed. This mode of operation is called the *byte mode.* Since the devices in this example are all relatively slow compared to high-speed devices such as magnetic-tape units, the channel is able to operate in the byte mode. However, the data-transmission

rate for a high-speed device is too fast to permit the interleaving of data from other input/output devices. Once it is initiated, the transfer of data to or from a high-speed device monopolizes a channel until it is completed. This mode of operation is called the *burst mode.*

DIRECT CONNECTIONS

Some computers feature direct connection of the input/output devices to the CPU. For example, it may be possible to attach a peripheral device such as a large-volume disk-storage unit directly to a computer without the connecting channel, but such a connection will eliminate the use of several channels for other input/output devices. In the Burroughs 2700/3700/4700 computers, no channels are required in the ordinary sense and each device is attached directly to the CPU. Thus each device can operate—read or write data— independently of any other device. No sharing of a channel for the transmission of data is necessary. The elimination of channel and channel control units may require more complex programming of input/output operations.

Figure 6–1
Input/Output Systems
(a) Selector Channels. In a conventional input/output subsystem, each channel can handle data transfers from only one piece of peripheral equipment at a time because there is only one path to the main system. Here, two out of eight peripheral devices can function simultaneously. Congestion results when several peripheral devices share the same link to the central computer.
(b) Direct Connection. In an input/output subsystem with direct connection of peripheral devices, various peripheral devices can function simultaneously because data from each follows a separate path to the central computer.

MAGNETIC TAPE

Magnetic tape is a primary input/output medium for computer data. It serves as a relatively fast (compared to punched cards), reliable means of entering data into the computer and also of retaining data records for long periods of time. For many years, magnetic tape was the sole medium for the retention of large, permanent data files. Today it remains a popular mode for data files because of its relatively low cost.

Magnetic tape is termed a *sequential-access storage medium.* To locate a data record, the tape must be read sequentially until the record is located. If another record must be found, the tape must be rewound and searched again. For example, to find record 101, records 1 through 100 must be read first. To find record 50 after record 101 has been located, it is necessary to read backwards from 101 to 50 (if the tape unit permits this) or to rewind the tape and begin a new search for record 50.

RECORDING DATA   The magnetic tape used with computers is similar to that found in home tape recorders. Two popular methods for

recording data on computer tape are: *non-return-to-zero (NRZI) recording* and *phase encoding.* In NRZI recording, the magnetic pulses recorded on the computer tape represent one-bits, while the lack of a pulse indicates a zero-bit. In phase encoding, however, both zero-bits and one-bits are recorded. Phase encoding provides greater reliability than the NRZI method. The tape is generally ½ inch wide; the length of a reel varies from 600 to 2,400 feet. The standard length is about 2,000 feet.

Data is recorded by a tape unit under the control of the computer or by a special keyboard device similar to a typewriter. (This device is discussed in Chapter 8.) A tape unit transfers data from the computer to magnetic tape and also transfers data from tape to the computer. A tape is considered to be divided into seven or nine tracks, or channels, which run the length of the tape. A unit of six or eight bits, called a *frame,* is recorded across the width of the tape; each one- or zero-bit in the frame occupies a separate channel. A frame is also called a *character,* although the data bits may not be interpreted by a program as a character but as a number.

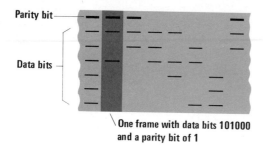

Parity bit

Data bits

One frame with data bits 101000
and a parity bit of 1

Figure 6–2
NRZI Recording on a 7-Track Tape

A special bit known as a *parity bit* is included with the character bits to provide a way of checking the accuracy of the data recording and to ensure accuracy in a subsequent reading of the data. If the tape unit records with *odd parity*, it will always record an odd number of one-bits in each frame. For example, in Figure 6–2, the first data character is 101000. There are two one-bits and, therefore, a parity bit of one is used to give an odd number of one-bits for the frame. If *even parity* is the recording requirement, the number of one-bits in a frame must be even. When a tape is read, the tape unit checks that each frame contains the right number of one-bits. If it does not, an error is signaled and corrective action can be taken.

THE MAGNETIC-TAPE UNIT   The basic design of a tape unit is similar to that of a home tape recorder. As Figure 6–3 shows, there is a *supply reel* and a *take-up reel.* The tape is threaded from the supply reel about a capstan, past the magnetic read/write head, about another capstan, and then wound around the take-up reel. The tape generally hangs down in two large loops in vacuum chambers on each side of the read/write head. The tape is stationary until an instruction to read or write data is given. The interval from the initiation of the tape motion to the time it reaches its full speed is called the *start time.* After data is transferred to or from the tape, the tape motion is halted. The time required to stop the tape is called the *stop time.* The group of data written at a given time is called a *block.* The mechanical necessity of starting and stopping the tape motion each time a group of data is recorded causes the formation of blank spaces between the data groups, or blocks. These spaces are known as *interblock gaps* (IBG's); the interblock gap for most tape units is either .75 or .6 of an inch.

The density of characters recorded on a tape is high; typical densities are 200, 556, 800, or 1,600 frames per inch. The rate of transfer of information is found by multiplying the speed of the tape—say, 75, 112.5, or 200 inches per

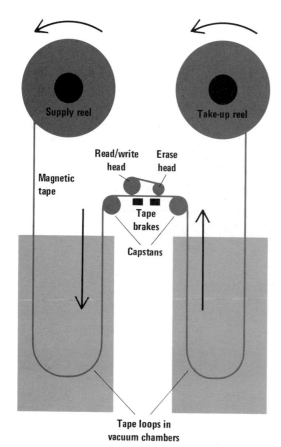

Supply reel

Take-up reel

Read/write
head

Erase
head

Magnetic
tape

Tape
brakes

Capstans

Tape loops in
vacuum chambers

Figure 6–3
A Magnetic-Tape Unit

Figure 6-4
The IBM 3420 Magnetic-Tape Unit

second—by the density per inch. Typical transfer rates are 30,000, 60,000, 90,000 and 320,000 characters per second. Because of differences in recording densities, in the number of bits per frame, in recording techniques, and so on, tapes written on one computer may not be readable by another computer.

The motion of the tape from the supply reel to the take-up reel is called the *forward motion.* Most tape units also provide for the reading of the tape backwards. The time required to reverse the tape motion must be considered if this feature is used. After the reading or writing of the tape has been completed, the tape is returned from the take-up reel to the original reel by rewinding at a high speed. The time required to rewind a full reel of tape varies from one to three minutes depending on the make and model of the tape unit.

LOAD POINTS AND END-OF-FILE MARKERS   A length of 10 to 15 feet of tape at the beginning of a reel is not used to store data. This protects the data on the tape from being accidentally damaged by the computer operator. A reflective spot of material known as the *load point* marks the beginning of the

Figure 6-5
The UNIVAC UNISERVO 12 Magnetic-Tape Subsystem

Figure 6-6
A Load-Point Marker

usable tape for IBM standard tape reels. When the tape is placed on the tape unit, photoelectric cells detect the load point and position the tape for reading or writing. A marker is also placed at the end of the reel to denote the end of the tape. This marker is also a reflective spot of material; it is known as the *end-of-file marker* and is placed about 18 feet from the physical end of the tape.

DATA BLOCKS AND RECORDS   A *file* is a collection of related data. For example, we can designate the collection of information on employees necessary for the production of weekly paychecks as the payroll file. A logical unit of data within a file is called a *record.* A record in a payroll file may consist of the employee's name, payroll number, Social Security number, salary, number of deductions, and so on. A *block* is a physical unit of data and may contain one or more logical records. The word *record* is sometimes used to indicate either a physical or a logical record. This double usage is confusing; in this text, a record will always mean a logical unit of information. Although it is physically possible to write less than an integral number of records in a block, it is not convenient in pro-

gramming to do so. If all the blocks in a file contain the same number of characters or words, the file is called a *fixed-length file.* If the amount of data given in individual records varies, the file is called a *variable-length file.* A tape file may consist of several tape reels.

Because magnetic tape must be read sequentially, the use of tape dictates that a file be organized in a logical sequence. For example, a file containing 1,000 records must be ordered by the identification assigned to each record. The file is then maintained with records ordered by the identification code in each record. The number of records placed in a block is determined by the quantity of data in the record and the uses of the data.

WRITE PROTECTION   Because it is important to prevent the accidental destruction of data files, a *write-enable ring* is commonly required by the tape unit. When the ring is inserted in the inner hub of the tape, writing is permitted. If writing is attempted on a reel without a write-enable ring, the unit will send an error signal and no writing will occur.

ADVANTAGES OF MAGNETIC TAPE   Magnetic tape has several advantages over other

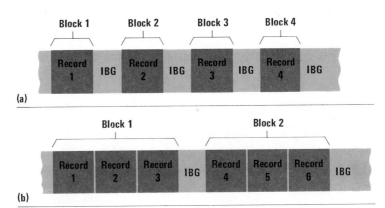

Figure 6–7
Records and Blocks on Tape

Figure 6–8
A Write-Enable Ring

data-storage mediums. It is a compact, reliable, and relatively inexpensive way of storing large amounts of data. A 2,400-foot reel of tape costs about $35; placing a comparable amount of data on punched cards would cost more than $300. Tape can be reused simply by erasing and writing over the old data; cards containing obsolete data must be discarded. There is no limit on the number of characters in a tape record, whereas a punched card has a physical limit of 80 or 96 characters. If a tape file overflows the number of reels allocated for it, any number of additional reels can be used. Magnetic tape also allows data to be inputted or outputted at a faster rate than card readers.

DISADVANTAGES OF MAGNETIC TAPE
Although magnetic tape is a reliable recording medium, it is vulnerable to damage from dust, heat, humidity, and careless handling by computer operators. It is also liable to damage from magnetic fields produced by large electric motors. A tape may break due to wear or a malfunction of the tape units. Splicing a tape does not produce a permanent repair; and because of the high density of recording, some data are generally lost. Data searches are always sequen-

THE COMPUTER ON THE OPERATING TABLE

SIM ONE is a six-foot manikin with a "skin" of resilient plastic that has been used since 1968 for anesthesiology training at the University of Southern California School of Medicine. It does not talk—yet. But it breathes, chokes, blinks, coughs, and regurgitates. By working on the manikin, anesthesiology residents can become skillful in the delicate and potentially dangerous technique of endotracheal intubation, before approaching a human patient.

Intubation is a technique frequently used in anesthesiology. It requires the insertion of a semirigid tube down a patient's throat and upper chest, between the vocal cords, for artificial ventilation of the lung. SIM ONE will respond to errors in the procedure just as a patient would—even to the point of "dying."

SIM ONE can also present symptoms of a patient in shock, such as lowered blood pressure, a vanishing pulse, and gasping for breath. Unless an emergency-room attendant does the right things quickly, SIM ONE will "die." But unlike a human patient, SIM ONE can be brought back to "life" by a flick of a switch. Computer programs have been carefully designed to simulate exactly the reflexes of a patient so that students may practice the same techniques repeatedly until they reach a professional level of skill.

When SIM ONE was first used, in 1968, it drew considerable attention because of the possibilities it opened for the use of simulated patients to teach difficult medical and dental procedures without risk. SIM ONE's versatility and that of its future descendants is limited only by the data fed into its computer system.

Adapted from *Computers and People*, "SIM ONE Entering Commercial Production," April 1974, p. 36.

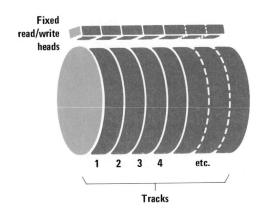

Fixed
read/write
heads

1 2 3 4   etc.

Tracks

Figure 6–9
A Magnetic Drum with Fixed Read/Write Heads

tial; that is, it is necessary to physically pass over earlier records to reach any specific record.

The correction of any item of data on a reel requires the rewriting of the entire reel onto another reel. This is not true when data-preparation devices are being used to transcribe data onto the tape; however, once the tape has been prepared, the correction of any information means that the entire tape must be rewritten with the corrected information. A punched card, on the other hand, can be corrected simply by repunching that one card and inserting the new card in the file. Lastly, the accuracy of data on magnetic tape cannot be verified visually, whereas reading the holes present in punched cards does provide a visual check.

RANDOM-ACCESS DEVICES

Unlike magnetic tape, magnetic disks and magnetic drums permit the retrieval of data records in any order. The time required to obtain a data record is independent of its location in the storage device; consequently, the access time for any data record is the same (or almost the same). Because data can be retrieved in any order, magnetic-disk and magnetic-drum storage units are known as *random-access memories* (RAM). Since the data from any location is obtained directly, without the reading of unwanted data, these devices are also called *direct-access storage devices* (DASD).

MAGNETIC DRUMS   A *magnetic drum* is a cylinder that is constantly revolving under several read/write heads. The reading or writing of a data record occurs when the physical location of the record on the drum passes under one of these heads. The data is then transferred to the central memory. Since the rotational speed of the cylinder is constant and the position of the read/write heads is fixed, the average access time is the same for each data position.

The entire drum surface is magnetized. Each read/write head covers an area on the drum and reads or writes data on that area as it revolves under the head. The band of area covered by each head is called a *track,* or *channel.* (See Figure 6–9.) The read/write heads write bits by magnetizing a spot on the drum. The presence of a magnetic spot indicates a one-bit; its absence indicates a zero-bit. Reading is accomplished by sensing the condition of magnetized spots.

Figure 6–10
A Fixed-Head Drum

Figure 6–11
The IBM 3330 Disk Subsystem

The read operation is said to be nondestructive since the condition of the data is not altered. Magnetic-drum storage is permanent, since a spot will retain its magnetic state indefinitely unless it is changed by a write operation. The contents of the drum remain unaltered even when the power is switched off.

If there is a read/write head for each band on the drum, and the position of the heads is fixed as described earlier, the average access time is quoted as one-half the time required for the drum to make one complete revolution. In order to reduce access time, some drums have more than one read/write head per track. Very large drums may be divided into *sectors* with only one read/write head per sector. If the data being accessed is not under a read/write head, the heads must be moved. The access time is then calculated as the average time it takes to position the heads plus one-half the time required for the drum to complete one revolution. The transfer time is very fast in comparison to the access time. For example, access time for a high-speed drum such as the UNIVAC FH-432 is 4.3 milliseconds, and the transfer rate is 1,440,000 characters per second. The capacity of this drum is 1,572,864 characters with 7,200 revolutions per minute.

Each location on a drum has an address; the content of any location is retrieved by specifying its address. For drums with movable heads, it is necessary to specify both the sector and the address. However, it is inefficient to retrieve data by reading the contents of first one location and then another, and so on. Each positioning of the drum for reading or writing at a particular location on the device is called an *access* to the device. An entire group (a block) of sequential locations is generally read or written on the drum at one access. This minimizes the time required to reach the desired position on the drum before the transfer of data can begin. The time required to reach the position on the drum before the transfer of data can be initiated is called the *access time.*

The primary advantages of a magnetic drum are its speed, the fact that data can be retrieved by directly addressing a location, and its reliability as a storage device. The main disadvantage is its cost. Magnetic drums, on the whole, are somewhat more expensive than magnetic tape or magnetic-disk units. A drum is useful as a high-speed storage device for intermediate data. Because it has a fixed storage capacity, the storage of permanent files (which will expand in time) will eventually require the acquisition of another drum at considerable expense. The cost of drum storage versus its advantages must be carefully weighed.

MAGNETIC DISKS   The magnetic disk is another random-access (or direct-access) storage device. A disk unit resembles a phonograph turntable on which several metal disks are stacked on top of one another but separated by spaces. (See Figure 6–11.) One or more arms (similar to phonograph arms) containing read/write heads move in or out to reach a specified position. The disks are constantly revolving under the arms, which are a hair's breadth from the surface of the disks. The surface of each disk is divided into concentric circles called *tracks* and pie-shaped segments called *sectors.* The location of data is specified by giving the disk face, sector, and track containing the information. Each track has the same storage capacity. For example, the UNIVAC 8424 disk subsystem has eleven disks and twenty disk surfaces per control unit; each surface contains 406 concentric circles, each of which has a capacity of 7,294 bytes. The disks make 2,400 revolutions per minute.

The movement of the arm to a particular point is relatively expensive in terms of time compared to the transfer of data to or from the core. Access time must be calculated as the time required to position the arm plus the average time it takes for the data needed to pass under the read/write head; this latter time interval is known as the *average rotational delay.* Transfer rates are generally very fast in comparison to access time. For example, the IBM 3330 disk-storage unit has a transfer rate of 806,000 bytes per second. It takes an average of 30 milliseconds to position an arm, and there is an average rotational delay of 8.4 milliseconds. To eliminate arm movement, some disks are manufactured with fixed heads. For example, the Burroughs Corporation manufactures a disk with sufficient read/write heads to make arm movement unnecessary. Thus, the time required to obtain data is only the average rotational delay plus the transfer rate, which

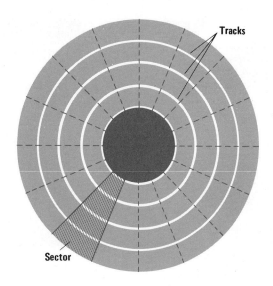

Figure 6–12
A Disk Surface Divided into Tracks and Sectors

Figure 6–13
A Burroughs Disk with Fixed Heads

Figure 6–14
The IBM 3336 Disk Pack

ranges from 100,000 to 500,000 characters per second.

Disks are high-volume storage devices with capacities ranging from 5.4 million bytes (for the IBM 2305-1 fixed-head disk-storage unit) to over 1 billion bytes (for the IBM 3330 Model 11 disk subsystem). Both permanent fixed-disk storage and removable disk packs are available. In fixed-disk storage devices, the disk surfaces are not removable from the disk unit. Disk packs are sets of disks that can be removed in the same way magnetic tapes are mounted and dismounted from tape units. For example, the IBM 3330 Model 11 disk subsystem may have up to eight *disk-storage* units connected to it. Each disk unit contains a disk pack, which is a set of ten disks with nineteen disk surfaces and a storage capacity of 200 million bytes. The total capacity of the subsystem is 1 billion, 600 million bytes. Furthermore, each disk pack may be removed and another disk pack mounted within the disk unit. This provides as much flexibility as magnetic tape storage. The main advantage of this type of disk storage is that data files can be expanded by purchasing extra disk packs rather than another disk unit at considerably greater expense.

Disk units generally have a number of advan-

tages. They can be used to store a large volume of data at a reasonably low cost, and there is direct access to their contents. Although the per-bit cost of magnetic tape is less, the data are always located in sequential fashion. The access time for a data block on tape depends on its location on the reel. Each record on a disk file has the same anticipated access time, although individual records have different access times depending on the current position of the arms. In contrast, each record on a drum with fixed read/write heads has the same average access time, since no arm motion is involved. Basically, a disk file has the same advantages and disadvantages as drum storage unless the drum has sufficient heads so that no mechanical arm movement is necessary. Disk packs offer a further advantage in that they make it considerably less expensive to expand storage capacity. Because the cost of disks has decreased in recent years and their reliability has increased, they have become the most popular direct-access device.

MAGNETIC CARD STORAGE   Magnetic card storage units, also known as data cell units, provide storage for a large volume of data at a low speed and a correspondingly low cost. This type of storage unit is represented by the IBM 2321 data cell drive. This unit can store up to 392 million bytes. Up to eight IBM 2321 data cell drives can be attached to a control unit to give a storage capacity of 3.2 billion bytes. Data is stored on a magnetic card 2¼ inches wide and 13 inches long. Ten of these cards are stored in a *subcell,* and twenty subcells are contained in a data cell drive. To read or write data on a card, the data cell drive rotates to reach the subcell required. Then the addressed card is drawn from the ten cards in the subcell and placed on a drum, which is spun under a read/write head. Access time ranges from a minimum of 100 microseconds (when the data card is already on the drum) to 600 milliseconds. The entire selection process is mechanical and requires substantially more time than in tape, drum, or disk units.

Figure 6–15
The IBM 2321 Data Cell Drive

"See, without me you're nothing!"

REFERENCES

Awad, Elias. *Business Data Processing.* Englewood Cliffs, N.J.: Prentice-Hall, 1971.

Bohl, Marilyn. *Information Processing.* Chicago: Science Research Associates, 1971.

Davis, Gordon B. *Computer Data Processing.* New York: McGraw-Hill Book Co., 1969.

Foster, Caxton. *Computer Architecture.* Englewood Cliffs, N.J.: Prentice-Hall, 1971.

In addition, the available booklets on specific manufacturers' equipment should be consulted.

QUESTIONS

1. What is a channel? How does a multiplexer channel differ from a selector channel?
2. What do the terms *random-access* and *direct-access storage* mean?
3. Define the terms *block* and *record* as they apply to magnetic tape.
4. Compare the speed, cost, and method of data retrieval of magnetic-tape and magnetic-drum storage.
5. Compare the IBM 2311 disk pack to the IBM 3300 disk unit. What are the advantages and disadvantages of each device? How fast are they, and how much data can they store? (See "Disk and Drum Drives: Part 2 — Large-Scale Drives," Franklin L. Tabel, *Modern Data,* February 1971, pp. 68-78.)
6. File A contains 100 records, each composed of 60 characters. File B contains 500,000 records with 200 characters per record. What storage medium would be most suitable for these files? What other information would you need to select a storage medium?
7. An insurance company has 60,000 policyholders and presently stores all its data files on magnetic tape. An anticipated increase in business should bring the number of policyholders up to 100,000 in the next three years. Fast access to the files is not a prime consideration, but the constant handling of the huge tape file has become troublesome. How else might this data be permanently stored? Argue the case for each storage medium.

CHAPTER SEVEN

Data Input/Output Devices

Figure 7–1
The Honeywell CRU 1050 Card Reader

In the previous chapter we discussed the most common devices for storing large data files: magnetic tape, drums, and disks. This chapter discusses the remaining input/output devices — card readers, card punches, paper-tape readers, paper-tape punches, and display devices such as line and character printers, cathode-ray-tube units, plotters, and audio-response units. These devices are used to input source data directly and obtain output accessible to human eyes and ears.

CARD INPUT/OUTPUT DEVICES

CARD READERS   Cards are a primary input medium for the computer. The *card reader* reads punched cards and transfers the data to the computer. Binary data on cards may be read and transferred directly. More commonly, however, the Hollerith code is translated by the card reader into an internal computer code; for example, the Hollerith code may be automatically translated to EBCDIC for computers such as the IBM System/370 computer.

The card reader consists of five basic parts: the input stacker, the first read station, the second read station, one or more output stackers, and the reject stacker. The deck of cards is placed in the input stacker. Each card is then read under the direction of the computer. As reading is initiated, the card moves past two reading stations that detect the absence or presence of holes by means of either wire brushes or photoelectric cells. The images of the card given at the two stations are compared to detect a possible *read error*. If the images do not match, the card is placed in the reject stacker and an error is signaled. Otherwise, the card is placed in the appropriate output stacker selected by the program. The data is translated, if necessary, and placed in the central memory. Card readers input cards at a rate of 100 to 2,000 cards per minute, depending on the make and model of the equipment. A typical speed is 1,000 cards per minute.

CARD PUNCHES   Cards may also be punched via the card punch on the computer. The cards produced by the card punch will have only rectangular holes; they will not have any printing. To obtain a line of printing on a card, the cards must be run through a device known as a *card interpreter*. Only cards containing Hollerith codes can be interpreted in this way. The card

Figure 7–2
THE IBM 2540 Card Reader/Punch

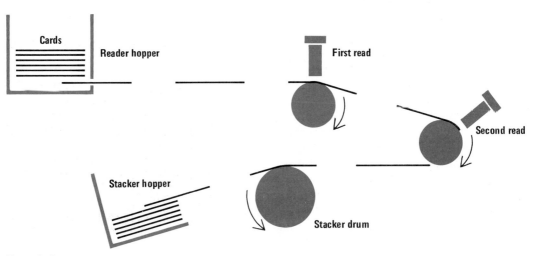

Figure 7–3
Diagram of a Card Reader

punch on the computer can also be used to punch cards containing only numerical data in a binary format; such cards cannot be interpreted by a line of printing.

Card punches must operate mechanically in order to physically punch holes through cards. Consequently they are slow devices; a typical speed is 300 cards per minute. Because of the slow rate for punching data, punched cards are not a popular output medium.

PAPER TAPE

Paper-tape readers are used to read paper tape prepared by keyboard devices such as teletypes and flexowriters. The paper-tape punch can produce tape to be read via one of these devices or by the paper-tape reader on the computer. Paper tape is punched with round holes across the width of the tape; each frame on the tape contains a character or unit of data. The middle of the tape is perforated with tiny holes, called *sprocket holes,* which run the length of the tape. Paper tape is classified by the number of channels, or tracks, provided; 5, 6, 7, and 8-track tape is available.

Characters are recorded in code on paper tape in the same way they are on magnetic tape, except that there is no parity bit. The particular pattern of holes punched is dependent on the recording device used. Any translation of the characters to the internal computer code is performed under the control of a computer program and not by the paper-tape device. The speed of paper-tape readers varies from 150 to 1,000 characters per second. A typical speed is 120 characters per second for a paper-tape punch.

Paper tape is not usually used as a primary input or output medium for large-scale computers because card readers are almost ten times faster than paper-tape readers. Paper tape is often the primary means of inputting and outputting data on smaller computers. Because card readers and punches are more expensive than paper-tape equipment, a smaller computer may utilize a

Figure 7–4
The IBM 3505 Card Punch

Figure 7–5
The IBM 1017 Paper-Tape Reader

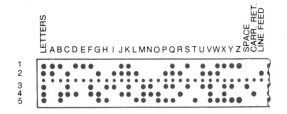
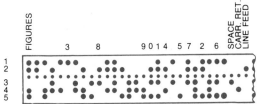

Figure 7–6
Punched Paper Tape

paper-tape reader and punch devices to lower the overall cost of the computer configuration. The introduction of the 96-column card on the IBM System/3, a small computer system, may alter this picture in the future.

The primary disadvantage of paper tape is the recording medium itself. Paper tape is one continuous strip of paper, and the correction or insertion of any single character is a time-consuming chore. The entire tape must be reproduced by the data-preparation device (e.g., the teletype) and the corrections entered in the new tape. Punched cards offer an ease of correction unequaled by any other medium. The tearing up of a punched card and the insertion of a new card is a joy compared to the tedious task of running a paper tape through a reader and carefully correcting the data. Paper tape also lacks the durability of punched cards.

DISPLAY DEVICES

The three basic display devices for the computer are line printers, character printers, and cathode-ray-tube display units. The plotter is a fourth display device useful in production of graphs and pictorial output.

LINE PRINTERS Character output devices such as a typewriter strike one character at a time. A line printer, in contrast, assembles all the characters on a line at one time and prints them with apparent simultaneity. Two printing methods are used: impact and nonimpact. Final printed output is also obtained by the use of microfilm printers. *Impact printers* strike hammers that press the paper against the appropriate type keys, whereas the *non-impact printers* produce a line of print by chemical or electronic means. *Microfilm printers* produce output on microfilm for subsequent processing and printing on paper.

Impact Printers The two most common types of impact printers are the drum and the chain printers. The *drum printer* utilizes a metal drum engraved with rows of characters. The drum is rotated so that each row of characters moves past a set of print hammers. There is a hammer for each print position on the line. When the characters reach the proper printing position, the hammers are actuated, causing the character to be pressed against the paper. Several activations of the hammers may be necessary to print one line. However, this process is so

Figure 7–7
The UNIVAC 0770 Line Printer

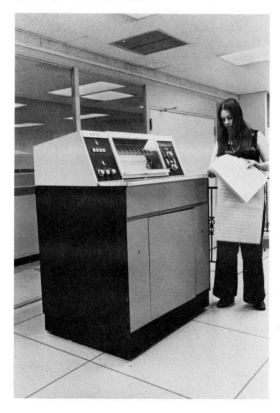

Figure 7–7
The UNIVAC 0770 Line Printer

rapid that it appears that an entire line has been printed by one simultaneous strike of the hammers.

Chain printers have a horizontal chain, generally containing five sets of 48 characters each, that moves continually past the print hammers. As the characters come into the proper position, the hammers are activated and the characters pressed against the paper. Because five sets of characters are provided, one revolution of the chain is usually sufficient to print a line. Both the character set and the type font can be changed by a substitution of the chain.

Both drum and chain printers provide high-speed printing. The rate of printing ranges from 600 to 1,000 lines per minute or more; the IBM 3211 chain printer operates at 2,000 lines per minute. The length of a line is typically 132 characters, although 120 and 148 are not uncommon. It is possible to obtain multiple copies of output at a single printing by the use of multiple-ply paper. Up to ten copies can be produced this way. Special forms are also available for printing jobs such as mailing-list labels or bank checks.

Two other types of impact printers are the wheel and the matrix printers. The *wheel printer* has a character wheel for each print position of

THE ENIAC: 1946–1955

The grandfather of electronic digital computers was born in a cellar of the Moore School of Electrical Engineering at the University of Pennsylvania during World War II. Built to replace a huge mechanical differential analyzer that calculated shell trajectories and artillery firing tables, it was a product of the war effort that was finished too late to contribute to winning the war.

The ENIAC (Electronic Numerical Integrated Automatic Computer) was proposed early in 1943 and funded through the ballistics and research laboratory of the U. S. Army Ordnance Corps. It took 30 months and 200,000 man-hours to complete. When it was dedicated in February 1946, it was capable of performing calculations at 1,000 times the speed of its mechanical predecessors.

The machine was constructed of 47 panels, each nine feet high, two feet wide, and one foot thick. It had something less than 19,000 vacuum tubes, plus 70,000 resistors and 10,000 capacitors, among its many components. It used over 150 kw. of power, and reportedly the lights in West Philadelphia would dim when it was turned on.

ENIAC was a synchronous decimal-arithmetic machine. Its cycle time was 200 microseconds, so it could perform 5,000 additions per second. Its word size was 10 digits plus a sign, and it could multiply two full words in 2.6 milliseconds. It could also subtract, divide, compare numbers, and take a square root.

Reading, computing, and writing were done simultaneously. Data could be inputted through dials and switches and outputted via a light display, but input and output were primarily produced through an IBM card reader and a summary punch.

The ENIAC used wired programs, and setting up a program could take weeks. The need for a stored program became apparent after construction had started, and this capability was eventually added.

The ENIAC died in 1955, a victim of competition from its own offspring. Its creators, J. Presper Eckert and John Mauchly, went on to build other machines, including the Universal Automatic Computer, or UNIVAC for short.

Adapted from "The ENIAC: 1946–1955," Datamation, June 1973, p. 122. Reprinted with permission of *Datamation*®, © copyright 1973 by Technical Publishing Co., Greenwich, Conn. 06830.

Figure 7–8
An Electrostatic Printer

the line. Each wheel is rotated to the proper character and then the entire line is printed. This simultaneous-printing method is comparatively slow. Wheel printers have speeds up to 150 lines per minute, with each line containing 120 characters. The *matrix printer* prints a character by activating selected wires to produce a pattern of dots.

Non-Impact Printers This type of printer does not employ print hammers, but forms a line image by chemical or electronic means. A variety of methods are used to produce characters on paper. The *electrostatic printers* use electrodes or other image matrix mechanisms to construct characters on sensitized paper. Another type of non-impact printer uses electro-optics to flash an optical image on photographic paper to form the characters. Still another type uses an optical-character mask to form characters on a print drum one page at a time; the drum then transfers the entire page onto the paper in a manner similar to that of photocopying machines. Since no striking hammers are used, non-impact printers are silent.

Although non-impact printers are faster than impact printers, the line images may be blurred.

Also, non-impact printing provides only one copy at a time, which can be inconvenient. Consequently, impact printers remain the most popular printing device.

Microfilm Printers *Microfilm printers* are devices that read data from magnetic tape, display the data on a cathode ray tube, and record the data onto microfilm. The microfilm may then be processed and the data printed on paper. The computer output must be produced in a special format suitable for the microfilm printer. The average line printer has a speed of 1,100 lines per minute, or less than 2,500 characters per second. The fastest line printer has a speed of about 5,000 characters per second. The average computer-output microfilm (COM) device operates at a speed of 50,000 to 60,000 characters per second, while the fastest has a speed of somewhat less than 120,000 characters per second. Its speed is more than ten times that of the line printer.

COM can record boldface or double-size characters for special information. Different character sizes may be available. If forms are required, they can be printed together with the data; no special form paper is necessary. The quality of the print-

Figure 7–9
A Microfilm Printer and Sample Microfilm

ing is very good and may include color and shading. If they are adequately indexed, data records stored on microfilm can be quickly retrieved by microfilm recorders. A typical retrieval time is less than 15 seconds. A firm with a high volume of data may choose to maintain its master records on microfilm without ever printing them on paper. Using a sophisticated retrieval system controlled by a computer, millions of documents may be stored and accessed quickly.

The primary disadvantage of COM is the inherent delay in the visual display of the microfilm. Film stock is less expensive than paper, so that costs are lower when a visual display on paper is not required. Because of its versatility, its speed, and the competitiveness of its cost with that of line printers, microfilm is becoming increasingly popular, especially where voluminous printing loads are encountered.

CHARACTER PRINTERS This type of printer provides *serial printing;* that is, it prints one character at a time. An example of a serial printer is an electric typewriter modified for use with a computer. Printed output known as *hard-copy output* is provided by striking the

appropriate keys against the paper. A serial printer is a slow device, printing less than sixteen characters per second. Another character printer is the *teletype,** which has a keyboard similar to the typewriter; it prints a maximum of ten characters per second.

A typewriter device can be·used as a remote terminal (see Chapter 18) or attached to a computer console as an input/output device. In either case, it serves as both a receiver and a transmitter of characters to and from the computer. Because a typewriter's speed is very slow, a medium- or large-scale computer will utilize one or more line printers for output data. On a small computer, a typewriter device may be the only means of producing hard-copy output.

The *console* is the means by which the computer operator can manually direct the computer. The console always has a means of displaying information from the computer and provides a way of entering small amounts of data into the computer. A cathode-ray-tube unit is sometimes supplied for the console rather than a typewriter device. A typewriter keyboard may not be furnished for some small computers; in that event,

* Registered trademark of Teletype Corporation

Figure 7–10
A Typewriter on a Computer Console

data can be entered into the computer at the console by manually pushing buttons or knobs on the console.

CATHODE-RAY-TUBE DISPLAY UNITS

The cathode-ray-tube (CRT) unit appears to be a television picture tube with a keyboard attached. Because the CRT device displays data electronically rather than mechanically, it can respond faster than any character printer. CRT units are popular as remote terminals. Because of its speed, a CRT device may be preferred for the computer console rather than a typewriter device. CRT units are divided into two basic types: those which display characters only and those which display graphical data as well as characters. The size of a display screen ranges from eight to twenty inches, depending on the make and model of the unit.

CRT devices both receive and transmit data. Some units feature a *light pen* that enables the operator to identify a particular point, line, or character in the displayed image to the controlling program. CRT display units are being utilized in a number of ways — for example, in airline reservation systems, in the display and modification of engineering drawings, and in man-

Figure 7–11
A CRT Display of Alphanumeric Data

agement information systems. The primary disadvantage of these devices is their high cost. However, the cost has steadily decreased as CRT units have become available from various manufacturers. The lack of hard copy may also influence some users against the choice of a CRT display device. It is possible to copy a CRT display using special nonprogrammed attachments such as the IBM 2285 display copier. Another disadvantage of CRT's is that they require more complex programming than simple typewriter devices.

PLOTTERS   *Plotters* are devices for drawing graphical output on paper. A plotter consists of a mechanical pen suspended over drawing paper. The movement of the pen is controlled by a program. The program commands are generally limited to commands to lift the pen, put the pen on the paper, and move the pen one increment in a specified direction.

A plotter is a versatile output device and has a large variety of applications. It is used to produce dress designs, maps, and anatomical drawings, and for many other purposes, as well as to produce routine graphs. Because the pen moves by small increments, alphanumeric data can also be drawn.

AUDIO-RESPONSE UNITS   A prerecorded set of spoken words can be stored for an audio-response unit. A spoken message selected from these words can be issued under the control of a program. This enables the computer to respond directly with words to an interrogation of a computer file. The standard telephone provides quick and easy access to an audio-response unit.

One prediction for the future is that data will

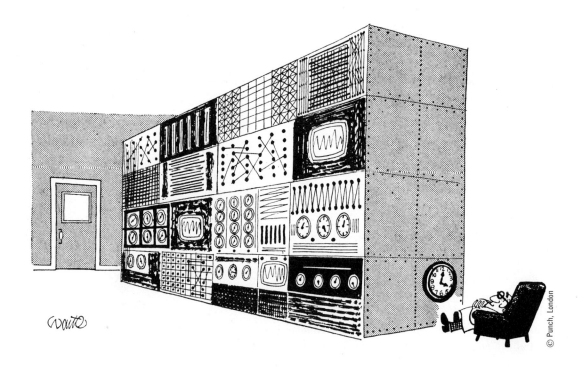

Figure 7–12
A Contour Map Produced by a Plotter

Figure 7–13
A Plotter

Figure 7–14
An Audio-Response Unit

be inputted vocally. So far, this prediction has not become a reality. However, a computer-controlled voice-recognition system to permit voting by phone is under consideration by the state of Washington. The technological advances necessary to enable computers to recognize voice prints and input vocal data directly may soon be here.

REFERENCES

Awad, Elias. *Business Data Processing.* Englewood Cliffs, N.J.: Prentice-Hall, 1971.

Bohl, Marilyn. *Information Processing.* Chicago: Science Research Associates, 1971.

Davis, Gordon B. *Computer Data Processing.* New York: McGraw-Hill Book Co., 1969.

Foster, Caxton. *Computer Architecture.* Englewood Cliffs, N.J.: Prentice-Hall, 1971.

"Computer Output Alternatives: An EDP Man Looks at COM." *Information and Records Management,* December 1973 and January 1974, pp. 52–60.

In addition, the available booklets on specific manufacturers' equipment should be consulted.

QUESTIONS

1. What are the advantages of using punched cards for input data? Compare the advantages and disadvantages of punched cards and paper tape for the preparation of input data. Consider the difficulties of correcting data and the accidental disarrangement of data records.
2. What is the computer configuration at your college? Give the size of the core, the characteristics of the computer (its speed, the length of a word, character length), and specify all the input/output devices. If you do not have a computer installation, design a hypothetical computer configuration and defend your choice of hardware.
3. Compare the characteristics of the various computers in the IBM System/370 series. In particular, contrast the System/370 Model 155 with the System/370 Model 165. (See Angeline Pantages and R. A. McLaughlin, "IBM System/370 Surfaces—But Is That All There Is?" In *Datamation,* August 1, 1970, pp. 58–59.)
4. What advantages does a character printer offer? What advantages does a CRT unit offer?
5. Describe the drum and the chain line printers. What features make the line printer invaluable as an output device?
6. Why should a firm with a computer installation consider the addition of a COM printer? Should the conventional line printer be eliminated if a COM printer is acquired? Why or why not?

CHAPTER EIGHT

Data-Entry Systems

The 80-column card and its recording device, the keypunch, have dominated the computer-input arena since the appearance of computers more than twenty-five years ago. Paper tape has never gained the popularity of punched cards because errors in paper tape are troublesome and time-consuming to correct. In the early days of computers, whenever a great volume of data was prepared on punched cards, it was customary to transcribe the data cards onto magnetic tape by means of a card-to-tape device that operated independently of the computer—that is, by means of an *off-line* device. The tapes would then be mounted on the computer's tape units and read directly by the computer. Since magnetic-tape units read data at a speed far exceeding that possible with any card reader, this procedure reduced the time required to process the data on the computer. This data-preparation method is still used by some computer installations today.

Although this method is generally satisfactory, two basic problems remain. First, the keypunching of cards is not an ideal data-preparation method, particularly for the transcription of a large volume of data, because it is a slow process. If an error is made anywhere in a card, an entirely new card must be created. Verification must be performed as a separate operation. Cards, once punched, cannot be reused. In a large-volume operation, the cost of blank cards is expensive. These factors gave rise to new input-preparation devices: the key-to-tape devices and the key-to-disk devices. Second, the transcription of data from original documents to punched cards or any other medium is time-consuming, it is expensive, and it may result in errors in the transcribed data. These factors caused the development and use of character-recognition devices: optical character-recognition (OCR) devices, magnetic-ink character-recognition (MICR) devices, and mark-sense devices. These two basic types of data-input devices will be discussed in the following sections.

KEY-TO-TAPE AND KEY-TO-DISK DEVICES

THE UNITYPER UNIVAC introduced the first key-to-tape device, called the *Unityper*. It was used in conjunction with the UNIVAC I and UNIVAC II. These two computers did not have card readers. Data was inputted and outputted on high-speed magnetic-tape units, and a line

printer was used to output hard copy. Consequently, data was often prepared on punched cards and then transcribed to tape via an off-line card-to-tape unit. The Unityper provided a direct means of preparing data on magnetic tape. It resembled an oversized typewriter with a tape-recording mechanism attached. Small tape reels of about fifty feet were used for recording data. After much success as the workhorse of the UNIVAC I and II systems, the Unityper was discontinued. The addition of card readers to the UNIVAC line of computers reduced the demand for the Unityper at that time.

THE DATA RECORDER In 1965, a key-to-tape device called a *data recorder* (Figure 8–1) was successfully produced and marketed by Mohawk Data Sciences. This device has a keyboard similar to that of a standard 80-column keypunch, a control panel of switches and indicators, an 80-position core memory, and a magnetic-tape handler for standard half-inch-wide tape. The operator keys in data, which is transferred and held in the core memory. Upon completion of a record, the data is transferred from the core memory and placed on tape in an 80-character block. If the operator detects an error while keying a record, it may be corrected by backspacing and striking the correct key. The correction is performed in the core memory so that the entire record, including the corrected data, is written on tape at one time. Many companies other than Mohawk are now manufacturing key-to-tape devices based on these same operating principles.

The data recorder offers a saving in data-preparation time, since a keying error detected by the operator can be quickly corrected on the spot. The production of magnetic tape for direct input to the computer means a reduction in the computer time needed for reading the data. The elimination of punched cards and the use of re-useable magnetic tape means a direct saving on the purchase of blank cards for punching. The use of tape rather than cards also means a reduction in the office space required for the storage of data. An indirect benefit has been the satisfaction of former keypunch personnel with the quiet environment provided by key-to-tape devices, a considerable contrast to the racket of the old keypunch room.

THE KEY-TO-CASSETTE DEVICE Although the key-to-tape device is highly success-

Figure 8–2
A Key-to-Cassette Terminal

ful, it has a tape reel that must be manually mounted and dismounted by the operator. The key-to-cassette, or key-to-cartridge, device offers the same features as the key-to-tape device but uses a tape cartridge or cassette containing about 100 feet of magnetic tape. The cartridges are later combined on a standard magnetic-tape reel by a special tape-cartridge reader for input to the computer.

MULTIPLE KEY-TO-TAPE DEVICES   In order to achieve greater flexibility in the preparation of data tapes, several key-to-tape or key-to-cassette devices may be controlled by a small computer. The use of the computer permits several operators to key data at individual *key-to-tape stations*, each handling a different job. Two cassettes at a keyboard can be used to verify data. As the data is verified, it is recorded on the second cassette and any missing data is inserted in proper sequence.

KEY-TO-DISK   Data can also be recorded directly on magnetic disks by the use of keyboard devices controlled by a small computer. The operator keys data at a keyboard station as in the case of the key-to-tape devices. Corrections and error recovery are performed by the operator

Figure 8–3
A Key-to-Cartridge Terminal—the IBM Model 50

Figure 8–4
A Key-to-Disk System with Multiple Keyboards

Figure 8–5
Another Key-to-Disk System
with Multiple Keyboards — the Keyplex by Honeywell

in conjunction with the data-recording program. Several key stations can be operating at the same time under the control of the small computer. After recording has been completed, the contents of the disk are generally written on tape for subsequent processing by the main computer. The key-to-disk device has become increasingly popular in recent years due to its flexibility and the relatively low cost per character recorded.

CHARACTER-RECOGNITION DEVICES

Although key-to-tape, key-to-cassette, and key-to-disk devices offer an improved means of transcribing data for the computer, they require the reading and recording of source data, which not only introduce the possibility of data errors but take time. When the data runs to hundreds of thousands of items per day, another means of transferring the information to the computer must be explored. The U.S. banking industry, faced with the clearance of 70 million checks per day, has turned to magnetic-ink character-recognition devices. Optical character-recognition devices and mark-sense readers are two other means of inputting data without transcribing it from source documents to another data form. The cost of character-recognition devices is substantially higher than that of other input devices, such as keypunch or key-to-disk equipment. It is estimated that a character-recognition device is economical only when over 10,000 input documents are processed per day — that is, when eight to ten keypunch operators are employed in the preparation of data for the computer. Currently, character-recognition devices represent a small percentage of the input devices in use. Computer scientists are predicting that optical character-recognition devices will have captured most of the market for input devices by 1980. However, the fulfillment of this prediction depends upon revolutionary changes in business procedures.

MAGNETIC-INK CHARACTER-RECOGNITION (MICR) DEVICES Magnetic-ink character-recognition (MICR) devices are very popular in the banking industry, which has been faced with a growing volume of personal checks that have to be rapidly processed daily. Industry-wide standards for the method of encoding data were necessary before the banking industry could adopt these devices, because as many as four banks could be involved in processing a single check. A set of standards was established in 1960.

Bank customers are issued checks magnetically imprinted with the bank number, the bank branch (if any), and an account number, using the E-13B font adopted by the banking industry as its standard. The checks also contain the customer's name and, in some cases, his address, printed in a conventional font. (See Figure 8–6.) When a check is presented for clearance, the amount of the check is encoded in magnetic ink. The MICR reader reads the checks and inputs the information to the computer directly or places the data on magnetic tape for subsequent

Figure 8–6
Data on a Canceled Check
(a) The Fourteen Magnetic-Ink Characters in Font E–13B
(b) A Sample of a Canceled Check

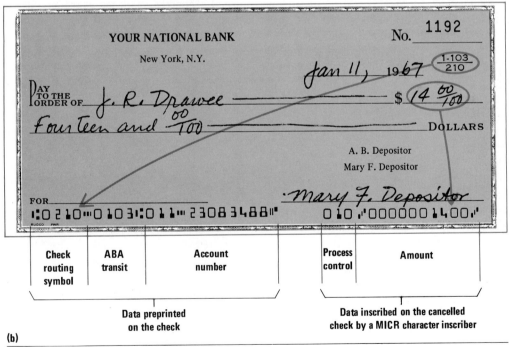

(a)

(b)

Source: (a) *IBM System/370 System Summary*, GA22-7001-3, pp. 7–21.

Figure 8–7
The IBM 3890 Document Processor

Figure 8–8
A Mark-Sense Reader

inputting to the computer. Some machines also sort the documents as the data is being processed. The IBM 3890 Document Processor (Figure 8–7) processes magnetically inscribed documents at a minimum speed of 2,400 documents per minute. Documents of various sizes and thicknesses can be read by this reader.

Magnetic-ink character recognition has two basic limitations. First, only the 10 numeric digits (0–9), an "amount" symbol, an "on us" symbol, a "transit number" symbol and a "dash" symbol are available in the E-13B font. Second, magnetic ink loses much of its magnetism immediately after imprinting takes place. The data may not be read correctly if the document is handled several times. The magnetic-ink character-recognition system was designed by and for the banking industry, and it has been successful in coping with this industry's data-entry bottlenecks. However, it has not been widely adopted in other fields. Instead, optical character-recognition (OCR) devices have been hailed as the solution to the problems of data entry.

OPTICAL READERS   There are four types of OCR readers: mark-sense, journal tape, document, and self-punching readers.

Mark-Sense Readers   A *mark-sense reader* scans pencil marks in designated areas on pre-printed forms or cards. (See Figure 8–8.) The mark is written with a soft pencil such as a No. 2 pencil. Formerly, mark-sense readers detected pencil marks by means of electrical brushes. Today, optical mark reading (OMR) is commonly used; optical reading permits creases in the card to be ignored. The marks are not characters, but merely fill-in marks in designated spaces. Mark-sense recording is a popular medium for recording brief individual responses such as meter readings or for scoring multiple-choice or true/false questions on tests. Mark-sense data recorded on cards may be processed by a reader that detects the marks and punches appropriate holes in the same cards. The punched cards are then fed to the computer. Another type of mark-sense reader detects the marks on a document and transmits the information directly to the computer. The mark-sense method has an established place in data recording, but it is not widely used except for the two purposes described above.

Journal Tape Readers   This type of OCR reader scans paper tape generated by accounting

machines, adding machines, cash registers, and similar devices. The data is recorded in a particular type font. By using a cash register that records transactions on paper tape in the required font, a retail firm can have all its data ready for the computer at the end of the working day.

Document Readers   These devices read documents printed in a special font and ranging in size from 2 by 4 inches to 8½ by 14 inches. Only one, two, or three lines are read on each document by an OCR reader designed for small documents. Larger documents are read by OCR readers called *page readers*. Pages range in size from 8½ by 11 inches to 8½ by 14 inches. OCR readers scan from 50 to 2,400 characters per second and process from 200 to 1,200 documents per minute.

Self-Punching Readers   Printed characters on cards are read and appropriate holes are punched into the same cards by self-punching readers. Unlike the data read by mark-sense readers, the information to be read is imprinted in a special type font, and not merely as a series of pencil marks. The punched cards are then ready for computer processing.

SCOFFLAWS DON'T GET FAR IN MONTREAL

Motorists take traffic tickets seriously in Montreal. They have no choice: A computer coordinates the collection of fines for motor-vehicle violations with the persistency of a bloodhound, levying increasingly severe penalties if the offender doesn't pay. It even issues "warrants for commitment" of dyed-in-the-wool scofflaws who disregard its mailed notices.

The computerized system, called SYCOM (System of the Municipal Court), is so reliable that the city recovers about 95 percent of fines for moving or parking violations. SYCOM handles about 750,000 parking and 250,000 moving violations each year in the city of Montreal, whose population is about 1,300,000. The central computer is a UNIVAC 1106 from Sperry Rand Corporation's Sperry UNIVAC Division.

Here's how the system works: Police officers return information on motor-vehicle violations each day at their own stations. The data is checked and entered into the computer's FASTRAND II memory. The 1106 then sends a notice to the motorist showing the date of the violation, the registration, year, and make of his car, and the time limit for paying the fine. If the fine for a moving violation isn't paid, the penalty is increased and the computer issues a summons for the motorist to appear before the Municipal Court. If he remains recalcitrant, he is "judged by default," and the 1106 issues a "Notice of Judgment" with a stiffer fine. Finally, the computer may issue a warrant to take the offender into custody.

SYCOM uses about 15 percent of the computer's capacity. The 1106 also handles the data-processing needs of some 27 urban departments.

Adapted from "Scofflaws Don't Get Far in Montreal," *Computers and People,* February 1974, p. 35.

Although we have divided OCR readers into four separate categories, an individual OCR reader may be capable of reading journal tapes in addition to documents printed in one or more type fonts with mark-sense data interspersed with the printed information. Magnetic-ink characters may also be recognized by the same device.

Type Fonts OCR readers are built to recognize one or more specified type fonts. Some readers are limited to type fonts designated by a particular equipment manufacturer. For example, NCR has its own optical type font for register receipts; the Farrington Selfcheck 7B type font is used for chargeplate imprinters; the banking industry has adopted the E-13B type font; and so on. However, there now exist two widely accepted standard type fonts: the OCR–A and OCR–B (Figure 8–11). The American National Standards Institute (ANSI) standard OCR–A has been adopted in the United States, whereas the international standard type font OCR–B is used in Europe. Initially the OCR–B font caused some difficulties because readers confused certain characters. Consequently, the more distinctive OCR–A font was generally adopted in the United States. Since OCR–A and OCR–B are the two accepted standard fonts, it is hoped that all others will become extinct in the future. The adoption of one or two standard fonts rather than a profusion of type fonts would save manufacturing costs. Typewriters and computer printers are available to print documents with an OCR-readable font. One standard font would eliminate the duplication of such data-preparation devices also.

Machine recognition of handwritten characters poses complex problems. For example, consider the writing of the numeral 5 and the letter S. There are OCR readers that recognize certain handwritten characters; an example is the IBM

Figure 8–11
OCR–A and OCR–B Type Fonts

OCR–A

IS AVAILABLE IN UPPER CASE AND WITH COMPATIBLE LOWER CASE AND SHOULD BE USED IN APPLICATIONS THAT ARE PRIMARILY HUMAN FACTORS INSENSITIVE.

The compatible lower case extends the available character set.

OCR–B

With lower case provides good human compatibility with some compromise for ease of machine reading. It is recommended for applications that are human factors sensitive.

Figure 8–12
The IBM 1288 Optical Reader

1288 optical reader, which can recognize all 10 digits (0–9) and the letters C, S, T, X, and Z block printed with a soft pencil to certain specifications. Figure 8–13 shows a sample OCR form for handwritten characters. No OCR reader is presently capable of recognizing all handwritten characters, but research is continuing in the hope of cracking this problem in the near future.

Applications of OCR Readers The oil industry was an early OCR user for the processing of credit-card billing. The fourteen largest oil companies are utilizing OCR readers and process up to 80,000 documents per hour. One company estimated that its available cash flow increased by $25,000,000 after it had used OCR readers for six months. The First National City Bank of New York has two OCR installations and employs one for stock transfers. Over 45,000 stock certificates are issued in eleven hours of operation. The Social Security Administration in Baltimore processes the names, Social Security numbers, and quarterly earnings of about 35 million wage earners by use of an optical page reader. It is estimated that the SSA has saved thus far over $750,000 by using the optical reader. The Field Enterprises Educational Corporation handles over 10,000 accounts receivable each day. Before the company switched to OCR, over 100 different forms were utilized. A carefully designed system employing typewriters with a 12F type font and an optical page reader has eliminated bottlenecks and speeded processing.

The Future of OCR The applications described above illustrate the tremendous potential of OCR. Why hasn't OCR fulfilled its promise of capturing the market for data-entry devices? The first commercial OCR system was installed in January 1956, when 600 computers were in use. An estimated 1,500 OCR systems and 80,000 computers are now in operation. OCR input constitutes roughly 2 percent of computer data input, and the dominant input device remains the keypunch unit. Two basic reasons exist for the failure of OCR. First, because most devices have been manufactured to read more than one type font, OCR readers are expensive. Many companies consider the cost of OCR readers excessive and not justifiable. With the standardization of type fonts to OCR–A and OCR–B, the cost should drop somewhat. The second and more important reason for the unpopularity of OCR is the failure of companies to take full advantage of its potential.

The simple replacement of keypunches by special typewriters that produce OCR-readable documents does not guarantee a more efficient operation. In the early days of OCR, many companies attempted to switch to OCR without a thorough evaluation and reorganization of their data-processing procedures. Consequently, the OCR installations could not achieve their objectives. Today, after these experiences, OCR manufacturers prefer to install complete OCR systems rather than merely OCR readers. Although the computer prophets forecast that OCR will have a majority of the data-entry market by the late 1970s, the cost of OCR devices must drop substantially and the data-processing community must be educated to have the technical acumen to obtain substantial results from OCR if this forecast is to be realized.

POINT-OF-SALE DATA ENTRY

The retail industry has two major data-processing problems: recording inventory information and sales. Since the 1950s, manufacturers have used machine-readable sales tags containing inventory data—stock numbers, sizes, colors, styles, and so on. Punched holes representing this data are placed in the tags by the retailer, using a *ticket recorder*. After an item is sold, the tag is retained by the retailer. Tags are then grouped in batches and sent to a central location for processing. Data may be transferred from tags to a computer-input medium such as magnetic tape. Alternatively, it is possible to read information on the tags directly into the computer by means of an on-line *tag reader*. Another type of tag system, called the *Meritag system*, utilizes magnetic-coded tags. The tag markings are read by a mark-sense scanner.

The recording of sales receipts is the second major problem of the retailing industry. One solution has been the use of cash-register receipts printed in OCR-readable type. Another approach to this problem is the *point-of-sale (POS) system*, which provides a keyboard device to record all sales information and produces both

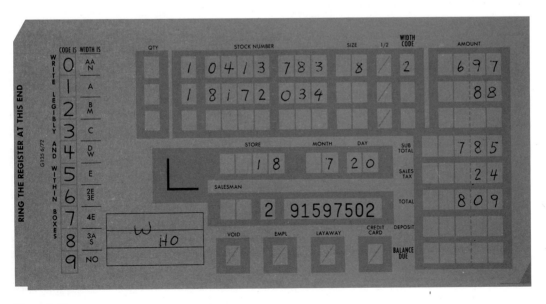

Figure 8–13
A Sample OCR Form for Handwritten Characters

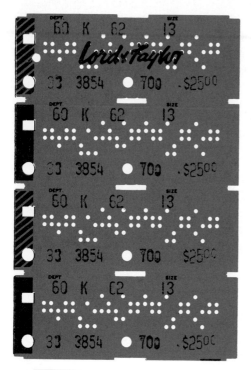

Figure 8–14
A Typical Sales Tag

Figure 8–15
Point-of-Sale (POS) Device—NCR

hard copy and data in machine-readable form on paper or magnetic tape. The hard copy becomes the customer's sales slip. All data written on the sales slip, such as the sales clerk's number, the customer charge identification, and the department number, are also recorded in an appropriate medium for subsequent processing by the computer.

SOURCE DATA AUTOMATION

Source data automation (SDA) means the capturing of information directly, at its source, for the computer. No additional steps are needed to transcribe the data to computerized form. Three recording systems—magnetic-ink character-recognition devices, optical character-recognition devices, and point-of-sale devices— offer the possibility of preparing data only once, at the original source, and sending this data directly to the computer. However, data are often transcribed from the source document to OCR- or MICR-readable forms; this is not SDA. Source data automation eliminates any extra time for data preparation and prevents the introduction of errors by the data handler, thus producing an immediate saving of money. A fourth way of capturing data at its source is by the use of remote terminals connected to a central computer. The operator keys information at the terminal and it is sent directly to the computer for immediate processing. This type of activity is called real-time data processing. The discussion of this topic is deferred to Chapter 18.

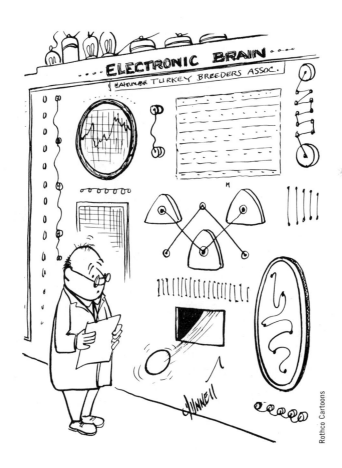

Rothco Cartoons

REFERENCES

Andersson, P. L. "OCR Enters the Practical Stage." *Datamation*, December 1, 1971, pp. 22–27.

Bauldreay, J. "Mark Reading." *Datamation*, October 1, 1970, pp. 34–38.

Chu, Albert L. C. "Source Data Automation: Shortcut to Computer Power." *Business Automation*, September 1971, pp. 16–22.

Chu, Albert L. C. "Data Entry." *Business Automation*, July 1971, pp. 18–27.

Dougherty, Geoffrey B. "Ready for OCR." *Data Processing Magazine*, April 1971, p. 34.

Dumey, Arnold I. "Computer-Addressed Letter Mail." *Datamation*, February 1972, pp. 32–35.

Hix, C. Frank, Jr., and Magsam, John E. "A Large-Scale Data Entry System for the IRS." *Datamation*, June 1970, pp. 106–109.

Rosbury, A. H. "Shared Processor Keyboard Data Entry." *Datamation*, June 1970, pp. 101–104.

Salzman, Roy M., and Niskanen, Anthony S. "Data Entry Systems." *Modern Data*, February 1973, pp. 28–43.

"OCR: The Evasive User's Recognition." *Business Automation*, January 1972, p. 14.

"Optical, Mark Sense Scanners." *Business Automation*, September 1970, pp. 110–15.

"Three Key-to-Disk Experiences." *Data Dynamics*, August/September 1971, pp. 17–22.

"Will Optical Scanning Now Catch On?" *Administrative Management*, May 1970, pp. 18–20.

QUESTIONS

1. What advantages do key-to-tape and key-to-disk devices offer with respect to the preparation of input data?
2. Prepare a table of the types of character-recognition devices and their applications. List at least two applications for each device.
3. By examining the current computer literature, find the operational characteristics of five OCR readers. List the manufacturer, model number, cost, type of reading capability, type fonts, and speed of scanning of each.
4. What is source data automation? What devices provide it? What are the advantages and possible disadvantages of SDA?

CHAPTER NINE

An Introduction
to Computer Software

Software is the essential complement to computer hardware. The term *software* has acquired several meanings in computer literature; but, essentially, it describes the "soft" portion of the computer installation, that is, the computer programs, which are executed by the hardware. Defined most narrowly, the term *software* indicates an *operating system,* a program designed to control the execution of other programs and achieve efficient use of the computer hardware. A broader definition of the term is that group of programs (including the operating system) which provides the means to utilize the computer hardware efficiently. Today, software has acquired a still broader meaning. It indicates all the programs required by an installation and, in particular, the programs needed to perform the primary tasks of the installation. For example, the software for an insurance company includes not only the operating system and associated programs, but also the file-handling programs used to maintain the records of the company, programs used to perform statistical analysis of the data, and related programs called *application programs.* Since the current literature gives the word software its broadest meaning, we will also adopt this usage.

Computer hardware is inexorably linked to computer software. Without programs, the hardware is merely a complex set of electronic gear with no problem-solving capability of its own. To perform even the simplest task, a program must be created and stored within the computer. Software is the fundamental ingredient that makes the innate power of the hardware available to the user.

Software—that is, programs—are written to be executed by the computer. To write a program requires the careful specification of a set of instructions to be executed by the computer. The group of instructions constitutes a program. The format and contents of individual instructions are determined by the computer language utilized for the computer. Since a programming language is necessary before software can be developed, this chapter briefly describes the historical development of programming languages and presents an overall survey of these languages. Further information on FORTRAN, COBOL, and PL/I is supplied in later chapters; BASIC and RPG are covered in the appendices. The latter portion of this chapter describes the software programs found at any major computer installation.

COMPUTER LANGUAGES

Computer languages are classified into three basic types: machine languages, assembly languages, and so-called higher-level languages. A *machine language* is defined by the operation codes and format of the machine instructions of the computer, whereas an *assembly language* is a symbolic representation of a given machine language. *Higher-level languages* evolved to overcome the inherent difficulties of machine- or assembly-language programming. Each type of language is discussed below.

MACHINE LANGUAGE   A program comprises a well-ordered set of instructions to the computer directing it to perform certain operations. The program is expressed by letters, numbers, and symbols according to a well-defined set of rules. The set of alphanumeric symbols and the rules combine to form the syntax of a programming language. A machine language is a language specified by the computer itself. A *machine instruction* contains two basic parts: (1) an *operation* to be performed and (2) the specification of one or more *operands,* such as machine locations, registers, channels, or input/output devices, upon which the operation will take place. The operation is specified by a numeric code called the *operation* or *"op" code.* An example of an instruction is a directive to add the contents of a machine location and a register location. The operation code is the numeric code for the addition operation, and the operands are the addresses of the register and the memory location. The operands are thus numbers indicating the addresses of computer locations, an address of a register, or a particular input/output device.

Since the computer deals only with binary numbers, the machine instructions must be expressed numerically, using only the digits 0 and 1. However, because binary numbers are cumbersome, almost impossible for humans to remember, and tedious to write, and because of the relationship between octal and binary numbers discussed in Chapter 3, machine-language coding is done using octal (or hexadecimal) numbers.

The precise format of machine instructions to be given depends on the make and model of the computer. It is not, basically, modifiable by the programmer. The exception to this statement is in microprogramming, where the set of basic machine instructions can be specified by the user with the aid of the manufacturer. Micro-programming is a feature frequently available in minicomputers. (See Chapter 10.) The interpretation of a machine-language program is a direct function of the computer hardware.

ASSEMBLY LANGUAGES An assembly language is one step higher than a machine language in the hierarchy of programming languages. Because machine-language programming proved to be a difficult and tedious task subject to much human error, a symbolic way of expressing machine-language codes was devised. In assembly languages, the operation code is expressed as a combination of letters designed to assist the programmer in remembering the function of the code. For example, the addition of two registers is indicated by AR in the assembly language for the IBM System/370 computers; the operation code is 1A in the hexadecimal number system used by these machines. Because the assembly-language codes were designed as an aid to the programmer's memory, they are *mnemonic codes*. Thus, assembly languages are categorized as *mnemonic languages*.

The addresses of the operands are also mnemonic. Rather than assigning a particular machine address to an operand, the programmer gives a symbolic name to a location and labels the location by that name. For example, the result of the addition of several numbers might be placed in a location called "SUM" by the programmer. Any reference to that location or its contents would then use the name "SUM." In machine-language programming, the programmer must determine a physical machine location for a quantity and write a machine address, such as 11472, in the machine-language instruction. Clearly, "SUM" is easier to remember than a number such as 11472.

Since the computer only "understands" and executes machine-language programs, the assembly-language program must be translated to machine language. This is accomplished by the use of a program called an *assembler*. The assembler accepts an assembly-language program as input and produces binary code as output. During the translation (or assembly) process, actual values are assigned to symbolic addresses. Any syntactical errors are detected by the assembler and printed on an output listing. The errors are then corrected by the programmer and the program resubmitted to the assembler. A program without syntactical errors is then executable, although testing is still necessary to prove the correctness of the programming code.

An example of an assembly-language program for the UNIVAC 1108 to solve the equation $y = x_1 + x_2$ is shown below:

ASSEMBLY LANGUAGE		MACHINE LANGUAGE
LA	1,X1	100020010000
AA	1,X2	140020010001
SA	1,Y	010020010002

Although assembly-language programming offers a vast improvement over octal coding for machine-language programs, it still is directly linked to a particular machine's operation codes and instruction reperloire. It requires the services of highly skilled programmers well versed in the language of a particular machine. A new computer ordinarily requires the learning of a completely different machine language. It also necessitates the manual conversion of all assembly-language programs to the assembly language of the new computer. This is a major expense in upgrading computer hardware. The costs of developing a program are high because of the time required to write a program, and testing the program is a long and complicated task

since corrections require the study and review of detailed machine instructions. Even the original programmer may need to study the logic and design of the program for hours in order to make a change in the program. A minor alteration of a program can easily introduce major errors. Formerly, the services of professional programmers were required for the solution of all problems. The people with the problems, such as data-processing personnel or engineers, were removed from the actual problem solving and intermediaries, the computer programmers, interposed between them and the computer. All these factors led to a search for better ways to use the computer and the development of higher-level languages.

HIGHER-LEVEL LANGUAGES   There are many different higher-level languages designed for a variety of applications. Each year at least one more programming language is added to the already overabundant collection of languages. The search for the perfect higher-level language is continual. Each higher-level language has its advocates, and the hope for the perfect language is still here. However, only a few of the many languages invented are in widespread use in business and industry. The popularity of other languages may grow, but the intrenchment and long-range use of some higher-level languages is certain. We will discuss the origins of only a small subset of higher-level languages—those most common in the business world.

FORTRAN   In 1957, IBM initiated a problem-oriented language that became one of the most widely used higher-level languages. FORTRAN (*For*mula *Tran*slator) was designed to provide a means to express scientific problems formulated in mathematical terms. The initial version of the language was expanded to include subroutines and other features, and a new version known as FORTRAN II was defined in 1958. Further refinements of the language led to the current version, called FORTRAN IV. Some computer manufacturers have added other features, including special data-handling features so that FORTRAN can be used in business data-processing applications. FORTRAN IV thus supplemented is known as FORTRAN V.

FORTRAN was an instant success in the scientific world. Today it remains one of the most commonly used higher-level languages in the world. It is available on over 150 different makes and models of computers. However, the explicit definition of FORTRAN initially varied from computer to computer. A standardized version of FORTRAN was defined by the *American National Standards Institute (ANSI)* in 1966. This institute was established to define and publish standards for computer hardware and software. It was originally called the American Standards Association (ASA), later changed its name to USA Standards Institute (USA), and finally changed to its present name. Consequently, references in the literature

"It says, 'You can fool some of the people some of the time, but you can't fool all of the people all of the time!'"

are to either ANSI, ASA, or USA FORTRAN, all of which are the same.

ANSI FORTRAN is approximately equivalent to FORTRAN IV; a subset of ANSI FORTRAN, Basic FORTRAN, roughly corresponds to FORTRAN II. Differences in FORTRAN language specifications from computer to computer still exist, but they are usually well documented in reference to ANSI FORTRAN. Generally only minor changes are necessary to take a FORTRAN program from one computer and execute it on another machine. Frederic Stuart presents detailed information on differences between the FORTRAN language as available on various computers in *FORTRAN Programming* (New York: Wiley, 1969).

To demonstrate the simplicity of FORTRAN, let us return to the equation $y = x_1 + x_2$. This would be written in FORTRAN as

$$Y = X1 + X2$$

ALGOL   In the late 1950s, interest developed in producing a precise and well-defined language that could be implemented in the same way on all computers. A program executed on one computer could then be taken, without making any change whatsoever, to another computer, executed, and produce the same results. It was with these aims

in mind that ALGOL (*Algo*rithmic *L*anguage) was first created in 1958 as a universal higher-level language for all computers. Whereas additional features were added to FORTRAN because of user demands, ALGOL was explicitly defined as a fully formed language. In 1960, ambiguity in the initial version resulted in a revised version known as ALGOL 60. Because the origin of ALGOL had its roots in Europe, it is a popular language there. It is also the preferred language for the publication of programs in computer publications, although FORTRAN has also become belatedly accepted by the computer societies. In the United States, ALGOL is used in academic communities but has never gained wide acceptance in industry or business. The equation of $y = x_1 + x_2$ is given in ALGOL as

$$Y := X1 + X2 \; ;$$

For further information on ALGOL, see Torgil Ekman and Carl Erik Fröberg, *Introduction to ALGOL Programming* (London: Oxford University Press, 1967).

COBOL   While languages for scientific and engineering disciplines were being formulated, another set of higher-level languages designed

"THE RAIN IN SPAIN FALLS MAINLY...."

Employing a small electronic device called a voice synthesizer, plus linguistic rules, two Michigan State University professors have programmed the university's main computer to talk. Its voice sounds like a man speaking with the enunciation of a long-distance telephone operator.

Dr. John B. Eulenberg, visiting assistant professor of linguistics and Oriental and African languages, and Dr. Morteza Amir Rahimi, associate professor of computer science at MSU, have been experimenting with the voice synthesizer as part of an ongoing project in artificial language development. The digitally controlled synthesizer is about the size of a breadbox, and much smaller than earlier voice synthesizers, which sometimes occupied whole rooms. Its electronic circuits imitate the effect of the human vocal tract. Electronic matches or near matches for the "phonemes," or basic units of speech sounds, can be created that combine to make words and sentences.

Eulenberg and Rahimi see their project as leading to improved computer-assisted instruction generally, and for blind persons particularly. A voice synthesizer could expand employment opportunities for blind persons in the field of computer programming, since a visually handicapped person trained in touch-typing could enter questions and requests on the computer using the keyboard, and obtain an instantaneous response both vocally and visually. The blind would thus be able to prepare and proofread letters, reports, and class assignments which had been fed to the computer in machine-readable form. Voice synthesizers could also be used to teach semi- or preliterate persons, . . . and to provide automatic navigation systems.

A typical demonstration of how the synthesizer works is provided by a program that acts as a calculator for the blind. For example, it will ask the user to type two numbers. After each number is typed, the computer repeats it aloud for confirmation, and then proceeds to announce the sum. Another program composes poems on the spot, using a list of words supplied by the operator. The computer then recites each poem aloud.

From "The Rain in Spain Falls Mainly . . ." *Computer*, April, 1974, p. 68. Reprinted from *Computer* Magazine, a publication of the IEEE Computer Society.

for business data processing was being defined and implemented. Some of the early languages designed for business data processing were AIMACO, FLOWMATIC, and COMTRAN. The use of these languages was discontinued when COBOL became available. In 1958, the Department of Defense brought together a committee of computer users, computer manufacturers, and universities to define a universal business language subsequently known as COBOL (*Co*mmon *B*usiness *O*riented *L*anguage). This committee, later known as the CODASYL committee, also monitored additions and revisions to the initial definition of the COBOL language. In 1968, the ANSI version of COBOL was defined.

COBOL is designed to serve the business community and consequently avoids the use of symbols or mathematical notations common to the mathematical and engineering disciplines. COBOL programs use English words and sentences. The language has special provisions for the definition of data files and the manipulation of data within a file. The equation $y = x_1 + x_2$ is written in COBOL as

ADD X1, X2 GIVING Y.

More COBOL language details are in Chapter 14.

PL/I   A recent development in programming languages was the definition and implementation of PL/I by IBM in 1966. This language is now used in both the United States and Europe. Initially PL/I was available only to IBM installations, but it has now become available to users of other computers. The name *PL/I* has no special meaning, although it is frequently interpreted as Programming Language/I. PL/I is a multipurpose language designed for the programming of both scientific and business data-processing problems. It has features drawn from FORTRAN, ALGOL, and COBOL. Until PL/I becomes widely available, it will be difficult to assess the impact of this language on non-IBM users. The equation $y = x_1 + x_2$ in PL/I is the same as it is in FORTRAN, except for a semicolon:

$$Y = X1 + X2 ;$$

For details on PL/I, see Chapter 15.

SPECIAL-PURPOSE LANGUAGES   In addition to programming languages designed to have a wide range of applications, there are symbolic languages developed to meet special needs. These languages attempt to incorporate the problem-solving techniques common to a

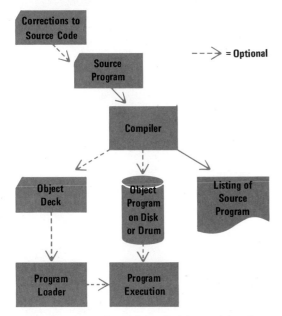

Corrections to Source Code

Source Program

- - -> = Optional

Compiler

Object Deck

Object Program on Disk or Drum

Listing of Source Program

Program Loader

Program Execution

Figure 9–1
The Compilation Process

particular type of problem. Problem-solving languages have developed for a vast range of applications, from the solution of differential equations to special data-processing problems. Although it is usually possible to utilize an algebraic-type language such as FORTRAN for a special problem, the special-purpose language provides an easier formulation of the solution and thus speeds the writing and testing of the computer program.

For example, a group of special-purpose languages was developed for simulation problems. *Simulation* is a numerical technique for conducting experiments on a computer which use certain types of mathematical or logical models that describe a real system. Examples of simulation languages are SIMULA 67, GPSS/360, and SIMSCRIPT. These languages allow the programming of simulation models on the computer. The finding of an optimal inventory-control point is an example of a simulation problem in the business world. The processes of ordering, reordering, supplying, and shipping goods can be simulated and a best choice made of a number of reorder points of goods or increased levels of production for a factory. For further information on programming languages and their historical

development, see Jean E. Sammet, *Programming Languages: History and Fundamentals* (Englewood Cliffs, N.J.: Prentice-Hall, 1969).

THE TRANSLATION OF PROGRAMMING LANGUAGES Because the computer executes a program expressed in binary numbers, any program written in any other form must be translated to an equivalent program in machine language. The original program is called the *source program,* or *source coding,* while its equivalent machine-language program is known as the *object program,* or *object code.* If the object code is punched on cards, the resulting cards are called an *object deck.* The translation from source language to object code is performed by computer programs. A program that accepts assembly-language programs as input and produces object code as output is called an *assembler.* A program that reads a program written in a higher-level language and produces an equivalent machine-language program as output is called a *compiler.* The process of translating higher-level languages into object code is known as *compilation.*

Assembly languages generally have a one-to-one relationship to the resultant object-code programs, although some assemblers provide special features; that is, a line of assembly-language coding is usually (but not always) translated into a single machine instruction. A single statement in a higher-level-language program typically requires several machine-language instructions. For example, our simple problem of finding y when $y = x_1 + x_2$ is written as one statement in FORTRAN but will produce three machine-language instructions on most computers. Because higher-level languages are more complex, it takes longer to compile programs in these languages than it does to assemble the same program expressed in assembly language. Conversely, a given program is shorter when it is expressed in a higher-level language than when it is written in an assembly language.

ADVANTAGES OF HIGHER-LEVEL LAN-GUAGES   Higher-level languages are defined without regard to an actual set of machine instructions. Thus they offer, potentially, a way to develop programs that are independent of any particular computer. It is for this reason that they are called "higher-level" languages; they are a level above the physical structure of the hardware. In actuality, the minor details of a higher-level language may differ depending on the computer for which it is used. In contrast to higher-level languages, an assembly language is completely dependent on the instruction repertoire and the instruction format of the computer for which it is defined.

Higher-level languages offer many obvious advantages. A programmer does not have to deal with the complex details of the computer hardware but can concentrate on the solution of the problem in terminology related to the problem. His or her efforts can be directed toward the analysis of the problem and not merely the task of programming. The time needed for the formulation of the problem, programming, and testing is substantially less for a problem in a higher-level language than for the same problem in an assembly language. Because higher-level languages offer independence from a particular computer, programs in these languages can be quickly converted when a new computer is introduced. The exception to this statement occurs when there are *machine-dependent* statements within a higher-level program. For example, a programmer may write a program that utilizes the basic word length of the computer being used.

The conversion of such a program to an equivalent program for another computer may require extensive changes if the word length of the new computer is not the same. The convertibility of a program may also depend on the amount of central memory utilized by the program, the number and kind of input/output devices required, and the numerical accuracy of the computations provided by the computer hardware. Consequently, a higher-level language program may become machine dependent.

Higher-level languages provide for a problem to be expressed in a fashion related to the formulation of the problem itself. Thus the problem and its solution are more clearly expressed by a program in a higher-level language. The logic of the program is usually easier to trace. Revision of the program is generally easier because of features inherent in the language.

Assembly languages offer none of the advantages of higher-level languages. Instead they place the full power of the computer hardware at the disposal of the programmer. If a problem requires certain manipulations not provided in any of the higher-level language available on the computer, it may be necessary to utilize an assembly language. However, it is often possible to supplement the higher-level language by writing self-contained portions of coding called *subroutines* in assembly language.

A clever programmer may produce a more efficient object code than the code produced by the compiler. However, the consensus today is that the average programmer writes programs with an average level of efficiency roughly equal to or less than that of the object code produced by compilers. Thus the execution time of the assembly-language program may be equal to or less than that of a similar program written in a higher-level language.

Assembly-language programming has several disadvantages. The program is more difficult to modify since it is written in a language related directly to the computer. The steps in the formulation of the problem are buried in a mass of machine instructions. Because the program is tied directly to a particular computer, the entire program must be rewritten for another computer (unless the new computer has a compatible machine language).

Because the cost of developing programs is high, programs are modified frequently, and the introduction of new computer hardware is an ever-present possibility, higher-level languages are favored over assembly languages. The battle over languages has largely ended, with higher-level languages the victors.

COMPUTER SOFTWARE

Although we have defined *software* in its broadest sense as any computer program, there is a category of programs common to most computer installations. The programs in this group are identified explicitly as software programs. They are (1) the operating system, (2) the assembler, (3) the compilers, (4) general-purpose subroutines, (5) sort/merge programs, (6) utility routines, and (7) other programs of a general nature. This set of software programs is typically supplied with the computer by the computer manufacturer. The software programs provided by UNIVAC for its 1100 series are listed in Figure 9–2.

Software is now often priced separately from computer hardware by the manufacturer. Today many firms specialize in the development of software and may supply the same items as the manufacturer, but possibly at a lower cost for improved versions of the same programs. These firms, known as *software vendors,* also offer software programs to supplement those supplied by the manufacturer and may provide generalized application programs such as a payroll program designed to meet the requirements of different organizations. An installation may choose to produce its own set of software programs or some subset of these programs. Because of the high cost of programming, this is seldom done today except in academic communities. Now let us discuss each individual item of software.

THE OPERATING SYSTEM The *operating system* is the program that controls and monitors the execution of all other programs. Without an operating system, constant human intervention is required to enter a program, initiate its execution, and manually record its successful or unsuccessful termination. Small computers may be operated with primitive operating systems called *monitors* if only one program is executed at any given time. Larger computers are designed to execute several programs with apparent simultaneity, sharing the computer hardware within the same block of time. An operating system is an essential item of software for such computers. It enables the

Figure 9–2
Software for the UNIVAC 1106 Series of Computers

UNIVAC 1100 SERIES OPERATING SYSTEM—
THE EXECUTIVE SYSTEM
SYSTEM PROCESSORS
    Collector
    FURPUR
    Postmortem and Diagnostic Processor
    DATA and ELT Processors
    SECURE Processor
    Text Editor (ED Processor)
    CULL Processor

LANGUAGE PROCESSORS
    UNIVAC 1100 Series Assembler
    COBOL
        ASCII COBOL
        FD COBOL
        DOD COBOL
    FORTRAN V
    Conversational FORTRAN
        FORTRAN Processor and the Executive System
        FORTRAN Language
    NU ALGOL
    BASIC
    Procedure Definition Processor
    JOVIAL
    SIMSCRIPT
    REENTRANT FORTRAN
    APL/1100 (A Programming Language)
    SIMULA

UTILITY PROCESSORS
    CUR to FUR Conversion (CON78)
    FLUSH
    SSG Processor
    UNADS (UNIVAC Automated Documentation System)

LIBRARIES
    Sort/Merge
    MATH-PACK
    STAT-PACK

APPLICATIONS
    APT 1100 (Automatically Programmed Tools)
    PERT
    GPSS 1100 (General Purpose System Simulator)
    Functional Mathematical Programming System
        (FMPS)
    DMS 1100 (Data Management System)
        Data Definition Languages (DDL)
        Data Manipulation Languages (DML)
        Data Management Routine (DMR)
        System Support Functions
    TIP 1100 (Transaction Interface Package)
    RPS 1100 (Report Processing System)

SOFTWARE INSTRUMENTATION PACKAGE (SIP)

SERIES 70 CONVERSION
    Software Conversion Aids
    Tandem Processor

Source: UNIVAC 1106 System, SYSTEM DESCRIPTION, UP-7685,
Rev. 2, © 1969, 1971, 1973 by Sperry UNIVAC.

computer to be used conveniently and with maximum efficiency. This topic is discussed further in Chapter 18.

ASSEMBLERS An *assembler* is a program that translates assembly-language programs into object programs. Since the machine language of a computer is dependent on the make and model, an assembler must be provided for each machine language. Because assembly language allows the programmer to use any hardware feature in writing programs, an assembler is a necessary item of software for each computer.

COMPILERS A *compiler* is a computer program that translates higher-level language programs into object programs. Each particular language requires its own compiler. If a higher-level language is to be utilized for writing programs on a particular computer, the compiler for that language must be available. Occasionally, a larger computer may be employed to compile programs for a smaller computer. For example, the IBM System/370 Model 165 could be used to compile COBOL programs for the IBM System/3 computer. The object code produced would be in the machine language of the System/3 computer

and the compiler would be executed on the IBM System/370 Model 165.

GENERAL-PURPOSE SUBROUTINES A *subroutine* is a self-contained portion of coding that performs an assigned task. The coding is written so that any program requiring that task may use the subroutine. For example, the coding for taking the square root of any number is ordinarily supplied as a subroutine because of its frequent use by scientific programs. Subroutines for various business applications are listed in Figure 9–3.

A program may also be structured as a set of subroutines linked by coding in the main program. This permits the logic of the program to be expressed more clearly and aids in the coding and testing of the program. For example, a payroll program may be written in which the computation of federal withholding tax is performed by a subroutine that accepts "gross pay" and "number of deductions" as input. Thus, any changes in the laws governing the federal withholding tax can be introduced within the withholding-tax subroutine. Similarly, the F.I.C.A. tax could be computed by a separate subroutine so that increases in this tax would cause modi-

Figure 9–3
An Example of Subroutines for Business Data Processing

Subroutines for Accounts Receivable

File inquiry
Discount
Cycle billing
Service charge
Check writing
Year-end processing

Subroutines for Accounts Payable

Discounts
Lost discounts
Cash requirements
Check writing
Batch balancing
Debit memo

Payroll Subroutines

Federal payroll tax
State payroll tax
City payroll tax
Deduction
Time calculation

General Ledger Subroutines

Budget comparison
Key business ratios
Accrual reversal

fications within the subroutine only and not the main body of coding.

SORT/MERGE PROGRAMS   A task common in business data processing is the rearranging of a data file in a different order. For example, the file containing the names of all the personnel of a firm may be ordered by a company-assigned number. It may be desirable to reorder the file by job classifications or by the employees' names. The process of rearranging a file into a different order is called *sorting.*

Two or more data files may be combined into one data file in a way determined by certain data in each data record; this process is known as *merging.* Because of the frequent demand for sorting or merging data files, these two procedures are usually in a program supplied with the standard software of the computer. The sort/merge program is general enough to permit the sorting or merging of any data files. This program is especially valuable for business data-processing applications.

UTILITY ROUTINES   These programs are special support programs designed for necessary but mundane tasks. Examples are (1) a program to copy the contents of a magnetic-tape reel onto another tape reel and (2) a program that reads cards as input and writes the data they contain onto magnetic tape or disk. If an installation frequently receives data from various locations on small reels of magnetic tape, a utility routine may be written to combine the data from the short tape reels onto one large reel of tape prior to processing by the data-handling program. In this case, the word *routine* is used to indicate a complete program that performs only one particular task.

MISCELLANEOUS PROGRAMS   Many programs may be developed at an installation to perform various programming tasks. Such programs may also be supplied by a computer manufacturer. For example, an entire package of statistical programs may be provided as part of the standard software. Special file-handling programs may be supplied to receive data and compute results. Before embarking on any programming task, it is always advisable to check the list of software programs and subroutines available for the computer. Hours of programming time may be saved by the utilization of a standard software program.

REFERENCES

Ekman, Torgil, and Fröberg, Carl Erik. *Introduction to ALGOL Programming.* London: Oxford University Press, 1967.

Glass, R. L. "An Elementary Discussion of Compiler/Interpreter Writing." *Computing Surveys,* March 1969, pp. 55–77.

IBM Corporation. *A PL/I Primer* [student text]. White Plains, N.Y.: IBM Data Processing Division, 1965.

Knuth, Donald E. *Fundamental Algorithms, Volume 1: The Art of Computer Programming.* Reading, Mass.: Addison-Wesley Publishing Co., 1968.

Maurer, Ward D. *Programming: An Introduction to Computer Languages and Techniques.* San Francisco: Holden-Day, 1968.

Murach, Mike. *Standard COBOL.* Chicago: Science Research Associates, 1971.

Rosen, Saul, ed. *Programming Systems and Languages.* New York: McGraw-Hill Book Co., 1967.

Rosin, Robert F. "Supervisory and Monitor Systems." *Computing Surveys,* March 1969, pp. 37–54.

Sammet, Jean E. *Programming Languages: History and Fundamentals.* Englewood Cliffs, N.J.: Prentice-Hall, 1969.

Stuart, Frederic. *FORTRAN Programming.* New York: John Wiley & Sons, 1969.

QUESTIONS

1. Define the term *computer language.*
2. What is the relationship between machine language and assembly languages?
3. What advantages do higher-level languages offer? What disadvantages?
4. Define the word *software.*
5. Define the terms *compiler, assembler,* and *operating system.*
6. What purposes does an operating system serve?
7. List the software programs and subroutines available at your college's computer installation. List any desirable items of software that are lacking at this installation.
8. Compile a list of the software programs and subroutines available for any particular computer such as the IBM System/3, UNIVAC 90/60, or DEC/System 10. This information is commonly supplied by computer manufacturers in advertisements given in computer magazines such as *Datamation.* Are there any additional software items desirable for a business data-processing installation but not supplied by the manufacturer of this computer?

CHAPTER TEN

Minicomputers

The wide-ranging effects of the industrial revolution on modern civilization are well recognized. Today we are witnessing another such revolution that in similar fashion is quietly but definitely affecting all of us. This revolution, in computing power, is well underway. Computers have proliferated in businesses, in government offices, in hospitals, in police data bureaus, and in all data-handling agencies. And now, with the introduction of the minicomputer (miniature computer), the possibility of a computer in every home and every business is truly here.

The high costs of computer hardware initially restricted the use of computers to the major business firms that had a large volume of data to be processed. Now that the cost of hardware has been reduced, almost all companies employing more than a hundred persons either rent or own a computer, utilize the services of a computer via service bureaus, or have a computer terminal for inputting data and receiving results in-house.

However, only two percent of the businesses in the United States have over a hundred employees. The minicomputer, with its much lower hardware cost, will affect all businesses and all individuals. It has been predicted that any business with five or more employees will utilize a computer within the next year or two.

In 1967, the first minicomputers were developed and installed. Five years later, the computer prophets were forecasting the presence of a minicomputer in every office and home. What are the reasons for such a rapid advance? The technological achievements in computer hardware have reduced the cost of hardware so that a small business can afford to rent or purchase a minicomputer. Further advances and subsequent reductions are predicted. Thus the minicomputer has become economically viable for smaller businesses.

The requirements of small businesses have resulted in a corresponding demand for computing power and data-handling capabilities. The overall operation of a small business has become more complex. For example, the government now requires more reports with detailed information. Wage rates have steadily increased, and skilled personnel are in short supply. The loss of a key employee may mean temporary chaos until a new employee is trained to fill the gap. The training period may be as long as six months. The management of the small business has become more intricate and requires the gathering, processing, retrieval, and analysis of substantial amounts of data. Rules of thumb and educated guesses are no longer sufficient to determine the most profitable level of inventory and corresponding increases or decreases of production. The volume of paperwork may exceed the capacity of the current staff of employees. For all these reasons, the small businessman has looked for help with his record keeping and has turned to a wide range of computing devices.

The minicomputer is the most flexible of the available miniature computing devices, but using it may require extensive changes in data-handling procedures. Although hardware costs are lower for minicomputers than for regular computers, the cost of developing software is high. A company must carefully weigh these costs before installing a minicomputer. It may be more advantageous for a business to retain its current data-handling practices with minimal alterations and obtain computing power from devices other than a minicomputer. The miniaturization of memories and central processor units has caused many other miniature computing devices to appear in the market. These devices can be categorized as hand calculators, accounting machines, or intelligent terminals. They have characteristics

similar to the minicomputer but lack the ability to store and retrieve data from files. However, each of these devices is exerting a tremendous impact on the overall use of electronic computing power. For example, more than eight million pocket calculators were sold in 1973. In the following section, there is a discussion of some of these devices. The details of minicomputer hardware and software are given later in this chapter.

MINIATURE COMPUTING DEVICES

The many different miniature computing devices available all share a common characteristic: the ability to perform calculations rapidly. Most devices also have a limited memory and the ability to execute a prewired or a stored program. Each type of computing device is designed to serve a special purpose, in contrast to the minicomputer, which is a general-purpose computer. These special-purpose miniature computing devices are discussed below.

ELECTRONIC HAND CALCULATORS

Formerly, calculators that were capable of performing arithmetic computations were so bulky and heavy that they were placed on a desk and seldom moved. Only computations could be done. No intermediate values, or only a few, could be stored, and computations could not be programmed. Today the electronic hand calculator is easily tucked into a pocket and its low price brings it into the reach of all. The ubiquitous slide rule for engineering students is now being replaced by electronic hand calculators. Most calculators provide for the automatic taking of square roots by a special key on the keyboard. Other special keys are available. Results are shown in numerals displayed electronically. The storage of intermediate results is frequently a feature of the calculator.

Hewlett-Packard now offers the HP-65 hand calculator (Figure 10–1), with a library of programs, for about $800. The programs are given on tiny magnetic cards to be inserted into the calculator. Each program may contain up to 100 steps. After a program has been entered, appropriate input values are keyed in and the computation is performed. It is also possible to develop individualized programs, using blank magnetic cards and appropriately keying the calculator. The calculator has 13 addressable memory locations. The standard packages of programs provided by Hewlett-Packard include programs for mathematical, statistical, medical, electrical engineering, and field-survey problems. Examples are programs for octal arithmetic, numeric integration, multiple linear regression, and forecasting for personal investments.

ELECTRONIC DESK CALCULATORS
Similar to the hand calculators, full-size desk calculators with memory and programmable features are now common. Full-size desk calculators no longer rely solely on keying by operators to control computations. The operator can use a standardized program and key-in the input. It is also possible to develop individualized programs for special computational tasks. Some calculators may be preprogrammed for special applications. The Hewlett-Packard 81, for example,

Figure 10–1
The Hewlett-Packard HP-65

Figure 10–2
The Canon Pocketronic

Figure 10-3
The Monroe 420 Hand Calculator

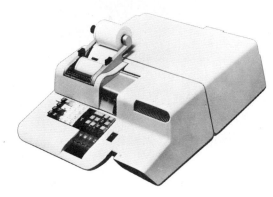

Figure 10-4
The Olivetti P101 Desk Calculator

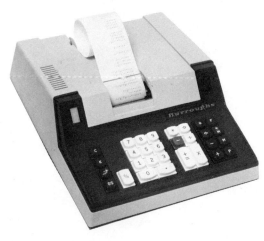

Figure 10-5
The Burroughs C6201 Desk Calculator

solves business problems involving the calculation of depreciation loans. It also provides a printout. The user may choose to create an individualized program to meet his special needs. A prime disadvantage of most of these calculators is the lack of hard-copy results. When hard-copy output is provided, the printing is so slow that it lowers the computational speed of the device. However, development of high-speed-printout capabilities is underway. The Canon Pocketronic provides this type of hard-copy output with a thermal printing mechanism, but the thermal paper needed for the machine is more expensive than, standard adding-machine rolls. Lowered costs, higher speeds, and a reliable means of printout should soon increase the popularity of the electronic desk calculator.

ACCOUNTING MACHINES   An *accounting machine* is a small computer with a central processing unit but without the ability to store and retrieve data from files. It is unit-record oriented and operated by a single individual at any given time. Input is entered via an alphanumeric keyboard and magnetic ledger cards, while output may be produced on a typewriter device or a magnetic ledger card. These cards have a ferrous-oxide backing that retains electrical impulses so that data can be recorded and accumulated.

The accounting machine executes stored programs prewired by the manufacturer. New programs may be entered by changing the entire program board. Accounting machines are electronic versions of the manual business machines. They are unit-record oriented since only one ledger card (or at most two) may be entered at a given time. No retrieval of data for cross-checking is possible. These machines are used for general-ledger accounting, the production of payroll checks, inventory control, and engineering computations. Because this type of machine is simpler to use than a minicomputer, a small business may elect to use an accounting machine rather than converting procedures to computer techniques. Personnel can be easily trained to use the

A MINI STANDS AMONG THE GIANTS

In the middle of a pristine Pacific Northwest forest, where the only noise for miles around used to be the wind caressing the fir trees, sits a computer. A Data General Nova 1200 is housed in a protective shed with its own power source. Its task? On-line monitoring . . . of tree growth!

Weyerhaeuser Co. is responsible for this odd-sounding, odder-looking computer application. If tree farming is ever really going to be farming—and not just seeding and harvesting—then there is much more to be learned about making trees grow. The project has established four points thus far: First, trees grow seasonally. The trees in the test plot grew only from March through September, and not at all during the rest of the year. Second, the height growth season is different from the circumference growth season. Third, trees shrink as well as grow. The test trees shrank during the day and grew at night; moreover, they shrank for weeks at a time during droughts. Fourth, fertilization, irrigation, and thinning can more than double tree yields.

What combination of growth-enhancement factors can most effectively and economically increase yields? Answering that question has involved turning a forest into an electronic technician's nightmare. Ten miles of wire link the growth-measuring devices attached to the trees from the computer which patiently records their readings. Bands to measure lateral growth surround the trees. Solar receptacles measure sunshine. Other devices measure air and soil temperature, relative humidity, and wind speed.

The bulk data is taken to Weyerhaeuser's central computing facility for "data reduction." Some data, such as information on malfunctions, can be obtained on-line, however, through the computer's console teletypewriter.

But why put a computer in the woods? Speed and accuracy, low operating costs (vs. the cost of manual methods), the production of highly usable data (90-percent usable data is typical; previously, 70 percent was considered excellent), timing information, and the rapid detection of malfunctions—these more than compensate for the high initial cost of the computer and its shelter and power problems.

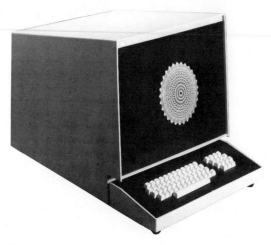

Figure 10–6
The IMLAC PDS4 Intelligent Terminal

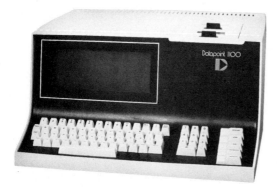

Figure 10–7
The Datapoint 1100 Intelligent Terminal

new machines, no programming is necessary, and no large-scale conversion of data and business procedures is required before they are installed. However, the prediction is that small businesses will eventually convert to minicomputers for more efficiency when the cost of the mini's decreases.

INTELLIGENT TERMINALS These devices are also computers but have a special role as links to a larger computer. They accept input on an alphanumeric keyboard and display the input as either typewriter output (hard copy) or on a cathode-ray-tube screen. They are called *intelligent* because they have the ability to check input data for errors, such as numerics outside an acceptable range, and perform other preliminary verifications of the data. Terminals have a CPU and a small memory to enable them to perform this task. They may also have peripheral devices associated with them. Data "edited" by a terminal is then sent via transmission lines to a large computer. Output is returned to the terminal and displayed on a CRT screen or as hard copy. An intelligent terminal differs from a conventional terminal such as a teletype or a CRT terminal, since these latter devices simply accept and transmit data. They have no computing power of their own, but merely operate under the control of a computer; a teletype is *not* itself a computer. The use of intelligent terminals is further discussed in Chapter 18.

SMALL BUSINESS COMPUTERS In addition to the computing devices described above, the computer professionals have chosen to label a subset of minicomputers *small business computers,* or *SBC.* Small business computers are designed to perform only business tasks. They are complete computers, with a CPU, an arithmetic/logical unit, a memory, and peripheral devices. They are capable of accessing data files stored on tape or disks and can perform all the typical business functions—payroll accounting, inventory control, and so on. Because SBC's can reference files, a program that processes in-

Figure 10-8
The Interdata 7/32

voices can update the inventory file, record salesmen's commissions, and issue bills to customers. An accounting machine, on the other hand, would require the execution of three separate procedures by the operator for each invoice. Because SBC's are truly minicomputers, we have chosen to treat them as part of the mini family rather than as special-purpose computers.

WHAT IS A MINICOMPUTER?

The structure of the minicomputer is the same as that of the computers described in Chapter 5. The miniaturization of the components has made the physical size of the minicomputer small, but it has the same basic structure: a central processing unit, an arithmetic/logical unit, a central memory, and peripheral devices. Technological advances in recent years have made possible both the miniaturization of components and large reductions in the cost of components. However, input/output devices are the most costly portion of the mini hardware. Therefore, special input/output devices for minicomputers have been designed, and are now in use. The minicomputer is a general-purpose computer that executes stored

programs. It can read and write data files. And by general accord, the term *minicomputers* implies that a minimum configuration costs less than $25,000. Certain key differences in hardware characteristics do exist between minicomputers and full-size computers—differences in word size, in arithmetic capabilities, and in input/output devices.

THE WORD SIZE Typically a minicomputer has a word size of 12 or 18 bits. A notable exception to this rule is the Interdata 7/32 computer (Figure 10-8), with a 32-bit word size. The limitation on word size results in a lower cost. The reduced number of bits also restricts the amount of memory directly addressable by a machine instruction. For that reason, most minicomputers have a maximum memory size of 32K or 65K words. The expansion of the word size in the Interdata 7/32 computer to 32 bits has permitted the memory size to expand to 1 million bytes of main storage. By using special addressing techniques, it is possible to have over 16 million bytes of memory in the Interdata 7/32.

THE CENTRAL MEMORY Because a semiconductor memory is physically compact, it

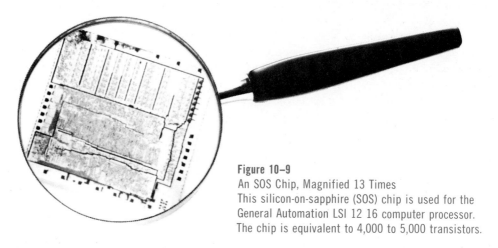

Figure 10–9
An SOS Chip, Magnified 13 Times
This silicon-on-sapphire (SOS) chip is used for the
General Automation LSI 12 16 computer processor.
The chip is equivalent to 4,000 to 5,000 transistors.

is the preferred type of memory for minicomputers. A core memory is less expensive than a semiconductor memory when the memory size is greater than 1,000 words. The cost of semiconductor memories is expected to drop dramatically as production increases, and it is predicted that this type of memory will be used in 50 percent of all computers within the next year or so.

The speed of the memory in minicomputers is comparable to or faster than that of the larger computers. Typical cycle times for memories range from .8 microseconds to 1.5 microseconds.

THE ARITHMETIC/LOGICAL UNIT
Minicomputers generally do not have multiplication or division operations in their standard repertoire of commands. These two operations are performed by subroutines when necessary. Because many instructions are required to do a multiplication, the overall computational speed of the minicomputer is substantially less than that of a large computer on which multiplication and division are standard operations performed directly by the hardware. Other logical commands common to full-size computers may be totally absent in the minicomputer. For example, the arithmetic commands—add, subtract, multiply,

and divide—for floating-point numbers are omitted. The reason for this lack of a full repertoire of commands is the desire to reduce costs.

MICROPROGRAMMING In order to overcome the disadvantage caused by the absence of machine operations and to provide greater versatility, most minicomputers offer microprogramming. This capability permits a sequence of instructions to be defined for each basic machine instruction. The execution of a microprogrammed machine instruction then automatically causes the execution of several individual (or micro) instructions. This permits a wide choice of instructions to be selected by the user for the minicomputer. The microinstructions are typically stored in a *read-only memory (ROM)*. Programs in a ROM cannot be written upon or altered by ordinary program instructions. The ROM is usually supplied by the manufacturer. Because a machine instruction in a microprogrammed computer may require the execution of several microinstructions, the microprogrammed machines are generally slower and also more expensive.

READ-ONLY MEMORIES Although a ROM's primary function is the storage of microprograms, it is sometimes used to store the applications programs for an installation. The contents of a ROM cannot be modified either by a loss of power or by other programs. The second advantage of a ROM is its speed. Its speed exceeds that of an ordinary memory, which must be both readable and writable. The primary disadvantage of a ROM is inherent in its nature; it cannot be modified. Consequently, it is usually supplied by the manufacturer, and if any changes are required the entire ROM module must be replaced.

PERIPHERAL DEVICES   The minicomputer generally supports all the devices mentioned as associated with full-size computers in Chapters 6 and 7. The standard tape units may be utilized, and random-access memories in the form of small fixed-head disks are common. However,

the addition of peripheral devices substantially increases the cost of the minicomputer. Standard input/output devices utilized by maxicomputers are relatively expensive compared to the basic cost of the CPU and memory of the minicomputer. For that reason, special low-cost versions of magnetic-tape and disk units have been developed for the minicomputers. However, lower costs also means lower speeds and smaller storage capacities.

Small Magnetic-Tape Units   The non-standard tape unit developed by the Digital Equipment Corporation (DEC) has become a very popular device for all minicomputers. The tape is shorter and the maximum number of characters stored is correspondingly less than on the full-size tape units. The DEC tape unit has proved to be reliable and has met the need for small

"It happened, J.B.! Last night
it finally happened!"

Figure 10-10
A DEC Tape Unit

Figure 10-11
A Tape Cassette

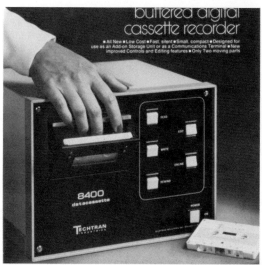

Figure 10-12
A Tape Cartridge

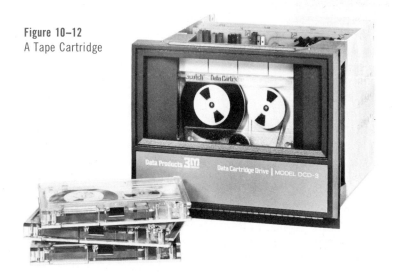

Figure 10–13
A Flexible Disk

amounts of data storage. Magnetic-tape cassettes are also available, similar to those used in home tape recorders. However, they are more reliable and may contain a minimum of 300K characters of data.

Another type of small tape unit is the magnetic-tape cartridge. These units offer ease of loading and a larger capacity. A cartridge marketed by 3M Corporation contains 300 feet of tape and records data on four tracks at a density of 1,600 bits per inch. Its storage capacity is 20 million bits, or roughly four times that of an average computer cassette tape.

Flexible Disk Units   A new type of disk, recently introduced, has proved a strong competitor with the conventional disk units. These flexible, or "floppy," disks of oxide-coated mylar are stored in paper or plastic envelopes. The entire envelope is inserted into the disk unit, effectively protecting the contents of the disk surfaces. The disk surfaces are rotated inside the protective covering. The disk head contacts the track positions through a slot in the covering. Storage capacities may be as great as 2.2 million bits. The disk units are relatively inexpensive, while the disks themselves are cheap. It is esti-

mated that eventually the disk envelopes will cost as little as 50 cents each. Because of their low cost and high speed, the floppy disks have increased in popularity and have even gained a foothold in the conventional disk marketplace.

Punched Card Devices   IBM introduced the 96-column card with the System/3 computer. Because of the low-cost card reader and card punch associated with it, this type of card has gained in popularity. For example, the Burroughs 1700 computer also offers the option of 96-column card equipment. Standard 80-column card devices are expensive and thus generally avoided for a minicomputer configuration.

A TYPICAL MINICOMPUTER CONFIGURATION   The basic configuration for a minicomputer would include a slow input/output device such as a teletype for both entering data and receiving hard-copy results, one or more tape units such as magnetic-tape cartridges, a flexible disk drive, and possibly a faster printing device such as a slow line printer that operates at a rate of 200 lines per minute. A minicomputer may be expanded with many input/output devices and the memory size increased. Thus, the cost

Figure 10–14
The PDP-8/e

Figure 10–15
The Varian V–74

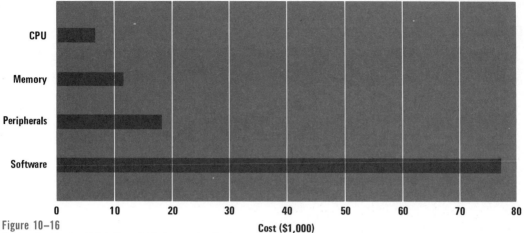

Figure 10–16
Costs of a Typical Disk-Based Minicomputer System

MINICOMPUTER SOFTWARE

Although many users compare minicomputers solely on the basis of hardware, the software cost of an installation is estimated to be 50 to 90 percent of the overall expense. As hardware costs decline, the cost of software in proportion to the total expense of the computer installation increases steadily. Because the overall cost of mini hardware is already low, the price of software becomes the overriding cost factor for a company acquiring a computer. Further, the resources of a small company do not allow for a large increase in personnel to perform in-house programming. Reliance on manufacturer-supplied software, including application programs, is very high. Because the development of programs requires highly skilled personnel, software costs have increased and not declined.

The amount of software available for minis ranges from nothing to everything. Since the performance of a computer is dependent on programs, the quality of software is of utmost im-

may equal or exceed that of the basic configuration of a full-size computer.

portance. The amount and quality of software is dependent, usually, on the manufacturer of the minicomputer. Some software houses also produce programs for particular minicomputers. The main items of software are programming languages and their supporting assemblers and compilers, the operating system, the utility routines, and the package programs supplied for applications such as inventory control and payroll accounting. Operating systems range from those which execute only one program at a given time (these are usually called monitors) to those which support multiprogramming activity. An assembler is an absolute necessity with a minicomputer. Since programs may require the use of the full power of the machine, compilers may be too slow and limited to handle the programming problems.

LANGUAGES The availability of higher-level languages varies. Typically, minicomputers offer scaled-down versions of the popular programming languages such as FORTRAN, BASIC, and COBOL. Business applications entail handling large data files, and COBOL is especially desirable for use in business programs. Because of its complexity, COBOL requires a machine with a large memory to translate all the features of the language. Since the minicomputers have small memories, a subset of COBOL is usually provided by the compilers rather than the entire language. Another linguistic alternative popular for business data processing is RPG. This language, in comparison to COBOL, is limited, but it permits the programming of many data-processing tasks. Other choices not as well suited for data processing are FORTRAN and BASIC.

Because no suitable higher-level language is available, the user may turn to assembly-language programming. As discussed in Chapter 9, assembly-language programming has major advantages and disadvantages for the user. The major advantage is that the machine's entire instruction repertoire is available to the user. The time required to translate an assembly-language program is minimal compared to the compilation time for a higher-level language such as COBOL. More efficient execution code may be produced, although this is dependent on the skill of the programmer. The major disadvantage is that the production of assembly-language programs requires a considerably longer time than the production of programs in higher-level languages.

Estimates run as high as four to seven times longer for the actual programming and testing time than for a comparable program in a higher-level language. Therefore, the choice of a minicomputer and its configuration must be based on its capability to both develop and execute programs. Since software costs exceed hardware costs, the available software must be carefully studied and weighed, as well as the hardware.

APPLICATION PROGRAMS   Many computer manufacturers and software vendors provide readymade programs for business applications. In general, these programs require adjustments to fit the individual user's data-handling requirements. These modifications are usually accomplished by the software supplier in conjunction with the user. If tailormade programs cannot be utilized, then the user must be prepared to incur the expense of software development. The mini user typically does not want to employ a staff of programmers. Instead he prefers to farm out the initial program development and then employ one or two programmers, at most, to maintain and modify the programs as needed. This limited staff also can be employed in writing other programs as required. However, the basic set of programs should be carefully scheduled so that delays in conversion are not experienced. The general recommendation to the small user is to purchase the major application programs in order to minimize the time and money expended on software development.

MINICOMPUTER APPLICATIONS

Minicomputers have a wide variety of applications. They are a handy computer to have in the home, they are a convenient way to control factory processes and to handle routine business data processing, and they are even used at racetracks to calculate odds. Where there is a computing need, the mini can often supply the computing power. Its uses are limited only by the human imagination. Only a few years ago, Honeywell was especially pleased to announce the use of a Honeywell minicomputer to control the Paris Metro subway system. Today this is considered to be a routine application. Now an experimental taxi system in London is a novelty. A magnetic-encoded ticket is inserted, and the taxi heads to its destination without a driver. The use of the

mini in school systems, for teaching purposes, is common. A Hewlett-Packard system for the Burnsville Elementary School District in Minneapolis provides special material for bright children who otherwise might be bored with school. In Los Angeles, a similar system is designed to meet the needs of slow achievers with drills and remedial work.

Minis are often used to monitor and control manufacturing processes. A computer performing this type of activity is called a *process-control* computer. These computers may have to withstand environmental conditions unthinkable for full-size computers. Tolerances of extremes of heat and cold and indestructibility under other forms of stress are built into some minicomputers. A PDP-8 recently set on fire by arsonists was retrieved unharmed. After the fire was out and soot and debris had been removed from the printed circuits, the computer was plugged in and ran correctly.

A minicomputer in every home may be still in the future, but some homes already have minis. The computer for playing games, filing income taxes, taking inventory of possessions, menu planning, and doing homework is the minicomputer.

THE FUTURE OF MINICOMPUTERS

Where do the minis go from here? The demarcation between minis and maxis is already blurred. The cost of computing power is decreasing and soon may be within the reach of all. The initial view of computers was that the cost of hardware was excessive and human personnel costs were minimal in comparison. Therefore, the overriding concern was efficient use of the hardware. This meant maximizing the number of programs executed in a given time and utilizing, as far as possible, the full capacity of the computer. Today the situation is reversed. Programming costs, and thus human costs, are high. As hardware costs decline, the luxury of an idle computer may become a reality. No one would argue that an office adding machine must be in constant use throughout the day for its purchase to be justified. Other office equipment stands idle much of the time, but is nevertheless necessary to the operation of the business. The day of the idle computer may be here soon. Multiprogramming may become obsolete, except for large time-sharing systems. The concern over the efficient use of hardware may evaporate as the minicomputer is accepted as a computational tool to be used as needed. Several minicomputers may prove more cost effective than one large-scale computer. As a consequence, minicomputers are rapidly gaining popularity and will be everywhere in our future.

REFERENCES

Auerbach on Small Business Computers. Philadelphia: Auerbach Publishers, 1973.

Austreich, Steven J. "Computers Advance the Art of Text Editing." *Administrative Management,* November 1973, pp. 71–73.

Cashman, Michael. "Small Business Computers." *Datamation*, June 1972, pp. 51–57.

Coury, Fred F., ed. *A Practical Guide to Minicomputer Applications.* New York: IEEE Press, 1972.

Cumpston, Charles. "Computers: Is Bigger the Answer?" *Administrative Management*, September 1973, p. 36.

Ford, Michael A. "Minimakers Better Get With It." *Infosystems*, December 1973, pp. 26–28.

Gardner, W. David. "Those Omnipresent Minis." *Datamation*, July 1973, pp. 52–55.

Gruenberger, Fred, and Babcock, David. "Speaking of Minis." *Datamation*, July 1973, pp. 57–59.

Hollingworth, Dennis. *Minicomputers: A Review of Current Technology, Systems, and Applications.* Rand Report R-1279. Santa Monica, Calif.: The Rand Corporation, July 1973.

Kenney, Donald P. *Minicomputers.* New York: AMACOM, 1973.

Meisner, Dwayne. "What to Expect When the Mini Arrives." *Administrative Management,* July 1973, pp. 14–15.

Murphy, John A. "Small Business Systems. What's Available?" *Modern Data,* November 1973, pp. 57–65.

Murphy, John A. "Floppy Disc Drives & Storage." *Modern Data*, February 1974, pp. 47–52.

Myers, Edith. "Small Business DP: User Experience." *Datamation*, June 1972, pp. 47–50.

Niskanen, Anthony S., and Rothenbuecher, Oscar H. "Small Business Systems." *Modern Data*, November 1973, pp. 53–56.

Zaffarano, Joan. "Calculators: The Programmables and 'Prepros.'" *Administrative Management*, August 1973, pp. 40–48.

"How to Succeed in Small Business DP." *Datamation*, June 1972, pp. 40–46.

QUESTIONS

1. What are miniature computing devices?
2. Why should a company select a minicomputer for data processing rather than one or more accounting machines?
3. What features distinguish a minicomputer from full-size computers?
4. What peripheral devices are especially suited to a minicomputer?
5. What factors should a company consider before selecting a particular minicomputer?
6. When should a company move up from a minicomputer to a full-size computer?

CHAPTER ELEVEN

Problem Analysis for Business Data Processing

In every aspect of our lives today, we are confronted by the process of recording information. The government maintains records of births, deaths, taxes, license plates, voter registration, and large quantities of other information. Stores maintain records of purchases in order to bill customers correctly and maintain a stock of goods. Libraries record the loan of a book together with the name and address of the borrower. Banks record each transaction by holders of checking and savings accounts. Everywhere we go there is a need for recording information.

Data is systematized information, and the recording, updating, and retrieving of data by some automatic means is called data processing. There are three types of data-processing activities: (1) routine data processing, (2) the analysis of scientific data collected from physical equipment such as laboratory devices, and (3) the analysis of data files. Business data processing is concerned with the routine handling of business data, which is of a semipermanent nature. But data processing is used as well in areas other than business. For example, medical records for a hospital placed in a computer data file will require constant updating. There will also be frequent requests for the retrieval of records. Processing that requires structured files and the updating of records is called routine data processing. Scientific data processing is concerned with the handling of data produced by physical devices such as those monitoring the Apollo moon shots. During these lunar expeditions, data was constantly transmitted to computers, recorded, and analyzed. The data was not organized immediately into records, nor was the file updated. We categorize this activity as scientific data processing. Businesses are concerned with the analysis of data files for the purpose of forecasting future sales and profits. Hospitals are interested in statistical analyses of data. These activities, and many others, are classified as a third type of data processing and not as routine data processing.

Although business data processing is concerned with the routine processing of business records such as those needed in the production of payroll checks, inventory records, and purchase orders, the problems encountered in business data-processing problems can be as complex as those encountered in mathematical and scientific analyses. The reason for this complexity is the lack of rigor in the statement of problems and the difficulties in defining the relationships between all the data elements in a problem. This difficulty in problem definition contrasts with the ease of defining scientific problems by the use of mathematical symbols and statements. There is presently an attempt to develop a formal language for the definition of data-processing problems to overcome these difficulties.

In this chapter we will attempt to present some guidelines for the analysis of business data-processing problems and their subsequent placement on the computer. Because these problems differ in size and complexity, there can be only general guidelines.

THE SOLUTION OF PROBLEMS BY COMPUTER

The solution of any problem by use of a computer requires several steps:

1. specification of the problem
2. analysis of the problem
3. design of the required computer programs and the data files
4. writing the program coding

5. testing the programs (also known as *debugging*)
6. documentation of the programs

In step 1, the problem must be clearly stated without regard to the subsequent use of the computer. Otherwise, a full picture of the problem may not emerge, but only a particular way to solve the problem on the computer. All aspects of the problem should be stated, and all possible details of the problem and its related data files should be specified. This step is typically performed by the persons directly connected to the problem together with the personnel who will implement the computer programs. For example, management in conjunction with accounting personnel may specify the requirements for handling purchase orders. However, these requirements should be stated not in terms of the existing manual operation but in terms of what processing must be performed, what data must be recorded and retained, and what output must be produced.

Step 2, the analysis of the problem in terms of computer processing, is usually performed by systems analysts working closely with the original problem posers. After the analysis has been performed, the problem is specified directly in computer terminology; the systems analysts then prepare an outline of program steps by drawing *flowcharts,* or pictorial representations of the program logic. Flowcharting is performed by systems analysts in many business organizations, but it may also be accomplished by the programmer who writes the program coding and tests the program. If a person only performs the coding of a program and is not involved in the flowcharting phase, he or she may be known as a *coder* and not a programmer. Finally, the program must be documented; this task is usually assigned to the programming group that performed the initial programming. These steps of writing, testing, and documenting programs are discussed in later chapters.

In this chapter we will discuss the design of the computer programs that comprise a data-processing system. The term *system* here indicates a group of programs and files that combine to provide the computer processing used for a particular data-processing task or a group of related tasks. The chapter is divided into three major sections: (1) a discussion of the design of data-processing systems, (2) a discussion of the updating of data files, and (3) an explanation

of the selection of a programming language for business data-processing applications. Before discussing the design phase, let us first review the terminology used in business data processing.

DEFINITIONS

Data are systematized items of information. For example, the name, height, weight, and phone number of an individual represent data, or information, about that person. Data regarding a particular person or physical item such as an item of merchandise are grouped to form a *record.* A collection of records containing the same type of data comprises a *data file.* For example, the personnel file of a company has a record for each employee of the company. Each record contains information about the employee, such as his or her name, address, date of employment, and Social Security number. The collection of these records forms a data file known as the personnel file. Because the records in this file are semipermanent, the file is called a *master file.* Whenever an employee terminates his or her employment, a correction must be made in the personnel master file. If a new employee is

COMPUTER DIAGNOSES HEART DISORDERS
FROM ECG DATA

A series of probabilistic computer programs—using a data base derived from 28,000 patients—has outperformed a group of trained cardiologists in diagnosing heart disease from electrocardiogram (ECG) data.

Analyzing ECGs from patients whose condition had already been confirmed, the system correctly identified disorders in 88 percent of the cases presented. The cardiologists' score was only 64 percent. The programs were developed by Dr. Hubert Pipberger, who is associated with both the Veterans Administration Hospital in Washington, D.C., and the George Washington University Medical School, where he is a professor of clinical engineering and medicine.

"Most of the people who have worked with computer analysis of electrocardiograms have tried to use the computer to simulate a physician," Pipberger said. "But we've tried to see whether the computer can do better than a physician."

An ECG is a record of how the heart's muscle tissue is functioning. The contraction of a muscle—like the transmission of a nerve impulse—is essentially an electrical process. An electric impulse propagates through the muscle, causing its fibers to shorten. The ECG shows the electrical disturbances associated with the contraction of heart muscle, as recorded by conductors placed on the patient's skin.

A typical ECG shows several distinct waves of activity during each heartbeat cycle. A record of these waves can provide considerable information about the heart's condition and activity. The important diagnostic parameters include the amplitude and direction of the waves and the time interval between successive parts of the wave series. Abnormalities in the formation of the contractive impulse, delays in its propagation within the heart, and other anomalies can help a trained observer identify the nature, location, and extent of many types of heart disorders.

The essential components of Pipberger's system are a three-channel ECG recorder, an analog-to-digital converter, the Varian 73 computer, and a package of programs that permits the computer to read an ECG and then identify a heart disorder by referring to a 28,000-patient data base. This data base, stored on disks and containing clinical information on patients with known types of heart disease, has taken some 13 years to assemble.

The program issues a printed list of conditional probabilities that the patient is suffering from a given heart disorder. It may, for example, tell the cardiologist that there is an 80-percent chance that the patient's right ventricular overload is due to a chronic pulmonary disorder, and that there is only a 6-percent chance that the overload is attributable to a diseased heart valve. The sum of all the probabilities listed must, of course, total 100 percent.

The cost-effectiveness of the system is now being analyzed by an independent evaluation team and compared with the cost-effectiveness of physicians in identifying heart disease. If the results are favorable to automated ECG analysis, it will probably become a regular clinical procedure in VA hospitals.

Figure 11–1
Data Fields

EMPLOYEE NO.	NAME	HOURS WORKED	HOURS OVERTIME
42B1812	Smith, John A.	40	3
43B8962	Jones, Abe	35	0
43A2361	Brown, Sam J.	40	8

Field

hired, an addition must be made to the file. Whenever an employee moves and changes his or her home address, the file must be altered to reflect this new data. Other changes may be necessary on individual records. The collection of data indicating deletions, additions, and changes to data records in a file is called a *transaction file* or *correction file*.

The items within a data record are called *fields*. Examples of fields within our mythical personnel record are the name of an employee, his or her home address, and his or her Social Security number. A field may be divided into *sub-fields*. For example, a home address may be divided into (1) a street number and street name, (2) a city, (3) a state, and (4) a zip code. A data record is considered to be a logical unit of data, and not a physical unit. Similarly, a field or sub-field is a logical subportion of the data record. A field or subfield may be expressed in one of the following ways: (1) by alphanumeric characters given in the alphanumeric code used by the computer, (2) by a binary integer, (3) by a binary number with a fractional part (a scaled number), (4) by a binary number in floating-point representation, or (5) by pseudodecimal numbers, also known as packed-decimal numbers,

available on some computers such as the IBM System/370 computers. The choice of a means of expression is dependent on the use of the field. If the contents of the field are simply recorded and printed when necessary (as is a Social Security number), alphanumeric representation is preferred. If the field is frequently used for computations in a computer program, binary representation may be preferred.

The data records in a file typically are ordered by a field or fields in each record. For example, the personnel file may be ordered by a company-assigned payroll number. Another possibility is an ordering by department number and then by a company-assigned payroll number. The fields by which a data file is ordered are called *keys*. A file may be reordered when desirable; the process of reordering the file by one or more keys is called *sorting*. For example, we may wish to reorder the personnel file by company department numbers, job classifications, last names, and then first names. In this instance, the keys are (1) the company department number, (2) the job classification, (3) the last name, and (4) the first name.

The physical organization of the data fields within each file record is called the *record format*, or *file format*. For example, the payroll number could be made the first physical field of the personnel record. Each record on a file has the same logical organization of data. The record format is designed to aid in the collection of data, the use of the data, and the subsequent retrieval of the data from the file. An example of a file containing records with no particular structure is the file of a book transcribed by a computer. Each page can be considered a record. Within each record data are organized into sentences. The beginning and end of the record may be portions of sentences. However, no record in this file necessarily resembles any other record. Such a file is called *unformatted*.

When the physical contents of each data field within each file record are identical in size and logical content, all the records in the file have the same number of characters or words. Such a record is called a *fixed-length record,* and the file, a *fixed-length file.* If individual records may contain differing amounts of data, the records are called *variable-length records.* For example, the file containing student records may be composed of variable-length records. Each student may have taken a different number of courses. The number of courses taken will be recorded for each student but may vary. Consequently the record may have a variable length. A *variable-length field* must contain special symbols to denote the beginning and end of the field. This ensures a proper interpretation of the data fields within the record. There are two ways to mark the limits of the variable-length field. The number of words or characters may be given preceding the field, or a special character may be used to denote the end of the field.

If the length of a group of data may vary up to a known maximum, it may be wiser to expand the

length of all the file records to this maximum. Whether this is wise depends on the difference between the size of the longest data record and the anticipated size of most of the data records. Fixed-length files are generally easier to create and manipulate than variable-length files, which require special precautions to ensure that sorting can take place as desired and that all data is interpreted correctly. Programming is also easier for fixed-length files than for variable-length files. Now that these terms for business data processing have been defined, we will continue our discussion of the design of data-processing systems.

THE DESIGN
OF DATA-PROCESSING SYSTEMS

When the demands for processing data exceed the capacity of a company to cope with them, or the retrieval or analysis of data is requested at a speed beyond that possible with the firm's present data-processing techniques, a computer data-processing system may be established. If the volume of data is small, the cost of establishing a data-processing system is usually greater than the benefits received from automating the data handling. The use of accounting machines may be a better cost-saving choice than introducing either a mini- or a full-size computer.

The design of a data-processing system depends directly on the nature of the data to be entered in the files and the purpose of establishing the system. If the management of a given firm wishes to have an accurate and reliable collection of data updated at frequent but scheduled intervals, the design of the system can be a routine one. If, in addition to the processing of data, the management wishes reports to be produced using data from the newly established file and other files, other factors enter into the design. Instead of periodic updating of data, the company may wish to update the file on a real-time basis. In real-time systems, whenever a change occurs in the data, such as a decrease in inventory caused by the shipment of goods to a customer, the file is immediately altered to reflect this change. This kind of adjustment calls for a design based on real-time handling of data and requires special hardware in addition to complex software programs.

A problem must be analyzed in light of the

management's aims in computerizing the data. All decisions on the final design of a data-processing system are interrelated. The format of the data file is dependent on the processing techniques for the file. The choice of the hardware is dependent on how the file will be structured to serve the purposes of management. All alternatives must be considered and the best one selected. Several key questions must be answered: (1) What data files should be established, and what data should these files contain? (2) How should the file record be organized? (3) What is the proposed size of the file, and what is its projected rate of growth? (4) Should the file be accessed sequentially or randomly? (5) How much of a delay is acceptable in processing and retrieving data from the files? These five questions are of primary importance in the design of any data-processing system. Each question is discussed separately below, but each answer is linked directly to the answers to the other four questions.

(1) WHAT DATA FILES SHOULD BE ESTABLISHED, AND WHAT DATA SHOULD THESE FILES CONTAIN? This is a crucial question, since all future processing depends on the data placed in the files. Precisely what data should be placed in the computer data files must be determined. Only data that is available in a computer file may be processed automatically. For example, a computerized personnel file may contain only the most important data on an employee while manual records are maintained to give further information, such as the number of children an employee has, references given by previous employers, and other information not directly related to the individual's present role at the company. Such information may be conveniently stored in a filing cabinet. But a choice must be made. If all the data from a personnel record are to be placed in a computer, the computer record will be longer and, therefore, more costly to maintain and process.

The data required by one department may also be necessary for a data file established by another department. For example, a payroll file may require each employee's name, address, Social Security number, and company-assigned number. A personnel file would also include this data. A decision must be made to establish separate files for the payroll and personnel departments or to integrate the data from these two departments in one file. This type of integration is usually possible, too, with data for other areas such as sales, purchasing, and inventory control. If files are integrated, their updating requires less time and less duplication of effort. Those retrieving data are ensured the use of a file corrected by various departments and containing all the information pertinent to an inquiry. This type of data file design is known as an *integrated data system* (IDS). An alternative is the maintenance of independent data files and the possible use of minicomputers by each department of the company.

(2) HOW SHOULD THE FILE RECORD BE ORGANIZED? After the data to be placed within a record has been determined, it is necessary to establish a format for the data record. The type of data and its usage are considered in designing the structure of the record and the mode of storing the data values. For example, an employee's Social Security number is never used in any computation; it functions only as an identifier and is used for such purposes as checking that a record matches the record sought or for identifying information on checks or company reports. Consequently, it is con-

venient to store Social Security numbers in alphanumeric form. If a data value will be used extensively in computations, it may be stored in binary form. However, a data value is frequently used both for computations and for output. The computations must be done with binary numbers, and the output display requires numeric characters in a computer code such as EBCDIC. Therefore, a choice must be made between binary form and coded representation. If the data is stored in a binary form, additional time is required by each program to convert it to numeric characters for output displays. If the data is stored in the record as numeric characters, it must be converted to binary form for computations, and a corresponding amount of time for conversion is required by each program using the data for computational purposes. In this case, the best choice is usually to store the data in binary representation or as packed-decimal numbers.

After the contents of the fields have been established, the actual structure of the record must be determined. Should the record have a fixed or variable length? The answer to this question is dependent on the inherent features of the data. For example, an employee may keep track

"Little Billy Malton, of Tarville, Ohio, deserves goods valued at $3.56."

of his work by charging each job to the department ordering the work. If this time charging by department is placed in a record, the record will probably be of variable length so that it can accommodate any number of jobs in a given day. If the maximum number of separate jobs that can be done in a day by an individual can be estimated, the record length can be set to accommodate this maximum number. Since all records will be extended to this length, the size of the file is increased and, similarly, the processing time is expanded. If the file will be of a relatively short length, this may not matter. The design of other file records may be easier, since no duplication of any group of data within a record is necessary. For example, a personnel record is a fixed-length record unless we permit some item that varies in length to enter it. If we wish to store the names of an employee's references, we might create a field of varying length. Or we could choose to allow a maximum of twenty names and add a special pointer to the manual personnel file to the records of any employees with a greater number of references.

The choice of a fixed- versus a variable-length record is important, since programming is generally easier for fixed-length records than for variable-length records. The processing time for the file, if it is sequential, is dependent on its size, which is determined by how much data is stored. The selection of data and the record structure together determine the amount of physical storage in the form of magnetic tapes or disks required for the computer.

A file is typically organized by a unique identifier. The updating of a data record is accomplished by the use of this identifier. Some careful thought should be given to selecting this identification field. For a personnel file, a company-assigned number or a Social Security number* could be the identification field. The inventory file may utilize part numbers. The identification field for a record must be unique and not duplicated by the identification field of any other record.

(3) WHAT IS THE SIZE OF THE FILE, AND WHAT IS ITS PROJECTED RATE OF GROWTH? This question is important because the physical size of the immediate file

* Legislation by Congress is likely in the future to safeguard individual privacy by making the use of Social Security numbers as identification fields illegal for any organization except the Social Security Administration.

must be estimated and the future growth rate evaluated. The choice of a storage medium is dependent on the proposed use of the file and its size, now and in the future. If a file will require 600 million characters of storage and must be accessed randomly, then the random-access device selected must be sufficiently large to accommodate the file. If a file will be processed sequentially about once a month but will grow at the rate of 2 million characters per year, magnetic tape is the obvious choice. If random-access processing is desired, then disk packs would be a suitable choice since more disk packs could be acquired as the file expands. However, the acquisition of disk packs without disk drive units would mean that thc whole file would not be available on the computer at a given instant.

The purpose of the file, its size, and the financial resources available interact to determine the storage medium. Although very fast random-access storage may be desirable, the money to pay for such storage may not be available. Consequently, sequential access may be chosen or a slower random-access device, such as a data-cell device, may be selected.

In designing a large file system, the amount of time for processing must be carefully considered. For example, with a tape file consisting of three reels it takes approximately nine minutes to read the data. If a 100-reel tape file is involved, it may take about five hours to process the entire file. Special precautions must be taken to prevent errors caused by the mounting of the wrong reels or the placing of an incorrect external label on a tape reel by the operator. The physical mounting and dismounting of that many tape reels poses problems. Therefore, it is desirable to index the file and also to place an index of the data records given on a reel at the beginning of each reel. Thus the program can select a desired reel without reading the entire file.

(4) SHOULD THE FILE BE ACCESSED SEQUENTIALLY OR RANDOMLY? The answer to this question depends upon the use of the file. It is also directly related to the storage medium selected for the data file and the time acceptable for updating or retrieving a record. If it is convenient to process a file sequentially, the storage medium selected will be magnetic tape as a general rule. However, a file stored on a random-access device may also be processed sequentially. In processing a magnetic-tape file, a specified time must be scheduled for the com-

puter processing, and there may be an interval of a day or several days between each processing of the file. A file stored on magnetic tape cannot be shared by several programs at once; but it can be read by only one program at a time. The chief advantages of using magnetic tape are its low cost and the ease with which a file can be expanded by adding another tape reel.

Random-access storage means that any record can be referenced directly in approximately the same amount of time as any other record. The updating of a file does not require the reading of the entire file, merely the selected records. Periodically the entire file should be rewritten to eliminate any wasted space caused by records that have been deleted. A random-access file is ordinarily available to all programs except when it has been written on a disk pack and dismounted from the disk drive unit.

Although random-access devices are the most popular storage medium today, they do have certain disadvantages. Random-access files cost more per character than magnetic-tape files. A file may grow beyond the capacity of a random-access device to handle it, requiring the acquisition of another random-access device at a greater cost than the cost of additional tape reels. Disk

packs offer a compromise solution, since more disk packs may be purchased; but then the entire file is not directly available at a given time on the computer. Data on disks is more vulnerable to destruction as a result of program or mechanical errors. To safeguard the file, it must be periodically written on magnetic tape.

(5) HOW MUCH OF A DELAY IS ACCEPTABLE IN PROCESSING AND RETRIEVING DATA FROM THE FILES? If the requirements of the data-processing problem demand the retrieval of data within seconds, random-access storage must be selected. The entire file must always be immediately available to the computer; that is, the file must be on-line and any program must be able to reference the file directly. If the data records must be on-line but need not be retrieved so quickly, slower random-access devices may be considered. There are now automatic control devices that select a tape reel from a tape library, automatically mount the reel, and automatically dismount it when it is no longer needed. Data-cell devices offer low-cost random-access storage with a slower speed of retrieval. If routine processing is sufficient to meet the demands of the users, then sequential

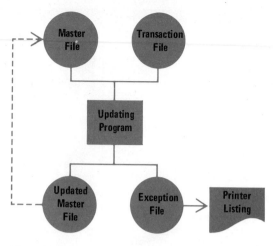

Figure 11-3
A General Flowchart of an Updating Program

MASTER FILE	TRANSACTION FILE	UPDATED MASTER FILE
Record 1	Delete record 2	Record 1
Record 2	Correct record 3	Record 3 corrected
Record 3	Delete record 4	Record 5 corrected
Record 4	Correct record 5	Record 6
Record 5	Delete record 28	Record 7
Record 6	.	Record 8
Record 7	.	
	.	

Figure 11-4
Updating a Sequential File

storage and magnetic tape may be an acceptable solution.

UPDATING A FILE

There are two basic functions that are performed for every computer data file: updating and the retrieval of information. The retrieval of data may be only from selected portions of the file. For example, it may be necessary to print all employee records from the personnel file for a single department of a firm or the records of all employees who have been with a company ten years or longer. Other functions may be performed only on a particular file. For example, a payroll file will be used periodically to produce paychecks for the employees of the company. Such a routine function may be incorporated within an updating program or it may exist as a separate program.

The updating of a computer file requires that a program be used to read the master file and the corrections to it and write an updated master file. Typically the program also will produce a printout listing exceptions to the corrections to the master file, that is, requests for correcting nonexistent records or placing erroneous data in the file.

Updating a file may involve three possible types of corrections: (1) the addition of new records, (2) the deletion of obsolete records, and (3) the insertion of different data into specified fields of selected records. These corrections may be collected in a correction file, or transaction file. If the file is updated periodically, the corrections can be grouped or batched and transferred to the master file at one time. The immediate correction of a master file whenever new data is received requires remote terminals and random-access storage; this type of processing is discussed in Chapter 18.

SEQUENTIAL PROCESSING   A master file may be processed either sequentially or directly. Sequential processing is required if the file is stored on magnetic tape but may also be used for a file on a random-access device. The updating process then requires the reading of each record from the transaction file and the matching of these records with the master-file records. The correction of the master-file records is then performed. Typically, new records are placed at the end of a master file. Because processing is sequential, the records on the transaction file must be in the same order as the records on the master file. Therefore, the transaction file is usually sorted prior to the execution of the updating program. (See Figure 11–4.)

DIRECT-ACCESS PROCESSING If a file is stored on a random-access device such as a drum or disk, it may be updated by *direct processing*. This means that the update program references only the necessary records and not the entire file. This is possible if there is a scheme for directly locating each record on the master file. Each record contains a pointer to the next record on the file. If a record is deleted, the record remains on the file, but the pointer to the deleted record is changed to point to the next valid record. Periodically, the file may be rewritten to eliminate wasted space and make it more compact. This method of processing is illustrated in Figure 11–5. Because all the references are performed directly, the order of the transaction file is immaterial. For convenience in studying the illustration, the transaction file has been ordered.

Figure 11–5
Updating a Random-Access File

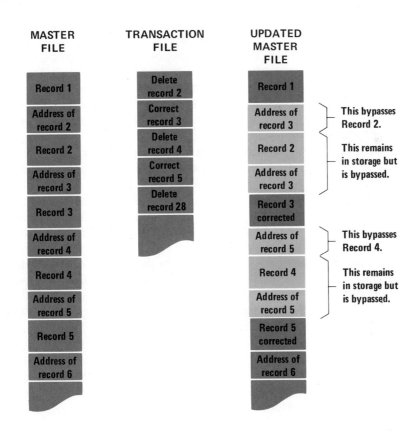

CHOOSING THE PROGRAMMING LANGUAGE

There are many possible choices for a programming language. One expert says that it doesn't matter what the language is as long as it is a higher-level language. On the whole, the computer professionals are in accord that a higher-level language should be used. The language chosen should suit the programming requirements and also must be available on the computer. There are two languages specifically designed for business data-processing applications: COBOL and RPG. COBOL is a versatile programming language and generally preferred over RPG for large data systems. RPG is designed to facilitate the generation of reports and, as such, is not as flexible and broadly based as COBOL. Other languages to be considered are any higher-level languages with file-handling capabilities. Another possibility is the addition of such capabilities via subroutines if no suitable language exists.

The choice of a language is also limited by the experience of the programmers who will write the programs. If there are no programmers available who are thoroughly familiar with COBOL, another higher-level language may be a wiser selection. If extensive computations are necessary, a mathematically oriented language such as FORTRAN, supplemented by file-handling subroutines, may be selected.

Five questions should be asked in choosing a programming language: (1) How will the files be read and written in this language? Are its features sufficient to provide all necessary file-handling capabilities? (2) Does the language provide for the handling of alphanumeric characters, singly or in groups? FORTRAN without the FORTRAN V features, for example, lacks this capability. (3) How does the efficiency of this language compare to that of the other languages available? That is, how does the compilation speed and the efficiency of the object code produced by the compiler compare with that of the other languages? (4) Does the language have features that simplify the testing of the program? (5) Is the language in general use on other computers? Otherwise, adoption of a different computer in the future may cause the rewriting of all programs in another language. The intelligent selection of a programming language means careful consideration of these questions before programming is initiated.

REFERENCES

Davis, Gordon B. *Computer Data Processing.* New York: McGraw-Hill Book Co., 1969.

Dodd, George G. "Elements of Data Management Systems." *Computing Surveys,* June 1969, pp. 117–133.

Gildersleeve, T. R. *Design of Sequential File Processing.* New York: Wiley Inter-Science, 1971.

Gruenberger, Fred, ed. *Information Systems for Management.* Englewood Cliffs, N.J.: Prentice-Hall, 1972.

Hanold, Terrance. "An Executive View of MIS." *Datamation,* November 1972, pp. 65–71.

Martin, James. *Design of Real-Time Systems.* Englewood Cliffs, N.J.: Prentice-Hall, 1967.

Patterson, Albert C. "Data Base Hazards." *Datamation,* July 1972, pp. 48–50.

Schubert, Richard F. "Basic Concepts in Data Base Management Systems." *Datamation,* July 1972, pp. 43–47.

Welke, Larry. "A Review of File Management Systems." *Datamation,* October 1972, pp. 52–54.

Wu, Margaret S. *Computers and Programming: An Introduction.* New York: Appleton-Century-Crofts, 1973.

QUESTIONS

1. What tasks are considered part of business data processing?
2. Define the following terms: file, record, field, subfield, sequential access, random access.
3. What are the six steps in solving a problem on the computer?
4. Company A processes all its data for 1,000 employees manually. It now wishes to computerize this data and process all paychecks by computer. What types of storage should be considered? Why?
5. Company B presently controls its inventory records by computer data processing. The inventory file presently occupies ten magnetic-tape reels. The company is considering another form of storage for the file to reduce the time necessary to update the master file. What storage devices should be considered? What advantages does each device offer?
6. Company C plans to perform all its data-handling activities by computer. What questions and answers must the firm consider before converting to a computer operation?
7. Company D plans to purchase a computer to process its business data. The computer to be used will have an operating system, a large subroutine library, an assembler, and compilers for FORTRAN IV and PL/I. What software problems does this firm face?

CHAPTER TWELVE

Defining the Program: Flowcharts and Decision Tables

Once the initial statement of a problem has been made, the overall design of the programming system may be formulated. The file structures are crystalized, the programming language is selected, and the general approach to the problem's solution is smoothed and polished to a state where programming may be begun. Before writing a single line of coding, the programmer mentally outlines the entire program and pictorially describes its logic. This pictorial description is called a *flowchart* or *block diagram.* Alternatively, the program logic may be presented in the form of a *decision table.* This chapter will discuss the techniques of constructing flowcharts and decision tables.

FLOWCHARTING

Flowcharting is an essential skill for the programmer and systems analyst. Preliminary planning provides a basis for the program, and the flowchart presents a more precise definition of it. The program itself represents the ultimate definition of the programming logic and steps. In simple programs, a programmer may choose to omit the flowchart and go directly to the coding stage. However, a flowchart is essential for more complex tasks. After the flowchart has been completed and reviewed for errors, coding begins with the flowchart serving as a guide. A good flowchart facilitates the writing of both good program code and a logically consistent program. After the program is put into operation, the flowchart is a prime resource for program documentation. Consequently, it should be as complete and accurate as possible.

To illustrate flowcharting, consider the problem of computing the payroll checks for 1,000 employees of a plant. The following steps would generally be required:

1. Get the data for an employee. If there is no more data, stop.
2. Compute the salary.
3. Calculate the deductions.
4. Compute the salary minus the deductions.
5. Write the paycheck.
6. Go to step 1.

These steps provide a basic outline for a payroll program. We have ignored details of the payroll file, computations for salary and deductions, checks for errors in the data, and so on, which

201

Figure 12–1
A Simplified Flowchart of a Payroll Program

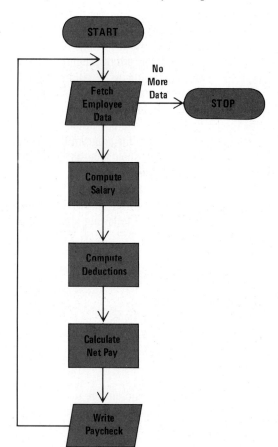

would be essential in an actual program, for the sake of clarity. The flowchart for this simplified program is given in Figure 12–1. The first box is labeled "Fetch employee data." If there is no more data, the program flows via the arrow at the right to a stop. Otherwise, it flows in a straight line until the employee's paycheck has been written. Then the program returns to step 1 and repeats all steps continuously until no more data exists. This repetition of program steps is called *looping,* or a *program loop.* The repetition of steps is an ideal task for the computer. A program usually contains several loops. Consider a program without loops, like that shown in Figure 12–2. What a tedious job its construction is for the programmer! There is an almost endless opportunity for making coding errors and possibly for the creation of program coding so lengthy that it could not be contained in the computer's central memory.

The tricks of constructing a good flowchart are an integral part of good programming procedures. Once constructed, the flowchart must be reviewed for logical errors, redundant steps, and a precise statement of the problem. The rules for boxes and arrows are a simple matter compared to the mental gymnastics required of the

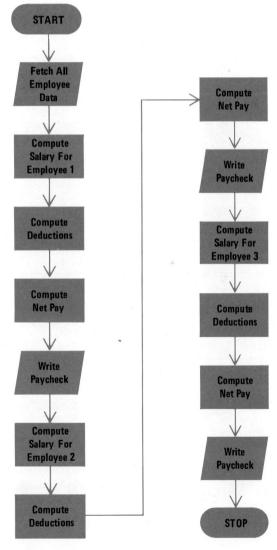

Figure 12–2
A Payroll Program Without Loops

flowcharter. He or she must think through the logic and conceive the *complete* program. The flowchart is an aid to this process and assists the programmer's memory of the program flow. The art of flowcharting and logical program design is usually learned under the direct supervision of experienced computer personnel.

ANSI STANDARD SYMBOLS   The American National Standards Institute (ANSI) has established standards for the symbols and boxes used for flowcharting. These standards are now widely accepted and used by the programming profession at large. The most commonly used symbols are given in Figure 12–3. The additional symbols provided are shown in Figure 12–4. Arrows are used to show the directional flow of the program. The shape of the box represents the type of activity to be performed. An input/output operation is represented by a parallelogram, whereas a decision is indicated by a diamond-shaped figure. A rectangle is used to contain a process, such as the addition of two numbers. Computer manufacturers provide flowcharting *templates* that contain the set of symbols used in flowcharting. The use of a template permits

Figure 12–3
Commonly Used ANSI Symbols

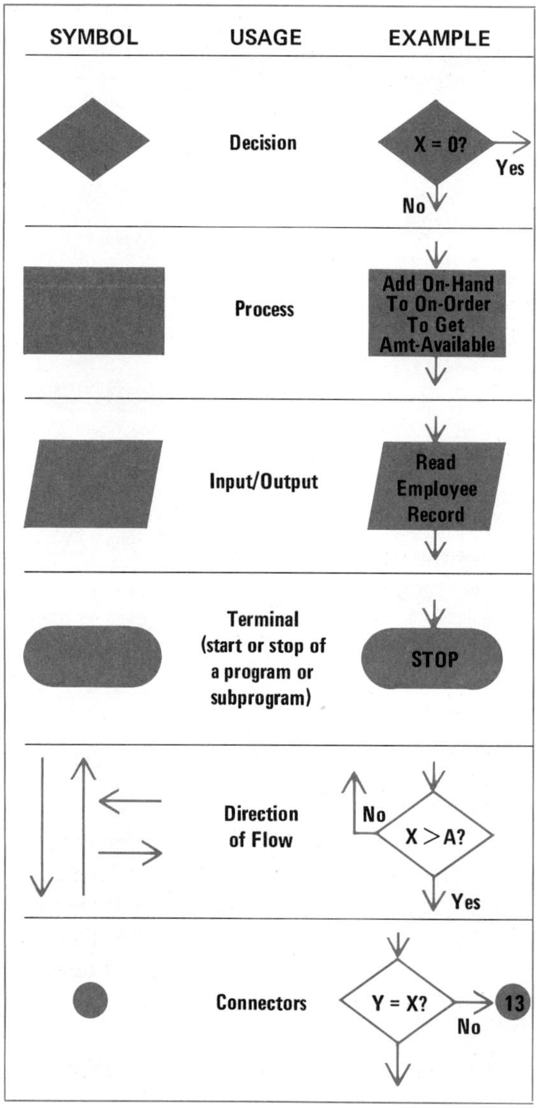

Figure 12–4
Additional ANSI Symbols

SYMBOL	USAGE	EXAMPLE
	Decision	X = 0? Yes No
	Process	Add On-Hand To On-Order To Get Amt-Available
	Input/Output	Read Employee Record
	Terminal (start or stop of a program or subprogram)	STOP
	Direction of Flow	No X > A? Yes
	Connectors	Y = X? 13 No

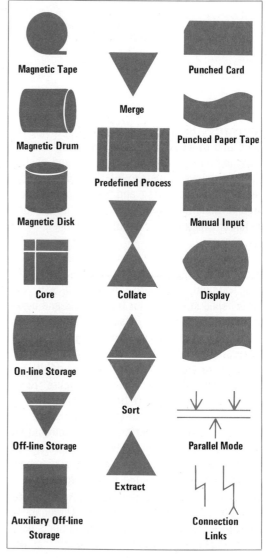

Magnetic Tape

Magnetic Drum

Magnetic Disk

Core

On-line Storage

Off-line Storage

Auxiliary Off-line Storage

Merge

Predefined Process

Collate

Sort

Extract

Punched Card

Punched Paper Tape

Manual Input

Display

Parallel Mode

Connection Links

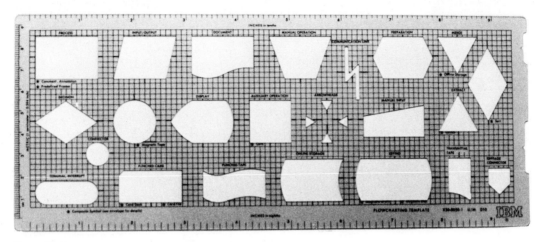

Figure 12–5
A Flowcharting Template

the drawing of a neater block diagram. Figure 12–5 shows the IBM flowcharting template that contains the ANSI symbols.

The contents of the boxes are important. Too much detail means that the flowchart becomes the program itself and not a quickly grasped pictorial version of the program's underlying structure. Such a detailed flowchart is frequently constructed after a program has been coded and tested. Although this type of flowchart provides some help in reading the program, it is not ideal. If too few details are given, logical errors may go undetected. Arriving at the proper amount of detail calls for a delicate balance. The flowchart must be sufficiently clear to enable the reader to grasp the logic of the program and aid in the examination of the actual coding, but it is not intended to displace the coding.

LEVELS OF FLOWCHARTING   There are two levels of flowcharting. First, the general flow of a program or programming system can be illustrated by a flowchart. This type of flowchart is also known as a *macro flowchart*. For example, the program to update a master file may require several types of input, such as exception cards (containing corrections to the data on the

transaction file), the transaction file on tape, and the master file on disk. It may produce an updated master file, a magnetic tape containing rejected transactions, and a listing of input errors together with a statistical analysis of the updated master file. The overall flow of such a hypothetical program is represented in Figure 12–6. Following ANSI conventions, circles have been used to represent tape-resident files and a cylinder used to indicate a disk-resident file. The detailed flowchart of this program might require several pages of block diagrams.

Second, as we discussed earlier, a flowchart is used to provide a graphical representation of a program. This more detailed flowchart is also known as a *micro flowchart*. For example, consider a program to read a set of 10,000 data cards and compute the sum of the numbers given on the cards, each of which contains one number. Let us assume that the program must also count how many numbers are less than or equal to zero and how many numbers are greater than zero. We can separate the solution to this problem into five steps:

1. Set the locations C1, C2, and SUM equal to zero.

Figure 12–6
A General Flowchart of an Updating Program

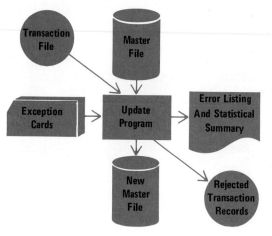

Figure 12–7
A Flowchart for Reading Data Cards
and Summing Numbers

2. Read a number. If there is no more data, print the contents of SUM and the two locations, C1 and C2. Stop.
3. Add the number to the location SUM.
4. Is this number less than or equal to zero? If yes, add one to the location C1. If no, add one to the location C2.
5. Go to step 2.

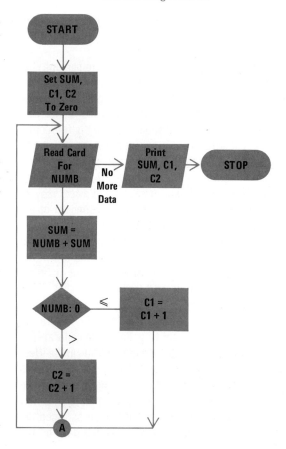

The flowchart of this problem is given in Figure 12–7. A colon (:) is used to indicate the comparison of a number with zero. We have arbitrarily attached names to the quantities manipulated by the program. We have placed each input number in a location called NUMB; the counters, C1 and C2, tally the numbers below and above zero. The name SUM is given to the location holding the sum of the numbers. These locations must be set equal to zero before they can be used by the program. Otherwise, their previous contents will be included in the summing process and an incorrect answer given.

The proper choice of boxes facilitates the reading of a block diagram. The address of a location (given by its name) and its contents are two different objects. In assembly-language programming, addresses of locations are manipulated as well as their contents. This type of address manipulation is achieved by other means in higher-level languages. To prevent confusion in notation, a location address is indicated by its name and its contents are specified by its name in parentheses. For example, NUMB indicates its address, whereas (NUMB) means the contents of that location. However, in higher-level languages, programmers often omit this more precise notation. The flowchart for the problem in Figure 12–7 can be drawn in many other ways, all of which may be acceptable. However, the statement in each box must always be meaningful and understandable to the reader of the flowchart.

Another example of a flowchart is shown in Figure 12–8. There, the problem is to find the personnel records for a list which contains less than 1,000 names and print the records. The program steps can be expressed in English as follows:

1. Read the list of names and store the total number of names in N.
2. Read a record from the personnel file. If there is no more data, go to step 6.
3. Does this record match one of those records being sought? If yes, go to step 4. If no, go to step 2.

Figure 12–8
A Flowchart of a Search for Personnel Records

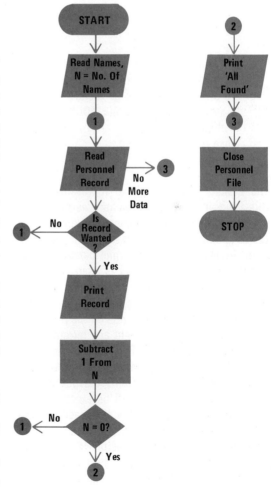

4. Print the personnel record. Subtract 1 from the number of records to be found.
5. Are any records left to be found? If yes, go to step 2. If no, print 'ALL FOUND' and go to step 6.
6. Close the personnel file.
7. Stop.

The flowchart is a graphical representation of this logic. In reading a flowchart we move from one box to another according to the direction of the arrows. However, it is not always necessary to draw an arrow directly from one box to another. Instead, a connective symbol is used to prevent the intersection of lines or confusing the connecting lines. For example, in Figure 12–8, if there is no more data available on the personnel file, the line flows to the right and terminates in a connector labeled "3." The program flow continues at the connector labeled 3 in the right-hand column of the flowchart; the box labeled "CLOSE PERSONNEL FILE" will be executed next. The labels given by the connectors need not correspond to the number of program steps as outlined above. It is also permissible to use alphabetic characters or a combination of alphanumeric symbols as labels for connectors.

Flowcharts usually require more than one sheet of $8\frac{1}{2}$ by 11 inch paper. At some installations, successive pages are joined together to form a scroll-like document. This is clumsy and difficult to store. A connector can be used to indicate where the program continues, and a page number may be written above the connector to aid in the study of the flowchart. For example, at the bottom of a page we might place a connector as follows:

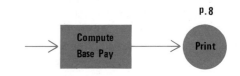

The flowchart continues at the connector labeled "PRINT" on page 8 of the flowchart.

GUIDELINES FOR FLOWCHARTING
The flowcharter has a wide range of freedom in drawing the block diagram. However, to produce an easy-to-read flowchart, the following guidelines should be observed:

1. The program should flow from top to bottom or left to right, with an arrow indicating

the direction of the flow from block to block.

2. The ANSI standard flowcharting symbols should be used.
3. Intersecting lines should be avoided, if possible.
4. To eliminate an excessive number of flowlines, connecting symbols should be used.
5. The operation expressed within a block should be clearly stated. Assembly language, in particular, should be avoided.
6. Special features of a language should not be used. The flowchart should not be tied to the structure of a particular programming language.
7. The flowchart should be neatly drawn, with the assistance of a programming template. The contents of the blocks should be legible.
8. The flowchart should be checked for logical consistency. (Are all the paths for a decision indicated? Are all connectors given?)
9. If a given step in the flowchart must be shown in greater detail, a separate flowchart should be drawn with the appropriate amount of detail.

The preparation of a flowchart is a time-consuming chore. Frequently, the coding of the program reveals errors in the flowchart or incomplete specifications for a particular area of the problem. Even more often, the original specifications are changed as the programmer begins to code or test the program. The programmer, under the pressure of a deadline and, usually, with an intense dislike of paperwork, proceeds to alter the program to fit the amended specifications. The flowchart then requires updating to accurately reflect the program code. Programmers often ig-

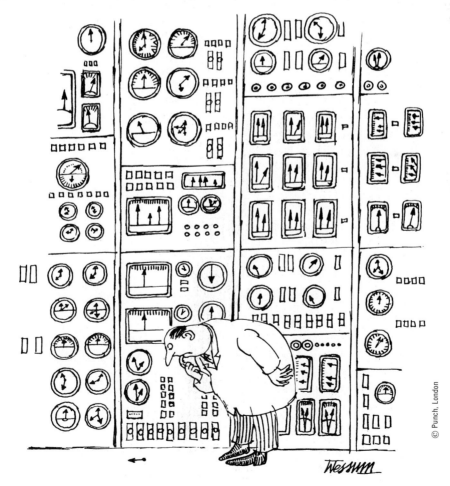

© Punch, London

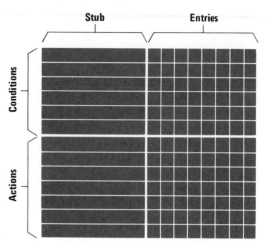

Figure 12–9
The Structure of a Decision Table

nore this latter step. Good management procedures require the completion of both a program that will work and a flowchart precisely describing the program's true structure.

DECISION TABLES

Decision tables are another way of specifying the logical structure of a program. A *decision table* is composed of conditional statements and program branches arranged in tabular form. Because it does not require block symbols, it can easily be prepared by a typist; and the decision table's simpler structure makes updating easier. Since conditions dctcrmining program decisions are given in English, they can be quickly understood by managers, engineers, and others, as well as by programmers. With a decision table, it is a simple matter to check that all options for a decision have been documented. The flowchart permits a wide range of language to express the action in each block. Because a decision table is constructed with English statements, the use of symbols, shorthand coding, and any direct use of programming-language coding are avoided. Decision tables have gained in popularity with

the advent of compilers that can translate them into a higher-level language. Examples of such compilers are FORTAB, which translates decision tables into FORTRAN, and DECTAB, which generates COBOL coding. Alternatively, the programmer may code directly from the decision tables, or he may choose to flowchart the logic first, using the decision tables as a guide, and then code the program.

THE STRUCTURE OF DECISION TABLES   There are three types of decision tables: limited entry, extended entry, and mixed entry. First, let us consider the design of a limited-entry table.

Limited-Entry Tables   A decision table is divided into four quadrants: a condition-stub quadrant, a condition-entry quadrant, an action-stub quadrant, and an action-entry quadrant. (See Figure 12–9.) The condition-stub quadrant contains a list of conditional statements or questions (called *stubs*). The statement "X = 0" in a condition-stub quadrant means "Is X = 0?" In our examples, we have chosen to phrase the items in the condition-stub quadrant as questions rather than conditional statements. In limited-

	1	2	3	4	5	6	7	8
Is Condition A met?	Y	N	Y	N	Y	N	Y	N
Is Condition B met?	Y	Y	N	N	N	N	Y	Y
Is Condition C met?	Y	Y	Y	Y	N	N	N	N
Action 1	X							
Action 2		X						
Action 3			X					
Action 4				X				
Action 5					X			
Action 6						X		
Action 7							X	
Action 8								X

Figure 12–10
A Sample Decision Table

entry tables, the condition-entry quadrant contains all possible replies to the question posed in the condition-stub quadrant. A condition entry may be a Y for YES, an N for NO, or a dash (—) to indicate a nonrelevant factor. The action-stub quadrant contains a list of actions (or *action stubs*). The action-entry quadrant shows whether or not an action will be executed. An X indicates that the action specified in the stub will be executed; a blank indicates that it will not be performed.

For example, let us examine the table in Figure 12–10, which shows the possible replies to three questions:

1. Is Condition A met?
2. Is Condition B met?
3. Is Condition C met?

To ensure that all combinations of Y and N responses have been tabulated the programmer computes the number of possible combinations, which is 2^n, where n is the number of items in the condition-stub quadrant. In this case, the total number of response combinations is 2^3, or 8. All the possible combinations have been given. The numbers 1, 2, 3, ... at the top of each column in the table each indicate a particular logical path which may be chosen depending on the status of Conditions A, B, and C. Each column represents a *rule* to be followed by the program. For example, rule 1 states that if Conditions A, B, and C are met then Action 1 will be executed; rule 2 states that if Condition A is not met and Conditions B and C are met, then Action 2 will be executed; and so on. The flowchart for this decision table is shown in Figure 12–11. It is overdetailed and difficult to follow.

Another example of a decision table is given in Figure 12–12. This table has three items in the condition-stub quadrant but only four possible combinations of responses. If Condition A is met, Conditions B and C are irrelevant. This reduces the number of responses by three and eliminates the need for the combination of Y and N responses in rules 3, 5, and 7 in the table in Figure 12–10. Because Condition C becomes irrelevant whenever Condition B is met, rules 2 and 8 are the same. Thus one more rule can be eliminated, leaving only four rules in the table in Figure 12–12.

Because a decision table can quickly become lengthy and too complicated, a program normally encompasses several decision tables. Each table is labeled by a name or a number. A *closed*

Figure 12–11
A Flowchart of the Decision Table in Figure 12–10

Figure 12–11
A Flowchart of the Decision Table in Figure 12–10

Figure 12–12
A Simple Decision Table

Is Condition A Met?	Y	N	N	N
Is Condition B Met?	--	Y	N	N
Is Condition C Met?	–	–	Y	N
Action 1	x			
Action 2		x		
Action 3			x	
Action 4				x

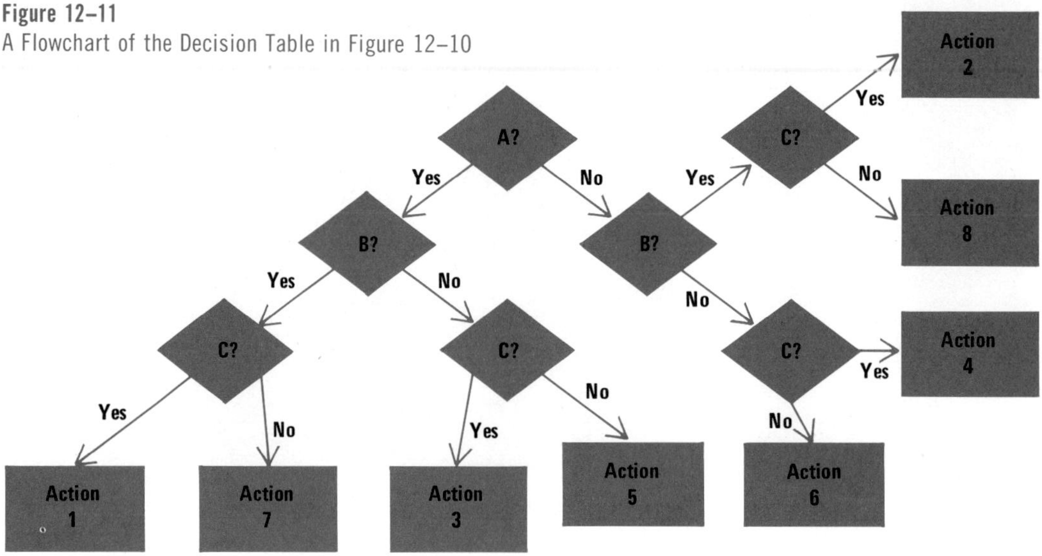

decision table is a table that is entered by one or more tables and returns control to the table that initially entered it. In effect, it represents a subroutine that can be used by any other decision table. An *open-end table* is a table that passes control to the next table in succession. It represents a set of coding in sequential order. It cannot be entered and exited by another table. A table can transfer control to an open-end table but control will not be returned; execution of the actions will continue with the next table in sequential order.

To show how tables are linked, two control instructions are used:

1. GO TO *table number or table name.*

This instruction written in an action stub directs the transfer of control to another open-end table specified by its name or number.

2. DO *table number or table name.*

This instruction written in an action stub transfers the logical flow from an open-end table to a closed table. After the action specified in the closed table is completed, control returns to the open-end table at the action stub following the DO instruction. This return of control is customarily indicated by the word "closed" or "return," written in the action stub of the closed table.

Extended-Entry Decision Tables **Extended-entry** tables permit the extension of the items in the condition-stub quadrant into the condition-entry portion of the decision table. For example, the items in the condition-stub quadrant in a limited-entry table could be

1. Is $x < 0$?
2. Is $x = 0$?
3. Is $x > 0$?

The extended-entry table expresses these three questions in a single statement: Compare x to zero. The entry side of the table is used to indicate the three possible conditions $x < 0$, $x = 0$, and $x > 0$. (See Figure 12–13.) A limited-entry table may use only Y, N, or – in the action-entry quadrant. The advantage to this type of table is the simplification that comes by reducing the number of items in the condition-stub quadrant. When the variables in a problem have multiple values, extended-entry tables are clearer than those with limited-entry.

Figure 12–13
An Extended-Entry Decision Table

(a) **A LIMITED-ENTRY TABLE.**

	1	2	3
Is $x > 0$?	Y	N	N
Is $x = 0$?	–	Y	N
Is $x < 0$?	–	–	Y
Action 1	x		
Action 2		x	
Action 3			x

(b) **AN EXTENDED-ENTRY TABLE.**

	1	2	3
Compare x To Zero	>	=	<
Action 1	x		
Action 2		x	
Action 3			x

PRESCRIPTION BY COMPUTER

Properly programmed, the computer can plot the trajectory of a rocket, keep track of a store's inventory, correlate census data and help predict weather more accurately. But can it be trusted to make the kinds of life-and-death decisions that doctors do? The answer may be yes, according to a team of scientists from Massachusetts Institute of Technology and Tufts–New England Medical Center in Boston. The researchers report in the *American Journal of Medicine* that they have taught a computer to exercise virtually the same clinical judgment that a physician must use in choosing a form of treatment. . . .

When the researchers began trying to write a decision-making computer program three years ago, says Dr. William Schwartz, chairman of the department of medicine at Tufts University School of Medicine and spokesman for the group, they discovered that little was known about how physicians arrived at their complex decisions. "Medical school . . . has paid remarkably little attention to the decision-making process." Thus he and his colleagues are analyzing how a doctor decides on such serious treatment as abdominal surgery.

A first-stage result of their study is a computer program that duplicates some of the mental processes of a highly skilled physician. Using acute kidney failure as an experimental model, the research group programmed the machine to weigh the risks and benefits of various tests and treatments and to consider such factors as the patient's attitude toward surgery.

The Boston group['s] study has also shown that computers could help doctors in their deliberations. That capacity was demonstrated when the computer was presented with the diagnoses of 33 hypothetical patients with 14 different serious kidney conditions. In all but two cases, the machine recommended the same treatment as did a pair of kidney specialists. In 14 of the 18 cases selected for further testing, the decisions reached by the computer were the same as those of the doctors. In each of the remaining cases, the computer's first choice was regarded by the doctors as a reasonable alternative.

From "Perscription by Computer," *Time*, January 28, 1974, pp. 54–55. Reprinted by permission from TIME, The Weekly Newsmagazine; © TIME Inc.

Mixed-Entry Tables This type of table combines features of the limited-entry and extended-entry table. Each item in the condition stub may assume the limited-entry or the extended-entry form. This combination permits the decision table to be as condensed as possible. An example of a mixed-entry table is given in Figure 12–14.

THE ELSE RULE To avoid having to write all possible Y and N combinations, the *ELSE rule* is employed. It covers all combinations not specified. An example of its use is shown in Figure 12–15. Unspecified sets of conditions are represented by the word "ELSE," and the action taken is indicated in the action stub. Because the ELSE entry eliminates the detailed outline of all combinations of conditions, it may permit the introduction of logical errors in the program. Consequently, it should be seldom used.

AN EXAMPLE OF A DECISION TABLE A problem especially well suited for expression in decision-table format is one in which there are several questions to be answered yes or no. The answers then can be tabulated as rules and the appropriate actions checked for each rule. For example, an insurance company may formulate rules for issuing automobile policies at various rates as follows:

"If the household has a driver under 25 years of age without driver training, the normal insurance rate plus a surcharge of 15 percent will be used. Otherwise, a surcharge of $7\frac{1}{2}$ percent will be used. If the automobile is driven to and from work each day, a round-trip distance of more than 10 miles, the normal rate plus a surcharge of 5 percent will be charged."

The decision table for this partial formula for calculating insurance rates is shown in Figure 12–16. Dashes (–) have been used to indicate when a yes or no answer is irrelevant. If a driver is not under 25, the question regarding driver education does not require an answer. For example, rule 3 states that if there is a driver under 25 with driver education and the automobile is driven to and from work a round-trip distance of

Rules For Calculating Overtime Pay	1	2	3	4	5
Is Number Of Hours Greater Than 40?	N	Y	Y	Y	Y
What Is Employee's Rank?		1	2	3	4
Pay Overtime		X	X	X	
Use Overtime Rate Of 1½ Times Base Rate			X	X	
Use Overtime Rate Of 2 Times Base Rate		X			

Figure 12–14
A Mixed-Entry Decision Table

Guidelines For Handling Loan Applications	1	2	3	4	5
Is Credit Record Excellent?	N	Y	Y	Y	Else
Is Annual Salary > $25,000?	N	Y	N	N	Else
Is Net Worth > $50,000?	N	Y	Y	N	Else
Approve Loan		X	X		Investigate
Reject Application	X				Investigate
Approve Short-term Loan				X	Investigate

Figure 12–15
A Decision Table with the ELSE Rule Applied

Rules For Figuring Insurance Rates	1	2	3	4	5	6	7
Is Driver Under 25?	Y	Y	Y	Y	N	N	N
Has Driver Under 25 Had Driver Education?	N	Y	Y	Y	-	-	-
Is Car Driven To And From Work?	N	N	Y	Y	N	Y	Y
Is Round Trip > 10 Miles?	-	-	N	Y	-	N	Y
Regular Rate	X	X	X	X	X	X	X
Surcharge Of 15%	X						
Surcharge Of 7½%		X	X	X			
Surcharge Of 5%				X			X

Figure 12–16
A Decision Table for Calculating Automobile Insurance Rates

10 miles or less, the insurance rate is computed as the normal rate plus a surcharge of $7\frac{1}{2}$ percent for the driver under 25. By adding more conditions, we could formulate rules for all possible combinations of yes and no responses. The more rules, the more complex the decision table. Many companies require that no more than 16 conditions be specified in a decision table to facilitate comprehension of the rules.

PRO'S AND CON'S OF DECISION TABLES   Decision tables are easy to prepare and can easily be updated by any programmer. Moreover, a final draft of a decision table can be prepared by any typist. The format of the decision table requires that all logical alternatives for a decision be given side by side. This facili-

tates the review and revision of the program logic. Decision tables lend themselves to independent review by personnel other than programmers. An especially attractive feature is the direct translation of decision tables by compilers.

Extensive work with decision tables is necessary for a person to become efficient at preparing them and familiar with the tricks of decision-table construction. Decision tables do not pictorially represent the program flow. Thus, the overall flow of the program may be more difficult to decipher. Many programmers dislike coding from decision tables since all the analysis has already been completed. This disadvantage can also be viewed as an advantage, from the standpoint of the problem originator.

REFERENCES

Chapin, Ned. "Flowcharting with the ANSI Standard: A Tutorial." *Computing Surveys,* June 1970, pp. 119–146.

Farina, Mario. *Flowcharting.* Englewood Cliffs, N.J.: Prentice-Hall, 1970.

London, Keith R. *Decision Tables.* Princeton: Auerbach, 1972.

McDaniel, Herman. *An Introduction to Decision Logic Tables.* New York: John Wiley & Sons, 1968.

Pollack, Solomon; Hicks, Harry T., Jr.; and Harrison, William J. *Decision Tables: Theory and Practice.* New York: Wiley-Interscience, 1971.

QUESTIONS

1. Draw and label the flowchart symbols for
   (a) input data read from a card,
   (b) the computation of $A = X + Y - Z$,
   (c) output data produced by a line printer,
   (d) the testing of X to see if its value lies between 0 and 100 inclusive,
   (e) a file stored on magnetic tape, and
   (f) a file stored on disk.

2. Draw flowcharts or flowchart segments for
   (a) a segment of a computer program to transfer data from punched cards to drum.
   (b) a program to compute the formula
      $A = \pi r^2$ for $r = 1, 2, 3, \ldots, 10$
   (c) testing a number to see if its value is 0, 100, or 1,000 and if it is negative.
   (d) reordering a stock item. If the stock of an item is equal to or below the reorder point, the item should be ordered.
   (e) mailing special advertising to charge-account customers. If the customer lives within 35 miles of the store, select his or her name from the file. If the customer charges over $100 a year, select his or her name. If the customer has opened his or her charge account within the last 90 days, select his or her name.
3. Prepare decision tables for problems 2(c) and 2(e).
4. Prepare a decision table for each of the following problems:
   (a) If the stock of item A falls below the reorder point of 100, check to see if item A is obsolete. If it is not, reorder item A. If item A is obsolete, substitute item B.
   (b) If $x < 0$, $A + B = C$. If $x = 0$, $A - B = C$. If $x > 0$, $A \times B = C$.
   (c) The combination of paychecks using rates of pay is controlled by column 80 in the individual record cards for employees. If column 80 contains a 1, compute the weekly rate. If column 80 contains a 2, compute the hourly rate. Then check column 79 to see if overtime pay is due. If so, verify that columns 76–78 contain numeric values. If not, write an error message.

CHAPTER THIRTEEN

Introduction to Programming Languages — FORTRAN

This chapter discusses first the general structure of higher-level programming languages and then proceeds to specific details of the FORTRAN language. Two other programming languages — COBOL and PL/I — are presented and compared to FORTRAN in succeeding chapters.

THE STRUCTURE
OF COMPUTER LANGUAGES

There are three basic parts in most programs:

1. reading the input data,
2. processing the data (that is, computing and manipulating the data as required), and
3. writing the results.

Each part may be complex and require several steps. For example, the input data may consist of several files stored on magnetic tape and/or disk and/or drum, plus additional data on punched cards or paper tape. Merely reading this data may involve several processing steps. Occasionally the input portion is omitted in special programs that generate their own input data.

An example is a program that generates test data internally. After testing has been completed, instructions to read actual data are inserted in the program.

The three basic operations listed above may be repeated many times in a program, not necessarily in the same order. For example, a program may consist of the three basic operations plus an operation that causes the repetition of a portion of the program:

1. Read the input data.
2. Process the data.
3. Repeat steps 1 and 2 until no more input data exists.
4. Write the results.

Any programming language must provide ways to specify the basic operations required by a program.

The most general programming language is the machine language of the computer itself. All the capabilities of the computer are available in this language. However, machine language, or its sister, assembly language, is difficult to master and time-consuming to use for programming and debugging. Higher-level languages entail more complex terminology but are generally easier to learn, faster to program in, useful in debugging, and a more meaningful record of the program. Fewer lines of coding are required in a higher-level language than in assembly language. The concentration of activity is centered on how to solve the problem rather than on the chore of coding. However, there is a price to pay for these attractive features. Higher-level languages generally do not allow the programmer to use all the features of the computer. For example, the manipulation of characters is not yet a feature of standard FORTRAN but is possible on any computer by the use of its machine language. FORTRAN V, an extension of ANSI FORTRAN, does provide for handling characters. Bit manipulation is not provided in most higher-level languages, although FORTRAN V and PL/I both offer such features. (The value of this machine feature is questionable today because of the speed and low cost of core storage.) Another disadvantage is that a program in a higher-level language must be translated into machine language by a compiler; a certain amount of computer time is necessary for each translation. Since a program is usually written, translated, tested, and then corrected, translated, and tested many times, the

compilation time may be a major portion of the computer time required for program development. Typically, the translation of assembly-language programs into machine language requires a relatively smaller amount of time. A third disadvantage is that the translated machine coding may not be as efficient as the machine-language program written by a programmer. These three arguments against using higher-level languages have lost their appeal with the development of large, high-speed memories and the lower cost of computers today. The computer profession has also come to realize that a programmer may not write better machine coding than that automatically produced by a compiler; in fact, some programmers may even produce less efficient coding.

There is a superfluity of programming languages, and more are still under development. Some languages also have special versions that incorporate new features and deserve an independent name. But despite the proliferation of languages, only a few are universally used: FORTRAN, COBOL, and ALGOL. (Two other languages—BASIC and RPG—are now widely used; they are discussed in the appendixes.) PL/I is a language developed by the major computer manufacturer, IBM, and available with the IBM System/360 and System/370 series of computers. Recently other manufacturers have produced compilers for PL/I. Conversational languages such as BASIC, APL, and CPS are assuming greater importance with the increasing use of remote terminals. Special-purpose languages such as DECTAB (used for the translation of decision tables), LISP (used for list processing), and GPSS/360 (used for simulation) are also available. These languages provide the programmer with an easier way of expressing a problem and thus aid in creating a working program faster than possible by programming in a general-purpose higher-level language.

A natural language, such as English, consists of a set of symbols whose relations are defined by grammatical rules. The definition of a programming language is given by a set of explicitly defined symbols and a set of rules which are explicitly stated. As far as is possible, any ambiguity in the definition of a programming language is avoided. A program expressed in a programming language is designed to be read by a program called a compiler, which translates it into the language of the computer. The rules of a programming language are formulated bearing in mind three viewpoints: that of the user (the person who will write programs in the language), that of the creators of the compiler (which will translate the language), and that of the computer. Because each has different aims, a programming language represents a compromise. The user would like maximum flexibility, freedom from precision, and a language in which he or she can write correct programs quickly. The compiler writers want program statements that can be rapidly and unambiguously translated into machine language. They must function within the restrictions of the machine language as defined by the computer designers. The limitations of the computer as designed by the computer engineers prevent complete harmony between these two groups.

All programming languages incorporate certain features. They must provide for the definition of data, the input and output of data, computations, internal manipulations of the data, control of programming loops, and logical decisions such as the comparison of two numbers and the choosing of a path in a program. These features of the language will be called its *operational characteristics*. In addition, a language is governed by the rules for writing it, that is, by its

SOME PIPES AND A MINI SING SWEET TUNES

A systems analyst is making some beautiful music with a minicomputer, a teletypewriter, a tape reader, and a pipe organ he put together with "some spare parts." Prentiss H. Knowlton has been operating his computerized pipe organ in a walled-in breezeway of his home since June 1973. He started playing after a year of putting the organ together and a year of interfacing it with the DEC PDP-8. He also plans to allow composition at the keyboard via a graphic display device with a hard-copy option and storage and retrieval of information from a high-speed disk.

The computerized seven-rank pipe organ has more than 400 pipes. Ordinary sheet music is programmed onto paper tape via the teletype. Any type of sheet music, such as a Bach organ concerto or an opera overture, can be used. The tape is read by the high-speed paper-tape reader and the computer analyzes the music on the tape for correctness, checking such things as the number of beats per measure. If it finds anything wrong, it types an error message on the teletypewriter so the tape can be corrected.

In addition to reading the tape, the computer analyzes the music, checking the tape for coding errors and merging multiple voices that can occur in a single measure. Then it plays the music.

Adapted from "Some Pipes and a Mini Sing Sweet Tunes,"
Computerworld, February 20, 1974, p. 2. Copyright by Computerworld,
Newton, Mass. 02160.

syntax. In discussing FORTRAN, COBOL, and PL/I, we will attempt to define their common features. We will also emphasize the special features of each programming language. Now, let us proceed to the discussion of FORTRAN.

ANSI FORTRAN

There are two formal definitions of the FORTRAN language published by the American National Standards Institute. The first version, called Basic FORTRAN, is an outgrowth of the original language known as FORTRAN II. The second version is an expanded version of Basic FORTRAN and incorporates additional programming features. This version is called, simply, FORTRAN; but the compilers actually translating it are known as FORTRAN IV compilers. Basic FORTRAN is a subset of ANSI FORTRAN; thus any program written in Basic FORTRAN is completely acceptable to any ANSI FORTRAN compiler. The multiple versions of Basic FORTRAN and FORTRAN IV provided by the computer manufacturers are not necessarily identical to those defined by ANSI. For the most part, the manufacturers have chosen to add some useful but nonstandard features of their own to the ANSI version of the lan-

guage. The inclusion of certain data-handling features has resulted in a version of FORTRAN called FORTRAN V. Differences from compiler to compiler are generally minor. However, it is not usually possible to take a FORTRAN source program from one computer, translate it on another computer, and execute the resulting program successfully. This problem occurs with all programming languages to some degree. Furthermore, a program can be written to be machine dependent even though it has been expressed in a higher-level language such as FORTRAN. Programmers should be encouraged and guided to write programs that function independently of machine features as far as possible. For a tabulated comparison of the FORTRAN language designed for different computers, see Frederic Stuart, *FORTRAN Programming* (New York: John Wiley & Sons, 1969). Now let us present the structural elements and the operational characteristics of ANSI FORTRAN, henceforth called simply FORTRAN.

STRUCTURAL ELEMENTS

The symbols available to express a FORTRAN program are limited to the upper-case letters A

Table 13–1

COLUMN	CONTENTS
1	The letter C is punched if a *comment* is written; comments are ignored by the compiler, but are printed on the output listing. If there are no comments, column 1 will contain a blank.
2–5	The statement number, if any, is punched here.
6	Column 6 is a continuation field and ordinarily contains a blank. If a statement will not fit on a single card, succeeding cards are used and punched in column 6. Column 6 may contain any alphanumeric character except zero.
7–72	A FORTRAN statement is punched in these columns. If more space is required, the statement is punched on successive cards, which contain a nonblank, nonzero character in column 6.
73–80	These columns, which are disregarded by the compiler, are reserved to permit sequential numbering of the program cards or for other information.

through Z, the digits 0 to 9, and the following characters:

CHARACTER	NAME
	Blank
=	Equals
+	Plus sign
−	Minus sign
*	Asterisk
/	Slash
(	Left parenthesis
)	Right parenthesis
,	Comma
.	Decimal point
$	Dollar sign

A basic component in FORTRAN is called a *statement;* several statements make up a program. Statements are generally prepared on 80-column punched cards. The card columns are assigned as shown in Table 13–1 above.

A statement may be assigned a number from 1 to 9999. Statement numbers may be assigned in any order and do not have to be in numerical sequence. Statements are executed sequentially unless a statement transfers control to another statement specified by its statement number.

To facilitate the writing of a FORTRAN program, special coding paper is often used. An example of a program written on a coding form is shown in Figure 13–1.

OPERATIONAL CHARACTERISTICS

Now let us turn to a discussion of the operational characteristics of FORTRAN. These characteristics include

- data
- computational facilities
- program loops
- input/output
- control statements

Other features of FORTRAN, such as subroutines and functions, are discussed in the last subsection.

DATA   ANSI FORTRAN provides for five different types of data: integer, real, double-precision, logical, and Hollerith (alphanumeric) data. Data are represented by constants or variables. FORTRAN V also offers another classification of data called *typeless data,** which can be manipulated as bits or characters.

Constants A *constant* is a specified data value that does not change during the execution of a program. *Integer constants* are numeric values expressed by the numeric digits (0–9) without a decimal point. A minus sign is used to indicate a negative value. For example, the numbers

2
−456
90000

are integer constants. The numbers

2.0
456.
90,000

are not valid integer constants, because of the decimal point in the case of first two values and because of the comma in the case of the last value. *Real constants* are written with a decimal point and may be expressed in scientific notation with an E written to indicate the power of 10 to which a number is raised. The following are examples of valid real constants:

VALUE	FORTRAN NOTATION
10,000,000,000	1.0E10
−.00000987	−0.987E-5
98,700	987.E2
2.	2.0
−99.	−99.

* UNIVAC FORTRAN V uses the terminology *typeless* constant or expression. Compilers by other manufacturers may employ other terminology.

Figure 13–1
A Sample FORTRAN Program on a Coding Form

U of I FORTRAN CODING FORM **University Computer Center**

PROJECT NUMBER 192008
PROGRAM TEST
PROGRAMMER JOHN P. JONES DATE 2/1/75
Punching Instructions: 0 = Zero, 1 = One, 2 = Two, Ø = Alpha O, I = Alpha I, Ƶ = Alpha Z
Verify ☒ no ☐ yes Page of Identification 73 80

C FOR COMMENT — STATEMENT NUMBER — Cont. — FORTRAN STATEMENT

```
C     EXAMPLE ØF FØRTRAN PRØGRAM
C     CØMPUTE AREA ØF CIRCLE FØR R=1,10
C     AT INTERVALS ØF 1/10
      WRITE(6,100)
  100 FØRMAT(5X,1HR,7X,4HAREA)
      R=1.0
   20 AREA=3.141596*R*R
      WRITE(6,101)R,AREA
  101 FØRMAT (2F10.1)
      R=R+.01
      IF (R.LT.10.01)GØ TØ 20
      STØP
      END
```

A decimal point must be written, but the use of the decimal exponent is optional. Only the numeric digits, the decimal point, the letter E, and a minus sign may be used to express a real constant.

Variables   A *variable* is referred to by an assigned name and may assume different values during the execution of a program. It designates a particular location in the computer memory. For example, the formula for the area of a circle, $A = \pi r^2$, has two variables, A and r. The letter π is a constant expressed in calculations as 3.141596. A *variable name* must begin with a letter and may contain up to six alphabetic or numeric characters. Variables that begin with the letters I, J, K, L, M, or N are assumed to contain integer values. The following are examples of integer variable names:

IN
JASON8
K123
LINK
M8
N2H5

All other variables are considered real. The following are examples of real variables:

ALPHA
X88995
SAMSON
PAY
VALUE

The convention for naming variables can be overridden by the use of either the IMPLICIT or the EXPLICIT statement. The *IMPLICIT statement* permits the designation of any letter as indicating a type of variable, provided the letter is used as the first character in the name. The *EXPLICIT statement* permits any legal variable name to be used for any type of data. Thus, for the convenience of the programmer, it is possible to have the location with the variable name X contain an integer number or to have all variable names beginning with the letter J classified as real variables.

Arrays and Subscripts   A variable name represents one memory location. For certain jobs, it is convenient to assign many locations to a single variable name. For example, a laboratory experiment may record the temperature of a fluid every minute throughout the day. Let us assume that all 60 values for a given hour are required at one time for computations. If we assign an independent variable name to each value, say TEMP1, TEMP2, TEMP3, etc., we will have 60 names. An *array* permits the assignment of a single name to a designated set of locations. In this case, the name TEMP could be assigned and the values identified as TEMP(1), TEMP(2), TEMP(3), and so on. The number in parentheses used with an array name is called a *subscript*.

The array TEMP is called a *one-dimensional array;* it represents a list of values that are stored sequentially in the computer memory. An array may also be two or three-dimensional, if two or three subscripts, respectively, are used to identify an element. Such arrays are also known as *matrices*. In addition to facilitating mathe-matical computations involving matrices, multiple-dimensioned arrays are convenient for the storage and retrieval of elements of data sets. For example, the 100 values of a data record from a file could be stored in the array RECORD; each specific location (called an element) would be referenced by the array name with the appropriate subscript. An element of an array can also be referenced by subscripts given as integer variables or expressions. For example, COST(I,J) refers to a specific element of the array COST which is determined by the current values of I and J. ANSI FORTRAN contains explicit constraints on the construction of the integer variables used as subscripts. These constraints are not required in many of the FORTRAN compilers.

The DIMENSION Statement   The DIMENSION statement is used to allocate memory locations for each array. Each array, with the maximum

"It just put itself at the top of the vacation list."

Figure 13–2
The Storage of Arrays in a Computer Memory.

(a) The one-dimensional array TEMP.
TEMP(1)
TEMP(2)
TEMP(3)

.
.
.

TEMP(9)

(b) The two-dimensional array COST.
COST(1,1)   →COST(1,2)   →COST(1,3)
COST(2,1)──┘ COST(2,2)──┘ COST(2,3)

values for each subscript in the array, must be listed in a DIMENSION statement. The arrays specified by a DIMENSION statement are said to be *declared* by that statement. For example, the array COST in Figure 13–2 has 6 locations. The maximum values of the subscripts are 2 and 3. The required DIMENSION statement is

DIMENSION COST(2,3)

The total number of locations assigned is computed by multiplying the subscripts; for the array COST, 2×3, or 6, locations are reserved. A DIMENSION statement may contain the declaration for more than one array. For example, consider the statement

DIMENSION COST(2,3), HEAT(4,2,9), LINK(100)

The array HEAT will be assigned 72 locations, and LINK will be allocated 100 locations. A reference to a specific location within an array is given by the array name and the correct subscripts. Examples are COST(1,2), HEAT(1,2,8), and LINK(50). An array is classed as either real or integer. The rules for variable names also apply to array names.

COMPUTATIONAL FACILITIES FORTRAN provides computational facilities by means of

the arithmetic statement. This statement has the form

$$\left.\begin{array}{c} variable \\ name \\ or \\ subscripted \\ array \\ name \end{array}\right\} = \begin{array}{c} arithmetic \\ expression \end{array}$$

Only one variable or subscripted array name may appear on the left-hand side of the equals sign. The equals sign indicates "replace by" rather than the equality of the two sides. For example, consider

$$X = (A + B - C^2)/4.0$$

The right-hand side of this arithmetic statement is evaluated using the current values of A, B, and C. The calculated value is then stored in the location denoted by the variable name X. If $A = 6.$, $B = 15.$, and $C = 3.$, the value 3.0 will be stored in the variable X. Another example is:

$$I = I + 1$$

The current value of I is incremented by one and

inserted in the location I. If, prior to the execution of this statement, I contained the value 5, the new value of I would be 6.

An arithmetic expression is formed by one or more variable names or subscripted array names, constants, parentheses, and symbols indicating an arithmetic operation. These symbols are

+	addition
—	subtraction
*	multiplication
/	division
**	exponentiation (raising to a power)

Arithmetic operations are executed according to an established priority. The statement is scanned from left to right and operations executed in the following order:

exponentiation,
multiplication and division,
addition and subtraction.

Parentheses are used as in mathematics and override these established priorities. For example,

$$A*B/C+D*E**2$$

will be computed as

$$[(A \times B)/C] + D \times (E^2)$$

By inserting parentheses, the meaning of the expression can be changed. For example,

$$A*(B/C) + (D*E)**2$$

indicates the computation to be

$$A \times (B/C) + (D \times E)^2$$

An exception to the left-to-right scanning is in exponentiation. For example, A**B**C will be evaluated as A**(B**C).

All arithmetic operations must be explicitly stated. Thus the term AB means the variable AB and not A*B. Two or more consecutive operations are not valid unless parentheses are used. For example, A+—B must be written as A+(—B). All variables, array names, constants, or other operands must be of the same type (all integer or all real). The mixing of types is called operating in a *mixed mode,* a feature permitted in some FORTRAN versions but not in ANSI FORTRAN. Examples of mixed-mode expressions (not valid in ANSI FORTRAN) are

$$A = Z + 2$$
$$I = J - Z(3,4)$$

However, an arithmetic statement may contain different types of data on each side of the equals sign. For example, the following statements are valid in ANSI FORTRAN:

$$X = I + 2$$
$$JACK = SAM(1,2) + 7.0*TIME$$

The expression on the right-hand side is evaluated and the result converted to the data type assigned to the variable name on the left-hand side. In the second example, if SAM(1,2) contains the value 1.5 and TIME contains the value 0.2, the right-hand side is evaluated as

$$1.5 + (7.0) \times (0.2), \text{ or } 2.9$$

The value 2.9 is converted to an integer and the fractional portion is dropped. Thus, JACK is set equal to the integer value 2.

PROGRAM LOOPS   A convenient way of expressing program loops in FORTRAN is provided by the DO statement. Loops can also be expressed by the IF and GO TO statements, which are discussed later. The general form of the DO statement is

$$DO\ n\ i = m_1,\ m_2,\ m_3$$

where n is a statement number indicating the last statement in the loop, i is an integer variable, m_1 is the initial integer value assigned to i, m_2 is the upper-bound value for i, and m_3 is the incremental value. If m_3 is not given, it is assumed to be 1. The values m_1, m_2, and m_3 must be unsigned integer values such that $m_2 > m_1$. The loop terminates when $i + m_3 > m_2$.

The following is an example of a loop using the DO statement.

$$\left. \begin{array}{l} DO\ 100\ I = 1,5,2 \\ \qquad . \\ \qquad . \\ \qquad . \\ 100 \quad X(I) = A(I) \end{array} \right\} \text{Program loop}$$

The DO statement directs the execution of the statements immediately following it up to and including statement 100. The loop is first executed with I = 1 and then with I = 3, and I = 5.

Table 13–2

```
1   DO 5 J = 2,5,1
    A(J) = B(J) + 1.0
    DO 10 K = 5,10,5
10  CRD(J,K) = A(J)/B(J) + 5.28* ST(J,K)     Inner loop   Outer loop
    DO 5 IN = 1,7,2
5   DATA(IN,J) = FALL(IN,J) − 25.0            Inner loop
```

The DO loop terminates when $I + 2 = 7$, which exceeds the final value of 5 for the loop.

DO loops can be nested within one another. This is particularly useful for computations with two- or three-dimensional arrays. An example of a DO loop containing two other DO loops is shown in Table 13–2 above. The DO loop begins with $J = 2$; the first value calculated is $A(2) = B(2) + 1$. Then the inner DO statement is executed for the values $K = 5$ and $K = 10$. That is, CRD(2,5) is set equal to A(2)/B(2) + 5.28*ST(2,5) and CRD(2,10) is set equal to A(2)/B(2) + 5.28*ST(2,10). The next inner DO loop is initiated with the values $J = 2$ and $IN = 1$. This loop is repeated with the values $IN = 2, 4,$ and 6 while J continues to have the value 2. This process is now repeated, starting from statement 1, until J has assumed all the values specified, that is, 2, 3, 4, and 5.

The DO loop is a powerful means of concisely stating program loops. It permits the sequential selection of all or specific elements of arrays to be used within the loop. The detailed rules governing the construction of nested DO loops are not relevant here.

INPUT/OUTPUT STATEMENTS FORTRAN provides three statements for program input/out-put; these are the READ, WRITE, and FORMAT statements. The READ and WRITE statements are commonly used in conjunction with the FORMAT statement. If no FORMAT statement is specified, the input/output statement is called *unformatted*. The forms of the READ and WRITE statements are

READ *(u, s) list*
WRITE *(u, s) list* } Formatted input/output

READ *(u) list*
WRITE *(u) list* } Unformatted input/output

where *u* is a unit number or an integer variable name designating an input/output unit, *s* is the statement number of an associated FORMAT statement, and *list* is a list of variables from which data will be transferred to the output unit or to which data will be transferred from the input unit. The following are examples of READ/WRITE statements:

READ (5,100) A, B, C5
WRITE (6, 78) I, J, ALPHA, K
READ (1) SAM, TOM
WRITE (2) LIST, ABLE, BAKER

The list of variables may also include an implied DO loop so that transfers of data to and from arrays can be expressed concisely. For example,

READ (5, 89) (RATE(J), J = 1, 10), TIME

will cause the reading of 10 values into the array RATE. The eleventh value will be inserted into the variable TIME.

The FORMAT statement consists of one or more FORMAT codes separated by commas. Parentheses are always used to denote the beginning and the end of the FORMAT statement. The format codes define all the types of variables possible in FORTRAN — integer, real, double-precision, and logical. In addition, there is a means of reading and writing alphanumeric information. There is also a format code (X) for skipping spaces. Each format code specifies the number of character positions to be treated as a unit (or field) for the input or output of a data variable. For example, the format code for integer variables is written

$$nIw$$

where w is the number of character positions. In the case of input, w positions are considered

to represent an integer number; in the case of output, w positions are allocated to the integer value of the variable. The n serves as an optional repeat counter. If n is not written, it is assumed to be 1.

When the data consists of real values, the format code specifies the total number of character positions and the number of digits to the right of the decimal point (that is, the fractional portion of the number). For example,

$$nFw.d$$

indicates a total of w positions with d positions to the right of the decimal point. The n serves as the repeat counter. The format code F indicates that the value is converted on output without a decimal exponent. The value of d denotes an implied decimal point for input data; if a decimal point appears, it takes precedence over the implied decimal point. For example, F6.2 indicates a total of 6 character positions with an implied decimal point between positions 4 and 5. The format code E indicates a conversion with a decimal exponent to be given. In programming input data, d can be used to express an implied decimal point.

Table 13–3

```
      READ (5,100) X, Y, Z          ⎱ FORTRAN
  100  FORMAT (F10.5, F5.1, F10.5)  ⎰ Statements

                          1 1 1 1 1 1 1 1 1 1 2 2 2 2 2 2 2 2 2 2 3
              1 2 3 4 5 6 7 8 9 0 1 2 3 4 5 6 7 8 9 0 1 2 3 4 5 6 7 8 9 0 . . .

                  9 6 7 1     2 . 6 7 8 1 . 5
```

An example of a FORMAT statement and the input data to be read is shown in Table 13–3 above. The variables will be set equal to the following values: X = 9.671, Y = 2.678, and Z = 1.5. Implied decimal points occur between positions 5 and 6, 14 and 15, and 20 and 21. The decimal point for the values of Y and Z has been given and overrides the implied decimal point.

Examples of the E and F format codes for output are shown below:

FORMAT CODE	OUTPUT	VALUE
F6.1	1234.5	1234.5
F10.5	¢¢¢1.50000	1234.5
E13.6	¢0.123456E 08	12345600.
E13.4	¢¢¢0.1234E−04	.00001234

where ¢ represents a blank position on the output.

The FORMAT statement is scanned from left to right. Each format code is matched with the appropriate variable given in the *list* of the READ or WRITE statement. If the *list* is shorter than the string of FORMAT codes, the input/output statement is terminated. If the *list* is longer, the scanning of the FORMAT statement is reinitiated according to certain rules regarding inner parentheses. An example of the matching of codes with variables in the *list* is given below:

READ (4, 30) A, B, C, (D(I), I = 1,3), K
30 FORMAT (F10.3, 2E15.4, 3F10.5, I3)

The data will be transferred as follows:

VARIABLE	FORMAT CODE	POSITIONS
A	F10.3	1–10
B	E15.4	11–25
C	E15.4	26–40
D(1)	F10.5	41–50
D(2)	F10.5	51–60
D(3)	F10.5	61–70
K	I3	71–73

Because character positions are used to denote the field for a variable and alphanumeric data can be both read and written as output, FORTRAN input/output statements have the flexibility to read any kind of data and produce a highly structured output. Typically, the basic input medium is the 80-column card; the usual output medium is the line printer, with 128 or 132 characters per line. The first character of the line is used to indicate that the printer should advance one or more lines or skip to the next page. There are four printer control characters:

CONTROL CHARACTER	MEANING
Blank	Advance one line
0	Advance two lines
1	Skip to the first line of the next page
+	Do not advance

FORTRAN programs can also read or write magnetic tape, drum, or disk, depending on the hardware facilities provided by the individual computers. Unit numbers are assigned by the particular computer installation to indicate the input/output devices available. For example, unit 5 is customarily the card reader, while unit 6 is the line printer.

CONTROL STATEMENTS The STOP statement is used to indicate the logical end of the program. It occurs at the logical end and may not be the last program statement. It is written

n STOP

where n is a statement number and is optional.

The END statement indicates the physical end of the program and must be the last statement in the program. It is written

END

The CONTINUE statement is a do-nothing statement. It is useful as the last statement of a DO loop in order to avoid having an IF or GO TO statement as the last statement. For example, in

```
      DO 10 I = 1, 100
      IF (A(I).EQ.20) B = B + 1.0
      IF (W(I).GT.A(I)) C = C + 1.0
10    CONTINUE
```

the CONTINUE statement marks the end of the DO loop. Otherwise, the IF statement would end the DO loop, contrary to the rules of FORTRAN.

The GO TO statement is a means of transferring control to another statement. It is written

GO TO s

where s is a valid statement number. Two variations of the GO TO statement are the assigned GO TO and the computed GO TO statements.

Basically these two statements permit a switching of control dependent on the value of an integer variable.

The IF Statement   FORTRAN provides the IF statement for the comparison of data values. There are two forms of the IF statement. The simplest form, called the *arithmetic IF statement,* is written

$$\text{IF } (a) \; s_1, \; s_2, \; s_3$$

where a is any real, integer, or double-precision-arithmetic expression and s_1, s_2, and s_3 are statement numbers. If $a < 0$, control is transferred to statement s_1; if $a = 0$, control is given to s_2; if $a > 0$, control is given to s_3. An arithmetic expression may consist of only one variable. For example, consider the statement

$$\text{IF } (X) \; 20, \; 25, \; 30$$

If $X < 0$, control is transferred to statement 20; if $X = 0$, control is given to statement 25; if $X > 0$, control is transferred to statement 30.

Another example, comparing the contents of the variable JACK with the value 10, is shown below.

$$\text{IF } (JACK - 10) \; 1, \; 40, \; 5$$

If JACK contains a value less than 10 (so that JACK $- 10 < 0$), the program branches to statement 1; if JACK contains the value 10, control is given to statement 40; if the contents of JACK is greater than 10, the program branches to statement 5.

The Logical IF Statement   The second type of IF statement is called the *logical IF statement.* Its form is

$$\text{IF } (e) \; S$$

where e is a logical expression and S is any executable statement except a DO statement or another logical IF statement. A logical expression may be either a relational expression or a logical expression or a composite of these two expressions. A *relational expression* is formed by

"Now all this stuff will finally begin to pay for itself—here's the formula for transmuting lead into gold."

two arithmetic expressions separated by one of the relational operators shown below:

OPERATOR	MEANING
.LT.	Less than
.LE.	Less than or equal to
.EQ.	Equal to
.NE.	Not equal to
.GT.	Greater than
.GE.	Greater than or equal to

Examples of relational expressions are

A.GT.500.0	A greater than 500.0
C.LT.X**2	C less than or equal to X^2
IN.EQ.KAT $-$ 1	IN equal to KAT $-$ 1

A *logical expression* is an expression linked by one of three logical operators:

.AND.
.OR.
.NOT.

Examples of logical expressions are

A.GT.B.AND.C.LT.D
I.EQ.5.OR.J.EQ.LL

The logical IF statement first determines the truth or falsity of the logical expression. If it is true, the statement S is executed. If it is false, the statement S is ignored and control is given to the next instruction in the sequence. The logical operators serve to bind together logical expressions. The use of the operator .AND. means that each of the expressions linked by the .AND. operator must be true for the total expression to be true; the use of the .OR. operator means that the entire expression is true if any of the individual expressions is true. The .NOT. operator serves to negate the expression. For example,

IF (.NOT.(A.GT.B)) X = X/10.5

means that if A is not greater than B the statement X = X/10.5 should be executed; otherwise, control is transferred to the next statement. Other examples of logical IF statements are

(1) IF (ALPHA.GT.BETA) GO TO 800
     X = X**2 + 1.5*BETA
     .
     .
     .

(2) IF (A.GT.2.0.AND.D.LE.25.0) X = X+1.0
DE = X + Y + Z + A
.
.
.

In the first example, the question "Is ALPA greater than BETA?" is asked. If the answer is yes, the statement "GO TO 800" is executed and the program continues at that statement. If the answer is no (that is, if the first part of the statement is false), the next instruction in the sequence, X = X**2 + 1.5*BETA, is executed.

The second example illustrates the use of the .AND. operator. If A is greater than 2.0 *and* D is less than 25.0, the statement X = X + 1.0 is executed. Both conditions must be true in order for this statement to be executed. Otherwise, control is immediately transferred to the next statement and DE is evaluated. Regardless of the path taken, control will eventually be given to DE = X + Y + Z + A.

OTHER FEATURES FORTRAN has many other features that facilitate the writing of programs. Coding that is useful for more than one portion of the program can be written as a subroutine or function, with parameters specified for each use. For example, the instructions for the calculation of the withholding tax for each employee of a firm can be written as a subroutine. Parameters for gross pay, the number of deductions, and so on can be submitted to the subroutine each time and the results returned to the main program for further calculations or writing as output.

In addition, FORTRAN has many built-in functions available for use in every program. A complete list of these functions is given in Table 13–4. Such common functions as those for square roots, sines, and cosines can easily be used by specifying the function name and the argument. For example,

X = SQRT(Y)

will cause the calculation of the square root of the value given for the variable Y. The result will be placed in the location designated by the variable name X.

It is possible also for the main program and the programmer-written subroutines to share

Table 13–4
Built-in FORTRAN Functions

FORTRAN FUNCTION	DEFINITION	SYMBOLIC NAME	TYPE OF ARGUMENT
Exponential	e^x	EXP	Real
		DEXP	Double
		CEXP	Complex
Natural logarithm	$\log_e(a)$	ALOG	Real
		DLOG	Double
		CLOG	Complex
Common logarithm	$\log_{10}(a)$	ALOG10	Real
		DLOG10	Double
Trigonometric sine	$\sin(a)$	SIN	Real
		DSIN	Double
		CSIN	Complex
Trigonometric cosine	$\cos(a)$	COS	Real
		DCOS	Double
		CCOS	Complex
Hyperbolic tangent	$\tanh(a)$	TANH	Real
Square root	$(a)^{1/2}$	SQRT	Real
		DSQRT	Double
		CSQRT	Complex
Arctangent	$\arctan(a)$	ATAN	Real
		DATAN	Double
	$\arctan(a_1/a_2)$	ATAN2	Real
		DATAN2	Double
Remaindering modulus[a]	$a_1(\bmod\ a_2)$	MOD	Integer
		AMOD	Real
		DMOD	Double

[a] This function is defined as $a_1 - (x \times a_2)$ where x is the largest integer whose magnitude does not exceed the magnitude of a_1/a_2. The sign of the integer is the same as the sign of a_1/a_2.

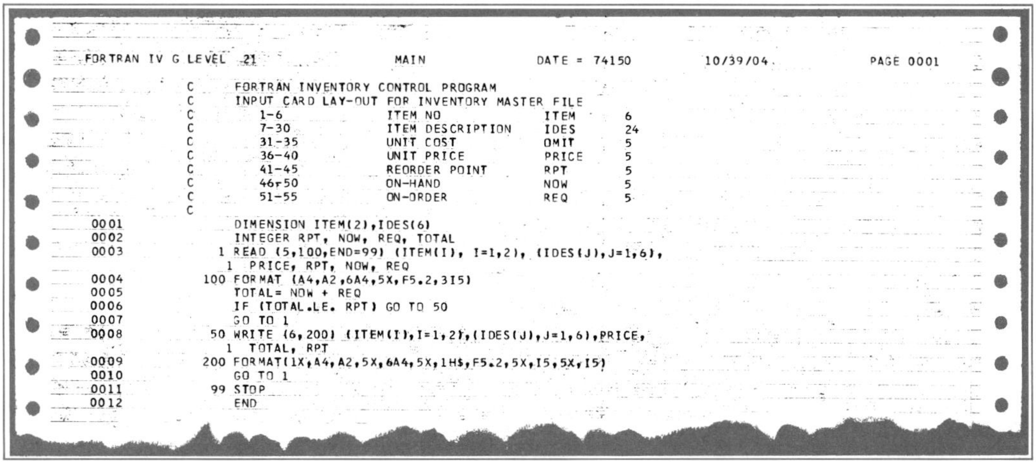

```
      C     FORTRAN INVENTORY CONTROL PROGRAM
      C     INPUT CARD LAY-OUT FOR INVENTORY MASTER FILE
      C       1-6          ITEM NO          ITEM     6
      C       7-30         ITEM DESCRIPTION IDES    24
      C       31-35        UNIT COST        OMIT     5
      C       36-40        UNIT PRICE       PRICE    5
      C       41-45        REORDER POINT    RPT      5
      C       46-50        ON-HAND          NOW      5
      C       51-55        ON-ORDER         REQ      5
      C
0001          DIMENSION ITEM(2),IDES(6)
0002          INTEGER RPT, NOW, REQ, TOTAL
0003        1 READ (5,100,END=99) (ITEM(I), I=1,2), (IDES(J),J=1,6),
             1 PRICE, RPT, NOW, REQ
0004      100 FORMAT (A4,A2,6A4,5X,F5.2,3I5)
0005          TOTAL= NOW + REQ
0006          IF (TOTAL.LE. RPT) GO TO 50
0007          GO TO 1
0008       50 WRITE (6,200) (ITEM(I),I=1,2),(IDES(J),J=1,6),PRICE,
             1 TOTAL, RPT
0009      200 FORMAT(1X,A4,A2,5X,6A4,5X,1H$,F5.2,5X,I5,5X,I5)
0010          GO TO 1
0011       99 STOP
0012          END
```

Figure 13-3
A Short Inventory-Control Program

storage areas. This is important in the case of programs that require large amounts of data. The EQUIVALENCE and COMMON statements provide this facility.

AN INVENTORY-CONTROL PROGRAM

A short FORTRAN program is shown in Figure 13–3. This program is a simplified inventory-control program that reads cards and prints items that should be ordered. The cards have the following format:

COLUMNS	CONTENTS
1–6	Item number
7–30	Description of item
31–35	Unit cost
36–40	Unit price
41–45	Reorder point
46–50	Quantity on hand
51–55	Quantity on order
56–80	Blank (not used)

A sample of four data cards is shown in Figure 13–4. The FORTRAN program reads the data cards and sums the quantity "on hand" and the quantity "on order." The sum is called TOTAL in the program. If the sum is less than the reorder point, the item number, item description, unit price, reorder point, and the sum of the quantity on hand and the quantity on order are printed. Otherwise, the next card is read. When there are no more cards, the program goes to statement 99 and stops. The FORMAT statement numbered 100 is used to specify the input-card format, while statement 200 determines the format of the printed line. The INTEGER statement is used to explicitly override the FORTRAN convention for naming variables. Thus, RPT, REQ, and TOTAL are integer variables rather than real variables. Notice that the statement numbers are not sequential. Comments are given to document the input-card layout. The output produced by the sample input (Figure 13–4) is shown in Figure 13–5.

FORTRAN V

The language specifications for ANSI FORTRAN are constantly scrutinized by the community that uses it. Proposals to incorporate additional features are always being made, but thus far ANSI

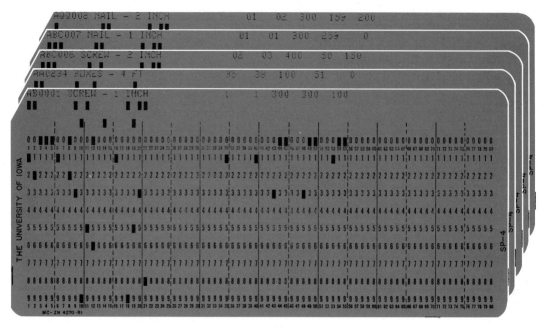

Figure 13–4
Sample Data Cards for an Inventory-Control Program

Figure 13–5
A Sample Output for an Inventory-Control Program

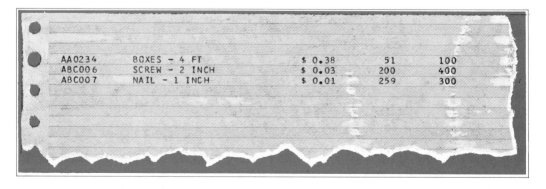

FORTRAN has not been extended to include the proposed features. Meanwhile, several computer manufacturers have issued FORTRAN compilers with character- and bit-handling capabilities; these versions of FORTRAN have been labeled FORTRAN V. Because FORTRAN V is widely used, it is anticipated that its features will eventually be incorporated into the standard FORTRAN specifications. Capabilities vary from compiler to compiler. The specifications for FORTRAN V discussed in the following material are for the UNIVAC 1100 series of computers. The transfer of a specified number of bits from a computer word (36 bits long in the UNIVAC 1100 series of computers) to any location within another computer word is accomplished by the FLD function. This is written

$$A = FLD\ (i, k, e)$$

where A is the name of the location that will receive the transfer of bits from the expression e. The number of bits is given by k, starting with the ith bit of the expression e.

FLD may also appear to the left of the equals sign in an arithmetic expression. The k bits are then extracted and aligned on the right, while the remaining bits are set to equal zero. The bits of the word are numbered from 0 to 35, with the leftmost bit being bit 0. For example, consider

$$FLD(18, 6, N) = Z$$

where Z contains the characters ABCDEF. Each character is six bits in length. Let N contain the characters PQRSTU. After the statement is executed, N will contain the characters PQRFTU. UNIVAC FORTRAN V also offers bit manipulation of expressions similar to that available in machine language.

THE PRO'S AND CON'S OF FORTRAN

As we have seen, the FORTRAN language is well-suited for programming engineering and scientific problems that can be expressed mathematically. It was not designed for the programming of business-type problems. Consequently, the language is defined in mathematical terminology. Its main deficiency is the lack of any commands to manipulate characters. For example, it is not possible to transfer any 10 designated characters from the array A to the array B directly unless the word length of the computer is 10 or a divisor of 10—that is, 5 or 2. FORTRAN V does provide for the transfer of characters. There are no special provisions for treating files and file records. These basic omissions in the language prevent FORTRAN from assuming a major role as a data-processing language. Furthermore, business personnel prefer a non-mathematical-appearing language such as COBOL (discussed in the next chapter).

REFERENCES

IBM. *IBM System/360 FORTRAN IV Language*. White Plains, N.Y.: IBM Publications, 1968.

Lee, R. M. *A Short Course in Fortran IV*. New York: McGraw-Hill Book Co., 1967.

Sperry UNIVAC. *UNIVAC 1100 Series FORTRAN V Programmer Reference*. Sperry Rand Corporation, 1973.

Stuart, Frederic. *FORTRAN Programming*. New York: John Wiley & Sons, 1969.

Weiss, Eric A., ed. *Computer Usage/360 FORTRAN Programming*. New York: McGraw-Hill Book Co., 1969.

Wu, Margaret S. *Computers and Programming: An Introduction*. New York: Appleton-Century-Crofts, 1973.

QUESTIONS

1. What is a programming language?
2. Discuss the advantages and disadvantages of the use of an assembly language as opposed to the use of FORTRAN.
3. Outline the operational characteristics of FORTRAN.
4. Describe the layout of a FORTRAN program card.
5. What types of data can be handled in FORTRAN?
6. What type of variable is each of the following FORTRAN variables?

IN	X4Y6
OUT	LENGTH
SAMSON	ZETA

7. Write a DIMENSION statement for the two-dimensional array TIME, which has 65 elements, 13 in each row.
8. Express the following arithmetic computations in FORTRAN:
   (a) $a + b - c/y$
   (b) $x = (y \cdot z)^3/(a - b)$
   (c) $\beta = (\sigma^2/\alpha^3) - \delta$
9. What actions will the following statements cause?
   (a) DO 10 I2 = 2, 10, 3
   (b) I = I + 2
   (c) X = (Y**2) *(A**4)
   (d) GO TO 105
10. Describe the two types of IF statements in FORTRAN.

CHAPTER FOURTEEN

COBOL

Table 14–1

COBOL ELEMENT	FORTRAN COUNTERPART
Symbols	Symbols
Literals	Constants
Programmer-supplied names	Variables, arrays, and statement numbers
Reserved words	Reserved words
PICTURE	None
Level numbers	None

COBOL is a higher-level language designed for the programming of business data-processing problems. It was evolved from several business languages — AIMACO, FLOWMATIC, COMTRAN, and others — that are now defunct. In May 1959, the Department of Defense called together representatives of the business community and the government to formulate a *Common Business-Oriented Language*, that is, COBOL. Since the government then required the provision of a COBOL compiler for any computer delivered to a government agency, COBOL gained instant popularity. FORTRAN is a language with a mathematical basis. COBOL, instead, uses English words and sentences to express a program. Superficially it appears easier to understand English statements than mathematical expressions, and therefore COBOL gives the appearance of being easier to use than FORTRAN. Quite the contrary is the case. The structure of the COBOL language is more complex, the rules of grammar are more abundant, and it is inherently more difficult for the novice programmer to learn COBOL and write correct programs. The opportunity for clerical errors increases with the number of characters written in a program. COBOL is verbose. It uses long statements, and the possibility of data errors due to misspelled words or errors in transcribing the program to computerized form is ever present. To offset these disadvantages, COBOL specifically provides the means to process data files. A portion of any COBOL program is devoted to a detailed description of the data files used by the program. A COBOL program may handle data records and manipulate each field within a record, if this is desired. These features are the prime advantages of the language. Because of the complexity of COBOL, only the highlights of its structure and operational characteristics will be presented. COBOL features will be contrasted with those available in FORTRAN.

STRUCTURAL ELEMENTS

COBOL has a complex structure based upon six elements and four divisions. The six elements and their FORTRAN counterparts are listed in Table 14–1 above.

The writing of a COBOL statement or command must begin in a position defined by COBOL. Positions 1 to 3 are used for the page number, written 001 (for page 1), 002 (for page 2), and so on. Positions 4 to 6 are reserved for the line number, written 010, 020, and so on. This way of writing page and line numbers permits later insertions of statements in the program without disrupting the sequence of numbers. Position 7 is reserved to indicate the continuation of non-numeric literals. An *A-margin* (or area) extends from positions 8 to 11 and a *B-margin* from positions 12 to 72. All division, section, and paragraph names must begin in position 8. All other entries must be written within positions 12 to 72. A statement or an entry can extend beyond a line. A period followed by a space indicates the end of a COBOL entry.

ELEMENTS   Although COBOL has six elements, we will initially discuss only the first three—symbols, literals, and programmer-supplied names. The remaining elements are more appropriately discussed in connection with the COBOL divisions presented later in this section.

Symbols   Symbols, reserved words, and level numbers are fixed elements in COBOL. (The other three elements are governed by COBOL rules.) The symbols available to express a COBOL program are the upper-case letters A to Z, the digits 0 to 9, and the following symbols:

SYMBOL	NAME
	Blank
.	Period
,	Comma
;	Semicolon
'	Quote
(	Left parenthesis
)	Right parenthesis
+	Plus sign
—	Minus sign or hyphen
*	Asterisk (** indicates exponentiation)
/	Slash used as divide sign
=	Equals sign
$	Dollar sign
<	"Less than" sign
>	"Greater than" sign

Literals   COBOL literals are similar to the constants in FORTRAN. A literal retains the same value throughout the execution of a program. Literals are either numeric or non-numeric. A *numeric literal* is composed of digits; the use of a plus or minus sign is optional. Integer values are defined by the absence of a decimal point. If a decimal point is given, it must not be the last character in the number. If the literal does not

Figure 14–1

A Sample COBOL Program on a Coding Form

U of I	COBOL CODING FORM		University Computer Center

PROJECT NUMBER **29086**		Punching Instructions	Verify □ no ☒ yes Page **3** of **5**
PROGRAM **SALARY**		0 = Zero 1 = One 2 = Two	Identification
PROGRAMMER **MARY E. BROWN** DATE **2/8/75**		Ø = Alpha O I = Alpha I Z̄ = Alpha Z	73 80

```
003 010  PROCEDURE DIVISION.
    020  START.
    030      OPEN OUTPUT FILE.
    040      WRITE SALARY-RECORD FROM HEADING 2 AFTER ADVANCING 0 LINES.
    050      PERFORM CALCULATIONS
    06|          VARYING MONTHLY-PAY FROM 500 BY 10
    07|          UNTIL MONTHLY-PAY IS GREATER THAN 1000.
    08|          IF TOTAL-A = CON-A AND TOTAL-B = CON-B AND TOTAL-C = CON-C
    09|          MOVE 'TABLE VALUES ARE CORRECT' TO SHOW
    10           WRITE SALARY-RECORD FROM MESG AFTER ADVANCING 2 LINES
    11|          ELSE
    12|          MOVE 'TABLE VALUES ARE NOT CORRECT' TO PRSNT
    13           WRITE SALARY-RECORD FROM DSPY AFTER ADVANCING 2 LINES.
    14      CLOSE SALARY FILE.
    15      STOP RUN.
    16
    17  CALCULATIONS.
    18      COMPUTE WEEKLY-PAY = 3 * MONTHLY-PAY / 13.
    19      COMPUTE ANNUAL-PAY = 12 * MONTHLY-PAY.
    20      MOVE WEEKLY-PAY TO WEEKLY IN SALARIES.
    21      MOVE ANNUAL-PAY TO ANNUAL IN SALARIES.
    22      ADD WEEKLY-PAY TO TOTAL-A.
    23      ADD MONTHLY-PAY TO TOTAL-B.
    24      ADD ANNUAL-PAY TO TOTAL-C.
    25      WRITE SALARY RECORD FROM SALARIES AFTER ADVANCING 1 LINES.
```

contain a decimal point, it is an integer. The following are numeric literals:

    25
    1.0
    −89123.1246
    +888
    +46.07

There is no provision for scientific notation as in FORTRAN.

A numeric literal represents a number that can be used in computations. A *non-numeric literal* defines alphanumeric characters. These characters can never be used in computations. A non-numeric literal is enclosed in quotation marks; consequently, a quotation mark within a literal must be represented in a special way on printed output. This is accomplished by writing the reserved word QUOTE. For example, to write

out 'EXAMPLE' with the quotes appearing on the output given by the DISPLAY verb, it is necessary to write

    DISPLAY QUOTE, 'EXAMPLE', QUOTE.

The following are non-numeric literals:

    '800'
    'ALPHA, BETA, GAMMA'
    '100%'
    'BALANCE SHEET'

The number 800 is not a computational number in the computer; it is represented by characters given in the character code of a particular computer.

Programmer-Supplied Names   Data names are assigned so that a program can refer to data by a name. Names are also used for paragraphs

"What d'you mean–'obvious to the meanest intelligence.' "

© Punch, London

to allow the transfer of control to a paragraph not in the normal sequence. Here, paragraph names serve the same function as statement numbers in FORTRAN. A name must be constructed according to the following rules: It must not be composed of more than 30 characters. Only letters, digits, and hyphens are permitted. A hyphen may appear only within the name and not at the beginning or end. The name must contain at least one alphabetic character. It must not be a COBOL reserved word. (See Table 14–2.) Examples of data names are

SALES-TOTAL
X123456
ANY-COMBINATION-IS-POSSIBLE

DIVISIONS   A COBOL program always has four divisions: an IDENTIFICATION, an ENVIRONMENT, a DATA, and a PROCEDURE division. Each division may be further divided into sections, paragraphs, and statements or independent clauses. A data entry is always terminated by a period followed by a space. The IDENTIFICATION, ENVIRONMENT, and DATA divisions have explicitly defined sections or paragraphs. The PROCEDURE division contains the executable statements of the program and is grouped into paragraphs defined by the programmer. In this division, paragraph names are assigned by the programmer. The IDENTIFICATION and ENVIRONMENT divisions have no counterpart in FORTRAN. The DATA division may be compared to the FORTRAN DIMENSION statement, which defines the storage allocation for data, and the FORMAT statement, which describes data for input and output processing. The PROCEDURE division is comparable to the FORTRAN executable statements that compose a program.

The IDENTIFICATION Division   This division, which is the simplest division of a COBOL program, serves only to identify the program. It may contain several paragraphs, but only the PROGRAM-ID paragraph is required. The program name must be enclosed in quotes. The programmer may include as much identification as he desires. The following is an example of an IDENTIFICATION division:

IDENTIFICATION DIVISION.
PROGRAM-ID. MASTER-FILE-UPDATE.
AUTHOR. JOHN JONES.
INSTALLATION. UNIVERSITY OF IOWA.

Table 14–2
IBM American National Standard COBOL Reserved Words

No word in the following list should appear as a programmer-defined name.

ACCEPT	COMMA	DATE-COMPILED	FILLER	LABEL
ACCESS	COMP	DATE-WRITTEN	FINAL	LABEL-RETURN
ACTUAL	COMP-1	DE	FIRST	LAST
ADD	COMP-2	DEBUG	FOOTING	LEADING
ADDRESS	COMP-3	DECIMAL-POINT	FOR	LEAVE
ADVANCING	COMP-4	DECLARATIVES	FREE	LEFT
AFTER	COMPUTATIONAL	DELETE	FROM	LESS
ALL	COMPUTATIONAL-1	DEPENDING		LIMIT
ALPHABETIC	COMPUTATIONAL-2	DESCENDING	GENERATE	LIMITS
ALTER	COMPUTATIONAL-3	DETAIL	GIVING	LINE
ALTERNATE	COMPUTATIONAL-4	DISP	GO	LINE-COUNTER
AND	COMPUTE	DISPLAY	GOBACK	LINES
APPLY	CONFIGURATION	DISPLAY-ST	GREATER	LINKAGE
ARE	CONSOLE	DIVIDE	GROUP	LOCK
AREA	CONTAINS	DIVISION		LOW-VALUE
AREAS	CONTROL	DOWN	HEADING	LOW-VALUES
ASCENDING	CONTROLS	DYNAMIC	HIGH-VALUE	
ASSIGN	COPY		HIGH-VALUES	MASTER-INDEX
AT	CORE-INDEX	EJECT		MEMORY
AUTHOR	CORR	ELSE	I-O	MODE
	CORRESPONDING	END	I-O-CONTROL	MODULES
BASIS	CSP	END-OF-PAGE	ID	MORE-LABELS
BEFORE	CURRENCY	ENDING	IDENTIFICATION	MOVE
BEGINNING	CURRENT-DATE	ENTER	IF	MULTIPLE
BLANK	CYL-INDEX	ENTRY	IN	MULTIPLY
BLOCK	CYL-OVERFLOW	ENVIRONMENT	INDEX	
BY	C01	EOP	INDEXED	NAMED
	C02	EQUAL	INDICATE	NEGATIVE
CALL	C03	ERROR	INITIATE	NEXT
CF	C04	EVERY	INPUT	NO
CH	C05	EXAMINE	INPUT-OUTPUT	NOMINAL
CHANGED	C06	EXHIBIT	INSERT	NOT
CHARACTER	C07	EXIT	INSTALLATION	NOTE
CHARACTERS	C08	EXTENDED-SEARCH	INTO	NSTD-REELS
CLOCK-UNITS	C09		INVALID	NUMBER
CLOSE	C10	FD	IS	NUMERIC
COBOL	C11	FILE		
CODE	C12	FILE-CONTROL	JUST	OBJECT-COMPUTER
COLUMN		FILE-LIMIT	JUSTIFIED	OCCURS
COM-REG	DATA	FILE-LIMITS	KEY	OF

OMITTED
OPEN
OPTIONAL
OTHERWISE

PAGE
PAGE-COUNTER
PERFORM
PIC
PICTURE
PLUS
POSITION
POSITIONING
POSITIVE
PRINT-SWITCH
PROCEDURE
PROCEED
PROCESSING
PROGRAM
PROGRAM-ID

QUOTE
QUOTES

RANDOM
READ
READY
RECORD
RECORD-OVERFLOW
RECORDING
RECORDS
REDEFINES
REEL
RELEASE

REMAINDER
REMARKS
RENAMES
REORG-CRITERIA
REPLACING
REPORT
REPORTING
REPORTS
REREAD
RERUN
RESERVE
RESET
RETURN
RETURN-CODE
REVERSED
REWIND
REWRITE
RIGHT
ROUNDED
RUN

SAME
SEARCH
SECTION
SECURITY
SEEK
SELECT
SENTENCE
SEPARATE
SEQUENTIAL
SET
SIGN
SIZE
SKIP1
SKIP2
SKIP3

SORT
SORT-CORE-SIZE
SORT-FILE-SIZE
SORT-MODE-SIZE
SORT-RETURN
SOURCE
SOURCE-COMPUTER
SPACE
SPACES
SPECIAL-NAMES
STANDARD
START
STATUS
SUBTRACT
SUM
SUPPRESS
SYNC
SYNCHRONIZED
SYSIN
SYSIPT
SYSLST
SYSOUT
SYSPCH
SYSPUNCH
S01
S02

TALLY
TALLYING
TAPE
TERMINATE
THAN
THEN
THROUGH
THRU
TIME-OF-DAY
TIMES
TOTALED

TOTALING
TRACE
TRACK
TRACK-AREA
TRACK-LIMIT
TRACKS
TRAILING
TRANSFORM
TYPE

UNIT
UNTIL
UPON
UPSI-0
UPSI-1
UPSI-2
UPSI-3
UPSI-4
UPSI-5
UPSI-6
UPSI-7
USAGE
USE
USING

VALUE
VALUES
VARYING

WHEN
WITH
WORDS
WORKING-STORAGE
WRITE-ONLY
WRITE-VERIFY

ZERO
ZEROES
ZEROS

DATE-WRITTEN. MAY 10, 1974.
DATE-COMPILED. MAY 17, 1974.
SECURITY. UNCLASSIFIED.
REMARKS. THIS PROGRAM READS THE OLD MASTER SALES FILE AND THE TRANSACTION FILE. IT PRODUCES AN UPDATED MASTER FILE, AN ERROR FILE, AND AN ERROR LISTING.

The ENVIRONMENT Division   This division is composed of the CONFIGURATION section and the INPUT-OUTPUT section. The CONFIGURATION section specifies the computer to be used to compile the program and the computer to be used to execute the object program. Generally, these computers are identical. It is also possible to indicate any special features of the object computer such as the number of tape units and the amount of core available. The INPUT-OUTPUT section provides information regarding data files and input-output devices. The optional FILE-CONTROL section assigns a programmer-supplied file name to an externally assigned file name and an input-output device. The words SELECT and ASSIGN are reserved words and must be used as in the example below. The symbolic names for the "ASSIGN TO" fields are specified by the particular COBOL compiler used. The optional I-O CONTROL section

defines input-output conditions or controls for files. For example, a programmer may specify the control for the end of a page for a print file in this section. An example of an ENVIRONMENT division is given below:

ENVIRONMENT DIVISION.
CONFIGURATION SECTION.
SOURCE-COMPUTER. IBM-370.
OBJECT-COMPUTER. IBM-370.
INPUT-OUTPUT SECTION.
FILE-CONTROL.
    SELECT INVENTORY-MF ASSIGN TO UR-2540R-S-SYSIN.
    SELECT PRINT-FILE ASSIGN TO UR-1403-S-SYSPRINT.

The DATA Division   The DATA and PROCEDURE divisions define the characteristics of the data and the program logic that manipulate the data. The DATA division provides for the explicit description of a program's data files and the contents of the file records. The PROCEDURE division makes provision for the manipulation of file records and individual fields, which may contain characters as well as numbers. The DATA division is divided into four sections: the FILE, WORKING-STORAGE, CONSTANT, and REPORT sections. The FILE section describes the structure of the input and output files. The format and contents of each data record are defined in detail. The WORKING-STORAGE section describes data records and fields that are necessary for processing but are not part of any input or output file. The CONSTANT section describes data records or fields that do not change during a program. Because there are other means of specifying these constants within the COBOL program, this section may be omitted. The REPORT section defines the format and contents of reports to be produced by a COBOL program.

The FILE section must describe the files and the format of the file records. The pertinent information about each file is the block size, the record size, the identification or label on the file, and the names of the records. The characteristics of the data records are then listed below the description of each file. An example of a file description is shown below:

```
FD   PAYROLL-MASTER
     RECORDING MODE IS F
     BLOCK CONTAINS 20 RECORDS
     LABEL RECORDS ARE STANDARD
     DATA RECORD IS PERSONNEL-RD.
```

The letters FD given in the A-margin indicate a general type of file rather than a file on random-access storage or a file to be sorted. The name assigned to the file by the programmer is PAYROLL-MASTER. The file contains fixed-length records, and therefore the recording mode is F rather than V (for variable-length records). Since there is more than one record per block, the clause 'BLOCK CONTAINS 20 RECORDS' has been used. If each block contains exactly one record, this clause is optional. The LABEL RECORDS clause is required. If the file label has been omitted, this clause is written

LABEL RECORDS OMITTED

COBOL also allows detailed information regarding the label to be specified. The name of the data record is then stated; in this example, the data record is identified as PERSONNEL-RD.

The next entry in this section is the description of the file record. Records are described using level numbers, data names, and the COBOL reserved word PICTURE. In addition to these basic elements, COBOL provides reserved words to describe data records: VALUE, USAGE, REDEFINES, OCCURS, SYNCHRONIZED, and JUSTIFIED. *Level numbers* denote the structure of the data

```
01   PERSONNEL-RD.
     02   NAME.
          03        LAST-NAME.
          03        FIRST-INITIAL.
          03        SECOND-INITIAL.

     02   PAYROLL-NUMBER.
          03        COMPANY-DIVISION.
          03        INDIVIDUAL-NUMBER.

     02   SOCIAL-SECURITY-NUMBER.

     02   DATE-HIRED.
          03        YEAR.
          03        MONTH.
          03        DAY.
```

record. They range from 01 to 49; special meanings are attached to the numbers 77 and 88. The highest level is 01, and it is assigned to the name of the data record. Each item within the record is then given the level number 02. (In COBOL, the word "item" is synonomous with "field.") A further breakdown of each item into subitems is given by additional items. For example, a record in a personnel file may contain the following information:

Name
    Last name, first initial, second initial
Payroll number
    Company division, individual number
Social security number
Date hired
    Year, month, day

The item containing the individual's name is further divided into three subitems: last name, first initial, second initial. Similarly, the date is divided into three subitems: year, month, day. The levels for this data record are defined in COBOL as shown in Table 14–3 above.

A PICTURE clause must be added to each of the level clauses shown in Table 14–3 in order to de-

scribe the type of data and the number of positions required for each item. The four characters listed below are used to present a "picture" of an input item, a working-storage item, or a constant:

CHARACTER	REPRESENTATION
9	Numeric digit
A	Alphabetic character
X	Alphanumeric character
V	Assumed decimal place

The repetition of any PICTURE character can be specified by writing the total number of characters in parentheses after the PICTURE character. The following are PICTURE clauses:

PICTURE 999V99
PICTURE AAXXX
PICTURE X(10)

In this example, the V denotes that two digits are assumed to the right of the decimal point. For input, 999V99 defines a field of 5 digits with 2 digits assumed to lie to the right of the decimal point. The use of the character V eliminates the need to record the decimal point for each number, thus saving data-preparation time. The definition

X(10) indicates an item with 10 alphanumeric characters.

For output, two commonly used characters are Z and $. Z causes the suppression of leading zeroes. Spaces are used in place of the zeroes. A $ causes the printing of a dollar sign; repetition of the dollar sign indicates that the dollar sign should be printed before the first nonzero digit and also marks a numeric position. Both the Z and $ have a dual function, since they both mark a numeric position. A comma (,) or an asterisk (*) can be written in the character position desired for output. The following brief table gives some examples of PICTURE clauses:

PICTURE CLAUSE	DECIMAL VALUE	PRINTED OUTPUT
PICTURE $999.99	000310	$ 3.10
PICTURE $$$$.99	000310	$3.10
PICTURE 9999.99	000310	0003.10
PICTURE ZZZZZ	00007	7
PICTURE 99999	00007	00007
PICTURE $9,999.99	234567	$2,345.67

The PROCEDURE Division This portion of the COBOL program contains the executable instructions of the program. It is composed of sections, paragraphs, and sentences. Each paragraph has a programmer-assigned name. Sentences are constructed according to the rules of COBOL and must terminate with a period. A COBOL verb or the reserved word IF must appear in each sentence.

OPERATIONAL CHARACTERISTICS

The characteristics of data in COBOL have already been discussed in connection with the structure of the language, and this knowledge is assumed here. Let us present the remaining operational characteristics: computational and manipulative facilities, program loops, input/output, and control statements. A list of COBOL reserved words used to implement these characteristics and the matching FORTRAN elements is given in Table 14–4.

COMPUTATIONAL AND MANIPULATIVE FACILITIES COBOL provides computational facilities similar to FORTRAN by means of the COMPUTE verb. When using the COMPUTE verb, the notation for arithmetic operations is expressed with the same symbols as in FORTRAN. Four other COBOL verbs for computational use are ADD, SUBTRACT, MULTIPLY, and DIVIDE.

Table 14–4
COBOL Operational Characteristics (Reserved Words) and Corresponding FORTRAN Elements

OPERATIONAL CHARACTERISTIC	COBOL RESERVED WORD	CORRESPONDING FORTRAN ELEMENT
Computational	ADD MULTIPLY DIVIDE SUBTRACT COMPUTE	Arithmetic statements
Data transfer	MOVE	Not available in ANSI FORTRAN. In FORTRAN V, a similar data transfer could be accomplished using the FLD function. Several FLD statements may be required to perform the data transfer accomplished by a single COBOL MOVE.
Program loop	PERFORM	DO
Input/output	OPEN } CLOSE }	Automatically performed by the FORTRAN program with the first READ or WRITE statement.
	READ WRITE	READ WRITE
	ACCEPT } DISPLAY }	No direct correspondence, but similar to READ and WRITE with I/O devices assigned for small amounts of data.
Control sentences	GO TO STOP RUN - - EXIT	GO TO STOP END CONTINUE
Comparison of quantities and branching	IF . . . ELSE . . .	IF

They are used as in the following sentences:

ADD A TO B.
ADD A, B GIVING C.
SUBTRACT ERROR FROM SALES-TOTAL.
MULTIPLY XA BY XB GIVING ALPHA.
DIVIDE YEARLY-PAY BY W.
COMPUTE C = A + B / C + D * E.

The first sentence indicates that A should be added to B and the sum placed in B. The GIVING clause in the second statement specifies the location C for the sum of A and B. The verb COMPUTE provides a compact way of expressing arithmetic operations. As in FORTRAN, the symbol * is used for multiplication and ** for exponentiation. The equals sign indicates not equality but "is replaced by." For example, consider the sentence

COMPUTE N = N + 1.

Here the contents of the location called N are added to 1 and the result inserted into the location called N. In a COMPUTE sentence, all operators must be imbedded in spaces. For example,

COMPUTE N=N+1.

is incorrect since spaces are omitted before and after the = and +.

The verb MOVE directs the transfer of data from one area to another area within the computer memory; thus, a data record or data item can be moved into a new location. This is a commonplace activity within data-processing programs. The verb MOVE can also be used to transfer literals to a data area. For example,

MOVE 700 to P-NUMBER.

causes the literal 700 to be stored in the area designated P-NUMBER. Another example of the MOVE sentence is

MOVE PAY-NAME TO PRINT-NAME.

The contents of the field called PAY-NAME will be placed in the field designated PRINT-NAME. The contents of PAY-NAME will be unchanged. The verb MOVE can be used in more complex ways for editing data. If the size and type of data in the data field being moved and the receiving data field correspond, the transfer is performed according to certain COBOL rules. If both fields are numeric, the PICTURE clause of the receiving field will determine the alignment of the decimal point. If the numeric item does not fit, it will be truncated or set equal to zero. If the receiving field is too small, a warning will be given by the compiler. If an alphabetic field is transferred to a larger field, it will be aligned at the leftmost position (that is, left-justified) and spaces will be inserted in the remaining positions.

In FORTRAN, transfers of data are accomplished by using the arithmetic statement in its simplest form — for example,

$$v_1 = v_2$$

where v_1 and v_2 are any variable or subscripted array names. Transfers of data to or from each individual location must be stated. Whole areas ot data cannot be moved by the execution of a single statement. FORTRAN V does provide for the movement of characters within a word to another word. In general, it does not have the power to move groups of characters specified by a single variable or array name to another area specified by a single variable or array name. Several FORTRAN V statements may be required to accomplish the data transfer made possible by the use of a single MOVE in COBOL.

PROGRAM LOOPS The PERFORM sen-

tence is analogous to the DO statement in FORTRAN. The verb PERFORM specifies the execution of a group of sequential paragraphs and lists the initial and ending paragraph names of the program loop. There are several options in the construction of PERFORM statements. For examples, consider the following sentences:

PERFORM PARAGRAPH-A THRU PARAGRAPH-B.
PERFORM PARAGRAPH-A THRU PARAGRAPH-B
    4 TIMES.
PERFORM PARAGRAPH-A THRU PARAGRAPH-B
    UNTIL ON-ORDER + ON-HAND > AVERAGE-
    USE*2.0.
PERFORM PARAGRAPH-A THRU PARAGRAPH-B
    VARYING X FROM 10 BY 5 UNTIL X IS
    GREATER THAN 1000.

The first sentence provides for the execution of the indicated set of paragraphs *once.* The second sentence causes the execution to occur *four times.* In the third sentence, the number of times the program loop is executed is dependent on the value of the variables ON-ORDER, ON-HAND, and AVERAGE-USE. When the value of ON-ORDER plus the value of ON-HAND exceeds the value of AVERAGE-USE*2.0, the loop is terminated.

The fourth sentence illustrates the control of the program loop by the variable X. X is initially set equal to the value 10. The program loop is then executed. The value of X is incremented by 5, and the program loop is repeated. This process continues until the value of X exceeds 1000.

INPUT/OUTPUT Because all files are completely described in the DATA division, COBOL input/output statements are relatively simple to write. Before referencing any input or output file, a program must first execute an OPEN sentence for that file. This opening of a file is a customary procedure for data-processing programs. In the case of input, the OPEN file sentence causes the identification information for the file (that is, the label record) to be verified. This ensures that the correct file will be processed. Otherwise, the operator may mount the wrong tape reel or disk pack without his mistake being detected by the program. If no label exists, this fact is noted in the DATA division. In an output file, the verb OPEN causes the writing of a label. The reading and writing of data records is accomplished by using the verbs READ and WRITE, as in the following examples:

READ INVENTORY-MF AT END GO TO FINISH.
WRITE NEW-INVENTORY.

After all the data have been processed for a file, it is necessary to close the file. In the case of output, this action causes the remaining data records in the computer memory to be written onto the file. In the case of input, it causes the file to be checked for an ending label, if any.

The verb ACCEPT provides for the input of small amounts of data from an input device such as a console or a card reader. The verb DISPLAY permits the printing of small quantities of information on a standard output device such as a console printer or line printer. Although other devices may be used, ACCEPT and DISPLAY are typically used with the console input device and the console printer respectively.

CONTROL SENTENCES Control Verbs The verbs GO TO and STOP are considered to be *control verbs*. The verb GO TO specifies the transfer of program control to a paragraph name—for example,

GO TO INCOME-TAX.

GRACE MURRAY HOPPER—COMPUTER PIONEER

Behind Captain Grace Hopper's desk in her Pentagon office is a counterclockwise-running clock, placed there to remind herself and her associates that "just because something has always been done one way in the past, that doesn't mean it always has to be done that way in the future." It was this outlook on life and science that led Captain Hopper to invent the first practical compiler for computers. "Nobody believed it could be done," says Hopper. "It was the obvious thing to do. Why start from scratch with every single program you write? Develop one that would over and over again do a lot of the basic work for you. Developing a compiler was a logical move; but in matters like this you don't run against logic, you run against people who can't change their minds. These individuals don't say it, but what they are thinking is 'let's not rock the boat.' I'm in the Navy and I like to rock the boat."

Captain Hopper prepared for her work in the computer field by graduating from Vassar College in 1928 with a degree in mathematics and physics and attending Yale on a Vassar fellowship to receive master's and doctor's degrees in the same subjects. She taught at Vassar until 1941, when she left on a faculty fellowship to study at New York University. In December 1943, she entered the U.S. Naval Reserve Midshipman's school at Northampton, Massachusetts. Upon graduation she was commissioned a lieutenant (j.g.) and ordered to the Bureau of Ordnance Computation Project at Harvard. "I didn't know what to expect. I walked into a room and Professor Howard Aiken said, 'Lieutenant, that is a calculating machine.' I looked at a monstrous device stretching 51 feet across a large room. It was Mark I, and I was stepping into history.

"During the war, we had little time to speculate about the future potential of the computer. In the postwar years, however, that was our favorite pastime at Harvard and at other small enclaves of computer activity in the United States. Do you realize that in the late 1940s you could have put all the computer people in one small room? Dur-

ing this period of blue sky-ing, I realized that great potential for computer usage lay in business data processing."

After the war, Captain Hopper joined the Harvard faculty as a research fellow in engineering sciences and applied physics at the computation laboratories, where work continued on the Mark II and Mark III for the Navy. In 1949, she joined the Eckert-Mauchly Computer Corporation (later the UNIVAC division of Sperry Rand Corporation) in Philadelphia as senior mathematician.

In addition to her work on the compiler, she played an important role in the development of COBOL, which in turn has enabled business to use computers far more effectively. She is presently engaged in a study of the various COBOL compilers and the lack of language standardization for the Navy. Since 1952, Captain Hopper has published more than 50 technical papers on automatic programming. She has many awards to her name, including the "1969 Man of the Year" award of the Data Processing Management Association. Since 1971, the Association for Computing Machinery has presented an annual award in her name to the young person who has contributed the most to computer science.

Speaking at a dinner for the 25th anniversary of the computer's invention held in Chicago in 1971, Captain Hopper closed by saying that she wanted to live until January 1 of the year 2,000. "I have two reasons. The first is that the party on December 31, 1999, will be a New Year's Eve party to end all New Year's Eve parties. The second is that I want to point back to the early days of the computer and say to all the doubters, 'See? We told you the computer could do all that!'"

The verb STOP is placed at the logical end of the program, accompanied by the word RUN:

STOP RUN.

Another form of the STOP sentence is

STOP 'WRONG DATA'.

This will cause the program to be halted temporarily and the literal 'WRONG DATA' to be displayed for the operator. This permits the operator to take corrective action prior to reinitiating the program.

The Conditional IF Sentence   The conditional IF sentence provides for the comparison of quantities and branching to a program path. It is comparable to the logical IF statement in FORTRAN. An example is

IF AGE GREATER THAN 65 GO TO RETIRED-INCOME.

The IF sentence also permits the use of the logical connectives AND, OR, and NOT. For example,

IF AGE GREATER THAN 21 AND LESS THAN 65 GO TO STANDARD-FORMULA.

In this case, if the value of AGE is both greater than 21 and less than 65, control is transferred to the paragraph STANDARD-FORMULA. If the value does not meet these requirements (say, AGE contains 70), control is given to the next sentence in sequence. The IF sentence may also be written with an ELSE clause—for example,

IF PAY IS LESS THAN 5000 SUBTRACT 1 FROM MINOR-COUNT ELSE ADD 1 TO MAJOR-COUNT.

AN INVENTORY-CONTROL PROGRAM

The inventory-control program written in FORTRAN in Chapter 13 (Figure 13–3) is shown as a COBOL program* in Figure 14–2. Because COBOL allows lengthy names for variable names, the input-card format is explicitly stated as part of the program; no additional comments are needed. Similarly, the print line is explicitly defined in lines 26 to 39 of the COBOL program. The data name WS-AVAILABLE is used to hold the sum of the quantity on hand and the quantity on

* Adapted from a program given in Mike Murach *Standard COBOL* (Chicago: Science Research Associates, 1971).

Figure 14–2
An Inventory-Control Program in COBOL

```
PP 5734-CB1 V3 RELEASE 3.1  1DEC72     IBM OS AMERICAN NATIONAL STANDARD COBOL     DATE JUN 4,1974


1


00001          IDENTIFICATION DIVISION.
00002          PROGRAM-ID. REORDER-LISTING.
00003
00004          ENVIRONMENT DIVISION.
00005          CONFIGURATION SECTION.
00006          SOURCE-COMPUTER. IBM-360.
00007          OBJECT-COMPUTER. IBM-360.
00008          FILE-CONTROL.
00009              SELECT INVENTORY-FILE ASSIGN TO UR-2540R-S-SYSIN.
00010              SELECT REORDER-LISTING ASSIGN TO UR-1403-S-SYSPRINT.
00011
00012          DATA DIVISION.
00013          FILE SECTION.
00014          FD  INVENTORY-FILE
00015          LABEL RECORDS ARE OMITTED
00016          DATA RECORD IS INVENTORY-CARD.
00017          01  INVENTORY-CARD.
00018              02 INV-ITEM-CODE            PICTURE IS A(6).
00019              02 INV-ITEM-DESC            PICTURE IS A(24)
00020              02 FILLER                   PICTURE IS X(5).
00021              02 INV-UNIT-PRICE           PICTURE IS 999V99.
00022              02 INV-REORDER-POINT        PICTURE IS 9(5).
00023              02 INV-ON-HAND              PICTURE IS 9(5).
00024              02 INV-ON-ORDER             PICTURE IS 9(5).
00025              02 FILLER                   PICTURE IS X(25).
00026          FD  REORDER-LISTING
00027          LABEL RECORDS ARE OMITTED
00028          DATA RECORD IS REORDER-LINE.
00029          01  REORDER-LINE.
00030              02 FILLER                   PICTURE IS X(5).
00031              02 RL-ITEM-CODE             PICTURE IS A(6).
00032              02 FILLER                   PICTURE IS X(5).
00033              02 RL-ITEM-DESC             PICTURE IS A(24).
00034              02 FILLER                   PICTURE IS X(5).
00035              02 RL-UNIT-PRICE            PICTURE IS ZZZ.99.
00036              02 FILLER                   PICTURE IS X(5).
00037              02 RL-AVAILABLE             PICTURE IS Z(5).
00038              02 FILLER                   PICTURE IS X(5).
00039              02 RL-REORDER-POINT         PICTURE IS Z(5).
00040          WORKING-STORAGE SECTION.
00041          77  WS-AVAILABLE                PICTURE IS 9(5).
00042
00043          PROCEDURE DIVISION.
00044          INITIALIZE.
00045              OPEN INPUT INVENTORY-FILE.
00046              OPEN OUTPUT REORDER-LISTING.
00047          BEGIN.
00048              READ INVENTORY-FILE AT END GO TO END-OF-RUN.
00049              MOVE INV-ON-HAND TO WS-AVAILABLE.
00050              ADD INV-ON-ORDER TO WS-AVAILABLE.


2


00051              IF WS-AVAILABLE IS LESS THAN INV-REORDER-POINT,
00052                  GO TO PRINT.
00053              GO TO BEGIN.
00054          PRINT.
00055              MOVE SPACES TO REORDER-LINE.
00056              MOVE INV-ITEM-CODE TO RL-ITEM-CODE.
00057              MOVE INV-ITEM-DESC TO RL-ITEM-DESC.
00058              MOVE INV-UNIT-PRICE TO RL-UNIT-PRICE.
00059              MOVE WS-AVAILABLE TO RL-AVAILABLE.
00060              MOVE INV-REORDER-POINT TO RL-REORDER-POINT.
00061              WRITE REORDER-LINE.
00062              GO TO BEGIN.
00063          END-OF-RUN.
00064              CLOSE INVENTORY-FILE.
00065              CLOSE REORDER-LISTING.
00066              STOP RUN.
```

order. The IF sentence on lines 51 and 52 compares this sum with the reorder point. If the sum is less than the reorder point, the input card is printed. At the end of the data, the program goes to END-OF-RUN, closes the files, and stops. The input cards and printed output produced are identical to the cards and output of the FORTRAN program.

A perusal of the COBOL program will quickly demonstrate the self-documenting features of the language. The COBOL program takes 65 lines (versus 14 lines for the FORTRAN program, plus 10 comments lines). However, the FORTRAN program without the comments cannot be easily read by anyone other than the original programmer. Moreover, the comments do not enhance its readability to the extent that it is as clear as a COBOL program, since FORTRAN limits variable names to six characters. The tediousness of writing long variable names in COBOL can only be evaluated by actually writing programs.

THE PRO'S AND CON'S
OF COBOL

Because COBOL was designed specifically for the writing of business data-processing pro-grams, it provides the necessary facilities for handling files, records, and data fields. It is a language widely used in business; and, presumably, it will gain in popularity in the years to come, if only because it is the only available business-data-processing language with sufficient versatility. RPG is a more limited language designed for the production of reports. (See Appendix II.) The Department of Defense has, in effect, closed the door on the development of other data-processing languages by computer manufacturers or software firms.

The disadvantages of COBOL are the complexity of the language structure and its sheer verbosity. There are computer installations where COBOL programs are written in an abbreviated form, necessitating programs that translate and expand the abbreviations for the COBOL compiler. Spaces are significant in COBOL, and the insertion of a space in the wrong place or the lack of a space can cause an error in the compiled program. A FORTRAN program may contain spaces for readability, but the FORTRAN compiler ignores them in interpreting programs. Since FORTRAN lacks any true capabilities for processing files, it cannot be considered for data-processing activities without the inclusion of appropriate routines written in assembly language. The business community generally prefers the use of English statements to the use of a mathematical-type language. The use of a supplemented FORTRAN language or PL/I (which offers character-handling capabilities) must be weighed against the intangible advantages of COBOL. A program in COBOL is usually felt to be well-documented because of the detail required for each COBOL statement. Whether it really is well-documented depends on the length and logical complexity of the program. The nature of COBOL requires the programmer to express details of all files and the structure of each record. This information is invaluable as a background to "reading" the program.

Due to the complexity of the language, COBOL programs typically require lengthy compilation times. Since the testing stage of a program may require several compilations of the program before a final version is obtained, the lengthy compilation time may be a minor factor in the selection of a language.

REFERENCES

Higman, Bryan. *A Comparative Study of Programming Languages.* London: MacDonald, 1967.

Lindahl, Tate F. *An Introduction to American National Standard COBOL.* Menlo Park, Calif.: Cummings Publishing Company, 1973.

McCracken, Daniel D., and Garbassi, Umberto. *A Guide to COBOL Programming.* New York: Wiley-Interscience, 1970.

Murach, Mike. *Standard COBOL.* Chicago: Science Research Associates, 1971.

Newell, John C. *American National Standard COBOL Programming.* New York: Holt, Rinehart and Winston, 1971.

Sammett, Jean. *Programming Languages: History and Fundamentals.* Englewood Cliffs, N.J.: Prentice-Hall, 1969.

Stern, Nancy B. and Robert A. *COBOL Programming.* New York: John Wiley & Sons, 1970.

QUESTIONS

1. Name the six elements and four divisions of COBOL.
2. Write the COBOL data description for a stock record that contains the stock number, quantity on hand, quantity on order, order number, date of order, and manufacturer's code number. The manufacturer's code number is composed of two subfields: an area code number and the manufacturer's assigned number.

3. What format will be produced on an output line if the following PICTURE clauses and data are used?

DATA	PICTURE
3456	$999.99
0025	ZZZZ
91345	$$9,999.99
00389	999.99

4. Write the equivalent COBOL statements for the following FORTRAN statements (altering the FORTRAN statement numbers, if necessary):

    DO 10 INK = 1, 25, 1
    IF (STOCK.LE.100) GO TO 200
    IF (INCOME.EQ.8000) GO TO 75

5. What function does the verb MOVE have? Give two examples of its use.
6. What special advantages does COBOL have over FORTRAN? What disadvantages does it have?

CHAPTER FIFTEEN

PL/I

FORTRAN has become one of the most popular programming languages, despite its inability to freely manipulate alphanumeric characters and its lack of provisions for interaction between the program and the operating system or real-time computing equipment. Because FORTRAN is essentially a language for programming mathematical-type problems, COBOL was designed to provide a programming language for business data-processing problems. But COBOL, too, lacks any special provision for real-time programming, and it is a clumsy language for certain types of problems. Because of the shortcomings of FORTRAN, the organization of users of large-scale IBM computers (called SHARE) and IBM formed a joint committee to expand FORTRAN. The committee decided that FORTRAN was inadequate and a new language should be developed. In 1964, the committee issued a report defining NPL (a *New Programming Language*), which was later renamed PL/I. IBM developed the first PL/I compiler in England in 1966. At the time, it was predicted that all computer manufacturers would develop PL/I compilers and PL/I would supplant FORTRAN and COBOL. Today it is easy to see that FORTRAN and COBOL were too well-entrenched to be replaced by another language. Furthermore,

the early PL/I compilers were too slow, due to the complexity of the language and the primitive state of the art of compiler development at the time. However, PL/I has had some measure of popularity at IBM installations, and with the development of PL/I compilers by other computer manufacturers it has become an established programming language.

The advent of structured programming has increased the popularity of PL/I. *Structured programming* is a programming technique that still has not been precisely defined by computer scientists. It appears to have three basic features:

1. The breakdown of the program into small logical blocks so that each block of code fits on a single page of printer output. (This feature may be optional in some cases.)

2. A restriction on GO TO statements. Instead of using GO TO statements, all (or almost all) branching is accomplished by IF . . . THEN . . . ELSE and DO statements. FORTRAN does not provide the IF . . . THEN . . . ELSE statement necessary for "GO TO"-less programming. COBOL does include the ELSE

option for the IF statement and thus allows structured programming in a limited manner.

3. A program design based on so-called *top-down programming.* In top-down programming, the entire program is designed and the control for the logical blocks is written first. The blocks then are coded and tied into the control program. If a block is not ready for testing, a dummy control block is inserted. This enables the structure of the entire program to be tested each time with all the currently completed blocks of coding. Without structured programming, a large program is typically divided into logical blocks, and each block is coded and tested independently. After all the blocks have been debugged, they are united by a control program. At this point, the usual experience is that the individual modules fail to work properly as a unified program. Top-down programming avoids this difficulty by insisting on the testing of the entire logical structure of the program concurrently with the development of the individual modules.

PL/I has some facilities for use in a multi-programming environment. It is a workable language for programming real-time applications. It incorporates data structures and apparatus for data manipulation from COBOL. The algebraic portions of PL/I are similar to FORTRAN but have the advantage of many optional features. The recursive facility of ALGOL has also been incorporated into PL/I. The structure of the language is related to the block structure of ALGOL and the paragraphs of COBOL.

Because PL/I is a complex language with multiple features for specifying computations and data handling, it provides default options. If a programmer does not specify a feature, PL/I automatically assumes a predetermined specification. This eliminates the necessity of writing additional burdensome code and provides the programmer with an adequate subset of the language. Although the full power of the language is not available with the subset, it permits the novice programmer to write PL/I coding after a short training period. If it is needed, the full power and range of the language is available for use by experienced programmers.

In the two previous chapters we discussed the

STRUCTURAL ELEMENTS

PL/I provides a choice of two character sets. The 48-character set does not have the full range of symbols available in the 60-character set; instead, a combination of symbols is used to represent a symbol available in the larger character set. Since keypunch devices do not always provide a 60-character set, the 48-character set is a practical compromise. The character sets include the upper-case letters A through Z, the digits 0 through 9, and the characters in Table 15–1.

The basic unit of expression is a statement. One or more statements are grouped to form a *procedure* headed by the keyword PROCEDURE. The other structural elements of a PL/I program are identifiers, delimiters, and keywords. A PL/I program is written in a free format. Its structure is not constrained by the physical limitations of an 80-column card. A PL/I statement can begin in any character position. A semicolon designates

structural elements and operational characteristics of FORTRAN and COBOL. We shall now discuss these features of PL/I.

Table 15–1
Additional Character Symbols in PL/I

48-CHARACTER SET	60-CHARACTER SET	CHARACTER NAME
		Blank
=	=	Equals sign
+	+	Plus sign
—	—	Minus sign
*	*	Asterisk
/	/	Slash
(	(	Left parenthesis
)	)	Right parenthesis
,	,	Comma
.	.	Period or decimal point
'	'	Single quote mark
//	%	Percent
.,	;	Semicolon
..	:	Colon
NOT	¬	Not
AND	&	And
OR	|	Or
GT	>	Greater than
LT	<	Less than
Omitted	_	Break character (underscore)
Omitted	?	Question mark

the end of the statement. However, software requirements at individual computer installations may place restraints on the program format. For example, the IBM/360 PL/I compiler requires programs to be prepared in columns 2 through 72 of punched cards. Column 1 is reserved as a control column, while columns 73–80 are not scanned by the compiler. These columns may be used for numerical-sequence numbers.

IDENTIFIERS   An *identifier* is a string of alphabetic, numeric, or break characters, the first of which must be an alphabetic character. An identifier may contain up to 31 characters. It is similar to the FORTRAN variable name. The following are examples of PL/I identifiers:

    ALPHA1234
    PAYROLL_FILE
    X
    SAMSON

DELIMITERS   A *delimiter* is a symbol or a combination of symbols that indicates an operation to be performed. Examples are the arithmetic operators or delimiters:

    +   add
    −   subtract
    *   multiply
    /   divide
    **   raise to a power (exponentiation)

A delimiter may also express a logical operation such as greater than or equal to, which is indicated by "GE" or "> =" in PL/I. Delimiters are also used for punctuation. For example, parentheses are used for enclosing lists; a semicolon is used to denote the end of a statement.

STATEMENTS   The basic unit in a PL/I program is a statement composed of identifiers and delimiters. PL/I statements are similar to FORTRAN statements. They may be executable

"It's really very simple, Edith. Inside is a very tiny mathematician."

Rothco Cartoons

statements such as arithmetic computational statements and logical comparisons, or statements that indicate input/output actions, alter the path of the program itself, or describe the program data. They also may be directives to the compiler such as the END statement, which indicates the physical end of the program to the compiler. The END statement may also be used as the logical end of the program, although PL/I also contains a STOP statement.

PROCEDURES A *procedure* is similar to a COBOL paragraph. It is composed of one or more PL/I statements and may be assigned an identifier. The first procedure in a program is always

NAME: PROCEDURE (OPTIONS) MAIN;

where NAME is an identifier assigned by the programmer. The execution of the program begins with the first executable statement of this procedure. Procedures other than the main procedure are termed *internal* or *external* to the main procedure. They allow the extension of the program into subroutines, either within the program or external to the program, in much the same way as FORTRAN subroutines.

OPERATIONAL CHARACTERISTICS

The operational characteristics to be discussed once again include data, computational and manipulative facilities, program loops, input/output, and control statements. Two special features of PL/I are presented in the last subsection.

DATA PL/I literals are similar to FORTRAN constants. In addition to floating-point (real) and fixed-point (integer) numbers, PL/I allows numbers to be expressed in binary form with the specification of a binary point, as follows:

PL/I BINARY CONSTANT	DECIMAL EQUIVALENT
10110B	22
−101B	−5
111.01B	$7\frac{1}{4}$
−1011.111B	$-11\frac{7}{8}$

PL/I also provides for character strings as data constants.

The DECLARE Statement Variables are classified by type in PL/I, in much the same way variables are classified as real and integer in FOR-TRAN. The DECLARE (or DCL) statement is used to define the type of number a variable will represent, as in the following example:

DECLARE NAME BINARY FIXED (20);

NAME has 20 bits and may be a positive or negative number. Binary floating-point data can also be specified—for example:

DECLARE GROSS WEIGHT BINARY FLOAT (16);

Strings of bits are also permitted as in

DECLARE BIT_STRING BIT(21);

BIT_STRING may have any combination of 21 bits.
PL/I provides default options so that variables not specifically declared are categorized automatically as to type. If an undeclared variable name begins with the letter I, J, K, L, M, or N, it is categorized as a binary fixed-point number (BINARY FIXED); this is the same as an integer variable in FORTRAN. An undeclared variable name that begins with any other alphabetic character is considered to be a floating-point number (DECIMAL FLOAT); this is the same as a real variable in FORTRAN. The precision of numbers can also be specified; the default options for precision are determined by the individual compilers.

The DECLARE statement is also used to allocate storage areas for arrays in much the same way as the DIMENSION statement is used in FORTRAN. An example of an array declaration is

DECLARE DATA (100, 20, 5);

DATA is a three-dimensional array with $100 \times 20 \times 5$, or 10,000, elements.

PL/I provides for the description of the range of subscript values by the use of the DECLARE statement. For example,

DECLARE A(−1:10, −5:5) FLOAT(6);

tells us that A is a two-dimensional floating-point array in which each element may have up to six decimal digits plus a sign. The first subscript ranges from −1 to 10, while the second subscript can have any integer value from −5 to 5. The total number of elements in the array is 12×11, or 121. ANSI FORTRAN does not provide for negative values as subscripts.

Data Structures   PL/I also makes provision for defining file structures similar to those in COBOL. A file record can be described by its fields, whose level is determined by the order of appearance of their names. Level numbers are used for clarity. For example, in

```
DECLARE 1 PAYROLL,
        2 NAME,
            3 LAST,
            3 FIRST,
            3 MIDDLE,
        2 PAYROLL_NO,
        2 RATE,
            3 STRAIGHT,
            3 OVERTIME;
```

the record name is PAYROLL. The three major fields of the record are NAME, PAYROLL_NO, and RATE. The field NAME is divided into three sub-fields called LAST, FIRST, and MIDDLE. A more complicated data structure using additional features of PL/I is given in Figure 15–1.

COMPUTATIONAL AND MANIPULATIVE FACILITIES   PL/I offers both computational and data-manipulation features that are more

Figure 15–1
A PL/I Record Similar in Structure to a COBOL Record

```
DECLARE
    1   PERSONNEL_RECORD CONTROLLED (P),
    2   NAME CHARACTER (16),
    2   CODE_STRING,
        3   SEX,
            (4 MALE,
             4 FEMALE) BIT (1),
        3   AGE,
            (4 UNDER_20,
             4 TWENTY_TO_50,
             4 OVER_50) BIT (1),
        3   HEIGHT,
            (4 OVER_6,
             4 FIVE_AND_A_HALF_TO_6,
             4 UNDER_FIVE_AND_A_HALF) BIT (1),
        3   WEIGHT,
            (4 OVER_185,
             4 BETWEEN_185_AND_120,
             4 UNDER_120) BIT (1),
        3   EYES,
            (4 BLUE,
             4 BROWN,
             4 HAZEL,
             4 GREY) BIT (1),
        3   HAIR,
            (4 BROWN,
             4 BLACK,
             4 GREY,
             4 RED,
             4 BLOND,
             4 BALD) BIT (1),
        3   EDUCATION,
            (4 COLLEGE,
             4 HIGH_SCHOOL,
             4 GRAMMAR_SCHOOL) BIT (1),
```

Source: IBM, *A Guide to PL/I for Commercial Programmers*. White Plains, N.Y.: IBM, 1966.

mathematically oriented than those of COBOL. In this section, we will briefly describe how computations can be programmed in PL/I and how characters can be manipulated.

Arithmetic Computations   PL/I provides for arithmetic computations written in FORTRAN-like fashion. For example,

X =(A*B — C*2)/(D**4.0);

is the same in either FORTRAN or PL/I except for the PL/I semicolon at the end of the PL/I statement. An additional feature in PL/I is the appearance of more than one identifier to the left of the equals sign. For example,

A, B, C = X + 2.5;

is equivalent to

A = X + 2.5;
B = X + 2.5;
C = X + 2.5;

Character Manipulation   The manipulation of character strings is provided in PL/I by the *attributes* (or keywords) VARYING and CHARACTER and the built-in *functions* LENGTH, SUBSTR, and INDEX. A character string is simply a group of alphanumeric characters that may include symbols. An example of a character string is

SOCIAL SECURITY NUMBER 123-45-6789

The words CHARACTER (CHAR is an acceptable abbreviation) and VARYING are used in conjunction with the DECLARE statement to name and describe the character string. An example is

DECLARE STRING VARYING CHARACTER(34);

The variable STRING is declared to vary in length to a maximum of 34 characters. If a string will be fixed in length, the attribute VARYING is omitted; the fixed number of characters in the string is given. For example,

DECLARE ALPHA CHARACTER(10);

indicates that ALPHA will always be exactly 10 characters in length.

Information on the length of the strings and the position of the characters within the strings is necessary for the manipulation of character strings. In PL/I, the position of each character

MINICOMPUTER MATCHES COLORS OF FABRICS

Precise color control plays a crucial role in a textile company's production and sales. A 1,000-pound batch of yarn that is one shade off a desired color must either be redyed or be sold at a reduced price. Avondale Mills of Sylacauga, Ala., one of the world's largest textile-dyeing operations, is using a Nova 1200 computer made by Data General Corporation to control a system that has cut offshade problems by 40 percent and has raised production 10 percent by increasing efficiency. The computer is the central processor of a direct digital control system made for dyehouses by Information Laboratories, Inc., of Charlotte, N.C. Their process control systems also are used in the petrochemical industry.

The key computer-controlled processing areas at Avondale Mills are the drug room, where dyes are mixed, and the individual dye machines. In the drug room, the Nova 1200 chooses the proper combination of 12 chemicals, selects the correct mixing tank, and notifies the operator when the mixing is complete.

Once the yarn has been loaded into one of Avondale's *kiers*, or dyeing vats, an operator in the central control room types instructions to the computer indicating which machine is ready for operation and which dye cycle should be used for that machine. The computer then takes over, first injecting the dye, then monitoring and adjusting the pressure and temperature within a vat so that a specific dye will react well with a particular fiber.

Seventy-eight of Avondale's 100 kiers are under computer control. Before the system was installed, an operator had to watch each dyeing machine constantly and try to maintain the proper temperature and pressure conditions by opening and closing valves at the proper time. Avondale managers find that the computer-controlled dyeing operation allows them to produce a product of unexcelled quality, and the operators now are working at other jobs where their skills are better used.

Adapted from "Minicomputer Matches Colors of Fabrics,"
Computers and People, February 1974, p. 37.

within a string is called its *index.* In the example below, the index of each character is shown:

| Character string: | EXAMPLE 1 |
| Index: | 123456789 |

The index of the letter M is 4; that is, it is in the fourth position in the character string. The length of the string is 9. In PL/I, the word LENGTH is used to obtain the length of a string, while the word INDEX will find the position of any character or group of characters within the string. For example, writing

N = INDEX(STRING,'123')

will cause the variable STRING to be examined to find the position of the characters "123." Then the location N will be set to contain the number indicating the beginning position of these characters.

The function SUBSTR provides for the transfer and handling of portions of a string, called *substrings.* The function SUBSTR must be written with the name of the string, the starting position of the substring, and the length of the substring. For example,

SUBSTR(SSN, 35, 8) = '12345 67'

specifies the replacement of 8 characters in the string called SSN starting in position 35. The characters "12345 67" will be inserted in the string beginning at position 35.

To concatenate strings means to chain two strings together. A bar (|) is used to indicate concatenation. For example, the statements

A = '12';
B = '345';
C = A ‖ B;

tell us that string A contains characters "12" while string B contains "345." C is a concatenation of the two strings and contains "12345."

PROGRAM LOOPS   PL/I provides DO and IF . . . THEN . . . ELSE statements similar to those in FORTRAN but with a few extras. The DO statement is more flexible. A DO loop is closed by writing an END statement:

DO P = −1 TO 100 BY 2;
   .
   .
   .

END LOOP ;

"The beauty of this baby is that there are a few small errors programmed into it, which helps to avoid total depersonalization."

The loop is executed for the values P = −1, 1, 3, . . . , 99. Another form of the DO statement provides for the execution of a loop while a certain condition is true—for example,

DO I = J TO K BY 3 WHILE (I<100) ;

The loop is executed for J, J + 3, J + 6, and so on until I exceeds K or until I equals or is greater than 100. The DO . . . WHILE statement can also be given with only the WHILE portion. For example:

DO WHILE (JOB = 1);

INPUT/OUTPUT STATEMENTS PL/I has both the input/output-processing capabilities of FORTRAN and the file-handling capabilities of COBOL. One of the input/output options in PL/I is related to the FORMAT statement in FORTRAN. PL/I also incorporates the data-record and data-file-handling provisions used to perform data-processing activities in COBOL. The words used for PL/I input/output operations are listed in Table 15–2. These are not reserved words. For example, READ may be used as the name of a file. The context of a word within a statement determines its interpretation by the compiler.

CONTROL STATEMENTS PL/I provides a GO TO statement to transfer control to another statement. Any PL/I statement may be labeled so that a GO TO can transfer control to it—for example:

GO TO HAND;

.
.
.

HAND: X = X + 1.5;

The STOP statement causes a program to terminate. The PL/I null statement is the counterpart of the FORTRAN CONTINUE statement. The null statement contains a semicolon only.

The IF . . . THEN . . . ELSE statement is similar to the FORTRAN IF statement but with the addition of an optional ELSE clause. Two examples of equivalent coding are given below:

Example 1:
    IF X = 2 THEN Y = Y + 1; ELSE Y = W;
    Z = Y**2;

Example 2:
    IF X = 2 THEN GO TO JACK;

Table 15–2
Corresponding PL/I and FORTRAN Statements

PL/I	FORTRAN
DECLARE	DIMENSION
DECLARE with EXTERNAL	COMMON
DECLARE with DEFINED or CELL	EQUIVALENCE
DECLARE with INITIAL	DATA
DECLARE with Precision	DOUBLE PRECISION
DECLARE with FIXED	INTEGER
DECLARE with FLOAT or REAL	REAL
DECLARE with COMPLEX	COMPLEX
DECLARE with BIT	LOGICAL
Assignment	Assignment
GO TO	GO TO
Assignment with label data	ASSIGN
IF . . . THEN . . . ELSE	IF (no equivalent for the ELSE portion)
DO	DO
STOP	STOP
DISPLAY	PAUSE
NULL STATEMENT	CONTINUE
CALL	CALL
RETURN	RETURN
PROCEDURE	{ FUNCTION { SUBROUTINE
ENTRY	ENTRY
GET or READ	READ
PUT or WRITE	WRITE
FORMAT	FORMAT
CLOSE	ENDFILE
No equivalent	REWIND
No equivalent	BACKSPACE
DECLARE with EXTERNAL and INITIAL	BLOCKDATA
DECLARE with ENTRY	EXTERNAL
GET/PUT with data-directed I/O	NAMELIST

```
Y = W;
GO TO JOHN;
JACK: Y = Y + 1;
JOHN: Z = Y**2;
```

In example 1, if the location X contains the value 2, then the value in location Y is incremented by 1. If X does not contain the value 2, then the contents of Y are replaced by the value given by W. This is expressed by an equivalent set of coding without the ELSE clause. In this case, the ELSE clause provides a more concise way of expressing the program action desired.

OTHER FEATURES   In addition to having the subroutine and function features of FORTRAN, PL/I permits the writing of recursive subroutines. This feature was a highlight of the ALGOL language when it was first formulated. PL/I also provides for interaction between the program and the operating system by a group of built-in functions.

Program Interaction with the Operating System
Among the functions available for interaction with the operating system are ON, TASK, EVENT, PRIORITY, SIGNAL, and WAIT. The ON function permits control to be given to the PL/I program when an error condition occurs. For example, the multiplication of two numbers may result in a product that cannot be contained in a computer word. This condition, which is called *overflow*, may be anticipated by the PL/I program by means of an ON statement. If an overflow condition does occur, then control is transferred to the PL/I program as directed by the ON statement.

The functions TASK, EVENT, PRIORITY, SIGNAL, and WAIT are designed to interact with a multiprogramming operating system. A PL/I program may request the execution of two or more tasks (called *subprograms*) simultaneously. The PL/I program then may ask the operating system if a particular task has been completed. If necessary, the PL/I program can wait for a particular subprogram to be completed by executing a WAIT statement.

Recursiveness   The recursive attribute may be specified for a subroutine, allowing it to call upon itself. This attribute can be extremely useful upon occasion. An example of its use is in the calculation of the factorial n for any number n. The factorial n is defined as $n! = (n)(n-1)(n-2)$ . . . (1) where 1! is defined as equal to 1.

To write a subprogram to compute $n!$ we may use the recursive attribute of PL/I and write

```
FACT:   PROCEDURE (N) RECURSIVE;
        DECLARE N BINARY FLOAT;
        IF N = 1 THEN RETURN (1);
        ELSE RETURN (FACT(N−1)*N);
END FACT;
```

This PL/I procedure is similar to a FORTRAN function and returns a single value as output. When $N = 1$, the value of 1 is returned. When $N = 2$, the ELSE clause is invoked and the subroutine calls upon itself; that is, it requests the execution of the procedure with N set to 1 by executing the call of FACT(1). For any value of N, a sequence of calls for FACT will be executed. Each time, the value (or argument) will be 1 less than the preceding argument until FACT(1) is invoked. The computation will then be completed.

AN INVENTORY-CONTROL PROGRAM

The inventory control program previously shown in FORTRAN and COBOL (in Figures 13–3 and 14–2) has been written in two different ways in PL/I to illustrate the duality of PL/I features, which have been drawn from both FORTRAN and COBOL. Figure 15–2 is a PL/I program with data descriptions and program statements similar to those of the COBOL program. The DECLARE statement (statement 4) describes the format of the record on the inventory file, while statement 5 defines the contents of the printer line. These statements are related to the COBOL statements in Figure 14–2. The name of the inventory file has been abbreviated to INVTORY, since PL/I accepts only the first seven characters of the file name as a unique identification. Contrast this to

Figure 15–2
An Inventory-Control Program in PL/I

```
            /* PL/I PROGRAM FOR INVENTORY CONTROL PROGRAM  */                           PAGE    2

STMT LEVEL NEST
                        /* PL/I PROGRAM FOR INVENTORY CONTROL PROGRAM  */
  1                     BALFWC: PROC OPTIONS (MAIN);
  2      1              DCL INVTORY FILE INPUT RECORD ENV (F(80) CONSECUTIVE);
  3      1              DECLARE PRINT FILE OUTPUT RECORD
                            ENV (F(132) CONSECUTIVE);
  4      1              DCL 1 INV_CARD,
                          2 ITEM_NO CHAR(6),
                          2 ITEM_DESC CHAR(24),
                          2 UNIT_COST PIC '999V99',
                          2 UNIT_PRICE PIC '999V99',
                          2 REORDER_POINT PIC '99999',
                          2 ON_HAND PIC '99999',
                          2 ON_ORDER PIC '99999',
                          2 FILLER_X CHAR(25);
  5      1              DCL 1 PRINT_LINE,
                          2 ITEM_NO CHAR(6),
                          2 FILLER_1 CHAR(5) INIT('     '),
                          2 ITEM_DESC CHAR(24),
                          2 FILLER_2 CHAR(5) INIT('     '),
                          2 UNIT_PRICE PIC '$Z99V.99(5)B',
                          2 ITEM_TOTAL PIC '99999(5)B',
                          2 REORDER_POINT PIC '99999',
                          2 FILLER_3 CHAR(65) INIT((65)' ');
  6      1              ON ENDFILE (INVTORY) GO TO END_P;
  8      1              OPEN FILE (INVTORY), FILE (PRINT);
  9      1              BEGIN: READ FILE (INVTORY) INTO (INV_CARD);
 10      1                  WS = INV_CARD.ON_HAND + INV_CARD.ON_ORDER;
 11      1              IF (WS<INV_CARD.REORDER_POINT) THEN GO TO OUTPUT;
 13      1                  GO TO BEGIN;
 14      1              OUTPUT:PRINT_LINE.ITEM_NO = INV_CARD.ITEM_NO;
 15      1                  PRINT_LINE.ITEM_DESC = INV_CARD.ITEM_DESC;
 16      1                  PRINT_LINE.UNIT_PRICE = INV_CARD.UNIT_PRICE;
 17      1                  PRINT_LINE.ITEM_TOTAL =WS;
 18      1                  PRINT_LINE.REORDER_POINT = INV_CARD.REORDER_POINT;
 19      1                  WRITE FILE (PRINT) FROM (PRINT_LINE);
 20      1                  GO TO BEGIN;
 21      1              END_P: END;
```

```
                    /* PL/I PROGRAM FOR INVENTORY CCNTROL PROGRAM */                                PAGE    2

STMT LEVEL NEST
                              /* PL/I PROGRAM FOR INVENTORY CCNTROL PROGRAM */
                              /* PL/I STATEMENTS SIMILAR TO FORTRAN */
                              BALFWC: PROC OPTIONS (MAIN);
     1                        DCL (REORDER_POINT, CN_HAND, ON_ORDER, WS) FIXED BINARY(31);
     2      1                 DCL (UNIT_PRICE) FLOAT BINARY;
     3      1                 DCL (ITEM_NO) CHAR(6);
     4      1                 DCL (ITE4_DESC) CHAR(24);
     5      1                 ON ENDFILE (INVTORY) GO TO END_P;
     6      1                 BEGIN: GET FILE (INVTORY) EDIT (ITEM_NO, ITEM_DESC, UNIT_PRICE,
     8      1                    RECRDER_POINT, ON_HAND, ON_ORDER) (A(6), A(24), X(5), F(5,2),
                                 3 F(5,C)) SKIP;
     9      1                    WS = CN_HAND + ON_ORDER;
    10      1                    IF (WS < RECRDER_POINT) THEN GO TO OUTPUT;
    12      1                    GO TO BEGIN;
    13      1                 OUTPUT:PUT SKIP ECIT (ITEM_NO, ITEM_DESC, '$', UNIT_PRICE, WS,
                                 RECRDER_POINT)
                                 (A(6), X(5), A(24), X(5), A(1), F(5,2), X(5), F(5,0), X(5),
                                 F(5,0));
    14      1                    GO TO BEGIN;
    15      1                 END_P: END;
```

Figure 15–3
An Alternate Inventory-Control Program in PL/I

the full name INVENTORY-FILE in the COBOL program. The line

2 FILLER_3 CHAR(65) INIT ((65)' ');

within statement 5 initializes the remaining portion of the printer line to spaces. (That is, it makes the initial values spaces.) CHAR is an abbreviation of CHARACTER; INIT indicates INITIAL.

PL/I also provides facilities for input and output handling similar to those in FORTRAN, as the program in Figure 15–3 shows. The file name (INVTORY) is given in statement 6. The input/output statements GET EDIT and PUT EDIT are used to input the inventory file records and print the output. Statement 8 shows the list of input variables

ITEM_NO, ITEM_DESC, UNIT_PRICE, REORDER_POINT,
ON_HAND, ON_ORDER

to be matched with the description of the data

(A(6), A(24), X(5), F(5,2) 3 F(5,0))

Thus ITEM_NO will be read as six alphanumeric characters, while UNIT_PRICE will be interpreted as a five-digit number with a decimal point assumed to lie between the third and the fourth digits. This FORTRAN-like PL/I program is considerably shorter than the COBOL-like PL/I program (Figure 15–2). The description of the record is explicit in the COBOL-like program. The GET and PUT statements do not provide this same ease of interpreting the record formats directly from the program statements.

Unlike the IF statements in COBOL and FORTRAN, the IF statement in PL/I uses the "<" sign. COBOL uses the English words "LESS THAN," while FORTRAN offers an abbreviation for "LESS THAN" (".LT."). The PL/I program also allows abbreviations such as CHAR for CHARACTER, DCL for DECLARE, and PROC for PROCEDURE. Abbreviations for lengthy words are permitted in some versions of COBOL.

THE PRO'S AND CON'S OF PL/I

PL/I is a general multipurpose language suitable for both scientific and business data processing. It provides for structured programming, a new technique for writing programs with fewer errors. Its main disadvantage is its complexity.

PL/I has a full repertoire of statements with many options. The number of options and default rules require more training for the programmer, and even so expert ability to handle all facets of the language may be lacking. FORTRAN is far simpler. COBOL is more complex than FORTRAN, but, overall, it is not as difficult a language as PL/I. However, PL/I is gaining in popularity due to its versatility. Its breadth of features is both its prime drawback and its chief selling point.

REFERENCES

Donaldson, James. "Structured Programming." *Datamation*, December 1973, pp. 52–54.

Fike, C. T. *PL/I for Scientific Programmers*. Englewood Cliffs, N.J.: Prentice-Hall, 1970.

Hughes, Joan K. *PL/I Programming*. New York: John Wiley & Sons, 1973.

IBM Corporation. *A Guide to PL/I for Commercial Programmers*. White Plains, N.Y.: IBM, 1966.

IBM Corporation. *A Guide to PL/I for FORTRAN Users*. White Plains, N.Y.: IBM, 1968.

McCracken, Daniel D. "A Revolution in Programming." *Datamation*, December 1973, pp. 51–52.

Miller, Edward F., Jr., and Lindamood, George E. "Structured Programming: Top-Down Approach." *Datamation*, December 1973, pp. 55–57.

Sammett, Jean. *Programming Languages: History and Fundamentals*. Englewood Cliffs, N.J.: Prentice-Hall, 1969.

Vazsonyi, Andrew. *Problem Solving by Digital Computers with PL/I Programming*. Englewood Cliffs, N.J.: Prentice-Hall, 1970.

Weiss, Eric. *The PL/I Converter*. New York: McGraw-Hill Book Co., 1966.

QUESTIONS

1. What advantages does PL/I have over FORTRAN and COBOL? What disadvantages does it have?
2. Prepare a chart comparing the major features of FORTRAN, COBOL, and PL/I.
3. Write equivalent PL/I statements for the following FORTRAN segments:

   (a) DO 10 IA=5,100,4
   (b) DIMENSION A(100,2), KAT(5,8)
   (c) IF (ALPHA.EQ.SAM) X=X+2
        GO TO 100
        X=X**2

4. What features does PL/I provide for character manipulation?
5. Explain the meaning of a "recursive subroutine." Give an example.
6. The Fibonacci series of numbers can be produced by using a recursive routine. The first two numbers in the series are 1 and 1. Successive numbers are derived by adding the previous two numbers. The series begins as follows:

$$1, 1, 2, 3, 5, 8, 13, 21, 34, 55, \ldots$$

Flowchart the computation for each element in this series, using a recursive procedure.

CHAPTER SIXTEEN

Program Testing

Every program must be tested before it can be used for production runs. The program-testing stage determines the reliability of the program. It is a common saying among computer personnel that the only error-free program is a program no longer in use. In other words, any program may contain an error undetected by testing and even undetected in months of production runs. Errors are subtle. The more complex a program is, the more likely it is that a "bug" will be discovered later in the life of the program. Because of this dire forecast of "bugs," it is essential that a program be tested thoroughly.

The testing of programs is also known as *debugging*. After all errors, or "bugs," have been removed, the program is considered to be "error-free" and ready for production use with actual data. The correctness of the program logic and its reliability in achieving true results must be considered in conjunction with the debugging of a program. Debugging includes more than the removal of program errors. It encompasses all the steps in the construction of a program. These steps are

- formulating the problem,
- designing the program,
- flowcharting the program or constructing a decision table,
- coding the program,
- testing the program,
- documenting the program, and
- making production runs (executing the program using actual data).

The steps prior to program testing are important in determining the usefulness of the program and the ease with which it can be tested.

The writing of a program can be compared to the writing of a letter which is then transcribed by a typist. Errors in the letter may be caused by either the writer of the letter or the typist. Typing errors can be detected by a perusal of the letter; they are then erased and the words intended by the creator of the letter are inserted. However, the correctness of the letter—of its grammar and its content—is determined by the creator. In a similar fashion, a program is designed and then implemented by a coder. Errors in coding can be eliminated after testing; but an error in the program's logical design or a failure to achieve desired results is not easily corrected. It may remain undetected because of faulty testing. Consequently, the steps prior to actual program test-

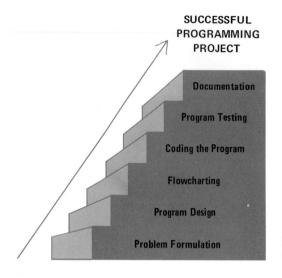

SUCCESSFUL
PROGRAMMING
PROJECT

Documentation

Program Testing

Coding the Program

Flowcharting

Program Design

Problem Formulation

Figure 16–1
Steps to a Successful Programming Project

ing are crucial in the creation of a good working program.

Program testing is an art. There is no formula or set of rules that can be followed rigorously for all programs. A unique testing procedure must be devised for each program. Although there are general guidelines, experience is the best teacher. Because of the interlocking of the steps required to construct a working program, let us briefly review program design, flowcharting, and coding from the standpoint of program testing.

DESIGNING THE PROGRAM

This aspect of programming was discussed in Chapter 11. The design of a program depends on the problem definition formulated by those who pose the problem to be solved. The choice of data media and data formats directly affects the design of the program. Such choices should be determined by an overall view of the problem, the desired results, the proposed use of the data, and the available computer hardware.

MODULAR PROGRAMMING A program should be designed so that it can be divided into

subprograms, or blocks. This is called *modular programming.* The use of subprograms permits each segment of a program to be checked out independently. The logical structure is clearly defined in terms of blocks. An error can be traced to a particular block; correction of the error usually affects only that block of coding and not the entire program. After all subprograms have been tested thoroughly, they are combined into a single entity which is then tested to ensure the correctness of the entire program.

Loopholes in the logic, data-handling errors, and complex branching in the program can be controlled better with modular-programming techniques. The modular approach to programming permits changes to be made more easily. The types of tests necessary to validate a program should be considered simultaneously with the design of the program. The formulation of tests is discussed in a separate unit later in this chapter.

STRUCTURED PROGRAMMING Structured programming is another technique for writing large programming systems that has recently gained some measure of popularity. It is related to modular programming but restricts the use of GO TO statements within a program. Preferably, a structured program should not contain any GO TO statements. An error rate of one per programmer man-year, or one per 10,000 lines of coding, has been reported by one spokesman — truly a remarkable achievement. This topic was discussed in Chapter 15.

FLOWCHARTING THE PROGRAM

After a program design has been completed, a flowchart or decision table that describes the program logic must be constructed. The flowchart should be carefully drawn and thoroughly reviewed prior to the writing of the program code. The standard ANSI flowchart symbols should be used for flowcharting. All paths should be traced. This pictorial representation of the program logic must be as complete as possible. Any loopholes

or lack of specifications in the design stage should be detected in the construction of the flowchart. A good flowchart is essential for the writing of good coding. It also serves to document the program after testing is over. These remarks also apply to decision tables.

CODING THE PROGRAM

Unfortunately, the achievement of a working program that performs the task intended is dependent on more than skill in coding the program. The three previous programming steps — the formulation of the problem, the design of the program, and flowcharting — have already determined the shape of the program and the form of its coding. If these steps have not been done correctly, the best coder in the world cannot

Rothco Cartoons

"I thought we had computers
to take care of all
this stuff."

construct a good program. He can write a program that is executable and produces results, but it may not solve the problem at hand. Discussion of the problem is the first step in programming. The usual difficulty at this point is the inability of the person with the problem to communicate it completely. No item—however small it may be —should be omitted in the discussion of the problem. The programmer should be aware that it is common for non-computer-oriented personnel to state a problem in terms of their limited understanding of computers. Only a complete discussion of a problem will produce a good program design.

A programming language is selected in conjunction with the design of the program. The programming language will affect both the design of the data files and the formulation of the flowchart. If a higher-level language is used, the flowchart can contain more general terms. The coder then writes the program using the flowchart or decision table as a guide.

Straightforward coding is preferable to tricky or ingenious coding. The age of the hotshot programmer is over. The programmer who writes fast, ingenious, and unintelligible code (unintelligible except to himself or other hotshots) has done a disservice to his employer. Almost every program is revised one or more times during its lifetime. The original programmer may not be available to make these revisions. Therefore, coding that can be quickly understood and easily amended is now preferred throughout the computer industry to the tight, unreadable code of the "genius" programmer.

DEBUGGING THE PROGRAM

It is a shock for anyone writing his first program to discover his own fallibility. The computer is an exacting taskmaster. It can only perform each step as directed by the program code. An entire program can be wrong because ot an error of one letter in a variable name or one digit in a number. The novice programmer is seldom consoled by the warning that a program rarely runs correctly the first time. He must learn the art of debugging and be prepared for a lengthy, frustrating, and time-consuming task. A program not adequately tested is of no value. Therefore, management must allow ample time for this stage of program development.

THE COMPILATION PHASE   After a program has been coded it is assembled, or *com-*

piled. The compilation of the program results in a program listing that shows the source coding and indicates any errors detected by the compiler. The error messages produced by the compiler are called *diagnostics.* Figure 16–2 shows a compilation of a FORTRAN program that contains several diagnostics. These error messages are about violations of the rules governing the language. Although the program may contain errors in logic, most compilers are not designed to detect complex logical errors. The compiler's function is to translate the source code to object code and note any incompatibility of the program code with the rules of the language. Generally, these types of errors are due to carelessness in writing the program or transcribing the program to a computerized medium — for example, to a keypunching error. If the error is minor, the compiler may attempt to circumvent it and produce an object program that may or may not be the program desired by the programmer. If the errors detected are considered to be major, no object program is produced. The programmer must correct these errors in the use of the language. He then resubmits the corrected program for compilation and obtains a new listing. This process continues until he obtains a program free of compilation errors. This program is now ready for execution with test data.

PROGRAM EXECUTION   The execution of a program has three possible results. First, the program may execute correctly and produce acceptable results. In this case, testing should proceed with the next set of data. Second, the program may not execute to completion; that is, it may terminate due to an improper instruction or because it exceeds the time allocated for execution. For example, an instruction to divide a number by zero will cause the termination of a pro-

Figure 16–2
A FORTRAN Program with Diagnostics

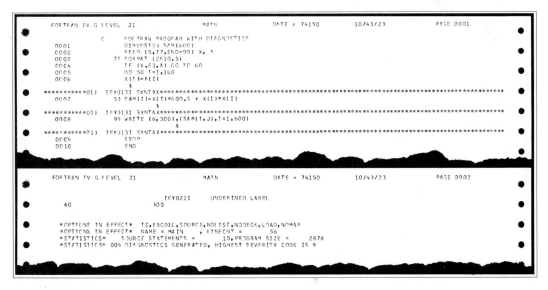

gram run. This is called an *error termination.* The third possibility is that the program will run to completion but will not produce the results expected. An example of this outcome is shown in Figure 16–3. The FORTRAN program was compiled without an error, but the output contains error messages produced during the execution of the program.

If a program has not run to completion or the results are incorrect, the coding must be checked for errors. This process is known as *desk-checking.* The type of error termination that occurs is an aid in locating the program bug. The possibility of errors in variable names, language rules, data input, and so on must be reviewed. If the error is elusive, the programmer may take a small amount of sample data and study the actions of the program using this data. He performs the role of a computer and keeps a running tally of the contents of locations. By checking the program results for each instruction, he can locate a hard-to-find error.

Another aid to debugging is the periodic output of calculated results. If output is written only at the end of a program, the abrupt termination of the program at some other point will not yield any information for debugging purposes.

If a program has executed to its terminal point, the results must be carefully checked. The results expected should already be known and be compared to those produced by the program. The output produced by the program must be sufficient for debugging purposes. If it is not, additional printed output should be produced by the program to aid in debugging.

TEST DATA A good understanding of the problem to be handled by the program is essential in designing test data. It is important to test a program with the aim of validating it as a tool

Figure 16–3
A FORTRAN Program without Diagnostics but with Erroneous Output

```
    FORTRAN IV G LEVEL  21               MAIN            DATE = 74155        13/29/01          PAGE 0001

                  C      FORTRAN PROGRAM WITH NO DIAGNOSTICS
                  C      BUT WITH ERRONEOUS OUTPUT
                  C      BECAUSE NO I3 VALUE IS WRITTEN
     0001                WRITE (6,200)
     0002            200 FORMAT (5X,2HI1,I5,9X,2HI2,I5,9X,8HI3=I1/I2,I5)
     0003              1 READ (5,100,END=99) I1, I2
     0004            100 FORMAT (2I5)
     0005                I3=I1/2
     0006                WRITE (6,200) I1, I2, I1
     0007                GO TO 1
     0008             99 STOP
     0009                END

      I1
      I1 1000         I2 2500         I3=I1/I2 1000
      I1  350         I2   41         I3=I1/I2  350
      I1    0         I257000         I3=I1/I2    0
      I1 8300         I2  990         I3=I1/I2 8300
  IHC215I CONVERT - ILLEGAL  DECIMAL  CHARACTER .

   83.   99

  TRACEBACK  ROUTINE  CALLED FROM ISN   REG. 14   REG. 15   REG.  0   REG.  1

            IBCOM                       C008E174  0008E100  00000000  00001036

            MAIN                        00C0936A  0108E010  FF000018  0009D760

  ENTRY POINT=  C108E010

  STANDARD FIXUP TAKEN , EXECUTION CONTINUING
      I1  830         I2   99         I3=I1/I2  830
      I1   84         I2    0         I3=I1/I2   84
      I1   64         I2   71         I3=I1/I2   64
      I1  102         I2  -15         I3=I1/I2  102
      I1   -9         I290000         I3=I1/I2   -9
      I1  -99         I2   20         I3=I1/I2  -99
```

Figure 16–4
A Flowchart of a Program

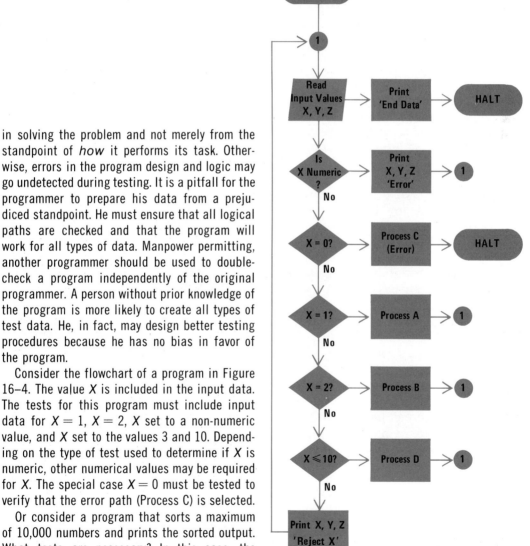

in solving the problem and not merely from the standpoint of *how* it performs its task. Otherwise, errors in the program design and logic may go undetected during testing. It is a pitfall for the programmer to prepare his data from a prejudiced standpoint. He must ensure that all logical paths are checked and that the program will work for all types of data. Manpower permitting, another programmer should be used to double-check a program independently of the original programmer. A person without prior knowledge of the program is more likely to create all types of test data. He, in fact, may design better testing procedures because he has no bias in favor of the program.

Consider the flowchart of a program in Figure 16–4. The value *X* is included in the input data. The tests for this program must include input data for $X = 1$, $X = 2$, *X* set to a non-numeric value, and *X* set to the values 3 and 10. Depending on the type of test used to determine if *X* is numeric, other numerical values may be required for *X*. The special case $X = 0$ must be tested to verify that the error path (Process C) is selected.

Or consider a program that sorts a maximum of 10,000 numbers and prints the sorted output. What tests are necessary? In this case, the

FARMING IN KANSAS BY COMPUTER

When Norm Gingrass wants to know whether he should plant less wheat and more milo, he reaches for his latest computer printout. Gingrass farms and raises cattle on nearly 2,000 acres in south-central Kansas. He is one of more than 170 Kansas farmers who have tied their operations into a computer-accounting system, K-MAR 105, developed by Kansas State University. For less than a dollar a day, the computer shows Gingrass which of his operations—cattle, wheat, and milo—are making money.

Each month Gingrass gets a computer printout through the Farm Management Association (FMA), which co-sponsored the pilot computer program with the university. The printout is an analysis of data supplied by the farmer —items bought or sold, the number of units, the price, and the farm operation involved. Because of the computer information, Gingrass has modified his farming practices. In the past year, he expanded his calf herd from 500 to 900. These are calves he feeds for a while, then sells to commercial feedlots for finishing. The printout shows him his break-even point, so he knows just what price he needs to show a profit. Gingrass dropped another cattle operation—raising calves on grass—because the computer showed it wasn't profitable enough. He found that milo was more profitable for him to raise than wheat. Whereas he used to plant 700 acres of wheat and 400 of milo, he has now reversed this ratio and will continue increasing his milo acreage.

The monthly printouts also give Gingrass detailed information on income and expenses both for his total operation and for each of four landlords from whom he rents part of his acreage. "A landlord often loses touch with what his farm is doing," Gingrass says. "At the end of the year, I can tell each landlord exactly how much he spent and what his income was. They seem to appreciate it." The income statements also help Gingrass in applying for loans and give added flexibility in tax management.

FMA fieldmen visit Gingrass about twice a year to help him interpret the printouts and make management decisions, and he says he's getting more proficient in using the computer information all the time. "It takes a year or two to get the grasp of it," he says. "It's a new thing, but they're kind of getting the hard spots out now."

Larry N. Langmeier, a KSU economist who helped develop K-MAR, predicts that more and more farmers will adopt computer-accounting systems. He says the system can be adapted to any type or size of farm operation, and "it gives the farmer a cold, hard, objective look at where to direct his effort." According to Langmeier, the university's interest is in refining K-MAR into an "optimum" system, rather than in becoming an accounting service as such, and it will probably limit its farmer clients to a maximum of 300.

Adapted from "Computer Makes Decisions for Kansas Cattle Farmer," an Associated Press story published in the *Iowa City Press-Citizen*, November 6, 1973.

amount of final output cannot easily be verified by visual means. Furthermore, a test using 10,000 numbers each time could be both lengthy and costly. Therefore, testing should be organized to progress from one stage to another. For example, the testing might have three phases:

1. Sort one number (to verify that the routine can accept the minimum input).
2. Sort 10 numbers. This small sort will test the program and permit many errors to be found and corrected before a large sort is performed.
3. Sort 10,000 numbers.

The manual preparation of 10,000 numbers for input is a time-consuming and tedious task. Instead, a computer program should be used to generate 10,000 numbers and pass them to the program directly. However, the selection of any 10,000 numbers at random would make it almost impossible to verify that the sorted output was correct and that no numbers had been lost. Therefore, the 10,000 numbers should be generated in a reverse order, starting with the value 10,000 and continuing down to the value 1. The program run would then yield the numbers 1 to 10,000 in order. This output could be verified automatically by having the program check that each number was one greater than the preceding number. A similar program could also be written to check that any sorted output was in sequential order. Another potential error in a sort is the incorrect handling of duplicate values. Consequently, a small quantity of input data containing duplicate values should also be tested.

In writing a program, the programmer must provide for checkpoints so that any error can be traced to its source. Periodic output during the execution of a program is far more valuable than a ton of output at the very end of the program. In addition to the required results, computational values used in creating those results should be printed. Small amounts of input that serve as parameters for the program should always be listed on the output. When the input data is minimal, it should be listed in its entirety to facilitate the tracing of an error.

Data-processing programs are especially difficult to verify. Consider the problem of testing a payroll program. Once the program executes correctly with *some* data, its functioning with all types of data must be checked as thoroughly as possible. Since a payroll program may have as many as 1,000 branches, it is clearly impossible to check all paths (that is, all possible combinations of the branches in the program) or to be absolutely certain that all the paths are correct. Here the program design is critical. All possibilities must be reviewed before coding the program. The program must be able to handle erroneous input data, it must cope with multiple deductions, it must treat the case of a zero paycheck (where the deductions exceed the salary), and it must have a path for a check that exceeds a maximum amount. Many other problems must be considered before the coding can be initiated. Finally, the program must be designed to defer judgments and ask for human intervention.

DEBUGGING AIDS Special debugging aids may be available, depending on the particular computer installation. A typical debugging aid is a *trace* that monitors each step of a program and shows the paths taken during the execution of the program. This information can be invaluable in tracking down an elusive bug. A trace routine is expensive in terms of the computer time it requires. Consequently, it is better to have the program furnish this information directly by the insertion of additional printed output. These additional output statements should then be bypassed or removed for production runs.

Another debugging aid is the listing of the symbolic program side by side with its object code. This listing may be standard output with some compilers. This information, combined with abnormal-termination information, enables an experienced programmer to track his error. Another common debugging facility is the listing of the contents of memory locations after the termination of the program. This listing is called a *memory dump*. The memory dump is used in conjunction with the object-code listing to locate a program error. The printing of specified memory locations at key points in the program also yields critical information for debugging; this type of listing is called a *snapshot dump*. A programmer should be aware of what debugging aids are available at his computer installation.

A programmer should use these professional debugging aids sparingly, for two reasons. First, many debugging tools assume that the user has a good knowledge of machine language and the octal or hexadecimal number system of the computer. Today, most programmers do not have the skills necessary to use these devices effectively.

"What I had in mind was
topographical elevations and circuit schematics."

Second, devices such as a trace routine can require enormous amounts of computer time. Consequently, the judicious placement of output statements that print the contents of key variables and furnish intermediate results may be more effective in debugging the program than the use of any special debugging aid. The brute force of the professional debugging aids should be reserved for a last resort, and they should be used with the assistance of experienced programmers familiar with the internal operations of both the computer hardware and software.

GUIDELINES FOR TESTING   Guidelines for program testing are given below. The list is not complete, since unique tests must be devised for each program. A judicious selection of tests is more valuable than many tests that are badly constructed.

1. The entire program should be tested; that is, all paths should be validated. The programmer should not assume that a path works because the coding is so simple and clear to him. Errors may occur in writing even the simplest coding.
2. The program must be checked with realistic data. For example, if the program processes 10,000 numbers, testing must include the input of 10,000 numbers, not merely 100 or 1,000.
3. Erroneous data values should be tested. For example, if a program computes the square root of X, then the path for a negative value must be checked. The program must reject a negative value and issue an error message.
4. The results of a test should be known to the programmer before the program is executed. He must be sure of the expected results and not guess that "they look okay."
5. Test data should be created automatically by means of a computer, if possible. The manual preparation of massive quantities of data is time-consuming and may introduce data errors.
6. A program that requires large volumes of data should be tested with small sets of data initially to save time and to enable the logical paths to be clearly shown. The final testing should include tests with a large volume of data.
7. The validation of program results should be performed by using the computer whenever

possible. The visual verification of large amounts of output is prone to human error.

8. If the original computer on which the program was run is replaced by another computer, the program should be completely checked out again. Differences in compilers and hardware factors such as word size may affect the running of the program on a different computer.

The final check of a program is ordinarily a run with actual data — that is, a production run. The programmer should verify the output of this run by comparing it to the results produced by a previously used program, by punched-card techniques or manually, and check that the program functioned as expected in all cases. If any change is made in a program, it must be thoroughly tested once again. The only exception is when a very simple correction is made; even this type of change may cause another portion of the program to malfunction.

QUALITIES OF A GOOD PROGRAM

The ultimate aim of testing is an error-free program that does an assigned task and produces correct results each time it is executed. All the steps leading to a production program should yield a "good" program and not merely a working program. What qualities make a good program? First, the program must do the task assigned and not some other task. The person with the problem must state it clearly, so that a program which incorporates all the features necessary to the solution of the problem can be designed. Second, the program should be efficient; that is, it should not require the entire computer memory or run in two hours when an improved design would require only half the memory and one hour of running time. Third, the program should handle all types of errors and issue clear, concise error messages. Fourth, the printed output should be formatted and labeled to facilitate reading. For example, the printing of 10 columns of numbers with no headings means that the reader must manually annotate the output listing, adding column headings. Fifth, in designing the format for input data, ease of preparation should be the first consideration. Sixth, the logical design of the program should be good. Complex switching logic should be avoided unless it is absolutely necessary. The easiest way to do a job is often the best way.

REFERENCES

Gruenberger, Fred. *Computing: An Introduction*. New York: Harcourt Brace Jovanovich, 1969, pp. 175–190.

———— *Computing: A Second Course*. San Francisco: Canfield Press, 1971.

———— "Problems and Priorities." *Datamation*, March 1972, pp. 47–50.

Mills, Harlan, and Baker, F. Terry. "Chief Programmer Teams." *Datamation*, December 1973, pp. 58–61.

Rustin, Randall, ed. *Debugging Techniques in Large Systems*. Englewood Cliffs, N.J.: Prentice-Hall, 1971.

Vander Noot, T. J. "Systems Testing . . . a Taboo Subject?" *Datamation*, November 15, 1971, pp. 60–64.

QUESTIONS

1. Why is program testing necessary?
2. What steps are required to obtain a program for production use?
3. During the testing stage, what are the three possible results of a program execution?
4. How does a programmer find an error in his program after a program test has failed to produce the desired results?
5. A program is written to compute the paychecks for a company employing 100 persons. Paychecks are computed on the basis of either an hourly, a weekly, or a monthly pay period. Deductions are made for federal income taxes, state income taxes, social security payments (FICA), the company pension plan, and hospitalization insurance in every case. Three other special deductions are optional. Outline the paths to be tested for this program. What special tests should be made to guard against the writing of erroneous checks by the computer?
6. A program has been written to compute the following formula:

$$TEST = X + Y/Z - B$$

where the values of X, Y, Z, and B are read as input. What special problems should be considered in the event of incorrect values of these variables? What types of numbers should be used as test values for these variables?

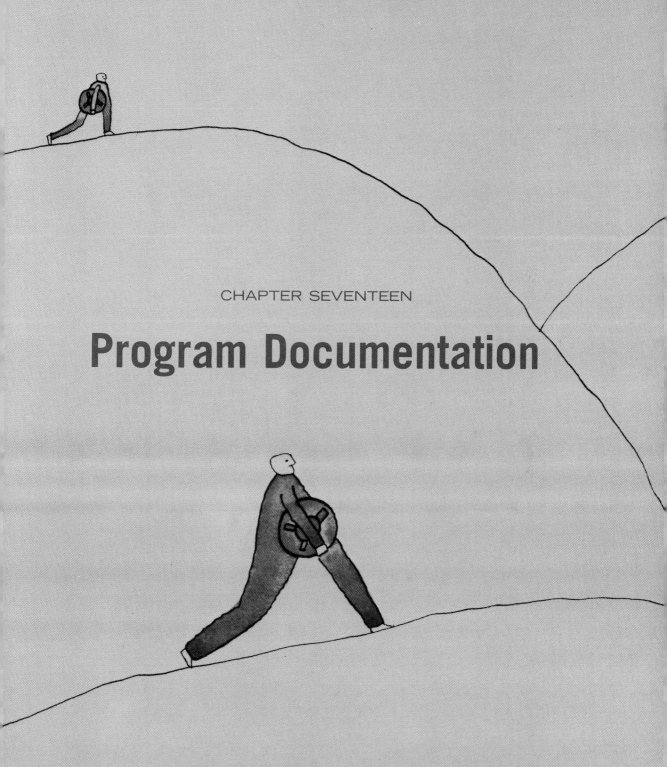

CHAPTER SEVENTEEN

Program Documentation

Programming tasks are complete only after the necessary documentation has been prepared. Although lip-service is paid to this final chore in a programming project, the time and effort allocated for documentation is seldom adequate. The design, coding, and debugging of a program are challenging to the skill of the programmer, but the deskbound job of writing a description of his or her activities which is something generally considered dull to perform. Thus, management must be alert to insist that adequate documentation be prepared before a program can be classified as operational.

DOCUMENTATION STANDARDS

In order to ensure adequate documentation for every programming task, management must establish standards for program documentation. These standards will vary for each installation, depending on the types of programs written, the programming languages employed, and the computer hardware and software available. Despite these differences, there are general guidelines for program documentation. Once the standards are determined at an installation, they must be rigorously enforced for all programming projects. The temptation to complete a programming project in a shorter time without providing the corresponding documentation is always present. But the omission of the documentation may have serious ramifications. The subsequent revision of a program without adequate documentation may cause the introduction of errors and lengthy delays. The conversion of a program to another computer requires a study of the program documentation. Without good documentation, conversion to another computer or the revision of the program may be an almost impossible task.

Documentation standards provide a checklist for the programmer and ensure that all the material needed will be furnished by the programming personnel. A standard format for documentation also facilitates a quick perusal of the information. Documents for production programs should be filed in a central location. For example, the flowchart and source-program listings produced by the compilation process for all programs of a particular department should be available and under the control of specific personnel at one location. If the number of production programs is sufficiently large, the employment of one or more technical writers to assist in the preparation of the documentation is an ideal arrangement. The person who has this job may also function as the program librarian who ensures that flowcharts and program listings as well as program descriptions (or *writeups*) are updated by the programmers after a program has been revised.

LEVELS OF DOCUMENTATION

There are many levels of documentation, all of which are necessary for a complete record of the program. Program documentation must meet the needs of all personnel connected with the program, from the manager, the problem poser, the programmer, and his associates, to the computer operator who must monitor the execution of the program. The various levels of documentation are discussed below.

RECORDS FOR COMMUNICATION In a large project that involves many programmers and personnel from other disciplines, the communication link between all individuals must be strong. A misunderstanding of any facet of the problem may cause endless difficulties in the later stages of the program. To ensure that information is being communicated accurately, documents giving a historical record of the planning phase are essential. They also enable management to check on the progress of the project at key points. Documentation of the entire programming project — the data, the problem posed, the chosen method of solution, and so on — may prevent disagreeable troubles later.

The standards required for a running historical record will depend on the complexity of the program and the number of personnel involved in the activity. Max Gray and Keith London (*Documentation Standards,* 1969) suggest the use of several forms to provide adequate information on the programming project from the planning stage to its completion. The feasibility of multiple documents is dependent on the particular installation. It is obvious that the entire problem must be stated from the viewpoint of the posers of the problem. The problem can be specified in a lengthy memorandum, in a report, or on a special form required by the data-processing department. As much detail as possible must be given. For example, documentation on the problem of producing payroll checks on the computer must include a description of how the payroll is presently prepared. Many times, existing methods are not sufficiently documented or clearly defined in an analytical fashion. In addition, the error-tolerance level must be stated and the time element (the scheduling of the task on the computer) must be considered. After a problem has been specified, management customarily imposes a schedule for the programming project. This schedule must give precise project-activity and completion dates. (The problem of estimating programming schedules is discussed in Chapter 21.) As requirements change, addendums to program documents must be written and circulated to all concerned personnel. In this way, a running commentary is provided by the initial statement of the problem and its subsequent revisions. If the problem to be solved is not communicated clearly to the programming staff, the resulting programming system will not satisfy the requirements of the posers. In addition to written communications, there must be conferences on the proposed programming project.

PROBLEM ANALYSIS The analysis of a problem for a program must be documented in order to create a record of how it has been solved. The terminology used is determined by the prob-

lem and should not be the jargon of the programmers. The formulas used for calculations and the numerical analysis of the task must be given for mathematical-type programs. For business programs, the flow of data and the way in which it is manipulated must be detailed. The inherent difficulties of the problem must be related and the proposed solutions stated.

After a problem has been precisely stated, it must be analyzed in terms of the computer. The method used to solve the problem (which may vary substantially from previous procedures) must be determined. For example, manual procedures for inventory control may be replaced by a real-time data-processing system. The entire system of handling and recording documents must be reviewed and a new system of documents and processing designed for the real-time system. The current data-processing system must be studied in detail to ensure that the new system will adequately perform all the tasks required. The format and the content of all input and output data files must be specified at this point in the project. The general flow of the programming system should be outlined by a block diagram. However, this diagram does not replace the detailed flowchart of the program which outlines

ENGLAND'S KIDNEY-MATCHING SERVICE

In Bristol, England, a computer-based kidney-matching service has topped the 1,000 mark. The service is operated for the National Tissue Typing Reference Laboratory by the South Western Regional Hospital Board.

The National Organ Matching and Distribution Service went into operation under the auspices of the Department of Health on February 1, 1972. It embraces 26 donor centers across the United Kingdom as well as three coordinating centers in Europe. It is involved in twice as many kidney transplants in proportion to population as are being done in the United States and handles at least 90 percent of all U.K. kidney transplants.

The service centralizes tissue-typing information on all patients awaiting kidney transplants at the participating centers and compares it with similar data on the donor. There is a severe shortage of donor kidneys, and the time between their availability and the transplant operation can be no more than 16 hours; ideally, it should be less than 10. Therefore, the service operates 24 hours a day, 365 days a year, with an on-call duty officer, computer operator, and tissue-typing serologist.

Because of the complexities of the matching process and the importance of speed, the service is feasible only with computer help. The key to the matching process lies in identifying antigens which, if present in the transplant and not in the host, would provoke the formation of antibodies in the host's blood, causing rejection of the kidney. These antigens are identified by blood sera known to contain specific antibodies. More than 100 blood sera are used nationally for reference purposes. The work of identifying them requires extensive computer support, as it involves comparisons of large matrices. The South Western Regional Hospital Board's computer center provides this support on a bureau basis, as well as running the matching programs immediately when a donor kidney becomes available. On the average this happens once or twice a day, but as many as eight matchings have been undertaken in a 24-hour period. Only 10 to 15 minutes elapse from the time the telephone rings in the computer center announcing an available donor to the time the duty operator calls the National Tissue Typing laboratory with the results of the computer run. The record time is four minutes.

The information provided by the computer lists the 10 best matches near the donor center, and also nationally (within the U.K.) and in Europe when necessary. It notes the quality of the match, the degree of urgency of need on the part of the waiting patient, the blood groups, and particular antibodies that have been identified. The National Tissue Typing laboratory chooses a recipient on the basis of this information, and then everything swings into action to get the kidney to the right place in time.

Adapted from "England's Kidney-Matching Service Tops the 1,000 Mark,"
Computers and People, February 1974, p. 38.

```
┌─────────────────────────────────────────────────────────────────────────┐
│                                        Date _____   │
│                                                                           │
│   File name _____ Program mnemonic_____    │
│                                                                           │
│   Storage medium _____     │
│                                                                           │
│   File ordered by _____                     │
│                                                                           │
│   Header label_____                     │
│                                                                           │
│   End-of-reel identification _____ End-of-file ID _____   │
│                                                                           │
│   Maximum record size_____ Fixed or variable_____    │
│                                                                           │
│   Records per block (maximum) _____ Maximum block size_____    │
│                                                                           │
└─────────────────────────────────────────────────────────────────────────┘
```

Figure 17–1
A File Documentation

the logic of the program. (See Chapter 16, Figure 16–4.)

The data-processing department may design special forms for this stage of documentation. A block diagram is useful in defining the overall characteristics of a programming system. The specification of the problem should be documented in a report or on a special form issued by the data-processing department. The data files to be used must be explicitly stated *before* a program is written. The data medium and the format to be used must be determined at this stage. Files and data records can be specified on forms similar to those in Figures 17–1 and 17–2. The term *position* must be defined for the installation; words, characters, or bytes may be used to delineate fields. Similarly, the unit for the record and block size must be defined as a word or byte. The programmer must complete the form for the record format by inserting the program mnemonics for each field. This enables another programmer to study the programming code with greater ease.

PROGRAM LOGIC Documentation must be given for the program logic to aid in subsequent revisions of the program. A typical program is modified several times during its lifetime. The original programmer may not be able to understand his own coding or make even a minor change without consulting the program documentation. This is especially true after a few months have elapsed since he last examined the coding. More frequently, the original programmer is no longer available. He has changed jobs or is preoccupied with another task. Thus another programmer must make corrections or revisions. Documentation of the program logic is also invaluable in converting an existing program for use on another computer.

Either a decision table or a flowchart must be prepared according to the standards given in Chapter 12. The ANSI flowchart symbols should be used in the preparation of the flowchart. All connectors should be clearly indicated. The flow of the logic should be from the top to the bottom of a page. Continuation to the next page should be clearly denoted. Any changes in the program logic during the coding stage should be reflected by changes in the flowchart. The detail given in the flowchart is dependent on the programming language. A program in a higher-level language does not require the same detail as an assembly-language program. In the case of an assembly-lan-

Date _____

File name _____ Record type (fixed or variable) _____ Maximum record size _____

Character Positions	Contents	Length	Data Type	Program Mnemonic

Figure 17–2
A Record Format

guage program, two flowcharts may be required; a general one giving the program logic and a more specific flowchart related to the actual program instructions. A flowchart for each subroutine in a program should also be provided.

A *storage map* is a useful device for the study of program coding. Such a map lists the names given to quantities in the analysis of the problem and the programmer-assigned names for these quantities. For example, the calculation of an individual paycheck may use the programmer-assigned name NETPAY for net pay, while the gross pay for the paycheck may be stored in a location with the programmer-assigned name GP. The form in Figure 17–2 provides space for the listing of programmer-assigned names for the contents of a file record. However, additional information for the cross-matching of names may be necessary to fully understand the program. Small amounts of input data used to control the running of the program are not listed on the data record form but should also be documented by the programmer; programmer-assigned names and the contents of the locations should be listed. Intermediate calculations and the names of storage locations should also be given by the storage map.

USER'S DOCUMENTATION The potential user of a program must be able to review the program writeup and determine what the program does, how it accomplishes its task, and how it can be used. All this information should be readily available, and the assistance of professional programmers should not be necessary to interpret the documentation. A program writeup is essential documentation for any program. It must provide sufficient information on such matters as how to prepare input data and how to use output listings. The format for program writeups should be standardized at each computer installation. A suggested format for writeups is given in Figure 17–3. The final program writeup should be reviewed with the user to ensure that it is both clear and complete.

TESTING PROCEDURES Testing procedures used to validate a program should be documented to answer any questions in the event of malfunctions. Any revision in the program may necessitate the running of all previous tests to ensure that no new error has been introduced. The record of tests is also useful for the testing of the program upon conversion to another computer.

Figure 17–3
A Format for a Program Writeup

I. An abstract of the problem.

This item should give a short description of the problem and its computer solution.

II. A description of the method of solution.

The method used to solve the problem should be stated in sufficient detail so that the potential user can determine if the method and program are suitable for the problem.

III. Program details.

This portion should provide the information needed for the preparation of input data and the interpretation of output data, as well as other information helpful in preparing for the execution of the program. It should be divided into several subsections, as follows:

a. Input data.

The input-data format and storage medium should be described here. The input-data files should be listed, with a description of their structure, the record format, and the storage medium. Format, storage medium, and data-preparation methods for even small amounts of input data should be described.

b. Output data.

The file structure, record format, and storage medium used for the output files produced by the program should be described here. The types of output listings provided by the program should also be described.

c. Intermediate output.

If the program produces any intermediate output files, the format and content of these files must be given.

d. Error conditions.

A discussion of the program's actions in error situations should be given here. For example, the handling of an erroneous input-data card should be described. A complete list of the situations treated as error situations is helpful to the user.

e. The operating procedure.

(1) Although this material is provided in a separate writeup for the operator, the user must know if the program uses standard procedures or requires special handling. Any program messages to the operator and possible operator responses to the messages should be detailed in this area.

(2) Any special control cards should be described here. Sample control cards should be listed to facilitate preparation of the cards.

f. A sample listing.

If possible, the program writeup should include samples of the program output. Several samples are desirable if the program has a variety of output options. If the samples are too bulky to fit in the writeup, suitable references should be made to the location of these output samples.

g. The running time.

It is helpful for the user to have a rough estimate of the running time. Any submission of the program for execution requires an estimate of the time required for execution. This estimate should be tied directly to the type of run performed—for example,

"This program executes in 10 minutes with an input of 1,500 employees on the personnel file."

IV. The programming language(s).

The source language used for the program should be specified. This information is significant when the program is submitted for execution. Also, the programming language used implies many features not explicitly stated in the program writeup.

V. The program listing.

The listing of the program in the source language (produced by the computer or assembler) should be filed and the location of the listing stated in the program writeup.

VI. The project personnel.

The personnel involved in the formulation of the problem and the program design should be listed. The programmers and analysts responsible for the implementation of the program should also be noted here.

A complete description of the tests used to validate a program should be given. The objectives of each test, the format and contents of the test data, and the results of the test run must be listed. A form for describing tests is shown in Figure 17–4. The output listings produced by the program tests should be attached to the description of each test run or filed in an appropriate location. The tests performed for each program should be summarized in a single document. Figure 17–5 illustrates such a summary.

OPERATING PROCEDURES Documentation must be provided so that operators can execute a program without assistance from the programmer. The information required will depend on the computer hardware and software used and also on the complexity of the program. An operator should be able to run the program without assistance from the programmer and handle any error situations by consulting the documentation. To facilitate the handling of programs by operators, standard operating procedures for both normal executions and error conditions should be established. Programs should not deviate from standard operating procedures without the special approval of the programming supervisor. The operator action required in the event of a program error or a failure by the input/output equipment such as an unrecoverable read error on tape should be covered by the standard operating procedures. An operator manual detailing the standard operating procedures should be prepared and placed on or near the computer console. The operating instructions for production programs should be included in this manual.

Figure 17–4
A Program Test Report

Program Test No._____

Program name_____   System_____

Test prepared by_____   Date_____
Purpose of test. (A brief description of the test—for example, "execute program with input data for all error paths"—is given in this space.)

Input files:

Additional input data:

Output files:

Output listings:

Program processing of test data:

Figure 17–5
A List of Program Tests

Program name_____ System_____
Prepared by_____ Date_____

Test 1. (A brief description of the test and its purpose is given in this space.)

Test 2.

Test 3.

Test 4.

Test 5.

Test 6.

Test 7.

Test 8.

Test 9.

Test 10.

Test 11.

Despite the differences between computers, certain guidelines can be listed for the operating-procedure writeup. The following items are required:

1. the program name, location, storage medium, and source language;
2. the loading procedure (if other than standard operating procedure);
3. the input-data files —
   the file name, storage medium, actual input device (if any), and program name for the device (if any);
4. other input data —
   the type of data, storage medium, physical location of the input device (if any), actual device (if necessary), and program name for device (if relevant);
5. output files —
   the file name, type of output device, specific device (if any), program name for device (if any), disposition of file, and external label to be placed on the file;
6. other output data —
   if cards are used, an estimate of the number of cards to be punched and directions for handling the cards;
   if printer listings are used, the type of paper (if special) and special instructions;
7. the initial console settings (if any);
8. the program messages and operator responses; and
9. the restart procedures, in the event of unrecoverable peripheral errors or abnormal terminations of the program.

"Herbert's been replaced by an electronic brain — one of the simpler types."

REFERENCES

Gray, Max, and London, Keith. *Documentation Standards.* Princeton: Brandon/Systems Press, 1969.

Magie, F. Stuart. "Documentation in a Financial Environment." *Software Age,* February 1969, pp. 32–39.

Ridge, Warren J., and Johnson, Leann E. *Effective Management of Computer Software.* Homewood, Ill.: Dow Jones-Irwin, 1973.

Rigo, Joseph T. "How to Prepare Functional Specifications." *Datamation,* May 1974, pp. 78–80.

Snyder, Robert G. "Programming Documentation." *Datamation,* October 1965, pp. 44–48.

QUESTIONS

1. Why is program documentation necessary?
2. Describe each type of documentation required for a programming system.
3. A program that produces the bills for customers of an electric company has been completed. Twenty-five tests were performed prior to its release as a production program. The program was written in COBOL. It is now necessary to modify the program because of an increase in the rates charged by the company. (a) What documentation items must be consulted? Why? (b) After the program has been successfully modified, what documentation must be changed?
4. Three programs composing a programming system have been written. Program A produces a master file A1 that is used as input to program B. Program B produces a master file A2 that is used by program C. The format of file A2 is directly related to the format of file A1. A change affecting file A1 is proposed. What documentation must be consulted? If no documentation was completed for program B, what difficulties may be encountered in altering programs A and C?

CHAPTER EIGHTEEN

Accessing the Computer

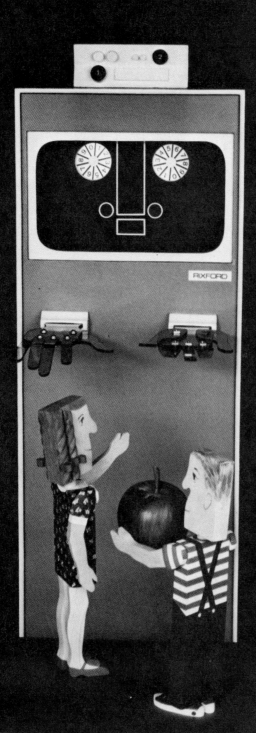

Using a computer to solve a problem means executing a program on the computer and printing or in some way transmitting its results to a location desired by the user. The three main ways of processing programs and data on the computer are: (1) conventional, or *batch,* processing, (2) real-time data processing, and (3) time-sharing. Real-time data-processing and time-sharing systems require the transmission of data to and from the computer, using communication lines and other special equipment. These systems are also called *teleprocessing systems.* The purpose of this chapter is to discuss the major ways of processing programs and data and the types of teleprocessing equipment now in use.

CONVENTIONAL PROCESSING SYSTEMS

In the early days of computers, there were no operating systems. The programmers were often the computer operators as well. They themselves pushed the buttons, observed the program run, and made corrections on the program at the computer console itself. There were no intermediaries between the programmers and the hardware; they interacted directly with the machine. They could observe the spin of the magnetic tapes, watch the lights flickering on the console, and intervene to restart their programs after an unexpected stop. (Even today, small computers and minicomputers are generally programmed and controlled by the same individuals, although these machines too may now be supplied with operating systems and other supporting software.)

Then operating systems were developed. It was too expensive and inefficient for humans to sit and fiddle with a computer. The computers, each valued at perhaps several million dollars, now were to be controlled by a program, and only highly trained personnel, called *operators,* were allowed to push buttons, mount tapes, and run programs. The programmers were no longer to work inside the computer room itself. They submitted their job, using a request form, and got their results without ever seeing the computer. They were allowed in the computer room only when trouble arose in connection with their programs; and, once there, no longer knew much about the situation as a whole. Computers were considered costly machines, programmers' time was deemed cheap, and operating systems and operators were introduced to ensure the most efficient use of the computer.

This conventional mode of operation is that which prevails today. Jobs are submitted by programmers, grouped, and executed on the computer. All the data for updating a file is grouped, or *batched,* and the file is updated periodically. Thus a file is only current at a given moment. It becomes out of date immediately after an updating run as soon as new data is received. Important files are usually updated every day, with new corrections held and processed the following day.

In the earliest operating systems, all compilations were performed together; after the compilations had been run, the programs to be executed were scheduled. This was the most efficient way of using the computer, since the compiler could be held in memory and executed repeatedly for the programs to be compiled. All the printed output would then be processed at one time. Programs would be scheduled for execution in the order considered to be the most efficient at the given computer center. This is called *batch processing*, since all jobs of a particular type are "batched" together.

After this mode of operation had been in use for some years, the development of larger computer systems combined with greater experience in software design led to the development of *compile-go systems.* These systems are now so common that they too are classed as batch-processing systems. In a compile-go system, a program is compiled and immediately executed, provided the compiled program has no fatal errors. The compiler may attempt to generate an appropriate object code in the event of minor compiler errors, and the program may be executed unless a programmer has specified that any type of error prohibits execution of the program. The

Figure 18–1
The Oldest Batch-Processing System

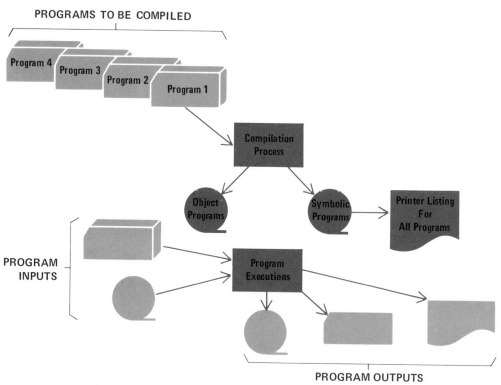

PROGRAMS TO BE COMPILED

Program 4
Program 3
Program 2
Program 1

Compilation Process

Object Programs

Symbolic Programs

Printer Listing For All Programs

PROGRAM INPUTS

Program Executions

PROGRAM OUTPUTS

operating schedule is then "compile program A, execute program A, compile program B, execute program B," and so on.

The next major software development was operating systems with multiprogramming capabilities. A conventional operating system executes only one program at a time. In a multiprogramming system, several programs may be executed simultaneously under the control of the operating system. A multiprogramming system became possible only because of a corresponding development in computer hardware. Computer hardware today usually permits the execution of instructions in conjunction with the transfer of data to or from an input-output device. More than one data transfer from an input-output device may be in progress at any given instant.

A typical multiprogramming system may operate as follows. It begins the execution of program A. Program A then requests the input of data from disk. The input of data from disk is initiated under the control of the operating system. While program A is waiting for its input data, the operating system begins the execution of program B. Program B executes instructions until it also requests data from an input device. Then the input for program B is initiated. Since program A

has not yet received its input data, program C is initiated. As program C is executing, the last item of input data for program A is received. Therefore, program C is interrupted and control is transferred to program A. Program A continues execution until it transfers data to an output device. Control is then yielded, and the operating system returns it to program B. This process continues until program A is terminated. As control is switched from program to program, a fourth program may enter the computer.

The number of programs controlled by an operating system at any given time is dependent on the availability of the core and peripheral equipment and the limitations of the operating system. If one program requires all the available core, then no other program can be executed along with it. This type of operating system relies on requests for the input and output of data and the completion of data transfers to switch control between programs. A chart showing the transfer of control between two programs is given in Figure 18–2.

The operating system is notified by a hardware interrupt that the transfer of input or output data to or from memory has been completed. An *interrupt* is a signal sent by a hardware

Figure 18–2
A Multiprogramming Operating System
under One Scheme

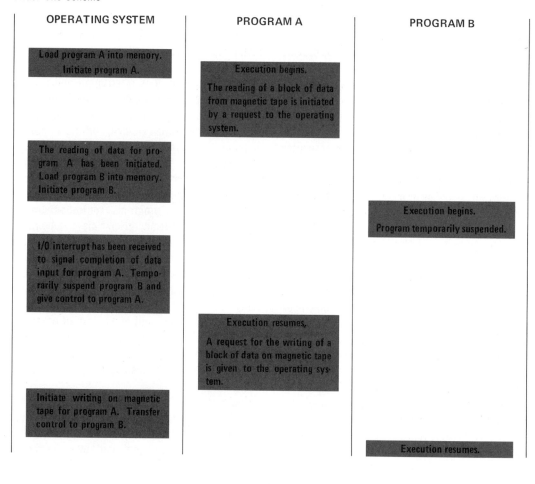

OPERATING SYSTEM	PROGRAM A	PROGRAM B
Load program A into memory. Initiate program A.	Execution begins. The reading of a block of data from magnetic tape is initiated by a request to the operating system.	
The reading of data for program A has been initiated. Load program B into memory. Initiate program B.		
		Execution begins. Program temporarily suspended.
I/O interrupt has been received to signal completion of data input for program A. Temporarily suspend program B and give control to program A.		
	Execution resumes. A request for the writing of a block of data on magnetic tape is given to the operating system.	
Initiate writing on magnetic tape for program A. Transfer control to program B.		
		Execution resumes.

device that interrupts the current program being executed and causes control to be transferred to a particular memory location. Since this location is under the control of the operating system, the transfer of control to the location directs the operating system to take appropriate action. In some multiprogramming operating systems, the programs under execution are continuously polled by the operating system. Each program is allowed a time slice of a fixed number of seconds, say, 10 seconds, after which control is transferred to the next program in the sequence.

In addition to the input/output interrupts that signal the completion of an input/output operation, a large-scale computer usually provides interrupts for certain types of program errors that can be detected by the hardware. These types of program errors are also known as *error conditions*. For example, if a program executes a divide operation with a divisor equal to zero, control is transferred to an assigned memory location. This location is under the control of the operating system, and thus the executing program can be terminated in an orderly fashion; another program execution will then be initiated by the operating system without causing any pause in the operation of the computer. Other

examples of conditions that cause error interrupts are described below:

1. The multiplication of two floating-point numbers whose product is greater than the largest number expressible by the computer creates an error condition called *overflow*. For example, 10^{50} times 10^{50} gives a product of 10^{100}, which is larger than the largest floating-point number possible for the IBM System/360 series of computers. Therefore, the attempt to execute the instruction to multiply 10^{50} times 10^{50} would cause an error interrupt.

2. Similarly, an arithmetic operation that results in a floating-point number too small to be represented in a memory location of the computer results in an error condition known as *underflow*. For example, 10^{-20} times 10^{-20} is 10^{-40}, which is too small a number to be represented in a memory location of the UNIVAC 1108.

3. If a program attempts to reference a location outside its allocated locations in the central memory, an *addressing error* occurs. An interrupt will cause the transfer of control to the operating system. Usually,

an error interrupt will occur only if the program has attempted to transfer data into a location outside its domain; the reading of a location (which does not cause the destruction of its contents) is generally ignored by the computer hardware and software. There are two types of addressing errors. The first is a request for a location outside the program's assigned memory locations but physically within the central memory. This is called a *memory-lockout* error and may occur with programs executing in a multiprogramming mode. The second is a request for a location address that is not physically available within the central memory. This occurs when a program has created a nonexistent address during its execution. Minicomputers may not provide hardware interrupts for all these types of program errors.

Multiprogramming means that more than one program is executed at a time. The term *multiprocessing* indicates that a computer has more than one central processing unit. A multiprocessing computer is always operated as a multiprogramming system. The processor units are operated concurrently. Thus the instructions of a program may be executed simultaneously with the instructions of another program.

TELEPROCESSING SYSTEMS

Data-transmission systems allow the transfer of data to a computer from a location remote from its physical site. The location may be only several hundred feet from the computer or several thousands miles across an ocean. This type of data transmission is known as *teleprocessing.* The computer, in turn, may send messages to the remote location. If data transmitted from another location is received directly by a computer, the communication link is called *on-line.* If the data is recorded on a storage medium such as magnetic tape, disk, punched cards, or paper tape and held for later processing by the computer, the communication link is termed *off-line.* On-line systems are further defined as (1) real-time data-processing systems or (2) time-sharing systems. The operation of on-line systems is discussed later in this chapter.

The transmission of data in a teleprocessing system is initiated either by a human operator stationed at a remote site or by the computer itself sending data to a remote site. Users of the system must enter their data at a data-entry device called a *terminal*. The data is then sent via telecommunication lines to the computer. The computer typically acknowledges its receipt of the data by sending a message back to the terminal. A computer may service many terminals, but each terminal requires its own telecommunication line. The physical characteristics of telecommunication lines and data-entry terminals are discussed below.

TERMINALS   Data is issued and received from a terminal linked to a computer via a telecommunication line. There are two types of terminals: intelligent and nonintelligent. An *intelligent terminal* is a minicomputer with a CPU and memory of its own. It may also have

peripheral devices such as a magnetic-tape unit, a disk drive, or other input/output equipment. An intelligent terminal provides the capability of editing and verifying data prior to transmitting it to the computer. An obvious error by a human operator can be detected by a minicomputer at a remote site, and an immediate correction can be made by the terminal user. A *nonintelligent terminal* is simply an input/output device. For example, a teletype has a keyboard for typing characters. Data can be sent or received. No prior editing at the remote site is possible. Any verification necessary must be performed by the computer receiving the data.

Data Displays   With both the intelligent and nonintelligent terminal, two basic types of data displays are possible. The first is via a device similar to a conventional typewriter. Data is

"Of course it's only the basic system."

Figure 18–3
A Teletype Terminal

transmitted by the depression of keys on the keyboard, and a hard copy of the information is produced. Output data is received on the device by the action of the keyboard, which again produces hard copy. One such device is the teletype shown in Figure 18–3. Data may also be displayed via a video-display device like that in Figure 18–4. This device also has a keyboard; but, instead of a paper roller and keys, it has a video-display tube resembling a television picture tube. The data to be transmitted is customarily displayed on the picture tube. The output data received is also pictured. If the data to be displayed exceeds the space available, the picture must be moved upward and the display changed so that all the data can be shown. A video-display device may be capable of displaying only alphanumeric characters; however, some devices also have graphic-display capabilities. Figure 18–5 shows pictures produced on such video-display devices.

The advantage of a video-display device as compared with a hard-copy device is its speed of transmission. The production of hard copy requires the mechanical reproduction of characters. The speed of mechanical reproduction is relatively slow—at most, 15.5 characters per

second. Since 2,560 characters per second can be produced on a video-display device, the popularity of the video device is most understandable.

Another data-transmission device is the touch-tone telephone. By depressing the numeric keys, the user can transmit data to a computer. Because only numeric data can be sent in this way, the device has a limited appeal. The computer may return messages to the user by means of audio-response devices. The transmission of audio messages directly from the user to the computer is still under development.

Batch Processing via Terminals   Another way of providing a connection to a computer is to use terminals for batch processing. For example, a combination card-reader and line-printer unit may be connected to a computer via a phone line, as shown in Figure 18–7. Whenever data must be transmitted, it is first punched on cards; then the card deck is placed in the card reader. The user dials the computer's phone number and the transmission of data is initiated. Hard-copy output data is produced by the line printer. The data-transmission rate is increased since it is no longer dependent on the manual depressing of the keys on the keyboard. The data may be col-

Figure 18–4
A Video-Display Device for Alphanumeric Data

Figure 18–5
Graphic Displays on CRT Terminals

Figure 18–7
A Batch-Processing Terminal — Line Printer and Card Reader Device

Figure 18–6
A Touchtone Telephone

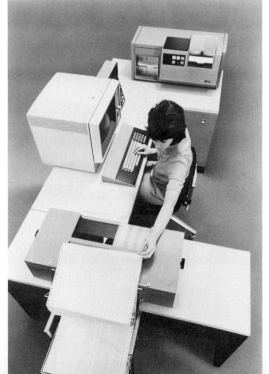

Figure 18–8
Analog and Digital Signals

lected in batches and then transmitted, if this is desired. No immediate response is required, since there is no one sitting at a keyboard awaiting a reply. This is a specialized form of the conventional batch-processing system.

COMMUNICATION LINES   In order to transmit data from a remote site to or from a computer, there must be a communication line (sometimes called a *telecommunication* line) to the computer. Often, an ordinary telephone line is used. A telephone is used to dial the computer and, after the connection has been made, the same instrument is used to send the data. Telephone lines are relatively inexpensive, reasonably reliable, sufficiently fast, and consequently a popular choice. Alternatives are telegraph lines, a share of a microwave circuit, or a share of a coaxial cable. A private telecommunication line may be obtained to reduce the number of errors in data transmission.

Analog vs. Digital Transmissions   Computers are digital devices, but most telecommunication lines transmit analog signals. All telephone lines, except those constructed most recently, transmit a continuous range of frequencies. This type of transmission is called *analog transmission.*

Digital transmission means that data is encoded as "ON" or "OFF" pulses that represent "1" and "0" and are interpreted as bits by the computer. Today the design of any communication facility for data transmission would automatically specify digital transmission. Because most telecommunication lines are still analog, a special device to convert digital data to analog signals and vice versa must be used; this device is called a *modem* or a *data set.*

Modems   A common example of a modem is the Dataphone. (See Figure 18–9.) The Dataphone is a telephone set that can be used to dial a computer. It converts the digital data leaving the computer into a range of frequencies suitable for transmission via an analog telecommunication line. At the receiving end, another modem converts the analog signal back to digital representation. The data set and the communication line must be coordinated; that is, every data set cannot be operated on every communication line. For example, modems designed for private voice lines cannot be used on public lines. The North American public network requires modems that are not suitable for use in other countries.

A modem for public lines must not interfere

Figure 18-9
A Dataphone

with the frequencies used by the network itself for signaling. On a private line, the modem has the entire band width and thus does not have to avoid the use of certain frequencies. The modem and communication line together determine the speed of data transmission.

Types of Lines   Telecommunication lines are categorized as simplex, half-duplex, and full-duplex. With *simplex lines,* data is transmitted in only one direction. With *half-duplex lines,* data is transmitted in only one direction at a given time but may be transmitted in either direction. With *duplex*, or *full-duplex lines*, data can be transmitted in both directions at the same time.

When a half-duplex line is used, there is delay when the direction of transmission is reversed. This delay is called *line-turnaround time.* Public telephone lines are half-duplex in operation. However, leased telephone lines provide the user with a choice of either half-duplex or full-duplex systems. Simplex lines are not generally used for data transmission, since no signal acknowledging receipt of the data can be sent; nor can the receiving machine signal its readiness to receive data. Currently, half-duplex lines are most common.

Line Speeds   There are three levels of speed for data-transmission lines.

- *Subvoice-grade lines* are slower than telephone lines. The rate of transmission ranges from 45 to 180 bits per second.
- *Voice-grade lines* are telephone lines commonly used to transmit voice messages. The usual rate is 600 or 1,200 bits per second. The use of ultra-high-speed modems will increase this rate as high as 10,500 bits per second. More commonly, modems yield an increased speed of 1,200 to 4,800 bits per second.
- *Wide-band lines* are faster than telephone lines. Another name for these lines is *broad band.* Typical transmission rates are 19,200, 40,800, and 50,000 bits per second. A rate of up to 500,000 bits per second, though possible, is not common. Even higher rates may be used.

Rates of transmission are measured in bauds. *Bauds* are the number of times the condition of a line changes per second. If a line's condition indicates the presence or absence of a bit, a baud is equivalent to the number of bits per

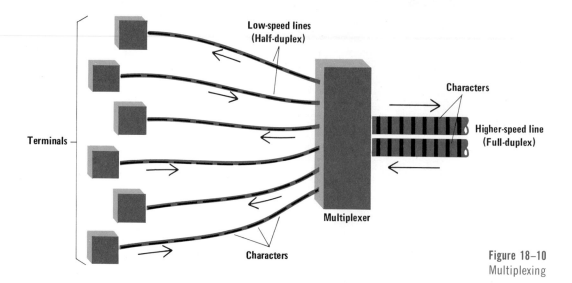

Low-speed lines
(Half-duplex)

Characters

Higher-speed line
(Full-duplex)

Terminals

Multiplexer

Characters

Figure 18–10
Multiplexing

second. However, a signal can be coded into more than two states — say, into eight possible states; thus, one line condition would indicate the presence of three bits. In this case, a baud would equal three bits per second. Because in the past bauds have been confused with bits per second, we have chosen to quote speeds in bits per second rather than in bauds.

Multiplexers Data transmitted from a terminal is usually sent at a speed considerably slower than that of the telecommunication line. A user may have several terminals, all of which transmit and receive data at less than the maximum rate of transmission on each line. To achieve greater efficiency, the smaller data streams can be joined to form a larger data stream using a higher-speed communication line. For example, several half-duplex lines operating at 75 bits per second can be linked to a device called a *multiplexer*. The multiplexer receives the data from each low-speed line and sends it on the high-speed line to the computer. It also receives data from the computer to be transmitted along an appropriate low-speed line to the terminal. A typical multiplexer may control 24 lines of 150 bits per second in this fashion. With multiplexing, *all* terminals may transmit *all* the time.

Multidrop Lines Another way of controlling several low-speed terminals is to use only one line. Only one message travels on the line at a time to avoid confusion. To send a message to a particular terminal, a special character preceding the message is used to identify the terminal to receive the message. The other terminals ignore the message. Such a line is called a *multidrop* line, since it "drops" the data at a particular terminal. (See Figure 18–11.)

Concentrators A third method of handling low-speed data transmission from several terminals is by the use of a concentrator. If the terminals are used by human operators, each character will be followed by a brief pause of perhaps three seconds; the user cannot react as fast as the communication line. Because of these intermittent delays, a concentrator is used to take data from the terminals and send the characters, intermixed, down a higher-speed line to the computer. The terminal that emitted each group of data must be identified. Similarly, data sent to the concentrator for dispersion to the terminals must indicate which terminal is to receive the data. (See Figure 18–12.)

SYNCHRONOUS VS. ASYNCHRONOUS TRANSMISSIONS Data transmission is

Figure 18–11
A Multidrop Line

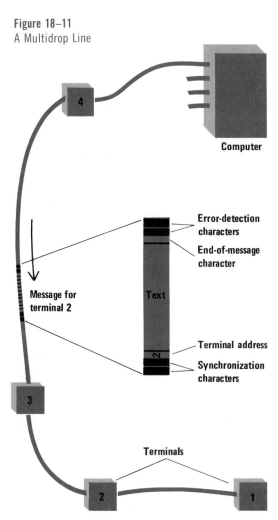

Computer

Error-detection characters

End-of-message character

Text

Message for terminal 2

Terminal address

Synchronization characters

Terminals

either synchronous or asynchronous. *Synchronous transmission* means that a block of data is sent continuously, without pause. For example, a group of 100 characters may be sent at a time, and for the duration of the data transmission the transmitting and receiving terminals must be in phase, that is, synchronized with each other. Synchronous transmission is the most efficient way of utilizing a communication line. There are no pauses between the bits in the block being transmitted.

The transmitting and receiving machines on many synchronous systems are controlled by oscillators, which must be brought exactly into phase with each other before data can be transmitted. Thus data sent via synchronous transmission must always begin with a *synchronization pattern* or *synchronization characters* to signal that synchronization must begin. The oscillators must remain in phase with each other throughout the transmission of the data. To check that synchronization is being maintained, synchronization characters may be sent by the transmitting machine every few seconds. The receiving machine is constantly looking for the appearance of the synchronization characters to ensure that the transmitter and receiver are in phase.

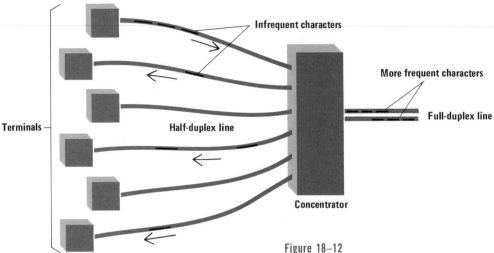

Terminals

Infrequent characters

Half-duplex line

More frequent characters

Full-duplex line

Concentrator

Figure 18–12
A Concentrator Taking Advantage of the Infrequent Character Transmissions from Terminals

Asynchronous transmission means sending one character at a time. Each character of data is preceded by a "start" signal and followed by a "stop" signal. There can be indefinite time gaps between the sending of characters. Between the transmission of characters, the receiving machine is in the "stop" mode. This type of transmission is also known as *start-stop transmission.* Machines for asynchronous transmission are less expensive to produce. Consequently, asynchronous transmission may be used even for terminals that transmit large quantities of data at a given time. For example, a card reader transmitting data to a computer does not have the stops between characters that a keyboard terminal does. However, the asynchronous mode may be used simply to reduce costs.

DATA-TRANSMISSION ERRORS Errors in data transmission can occur when data is sent over telecommunication lines. A bit can be changed from 0 to 1 and vice versa because of *noise* on the lines. In addition to the constant background noise, there are occasional sharp-noise impulses. Consequently, the error rate and ways to handle data errors must be carefully considered in teleprocessing system designs.

A typical error rate is one bit in 100,000 on a good-quality telephone line with conservative modems. When the modems are designed to maximize the data-transmission rate, smaller variations in signal condition are used and thus the signals are more prone to misinterpretation. The error rate then increases.

When communication lines especially designed for data transmission are used, a lower error rate is possible; one error in 10 million bits or 100 million bits is more typical. However, because most telecommunication lines were not designed for data transmission, the higher error rate must be considered and treated.

There are various ways of handling data errors. Data-checking codes may be transmitted periodically along with the data. Such codes are called *error-detecting codes.* The system used to encode characters may contain self-checking features. Another common way of checking for errors is to send all data received back to the sender. The sending device checks to see if the bits returned are correct. This method is called *loop* or *echo check.* After a data error has been detected, it is advisable to provide an automatic means of retransmitting the data rather than having it rekeyed by the terminal operator.

REAL-TIME DATA PROCESSING

The development of real-time data processing stemmed from the need of the airline industry to have fast access to up-to-date information at locations remote from the central location of the data. The airlines both required and had the resources to develop a real-time data system, and now many other industries are involved in real-time data processing. The realization of the full potential of this type of processing is still to come; someday all conventional data-handling systems may be replaced by real-time systems. The real-time data system has a basic point of difference from the conventional system of data processing. The data is transmitted directly from its point of origin to the computer, and results are sent directly to the location where they are required. No intermediate data-preparation or data-transmittal steps are necessary.

UPDATING A FILE ON A REAL-TIME DATA SYSTEM
To illustrate the differences between a conventional data-processing system and a real-time system, let us consider the differences in the updating of a master file. In a con-

ventional system, the transactions used to update the file are collected for a computer run of the updating program. The updating run may be performed at fixed intervals, perhaps even as often as once a day for a file that requires frequent updating. However, the transactions for the file must be recorded in some fashion and then converted to a computerized medium such as punched cards. The punched cards and the current master file are submitted as input to the updating program. The resultant master file then becomes the current master file. Once the updating run has been made, any new correction to the master file must be held for the next run. In fact, prior to the run, there is a cut-off time when no further transactions can be accepted for that run because of the need to convert the updating information to computerized form. The file can only be current with respect to an agreed-upon time. Therefore, it is not absolutely up-to-date.

In a real-time data system, on the other hand, a correction or addition to the file is received by phone and a clerk immediately sits down at a terminal and keys in the necessary information. The data is transmitted to the computer, and the appropriate program is activated. The master file is updated and becomes current as of that moment. No intermediate preparation of data is necessary. The accuracy of the data is verified by the computer program. As many as possible validation checks are made. Self-checking control numbers are used to ensure accuracy in the keying of the data by the terminal operator. The receipt of the data by the computer is acknowledged by a message sent to the terminal. The next interrogation of the file will produce a response based on the inclusion of this latest transaction in the file. There is no delay in the insertion of information in the master file.

AIRLINE RESERVATION SYSTEM   The chief ancestor of all real-time systems is the airline reservation system. The airline industry has the problem of maintaining current records regarding passengers on flights. If a flight is full rather than half-full an airline may increase its profit tremendously, since a half-load of passengers requires almost as much money to transport as a full load. The airlines have a perishable inventory. Once a flight has been made, the empty seats on it can no longer be sold. They are lost forever as a means of revenue. The airlines, faced with the problem of storing and retrieving pas-

senger information, turned to the computer for a solution. One of the oldest airline reservation systems is the American Airlines Sabre system. Today all major airlines have a computer reservation system or are planning to install one.

Consider the problem of manually booking a passenger on a particular flight. Mr. Smith is in Chicago and wishes to fly to Washington, D.C., on Friday. The reservations agent at the airline must make a phone call to the central data location to inquire if a seat is available. If the reply is yes, Mr. Smith then books his seat on the flight he desires. However, on Thursday, Mr. Smith decides that he will not fly on Friday evening. He would prefer to go on Friday morning. Again the agent must call, this time to cancel the seat originally reserved and book another on the required flight. In the last 24 hours before a flight, a number of cancellations and reservations are received for each flight. A tremendous amount of clerical detail must be handled. In the past, for overseas flights, it was necessary to wait up to a week for space to be confirmed. It was not possible to confirm a reservation for a flight just prior to take-off that day. Popular flights were overbooked, since cancellations were expected. Passengers could arrive and find that no seats

Figure 18–13
An Airline Reservation Terminal with Display

were available, because of overbooking. Disgruntled customers were a frequent result of this practice. Alternatively, the cut-off of reservation bookings prior to the flight resulted in empty seats on flights that could have been full. This meant a loss of revenue to the airlines. As the volume of passengers and the number of flights increased, the airlines were confronted with a data-processing problem of great magnitude. The solution was real-time data processing.

An airline reservation system functions with hundreds of terminals located at different sites all over the country (or the world, in the case of an overseas airline). The terminals may be conventional hard-copy keyboard devices or video-display terminals or special terminals designed for use with a reservation system. Each request for a flight reservation can be handled accurately in a matter of seconds. A prospective customer calls the airline office and requests information on a flight. After he has selected a flight, his reservation is quickly confirmed and any special details (e.g., any dietary restrictions, or a request for a car rental at the destination airport) are noted. A typical airline seat is sold and cancelled two or more times before the flight takes place. The airline has a centralized computer system with all terminals hooked directly to the computer. Information is transmitted quickly, and data is retrieved in a matter of seconds from a flight passenger's file. Since information may be misfiled, the passengers are located by name.

Once computer systems were established, the airlines found many other uses for them. Weather data, the scheduling of flight crews for planes, requests for special menus, V.I.P. treatment for important passengers, and so on could all be handled on the computer. The expense of a real-time data system was justified by increases in revenue due to increases in the number of passengers per flight. Today, no major airline can be competitive without an automatic passenger-reservation system. A passenger now expects a quick response to his inquiry regarding flights; he wants his reservation to be verified quickly, and bumping passengers from flights is no longer acceptable.

INTEGRATED DATA SYSTEMS   An integrated data system is often proposed whenever a real-time data system is to be implemented. An *integrated system* is achieved by the reduction of company data files to a set of files in which there is no duplication of data. This reduces the number of files to be searched when data is needed and hence the computer time spent to locate information. It also reduces the number of data-storage units needed. In an integrated system, all departments of a company reference the same set of files. The responsibility for updating a file may be divided between departments if the data for updates is received at various company locations.

In conjunction with integrated files, a *management-information system* may be proposed. By this we mean a system that gives management quick access to data in a summary form. For example, the management of a firm may wish to obtain a sales forecast for the following month. In order to do so, it must know the current sales figures, the previous sales figures for the month in question, and other pertinent data. The sales manager uses a remote terminal to send an inquiry to the company computer. Within a brief time, the appropriate figures are returned to the terminal. This type of summary information is valuable only when the files used to summarize the information are up to date. Management has discovered the advantages of current information, having worked with obsolete data in the past. Now decisions with regard to the production and

stocking of goods, and similar matters, can be based on current information. Remote terminals for interrogation of the files assist the various department heads to seek and obtain responses directly from the computer.

CHARACTERISTICS OF REAL-TIME DATA SYSTEMS   A system that is classified as real-time has certain well-defined characteristics, and it offers features not found in a conventional system. *First,* it offers the man-machine interaction that disappeared from the computer scene with the advent of sophisticated operating systems. By using terminals, programmers or clerks may interact directly with the computer. No other person must serve as an intermediary in order for them to access the computer. For example, an airline reservations agent can interrogate the company computer and receive a response without the assistance of any computer personnel. *Second,* the response time of the computer can be specified within certain limits. It is difficult to state precisely these limits, for they depend upon the application. A response time of three seconds or less is desirable. Any longer wait on the part of a human operator causes him to become impatient. A response time of five minutes may be deemed adequate if the return of information is not critical. However, the response time must be sufficiently brief so that the response directly affects the environment. For example, the response of a computer to questions about available flights allows a prospective passenger to select his flight. If the response time is too long, the passenger may hang up and call another airline. *Third,* different persons in different locations may use the same computer. The computer can respond to many inquiries, answering them all promptly.

A real-time data system requires certain hardware and software to function. The hardware selected should be expandable because the use of the system may increase over time. The software must be able to handle a variety of inquiries. The steps in the man-machine interaction must be simple and intelligible to all users. A complex scheme for addressing the computer would only defeat the purpose of providing direct access to the data files.

PRO'S AND CON'S OF REAL-TIME DATA SYSTEMS The prime advantage of a real-time data system is that it provides immedi-

ate access to current files. This means the difference between profit and loss for airlines, and also for companies making decisions on production schedules, inventory controls, and so on. The benefits of real-time data processing are more difficult to measure in terms of dollars and cents unless detailed studies are made of the cost of the system replaced by the real-time system, the cost of the real-time system, and the benefits gained because of the real-time system. Intangible advantages are quickly discernible, but more difficult to measure. A real-time system provides direct control of data. Moreover, data is handled only once, and not several times. Thus the frequency of data errors in the files is reduced. Up-to-date information means better control of company functions.

The disadvantages of real-time systems are all cost-related. It is more expensive to install the hardware and software for a real-time data-processing system. The development of software is very expensive and requires a large amount of time. The bugs in the system may be tiresome and frustrating to overcome. The software programmers and the company supplying the data-transmission equipment must work together to produce an effective real-time data system.

MARVEL OF THE BRONX

The 29 fourth-graders in Room 317 at P.S. 106 in the Bronx are pretty much in agreement about their assistant teacher, Leachim. They all think he is very smart and has a remarkable memory for their individual habits, failings, and hobbies. They like most of his jokes and the way he sings, "even though he has a bad voice," and they have learned to put up with his occasional cross moods. Most important of all, the children think of Leachim as their friend, as well as a good teacher. All of which is quite an achievement for a robot with an oaken body and head, a meter-like mouth and blue light-bulb ears.

Leachim was created for teacher Gail Freeman by her husband Michael after she complained repeatedly about the time she had to spend with her students on drill and review. A doctoral candidate and professor of management sciences at Bernard Baruch College, Michael spent 18 months and $1,000 to design, build, and program Leachim (Michael spelled backward, more or less), a 5 foot, 5 inch, 200 pound humanoid with black plastic arms and legs. Although his legs are motorized, he is chained and bolted to a table for security. The robot's brain is a computer, made partly from components cannibalized from an RCA Spectra 70. Plugged in and turned on, he can lecture to the entire class. He can also recognize students by their voices and, in his own peevish-sounding tones, can simultaneously question five different students wearing earphones and take their pushbutton replies.

Leachim's brain is packed with a fund of information that includes the contents of Compton's *Encyclopaedia,* Webster's *New World Dictionary*, a Ginn science book, a thesaurus, and a Macmillan reading series. He has also been programmed with biographical information on the 29 students, including their reading levels, math scores, and hobbies. As he works with the students, Leachim keeps track of their progress and changing scores, sometimes asking extra questions of the faster learners and drilling slower ones on older material. After about six months, he will have to be reprogrammed to keep up with the class.

Last week Leachim addressed Lisa Ilario, 9, as she sat down in front of him and put on her earphones. "My name is Leachim," said the robot. "You are doing Segment 10. Try to follow my directions carefully. If a classmate drops a pin on the floor, what would you pick it up with? Answer A: a screwdriver. Answer B: pliers. Answer C: a wrench." Lisa punched button B on Leachim's chest. "You are correct," said the robot. "Pliers will help you lift and squeeze things." "He's very polite," says Lisa. "He says 'thank you' and 'please.'"

After sports fan Warner Brown, 10, correctly selected from a list that lit up on Leachim's visual panel the word barometer as the one associated with weather forecasting, the robot rewarded him with brief observations about New York basketball and football teams. "You did very well," Leachim added. "I hope you enjoyed working with me. I like Joe Namath. I'm sure you do too." But if pupils take too long to answer, Warner explains, "Leachim says, 'You are not listening. Choose an answer now.' If you still don't, he'll say, 'I'm getting annoyed.'" Leachim's repertory includes the national anthem, the pledge of allegiance (during which he stops and asks what "indivisible" means), the fable of the boy who cried "Wolf!", a few words of Spanish, and a joke: "You are thinking so hard I can see smoke coming out of your ears."

Both Leachim's humor and his moments of testiness are deliberate. "He is geared to Gail's understanding of the children's tolerance levels at this age and what should be expected of them," says Michael. The robot's ultimate gesture of impatience is one many teachers would envy: He just turns himself off.

Adapted from "Marvel of the Bronx," *Time*, April 1, 1974, p. 48. Reprinted by permission from TIME, The Weekly Newsmagazine; © TIME Inc.

Companies without sufficient computer experience may find themselves caught in a morass of software that is both late and ineffective. The difficulty of developing good real-time software means that experienced and competent programming personnel are an absolute necessity in creating a workable and desirable system. The cost factor may be small compared to the tangible advantages such as increased profits or the intangible advantages such as speedy transactions and data records under up-to-date control. The elimination of the need to transcribe data to another medium may actually reduce costs, since one or more data steps will have been eliminated. However, the traditional view is that real-time hardware and software are more expensive than conventional systems.

TIME-SHARING

In a *time-sharing system,* many users at remote terminals have access to a central computer and a specific group of programs. Time-sharing includes real-time data processing as well as the use of the computer for conversational programming and computer-assisted in-struction. All forms of time-sharing call for the interaction of the user with a computer by means of a terminal. The user sends information to the computer, and the computer responds in a matter of seconds. The dialogue between the individual and the computer continues until the task is completed. In the case of real-time data processing, the user is always busy interrogating or updating files. In conversational programming, the user writes a program at the terminal, corrects it, and tests it by directly interacting with the computer. In computer-assisted instruction, the computer "teaches" the user by sending material to the terminal that requires constant interaction between the user and the computer.

Special computer hardware and software are required for a computer to function as a time-sharing system. The computer must have sufficient core storage to accommodate a large, sophisticated operating system and many programs at the same time. The hardware must be capable of interacting with many terminals so that the input-output devices function with apparent simultaneity. Today this type of sophisticated hardware is common. The software for a time-sharing system is complex and must be thoroughly checked prior to production use. The system must be able to poll many terminals continuously. A computer may be used as a *dedicated system* and execute time-sharing programs only. However, most computers run programs in a batch mode and also handle the processing of several terminals. The batch-mode jobs are said to be executed in the background of the time-sharing activity (called the *foreground jobs*). The foreground programs have priority over jobs run in the background. Thus users of the time-sharing system are guaranteed a quick response by the computer.

CONVERSATIONAL PROGRAMMING

In the early years of computers, programs were debugged by the programmer, who sat at the console and interacted directly with the computer. When his program stopped, he could sit and find the error and insert new coding into the program at the console. Only if an error were elusive and time-consuming to detect did the programmer retire to his desk to track it down. The computer was used as a tool in debugging directly. With the arrival of operating systems and in the belief that the computer time was a good deal more expensive than the programmer's time, the programmer began writing and debugging the computer at a desk distant from the computer. Now we are in a third era, that of time-sharing. One feature of a time-sharing system is that it gives users the opportunity to write and debug programs at a remote terminal. This mode is called *conversational programming.*

In conventional programming, the programmer prepares the coding at a desk. Next, the coding is transferred to some computerized medium such as punched cards and submitted for compilation and execution. The job is returned to the programmer by the computer-center personnel; errors are corrected and the job resubmitted. This cycle continues until the program has been thoroughly checked.

In conversational programming, the programmer prepares his coding by typing it directly on the keyboard at a remote terminal. As the coding is entered, any error in the programming language is detected and displayed to the programmer. He can then immediately correct his error. After the programmer has completed his coding, the program is compiled. Any further errors detected by this process can be displayed on the terminal and promptly corrected by the programmer. The programmer can then request execution of the program and supply test data directly on the terminal. The program is executed, and the results are immediately available to the programmer. He can correct any programming errors and execute the program once again.

This system of programming presents tremendous advantages for the one-shot programs written by engineers or other technical personnel. Such people want a response promptly; they generally have short programs to write, and they do not wish to learn complicated programming terminology. The elimination of the middleman, the programmer, means that methodology can be determined directly by the poser of a problem. Without tying up the entire computer, the poser can sit and think at the keyboard of the terminal, free to create the program and correct it as the design progresses. After the program has been written, the results can be checked and a final run made. The burden of submitting programs to the computer center, the time spent waiting for the completion of a run, and finally the resubmission of the program to the computer center— all these have been eliminated. One of the first conversational programming systems was JOSS, used at the Rand Corporation. Engineers would stay after hours to use JOSS at the time it was scheduled to be available on the computer. An-

other well-known system is the BASIC programming language used at Dartmouth College; its language is discussed in Appendix I. Conversational programming is quite popular at colleges and universities. An example of a program for a conversational programming system is shown in Figure 18–14.

The advantages of conversational programming are quick responses and the elimination of turnaround time. However, for large programming jobs, it is clearly less efficient to sit down at the console or terminal and write a program. The amount of time devoted to program design, flowcharting, and good coding is significant for a large production job that will be used frequently. For short, one-shot applications that do not require involved coding, conversational programming systems are more convenient and less frustrating. Time-sharing and conversational programming systems are expected to continue to gain in popularity with reductions in the cost of terminals and the other computer hardware necessary for a successful system.

COMPUTER-ASSISTED INSTRUCTION
Another application of time-sharing is educational computing, or *computer-assisted in-*

Figure 18–14
An Example of a Conversational Programming Language Program

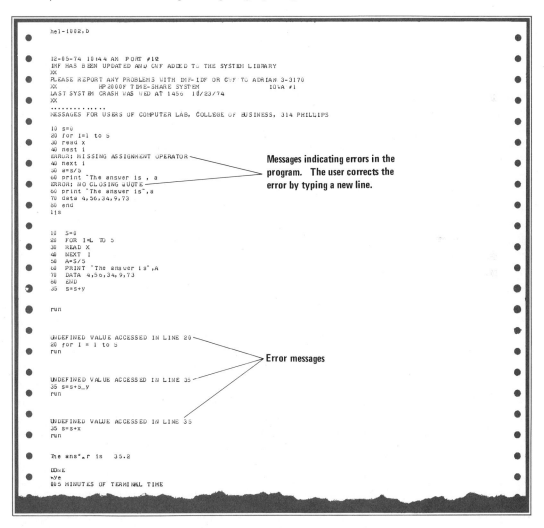

Figure 18–15
A Child at a CAI Terminal

struction (CAI). Today there are classrooms where each student is seated at a desk which also contains a terminal with a large display screen and a keyboard. Each pupil is working at his own pace—either learning a new lesson or being drilled on the previous lesson. Some students may be testing their knowledge, using tests administered by the computer. The computer responds rapidly to the demands of the students and also keeps a running tally of each pupil's performance. It may also have the ability to project slides requested by the CAI program. The teacher is free to plan a special lesson or assist the students who are not doing well according to their computer test scores.

A major problem encountered with CAI is the difficulty in producing imaginative lessons. The student selects a lesson and answers questions given on the terminal. If he answers incorrectly, the program attempts to teach him and lead him to the right answer. If this effort is unsuccessful, the program may reverse itself and begin to review previous material. Thus the student is able to proceed at his own pace without competition from other students.

Imaginative programming can result in good CAI programs. However, many CAI programs may be dull and hold no interest for the brighter student. The computer excels as an untiring teacher that can repeat question after question without exasperation. But the entire CAI program must be designed to stimulate the student. An example of how a student interacts with a CAI program is shown in Figure 18–16.

The advantages of CAI are readily apparent. Lessons can be drilled endlessly. It offers individualized instruction to each student. The disadvantages are the need for well-prepared CAI lessons. The questions asked of the student, and the replies, must be carefully thought out. The time needed to prepare CAI programs varies, but it is estimated to be considerably more than the time needed to write conventional lessons. CAI lessons must be use-tested and revised frequently to update the material and sustain the interest of the users. Terminals and computer hardware are still expensive when compared with the cost of conventional teachers. However, the anticipated development of cheap terminals and the creation of many CAI lessons to be distributed throughout the country may hasten the day of CAI in the classrooms of the nation. Judicious use of CAI may lead to better teaching and better-educated students.

Figure 18–16
Interaction with a CAI Program

COMPUTER:	YOU ARE A MANAGEMENT CONSULTANT CALLED IN TO ADVISE A TOY COMPANY ON A PROPOSAL TO CHANGE THEIR SCHEDULE OF PRODUCTION. IN THE PAST THE COMPANY'S PRODUCTION SCHEDULE HAS BEEN SEASONAL, REFLECTING THE HIGHLY SEASONAL PATTERN OF SALES. THE COMPANY IS CURRENTLY CONSIDERING THE ADVANTAGES AND RISKS INVOLVED IN A POSSIBLE SHIFT TO A LEVEL SCHEDULE OF PRODUCTION OVER THE YEAR. YOUR JUDGMENT IS BEING SOUGHT. ASK FOR THE INFORMATION YOU WANT BY TYPING IN ITEMS FROM THE VOCABULARY YOU HAVE BEEN GIVEN. . . .BEGIN YOUR INVESTIGATION AS SOON AS YOU ARE READY.
STUDENT:	MACHINE MAINTENANCE COSTS?
COMPUTER:	THE ESTIMATED MACHINE MAINTENANCE COSTS ARE $23,000 FOR SEASONAL PRODUCTION AND $10,000 FOR LEVEL PRODUCTION. . . .
STUDENT:	PRO FORMA INCOME STATEMENT?
COMPUTER:	YOU HAVEN'T GOT ALL OF THE DATA NEEDED TO MAKE UP THE PRO FORMA INCOME STATEMENT. YOU DON'T KNOW THE COST OF GOODS SOLD.
STUDENT:	COST OF GOODS SOLD?
COMPUTER:	THE COST OF GOODS IS 60% OF LAST YEAR'S SALES.
STUDENT:	PRODUCTION VOLUME?
COMPUTER:	THE PROJECTED PRODUCTION VOLUME? THAT'S YOUR PROBLEM. TELL ME WHEN YOU KNOW.
STUDENT:	INCOME TAXES?
COMPUTER:	DO YOU MEAN FEDERAL INCOME TAXES?
STUDENT:	YES.
COMPUTER:	THE FEDERAL INCOME TAXES ARE 50%.
STUDENT:	PROJECTED SALES?
COMPUTER:	THE PROJECTED TOTAL SALES FIGURE IS $1 MILLION. WOULD YOU LIKE TO SEE THE PROJECTED MONTHLY SALES ALSO? . . . NOW THAT YOU HAVE OBTAINED THE PRO FORMAS, YOU CAN STATE YOUR DECISION FAVORING EITHER SEASONALLY VARYING PRODUCTION OR LEVEL PRODUCTION THROUGHOUT THE YEAR — WHENEVER YOU'RE READY. MEANWHILE, TYPE "HELP" IF YOU BECOME TROUBLED BY ANY OF YOUR FINDINGS.
STUDENT:	DIRECT LABOR COSTS?
COMPUTER:	THE ESTIMATED DIRECT LABOR COSTS ARE $217,000 FOR SEASONAL PRODUCTION AND $170,000 FOR LEVEL.
STUDENT:	HELP!
COMPUTER:	WHAT FINDING BOTHERS YOU? IS IT YOUR PRO FORMA INFORMATION?
STUDENT:	YES.
COMPUTER:	YOU CAN HAVE REVISED PRO FORMAS IF YOU THINK OF SOMETHING THAT WOULD CHANGE THEM. WHAT NEW FACTOR IS RELEVANT?
STUDENT:	OVERTIME COSTS.
COMPUTER:	IT'S FORTUNATE THAT YOU HAD SECOND THOUGHTS HERE. THE OVERTIME AMOUNTS TO $60,000 FOR SEASONAL PRODUCTION AND NONE FOR LEVEL. THESE NEW DATA SHOULD CHANGE YOUR PRO FORMAS AND HAVE VERY SIGNIFICANT EFFECTS ON YOUR DECISION. . . .
STUDENT:	SEASONAL PRODUCTION.
COMPUTER:	NOW THAT YOU HAVE MADE A DECISION, LET'S CONSIDER IT IN THE LIGHT OF THE RELEVANT FACTS. . . . CONSIDER THESE PRO FORMAS CAREFULLY. THEN TELL ME — ARE YOU STILL HAPPY WITH YOUR CURRENT DECISION?
STUDENT:	YES.

(continued)

COMPUTER:	TELL ME AGAIN, JUST TO BE SURE THAT I UNDERSTAND, <u>WHICH</u> PRODUCTION SCHEDULE DO YOU RECOMMEND?
STUDENT:	SEASONAL PRODUCTION.
COMPUTER:	LET'S CONSIDER A HYPOTHETICAL QUESTION. IF YOU WERE GUARANTEED THAT YOU WOULD NOT BE CAUGHT WITH A LOT OF UNSALEABLE INVENTORY, WOULD YOU CHANGE YOUR DECISION TO ONE IN FAVOR OF LEVEL?
STUDENT:	NO.
COMPUTER:	THEN LET'S CONSIDER WHETHER OR NOT WE ARE AGREED ON AMOUNT OF SAVINGS THAT WOULD RESULT. ASSUMING ALL THE INVENTORY WERE SOLD, HOW MANY THOUSANDS OF DOLLARS IN SAVINGS WOULD RESULT FROM GOING TO A LEVEL PRODUCTION SCHEDULE?
STUDENT:	110.
COMPUTER:	THAT'S ABOUT RIGHT. THE ACTUAL VALUE, DETERMINED FROM DIRECT LABOR COSTS, OVERTIME COSTS, WAREHOUSING COSTS, AND MACHINE MAINTENANCE COSTS, IS $108,000. THAT'S A LOT OF MONEY. DOESN'T THIS CHANGE YOUR DECISION?
STUDENT:	NO.

REFERENCES

Brown, Robert R. "Cost and Advantages of On-Line DP." *Datamation,* March 1968, pp. 40–43.

Fano, R. M., and Corbato, F. J. "Time-Sharing on Computers." *Scientific American,* September 1966, pp. 129–140.

Gold, Michael M. "Time-Sharing and Batch-Processing: An Experimental Comparison of Their Values in a Problem-Solving Situation." *Communications of the ACM,* May 1969, pp. 249–259.

Hammerton, James C. "Business Time-Sharing: User-Economics." *Datamation,* June 1969, pp. 80–81.

Jenkins, William E. "Air-Line Reservation Systems." *Datamation,* March 1969, pp. 29–32.

Karplus, Walter J., ed. *On-Line Computing.* New York: McGraw-Hill Book Co., 1967.

Martin, James. *Design of Man-Computer Dialogue.* Englewood Cliffs, N.J.: Prentice-Hall, 1973.

Martin, James. *Design of Real-Time Systems.* Englewood Cliffs, N.J.: Prentice-Hall, 1967.

Martin, James. *Introduction to Teleprocessing.* Englewood Cliffs, N.J.: Prentice-Hall, 1972.

Orr, William D., ed. *Conversational Computers.* New York: John Wiley & Sons, 1968.

Suppes, Patrick. "The Uses of Computers in Education." *Scientific American,* September 1966, pp. 207–220.

Sutherland, Ivan E. "Computer Inputs and Outputs." *Scientific American,* September 1966, pp. 86–96.

QUESTIONS

1. What advantages do operating systems offer?
2. What is batch processing?
3. Define the term *multiprogramming*.
4. What is teleprocessing?
5. Describe the types of telecommunication lines available.
6. What is the least expensive teleprocessing equipment? Why?
7. What is real-time data processing? What advantages does it offer?
8. Why did the airlines choose to implement a real-time data-processing system?
9. What is an integrated data system?
10. Describe the programming procedures for a problem using conversational programming.
11. Discuss the use of CAI for teaching college students English literature and the Russian language. Compare the difficulties of using CAI at the college level with the ease of using it to teach arithmetic to second-grade pupils.

CHAPTER NINETEEN

Management and the Computer

Figure 19–1
The Interaction between a Customer
and a Manufacturer

The widespread current use of computers for data processing is a response to the need of business to handle, store, and process a fast-increasing volume of data. Modern business methods call for a dynamic flow of information from customer to central office to plants and to other companies. While a transaction could be described as a simple relationship between a customer and a supplier, as in Figure 19–1, in reality the picture is more complex. The record-keeping activity of a company requires the control of manufacturing schedules, inventory levels, and warehouse stock in addition to the fulfilling of routine orders from dealers. This dynamic flow of information is shown in Figure 19–2.

The computer serves as a supplement to human skills and endeavors. It performs arithmetic calculations and makes logical choices based on the comparison of two or more numbers. These qualities are also supplied by a clerk operating a desk calculator. However, the computer has two distinct advantages. First, it can process data under the control of a program. It will faithfully perform the same actions with regard to the first record as it will with regard to the one millionth record (provided the program is correct). Second, it allows the retention of large

amounts of data for processing. Once stored on a computerized medium, data is available for modification and retrieval. The computer functions as a tireless robot that can process vast quantities of records without error. Its actions are directed by programs produced with the cooperation of problem analysts, systems analysts, and programmers. However, the successful utilization of the computer depends not only on these three categories of personnel; the main responsibility for its success is in the hands of top management.

WHY A COMPUTER?

Management may decide to install a computer for a variety of reasons. Primarily, a company studies a computerized data-processing system as a replacement for manual or punched-card methods as a means of lowering costs. As the volume of records to be processed increases, the cost of processing each record with manual or semi-manual methods increases; in contrast, the cost per record decreases with the introduction of computer data-processing techniques for large-volume files. However, a company may find

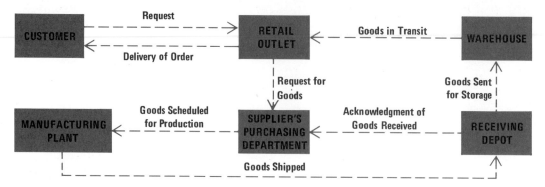

Figure 19–2
The Information Flow Caused by a Customer's
Request for Goods

Figure 19–3
Manual and Computer Processing Costs

The manual cost of processing records increases with the number of records because additional personnel must be hired to handle the increased volume. In contrast, the initial cost of a computer and of the development of computer data-processing programs is high. When this cost is divided by the number of records processed, the cost per record falls as volume increases. However, there is a limit on the number of records that can be processed within a given unit of time. Management must anticipate any increase in data volume that may tax the capacity of the computer system. Before the point of maximum capacity is reached, a more powerful computer system must be installed to handle the workload.

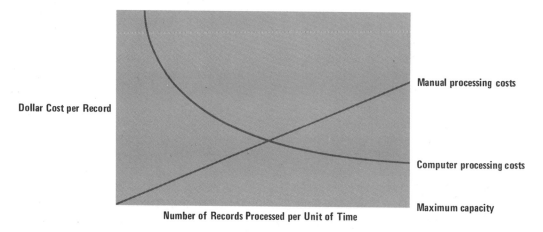

that the installation of a computer does not lower its costs; instead, costs increase as the computer is used to perform more than the routine data-processing activities initially assigned to it. A computer may stimulate management to demand more imaginative ways of using it—for example, for real-time data processing or to obtain summary information that was too difficult or time-consuming to obtain with manual data-processing methods. Consequently, the cost study for a proposed computer installation must be carefully reviewed to ensure that it takes into account future uses of the computer.

The second basic reason for converting to computer data processing is to improve the efficiency of record handling. As the number of records increases, the sheer physical problem of handling each individual record becomes detrimental to the speedy processing of data. The recording of data and the subsequent retrieval of information pose serious problems for data-processing systems. Accuracy in manual methods also tends to decline with an increase in the volume of records. The requirement of efficiency alone may be sufficient to cause a firm to invest in a computer for processing. As we saw in Chapter 18, it was the airline industry, confronted with a need to keep passenger records current and to retrieve data instantaneously, that pioneered real-time data-processing systems.

A third reason for turning to a computer is simply because a competitor is using one. While it is true that the use of a computer may be necessary for effective competition, the selection of a computer on such grounds is not justified. It may, in fact, lead to improper use of the computer, a loss of efficiency, and increased processing costs.

THE FEASIBILITY STUDY

Once management has decided to analyze the benefits of a computer, it must answer several questions. Four initial questions are

1. Is a computer necessary?
2. If so, what jobs will be placed on the computer?
3. Should a computer be purchased or rented, or should the use of a leased time-sharing facility (that is, a computer off the premises) be considered?
4. If the company chooses to acquire its own

computer, by lease or purchase, which computer should be chosen?

To answer these questions, a company must embark upon a computer feasibility study, a detailed study of the company's activities, in order to justify the choice of a computer for data processing. It must also provide a master plan for the selection and use of a computer. Several options exist regarding the selection of a computer. First, the company must determine if it wishes to establish its own computer facility, purchase computer time at another installation, or enter into a time-sharing agreement. The popularity of computer networks is growing, and a small company may find that it is to its advantage to lease time on a computer and direct all programming and data-processing activities via a remote terminal at its own site.

Typically, a large company will find that having its own computer installation is economically more advantageous. The control of its own computer has several advantages. An onsite computer is more convenient for programmers; the computer hardware and software are under the company's direct supervision; and the special hardware and software features required for the firm's

computer applications, which may not be available at another site or via time-sharing arrangements, can be provided.

SELECTING A COMPUTER Once a company has decided on its own installation, it is faced with the problem of selecting a computer appropriate for its needs and determining whether purchase or lease agreement is most beneficial for its purposes. The selection of an appropriate computer requires an intensive analysis of the company's needs for data processing. All jobs—current and future—that will be handled by the computer must be studied and defined as explicitly as possible. Having studied its own requirements and the projected future volume of data, the company must decide on a small, medium-sized, or large-scale computer. All computers available within this range should then be studied intensively.

The job of selecting the proper computer is an intricate one and should be delegated to skilled computer personnel. If there are none within the company, a consultant firm may be contracted to perform a feasibility study. The disadvantage of engaging an outside consultant is that it too may have biases and propose a computer based on those prejudices. Thus, the company may be forced to depend on its own managers to select a computer. Without sufficiently competent personnel, this may lead to an overreliance on the various computer manufacturers. Naturally, the computer manufacturers' representatives have a bias toward their own equipment. The problem of selecting a computer is a difficult one and should occupy the company for a period of one year to 18 months. A hasty study may lead to an inadequate computer center and improper use of the computer.

LEASE VS. PURCHASE AGREEMENTS
A company must decide whether to lease or purchase a computer. In order to make this decision, the project team responsible for the feasibility study must obtain a detailed cost outline for purchase or rental of the computer systems being considered. The usual breakeven point for purchase agreements is five years. If the computer will be retained for five or more years, a purchase agreement generally offers an economic edge over leasing. Maintenance costs are usually priced separately for a purchased computer. The maintenance costs of a leased computer are ordinarily included in the rental cost.

The purchase of a computer must be carefully considered, even if it appears overwhelmingly preferable in terms of the financial outlay. Advances in computer hardware technology are rapid; technical obsolescence of a computer system is possible within a five-year period. Also, because of expanded computer usage, it may become necessary to alter a computer configuration. Peripheral equipment such as tape units, disks, and drums may be changed because of software demands or an increased data volume. The financial arrangement for altering the configuration for a purchased computer should be reviewed with the manufacturer. This type of alteration is common about every two years or so. A company may also find in the future that the central computer is not adequate for an increased workload. Any cost savings from a purchase agreement must be evaluated in light of possible future disadvantages.

HIRING THE COMPUTER MANAGER
At the same time the computer feasibility study is being done, the top computer executive should be hired to assist in the planning of the computer center. The qualities required for a computer executive are, in many ways, identical to

those required for other top management personnel. A manager must be a capable administrator, able to communicate with other personnel and to direct and plan activities. Also, a manager's communication skills must be superior, since there will be exchanges with managers from all departments in the company. Tact and negotiating ability are important qualities, as is a broad knowledge of the jobs to be placed on the computer. Furthermore, the manager should have the technical ability to direct the activities of computer personnel. Because many of the people under the manager will hold college degrees, the computer manager should also have such a degree, along with experience in the supervision of employees. A computer background could be acquired by a manager who was willing and able to study and learn. The necessary computer knowledge could be gained by attending training courses offered by computer-education firms, courses offered by a university's graduate school of business, or IBM management seminars. Because of the rapid changes that take place in both computer hardware and software, it is expected that a computer manager will continue his study of the computer field by regular participation in professional development programs.

One of the first problems encountered by top management is where to place the top computer executive within the management structure. Companies use a variety of structures; but most often, the top computer executive reports directly to either the president or a vice-president of the company. The computer manager must be sufficiently high in the management hierarchy to cope with the difficulties of communication with other departments. Two sample charts of company structures are shown in Figures 19–4 and 19–5. The initial placement of the computer manager may change as more computer applications are

Figure 19–4
An Organizational Structure with the Top
Computer Executive a Manager

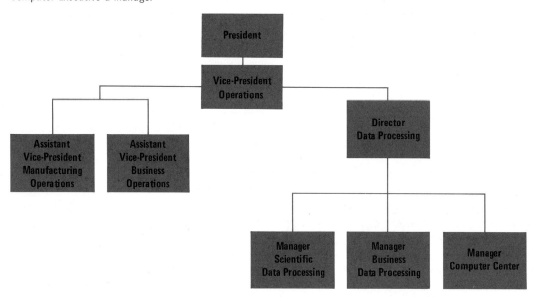

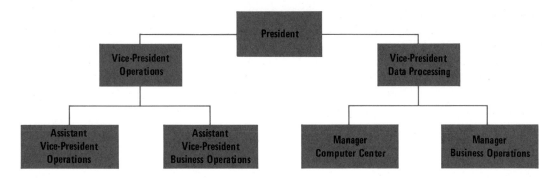

Figure 19-5
An Organizational Structure with the Top
Computer Executive a Vice-President

found, a larger computer is installed, and the budget allocated to the computer department increases. The computer center itself is basically a service department and has no role other than to provide assistance to other areas within the company. When programmers are employed by more than one department, the control of the computer center by a manager of a particular department may lead to internal conflicts. A preferred arrangement is to have an independent computer center with the manager reporting directly to an official of top management.

PLANNING THE COMPUTER FACILITY

Proper planning is essential for the installation of a computer. The planning must be complete and explicit, with sufficient time allowed for it. Each aspect of computer activity must be scheduled. The phasing in of the computer is a particularly critical period; it should not be slighted in the schedule. Frequently, management experiences frustration in the early use of the computer because the phasing-in stage has not been properly planned and the time allowed for it has not been adequate.

Management must also be aware that installation of the computer and conversion of data records to a computerized form mean that there is no retreat from the use of the computer for data processing. If a hopeless jumble results, the manual records may no longer be useful since all updating will have been performed by use of the computer. The manual records will be out of date, and the people responsible for maintaining these records may no longer be employed by the company. To go back to the old system will be costly and possibly more difficult than moving forward to computer processing.

SCHEDULING THE COMPUTER PROJECT The installation of a computer requires a master plan relating all the diverse tasks involved. A critical-path chart showing the relationship of these tasks is given in Figure 19-6. Delays in accomplishing certain tasks will directly affect the schedule of the computer project. As time passes, other tasks will occupy key positions and be able to delay the entire project. A brief explanation of each major activity is given below.

Ordering the Computer   After the feasibility

Figure 19–6
Critical-Path Outline of Tasks Involved in
the Installation of a Computer

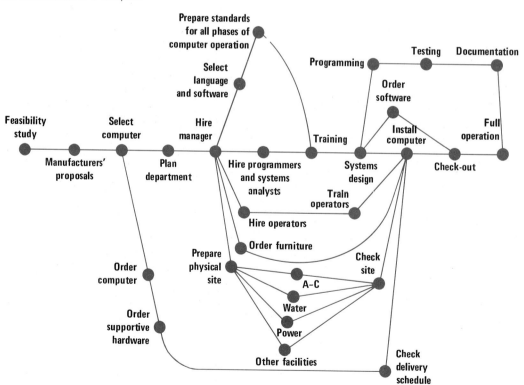

DON'T SPEED — THE COMPUTER IS WATCHING YOU

Professor T. C. Helvey, professor of cybernetics at the University of Tennessee, believes he has a surefire way to enforce the proper speed limits on the nation's highways:

You're driving along at 80 mph when a transparent red flashing sign appears on your windshield reading "slow down." Since there isn't a patrol car in sight, you keep going at 80 until you realize that all other traffic is making way for your car and there's another red flashing sign on the back windshield telling everybody on the road you're a hazard. You arrive home in record time, only to find that a computer has picked up your code number and a traffic ticket is awaiting you.

Helvey claims all this could be as commonplace as the traffic light in the next decade. Computers will set speed limits in the future for every car, for every driver, and on every highway at all times. Every driver will be given a small metal license tag bearing his name and the speed rating he is licensed for. The tag will be dropped into a slot of a minicomputer mounted on the car, without which the car won't start. If the car exceeds the driver's licensed speed limit, warning lights will flash and the central computer at the police station will automatically receive a report of the violation. Sensors embedded in the pavement will also feed speed-limit information into the computer to be checked against the car's actual speed.

If this all seems very unreal and far distant, it should be noted that a major freeway in Chicago already has electronic sensors imbedded in the pavement at half-mile distances.

Adapted from "They'll Probably Disconnect It Like Seatbelts,"
Computerworld, January 9, 1974, p. 39.

study has been completed, the computer must be ordered and the computer configuration must be specified in detail to the manufacturer. The computer manufacturer will tentatively schedule a delivery date to be confirmed later. After placement of the order, the representatives of the computer manufacturer usually will be available to assist in planning the physical site for the computer, to train computer personnel, and to advise about the conversion of the present data-processing system to a computerized system.

Planning the Data-Processing Center Management must begin the planning of the data-processing center soon after the order for the computer has been placed. Funds must be allocated for the center, a physical site for the computer provided, and the initial planning for the computer systems begun by a management group.

Hiring the Data-Processing Manager The data-processing manager must be selected as soon as possible. He or she plays a vital role in the planning for the data-processing center and is responsible for the preparation of the physical site. Suitable air-conditioning devices must be selected to ensure that the air-conditioning and humidity requirements of the computer are met. The data-processing manager must plan the physical layout of the computer and its peripheral elements. The manager must order any furniture necessary for the center, and lastly, must take a hand in hiring the operators, programmers, and systems analysts needed (or in training qualified individuals within the company).

Systems Planning The final goal of systems planning is the implementation of several computer programs that perform a selected group of data-processing activities. To achieve this, several separate but interrelated tasks must be accomplished. Standards for all phases of the computer operation must be established and documented in a standards manual. The programming language must be selected and all the necessary software placed on order. The data-processing systems to be implemented must be designed. Flowcharts or decision tables documenting the logic must be prepared. Then the programming of the data-processing systems can begin. Arrangements for testing programs on a suitable computer must be made for the interim period prior to the delivery of the computer, and there must be plans for acceptance of the computer hardware and software. A final shakedown of the in-house computer programs should be scheduled so that confidence in the systems will be high.

Training Training for computer personnel is essential. The amount of class time needed by programming and systems analysts will depend on their previous experience. Systems analysts and programmers should also be given an overall orientation to the jobs that will be done on the computer. Operator training must include actual hands-on experience with the computer.

Since the failure rate for new computer installations is high, proper planning is essential for success. A delay in the use of the computer because programs are not ready is common. Even more disastrous is the opening of the computer center with undebugged programs. Management tends to underestimate both the time and the money necessary to set up a successful computer center. An outside consulting firm may aid by reviewing the plans and supplying a more realistic schedule for the computer project. Management must review its own planning and implementation to ensure that realistic schedules have been established. The implementation of an unsuccessful computer system on the day promised is hardly a happy introduction to the use of the computer.

TYPES OF DATA SYSTEMS

Once the commitment to a computer has been made, the planning for the computer systems must begin. The direct conversion of old manual or punched-card systems to a computerized sys-

"I like to think that in its simple way,
it's fond of me, too."

tem will not result in the most efficient use of the computer. A complete rethinking of the old systems is an essential step in computer planning. For example, the use of OCR equipment may be the most efficient way of handling an increasing volume of orders. If this is so, the forms, the preparation of the data, the rejection of the OCR forms by the OCR reader and the handling of rejections, and the entire processing scheme must be designed afresh, without regard to the old system. If this is not done, the computer system is doomed to be less efficient than the manual system. Costs may soar due to the ineffectual use of the computer.

There are three distinct types of data systems. The first system is based on the maintenance of files for each department by each department. No common data files are established. This is merely a computerized version of the old manual system. Another system, commonly known as the *integrated system,* is based on the use of common files by the various departments. This means that the repetition of data in individual files is eliminated. In order to achieve an integrated system, it is necessary to review all the data files, and their uses, and determine how the various sets of files can be reorganized into one

set. For example, the payroll and personnel files can be combined into one file in which the necessary payroll and personnel information for each individual is given in one record. The data in the record may be listed as follows:

Name	
Social security number	} Shared data
Address	
Date employed	} Personnel data
Base salary	} Payroll data

In the same way, inventory files may be expanded to include data on suppliers.

The third type of data-processing system is the management-information system. By this we mean both an integrated system with up-to-date data and a system in which reports or individual data records are available on demand to management via a time-sharing facility. Management can request any item or report specified within the limits of the management-information system and receive a virtually instantaneous response. Thus management can make decisions based on current conditions. A quick downturn in sales can be detected immediately rather than after a wait of 30 days, as is usual with summary reports supplied via conventional methods. A management-information system must be designed with the assistance of management. Much of the information spilled off by the computer is not needed or readily digested by management. A summary report of 800 pages is not useful to management as a tool in making decisions. Such a lengthy report may serve as a reference, but not as a summary sheet and a planning tool. The selection of data from files is a key concern in planning an information system. Summary reports must be short enough to be read. Management may feel it already has too much information crossing its desk. The determination of what information is needed, its form, currency, and its frequency are all factors in the development of a computer data-processing system.

THE HUMAN ELEMENT

The success of a computer installation depends on more than the technical and organizational expertise of top management and the computer personnel. Directly involved with each facet of a proposed computer project and the jobs to be automated are people who may be reluctant to deal with the computer and its personnel. These workers may fear that the computer is eliminating the need for their skills; they may resent the computer and its representatives, who sometimes lack "tact" and communication skills, and they may distrust the computer as a tool for performing particular jobs. People in middle management often evince negative views on computers. They fear the loss of certain responsibilities, status, or even their jobs. They often are not willing to learn new skills and may choose to find other jobs rather than attend school.

The effectiveness of the computer can be degraded by a lack of cooperation from employees outside the computer center. For example, in company A, the time required for the preparation of payroll checks increased with the use of the computer. Upon investigation, it was found that the head of the payroll department had ordered the manual preparation of all paychecks to ensure the accuracy of the computer output. In company B, the systems analyst assigned to study a data-processing activity encountered heavy resistance. False information was provided to him. The final computer programming system did not do the task required, to the delight of the uncooperative personnel. The computer was once again foiled.

Management must overcome the resistance of its own personnel by a well-planned orientation program. The facts about the computer installation should be presented to all employees. Since a computer is usually installed because of increased data volume and a corresponding expansion of the company, increased job opportunities should be emphasized. The computer should be propagandized as a tool to aid data-processing personnel in performing their tasks. It is a means of relieving them of much menial activity. The cooperation of all company employees should be enlisted for the success of the computer center.

REFERENCES

Brandon, Dick H. "The Need for Management Standards in Data Processing." *Data and Control Systems,* September 1966, pp. 26–29.

Rothery, Brian. *Installing and Managing a Computer.* New York: Brandon/ Systems Press, 1968.

Sanders, Donald H. *Computers and Management.* New York: McGraw-Hill Book Co., 1970.

Withington, Frederic G. *The Real Computer: Its Influence, Uses, and Effects.* Reading, Mass.: Addison-Wesley Publishing Co., 1969.

QUESTIONS

1. Why should a business firm choose to use a computer?
2. List the major steps used in planning for a computer installation.
3. Discuss the three types of data systems.
4. Why should management enlist the support of all computer personnel? What methods can be employed to win their support?
5. A firm presently employs 50 clerks to process the billing for the company. All billing is performed with the aid of punched cards. So far, there is no computer at the company. What advantages does a computer system offer? How can management select the right computer for this task? What else should management consider in its choice of a computer?

CHAPTER TWENTY

The Data-Processing Center

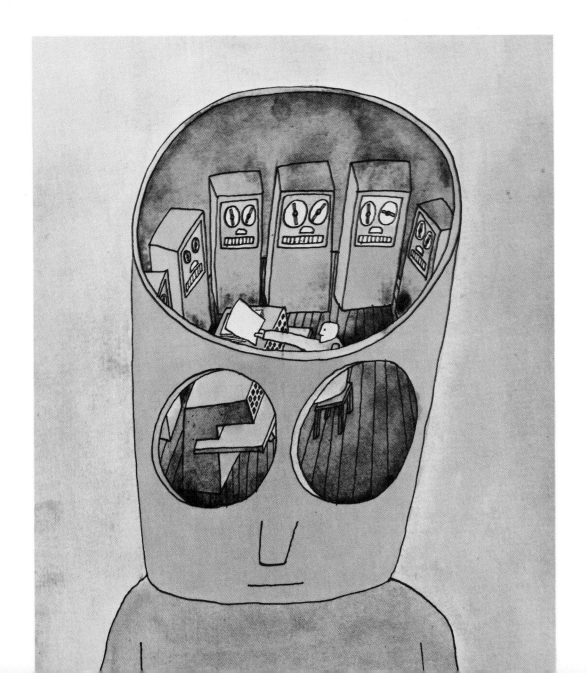

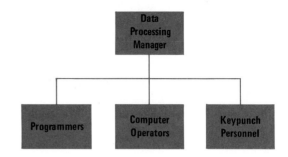

Figure 20–1
An Organization Chart for a Small-Scale Computer Center

A data-processing center may assume a variety of roles, depending on the company and its organizational structure. Thus the phrase "data-processing center" may create some confusion for one reading the computer literature. In this chapter, we shall view the responsibility for the operation of the computer and its operating personnel as vested in the *computer center.* The broad range of activities that includes programming will be considered the purview of the *data-processing center.* The computer center may be incorporated into the structure of the data-processing center, or it may function independently of the data-processing manager and report directly to top management.

Once a company has decided to use a computer, the organizational structure and the chain of authority for computer operations and related activities must be determined. The complexity of the organizational structure depends on the size of the computer and the number of computer personnel to be hired. A small computer does not require a complex organization. The computer-center manager may direct the work of programmers and systems analysts as well as computer operators. In fact, the lines of role action may be blurred, so that programmers operate the com-

puter directly and the computer-center manager also functions as a systems analyst/programmer. A distinction between systems analysts and programmers may not exist. This type of organizational structure is represented in Figure 20–1. The number of programs to be developed and the number of computer personnel is small; the computer is operated by the programmers, and all computer personnel work together to program and test systems.

A medium- to large-scale computer system requires more personnel to develop and maintain data-processing systems. The computer hardware is more difficult to operate. The number of files may be large, and a librarian may be required to control the labeling and ensure the accuracy of the files. Typically, a division of labor exists, with programmers, systems analysts, and computer operators functioning independently of one another and with the data-processing manager coordinating their activities. This type of organization is illustrated in Figure 20–2. In this structure, the operation of the computer center is supervised by a manager, who directs the computer operators and data-preparation personnel. He ensures that computer jobs are run accurately and efficiently. Work is submitted to

371

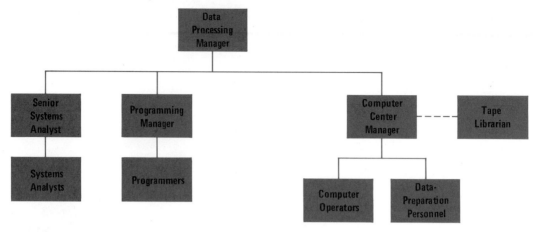

Figure 20–2
An Organizational Structure Separating the Functions of Systems Analysts, Programmers, and the Computer Center Personnel

the computer center, and completed jobs are returned to the programmers or those individuals responsible for running production jobs. The computer manager reports, in turn, to the top data-processing executive. The direction of the programmers is assigned to a programming manager, who is responsible for the scheduling of jobs and their completion. The systems analysts are directed by a senior systems analyst who guides their activities and acts as a liaison with the top computer executive.

In a large organization with many data-processing systems, the need for an additional division of responsibility, as in Figure 20–3, may exist. As programs are developed, constant maintenance work is required, both to correct minor errors and to insert additional features. This maintenance activity may be the responsibility of a special group of programmers. This is particularly desirable when programmers are reluctant to continue to modify their programs. Minor modifications to programs are unappealing to many programmers, who resent interruptions of their main creative activity—developing new programs. If the maintenance task is assigned to a special group, programmers are always available for this activity; furthermore, the control of

up-to-date documentation is centralized within this group. If budgeting permits, a documentation librarian may be hired to aid in the preparation of documentation, oversee the typing of reports, and ensure the completeness of the documentation files. Such a person would be an invaluable asset to the maintenance group. A technical writer could also assist programmers documenting the initial development of systems. Since computer personnel typically resist documentation requirements, a technical writer would aid substantially in the production of readable and accurate documentation.

In a large computer installation, the handling of software from the computer manufacturer or software houses can represent a separate task for another group of programmers, called *systems programmers*. This terminology is confusing since the same phrase is also used to denote systems analysts. These "systems programmers" monitor the release of new software, check the software before making it available to the computer center for use by other programmers, report errors in the software to the appropriate sources, and aid other programmers in debugging programs whenever a system error is suspected. Computer manufacturers generally

Figure 20–3
An Organizational Chart for a Large-Scale Computer Center

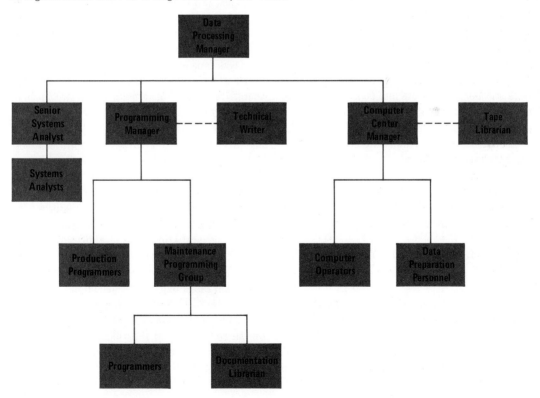

provide a programmer-analyst of this type to assist in the use of manufacturer-supplied software. These individuals are sometimes known as *systems engineers.* In addition, it is generally necessary for a firm to have at least one or two programmers who are familiar with the software and the internal operations of both the software and the hardware so that they can interpret software and hardware errors and communicate with the manufacturer's representatives.

It should be emphasized that the size of a company does not determine the organization of the computer department. The size of the computer, the number of programs to be developed, and thus the number of computer personnel to be employed determine the type of structure required for the data-processing center.

HIRING COMPUTER PERSONNEL

The establishment of a data-processing center requires the employment of systems analysts, programmers, computer operators, and data-preparation personnel such as keypunch operators. The qualifications of these personnel are detailed below.

SYSTEMS ANALYSTS The systems analyst defines a problem for the computer and specifies it in detail for the programmer. The analyst must communicate with non-computer-oriented personnel outside the data-processing department, in addition to guiding the programmers who code and test the programming systems that are designed. In addition, a systems analyst should have the background necessary to cope with the problems given to him for solution; this knowledge may be acquired by on-the-job training. A college degree in an appropriate major, such as accounting, business administration, or economics, ensures that an individual has been exposed to problem solving and presumably has developed the analytical skills it requires. For scientific work, a degree in engineering, mathematics, or statistics is preferable. A systems analyst must have an analytical mind able to understand a problem and break it down into individual tasks to be performed on the computer. Such an individual must be able to conceive a mental picture of how the problem will be solved by the computer, and thus must be creative and imaginative. The analyst's communication skills must be expert, to keep open lines of communication with those who posed the problem and those who must perform the actual coding. An ample supply of tact is desirable. This type of individual is in short supply. Dick Brandon, in *Management Planning for Data Processing* (Princeton: Brandon/Systems Press, 1970), estimates that only 1 person out of 100 in the general population is suitable for this job, and only 1 college graduate out of 10. A shortage of over 120,000 systems analysts is estimated for the late 1970s.

Preparation for the position of systems analyst calls for approximately 26 weeks of training on the job. The analyst must have a thorough knowledge of the computer hardware and software and be able to program in the particular computer languages used at the installation. In addition, it is important for the analyst to learn about the company's special problems; in view of this, a case study of the given computer application should be made. Since a systems analyst produces the initial specifications for a problem in terms of the computer, the analyst must be competent in the computer area and not merely in the problem area. If a systems analyst lacks a working knowledge of the computer and the languages in use at the company, the programs evolved will be poorly designed and

inefficient. Finally, the analyst must also be able to schedule and organize his work well. The position of systems analyst is frequently a stepping-stone to management.

PROGRAMMERS   The job of a programmer differs considerably from that of a systems analyst in that it does not require as broad a base of knowledge. A programmer generally works from the flowcharts or decision tables supplied by a systems analyst and codes programs for the computer system. A well-developed analytical ability is important, to uncover flaws in the logic of the systems analysts. A programmer must be able to design tests of computer programs, document programming activity, and have the logical ability to trace a path through a computer program. Thus, the prime qualification is logical aptitude, whether or not the programmer holds a college degree. The latter is important only for scientific work; however, companies frequently require a college degree as a means of selecting applicants for programming positions.

A programmer must be able to sustain interest in a program for many weeks and follow through on his job. Since programming requires a high degree of mental concentration, it cannot be

COMPUTER-GENERATED SEASCAPES

An unusual computer-generated color video display will be used to present a realistic, sweeping panorama of seascapes as seen from a ship's bridge. The Image Generation and Display Subsystem (IGADS) is being built under a $3.5 million contract awarded to Philco-Ford's Western Development Laboratories Division by the Sperry Rand Corporation. The huge subsystem is part of the Computer Aided Operations Research Facility being engineered by the Sperry Systems Management Division in Great Neck, New York, for the U.S. Maritime Administration. It will be installed in the National Maritime Research Center at King's Point, New York.

When completed, the facility will be used to improve the efficiency and competitive position of the U.S. Flag Merchant Fleet, to evaluate port and terminal designs, increase the safety of ships at sea, substantiate environmental-impact evaluations, and establish maritime-industry standards through improved technology and operational procedures.

The facility's simulated ship's bridge will make it possible to analyze ship operations in a wide range of environments—for example, by simulating hazardous conditions at sea and in harbors, harbor approaches, and channels.

The facility will consist of a full-scale model of a ship's bridge that looks out on IGADS, a cylindrical display 12 feet high by 120 feet long that has a 240-degree field of view from the bridge.

IGADS is unique in that its images will be in full color, and the "hidden" lines visible in most computer-generated scenes will be removed to provide three-dimensional realism. The ship's bridge will be equipped with steering gear, an engine-room telegraph, a radar console, communications facilities, and other standard instrumentation, all connected to a central computer that simulates ship dynamics and environmental factors. The central computer will also feed information to the IGADS computer on the position of the sun, fog conditions, ship positions and headings, and similar data for up to six other ships "moving" in the research ship's area. The IGADS computer will combine this information with data it stores on objects located in various harbors, channels, and approaches. It will then generate a changing scene on the display that duplicates what a pilot would see from the bridge of a ship.

Adapted from "Computer Generates Seascape," *Computer,* April 1974, p. 69. Reprinted from *COMPUTER* Magazine, a publication of the IEEE Computer Society.

treated strictly as a 9-to-5 job. In earlier days, a programmer was often obliged to work night and early-morning shifts to complete a program. Although this practice has become less frequent, except in the development of software, the determination and will to finish a programming task is essential for success. Programmers generally lack good communication skills. They are typically loners and prefer to work autonomously. Brandon estimates that 1 out of every 10 persons in the general population has the ability to work as a computer programmer.

COMPUTER OPERATORS A computer operator is responsible for the actual execution of programs: supervising the running of the computer, mounting the disk packs or magnetic tapes required for programs, monitoring messages from the computer, and holding responsibility for the successful running of the program. If the program terminates abnormally, the operator must supply whatever information is pertinent to the programmer. The complexity of the operating systems for large-scale computers requires an on-the-job training period of approximately five to eight weeks. A computer operator must understand the functioning of the operating systems and his role in the event of abnormal occurrences. Typically, the computer operator is a high school graduate and may aspire to be a programmer. An overqualified individual may function poorly as a computer operator, since the routine of the job can be monotonous. Therefore, unless it is company policy to promote from within, a person with programming qualifications may be a bad choice. Brandon estimates that one out of every two persons could be trained as a computer operator.

DATA-PREPARATION PERSONNEL The punched card remains the basic medium for computer input. However, other data-preparation devices, such as key-to-tape or key-to-disk devices, and direct input via special typewriters with OCR type fonts are gaining popularity. Personnel involved in data preparation must be ready to perform the monotonous task of keying data or programs. Basically the same skills are required as for a typist. Keypunch operators generally acquire their training at trade schools. Personnel who will use other data-preparation devices require on-the-job training by the company or the manufacturer of the input-preparation device. The rotation of personnel may alleviate some of the tedium of data preparation, and competent keypunch personnel may sometimes assist programmers by detecting errors in data formats or program statements since they, having prepared the data, are familiar with the format and general style of programs. The supply of personnel trained in data preparation is sufficient for today's data-processing operations.

THE MORALE PROBLEM

The computer professional has traditionally occupied a choice position in the job market. High in demand and short in supply, these professionals have had the pick of jobs and therefore changed jobs frequently in search of both more interesting work and higher pay. Consequently, problems for companies include not only how to retain computer personnel but how to survive without them—that is, how to ensure that the termination of any one employee does not drastically affect any given job. This is accomplished by strict control of standards and documentation. This topic is discussed in Chapter 21.

The task of retaining computer systems analysts and programmers is complicated by two main problems, which, though occurring in other professions, are particularly common in the computer field. First, systems analysts and programmers enjoy new challenges, which are found in new problems to be placed on the computer. If all the problems they handle fall into the same category, they will master the technique of solving them and find it boring to perform basically the same job over and over again. Their work will no longer challenge their creative skills as computer professionals. They then are likely to leave

"We've lost the main processing unit."

the company to seek other employment in order to maintain their professional standing and once again enjoy the challenge of solving new problems. Management must be alert to this problem and seek fresh approaches to computer jobs. A programming group willing to perform routine maintenance must be established to ensure continuity when the original programmers are no longer with the company. The possible generalization of a computer system to perform many different but related tasks should be evaluated. Primarily, management must ensure that the standards for programming systems have been met, that documentation is adequate, and that there are programmers who know about many programs, to perform maintenance activities. When a system is the sole responsibility of a single programmer, the loss of that programmer usually causes serious difficulties in the use and maintenance of that system.

Second, the computer professional works in an ever-changing field. As new computer hardware appears, as new languages come into use, and as time-sharing increases in popularity, the systems analyst or programmer wants to be part of these new developments, not only in order to learn new things, but to avoid technical obso-

lescence. If a computer professional does not keep abreast of the field, hard-earned skills may no longer be marketable. Poor morale for this reason may be alleviated by encouraging computer personnel to attend professional seminars, offering classes at the company itself, and promoting the continuing education of personnel.

Since computer applications at a large company undoubtedly will be stagnant for only a brief period before changes such as conversion to an OCR system, the development of a management-information system, or the updating of the computer hardware occur, it is advantageous to keep the computer professionals within the company up to date on such developments and retain them as employees. If this type of continuing education is not available, the computer personnel will seek it elsewhere, perhaps by changing employers.

It is appropriate to comment here on the attitude of a typical company in requiring specific job skills for a job applicant. For example, an advertisement for a job may ask for a specific knowledge of COBOL, the IBM 360/65, and the operating system OS/MFT. Yet a systems analyst with a thorough knowledge of another computer and its operating system can be quickly trained to do a job requiring familiarity with an IBM 360/65 and COBOL. Intelligent individuals are retrainable, and an ad like that described above serves only to foster job hopping within the computer profession. Otherwise, an individual becomes unemployable due to the locked-in position of industry, and job hopping becomes the only way for a person to ensure that a given set of computer skills remain marketable. A company should seek individuals who have analytical ability and competence in the computer area and who are ready and able to learn specifics, regardless of the particular computer configuration or language to be used.

MANAGING
THE COMPUTER CENTER

The computer center is basically a service center that accepts requests for the execution of a computer job and returns the completed work. This type of computer operation is called a *closed shop,* referring to the fact that the actual operation of the computer is closed to all except operating personnel. When programmers are also permitted to operate the computer, the computer center is classified as an *open shop.* Management must determine whether a shop will be open or closed. The reasons for barring programmers from executing their own programs are related to the economical use of the computer. First, programmers tend to treat the computer as a useful device for debugging programs. They often prefer to debug at the computer console rather than to return to work out the problems at their desks; this makes for inefficient use of the computer. Second, a programmer generally is an inefficient operator and has a salary higher than that of a person hired as an operator. Third, medium- to large-scale computers have sophisticated operating systems that execute programs placed in the job stack and do not stop between program executions. The aim of the software is to maximize use of the computer hardware so that there is never a halt in the computer's operation.

The space, personnel, and equipment required for the computer center must be planned carefully, keeping in mind the tasks assigned to it. The computer center manager must be alert to new developments in the computer fields. The needs of the company will change with time; the computer configuration will require updating, the data-preparation equipment will need expanding, and established procedures will have to be revised.

COMPUTER OPERATIONS   The work of the computer center is divided into two basic functions: computer operations and data preparation. The flow of work must be supervised by a *scheduler,* who groups the jobs submitted and may place a priority on a particular job. For example, the payroll program must always be run and printed by a specified date. Procedures must be established for the submission of a job and for the handling of files. A large computer center may own and store several hundred tape reels, plus several disk packs. A *tape librarian* who records the tape reel numbers is then necessary. The location of production programs is also a responsibility of the tape librarian. The tape librarian may be assigned the responsibility of sending tape reels for cleaning. A clerk may also be required for the input/output window of the computer center. This individual accepts jobs, answers questions on procedures, and returns the work on request. The clerk may also perform some routine typing. The computer center requires sufficient space for the acceptance of jobs, the set-up of job carts, and the storage of job output, tape reels, and disk packs.

DATA PREPARATION   The data-preparation room houses the data-preparation equipment and associated equipment as well as, usually, a voluminous amount of data-preparation supplies. Typically, data-preparation equipment consists of keypunches with a card printer, a card sorter and/or collator, and a card interpreter. In view of the relatively high cost of the card support equipment, many installations prefer to do card listings, sortings, and so on, on the computer. Cards are commonly interpreted by a run on a combination keypunch/interpreter. If more than four data-preparation clerks are employed, a supervisor of the data-preparation room is needed. As the number of keypunch devices increases, a supervisor for each group of personnel operating the keypunches may be needed. The doubling of employees does not merely require a simple multiplication of space. Other factors, such as noise, employee relationships, and the scheduling of work must be considered.

Key-to-tape and key-to-disk devices have gained much popularity in recent years. They resemble the standard typewriter more closely than the keypunch device and offer ease of correction and a relatively quiet keying operation. When the data volume becomes excessive, the economic feasibility of other means of inputting data must be reviewed. The best way to handle a very high volume may be to introduce OCR devices or direct keyboard entry systems with on-line computing capabilities.

HUMAN ERROR   Human error is one of the main obstacles to the complete success of computer operations. Operators drop cards, program listings are torn or mislaid, wrong tape reels are mounted, and other human errors occur. Minimizing human error is a prime concern of the computer center manager, who must be constantly alert to such possibilities. The physical layout of the center, the placement of output, the handling of jobs, and all the details of the center's actions must be monitored with a view to reducing human error. Good supervision and good employee morale are essential for the smooth operation of the computer center.

REFERENCES

Brandon, Dick H. *Management Planning for Data Processing.* Princeton, N.J.: Brandon/Systems Press, 1970.

Horniman, Alexander B. "Expanding Role of the Data Center Manager." *Data Management,* August 1972, pp. 16–21.

Rothery, Brian. *Installing and Managing a Computer.* Princeton, N.J.: Brandon/Systems Press, 1968.

Sanders, Donald H. *Computers and Management.* New York: McGraw-Hill Book Co., 1970.

Szweda, Ralph A. *Information Processing Management.* Princeton: Auerbach Publishers, 1972.

Weinberg, Gerald M. *The Psychology of Programming.* New York: Van Nostrand Reinhold Co., 1971.

Wight, Oliver. *The Executive's New Computer: Six Keys to Systems Success.* Reston, Va.: Reston Publishing Co., 1972.

QUESTIONS

1. Define the functions of the computer center.
2. What is the role of maintenance programmers?
3. What services does the systems-programming group provide?
4. Define the qualities and background needed by the following employees:
   (a) systems analysts
   (b) programmers
   (c) computer operators
   (d) data-preparation personnel
5. How can management minimize the turnover among computer personnel?
6. Define the terms *closed shop* and *open shop*.
7. A large data-processing center has 50 employees and a large-scale computer installation. Draw a chart illustrating a possible organizational structure for this center. What special problems will be encountered with a division of 50 employees or more?

CHAPTER TWENTY-ONE

Control and the Computer

The computer represents a tool for solving problems. Since it performs its tasks internally, by executing the instructions of a program, it is sometimes looked upon as a mysterious "black box." Input data are fed into the box, where they are processed, and results are passed to the outside world. How this mysterious process can be controlled is an area frequently neglected by management. Executives who attempt to control it encounter the jargon of the computer professionals, delays in programs, and sometimes disastrous errors in programs already "thoroughly debugged" and "error-free." Despite the lack of a thorough grounding in computers, management must be in control of the data-processing operation.

There are five basic areas where controls are applied to eliminate or minimize problems in the use of the computer. *First,* management must have control of program development and be able to predict a reasonable completion date for programming systems. *Second,* there must be controls to ensure that production programs run without errors, that is, that they perform correctly the task they are designed to do. *Third,* controls must be established to ensure good data, for data submitted for processing must be as accurate as possible. *Fourth,* the programming system must be controlled to prevent unauthorized uses of data or the illegal transmission of monetary funds — for example, the issuance of an unauthorized payroll check. And *lastly,* physical materials must be controlled to prevent harm from natural disasters such as floods or fires or more commonplace losses of data due to hardware or human errors. Duplicate copies of major data files and programs must be available so that they can be swiftly recovered in the event of such disasters. Management must have controls in these five areas or suffer the consequences.

SCHEDULING PROGRAMS

A variety of methods are available to estimate the length of time needed to complete a programming task. Some authorities provide formulas to calculate the amount of time by estimating the number of coding lines and the ability of the programmer. The accuracy of the input values for the formulas depend on the judgment of the user of the formula. He must already have made a comprehensive evaluation of both the program and the programmer in order to calculate a com-

Table 21–1

STAGE	PERCENTAGE OF TOTAL TIME REQUIRED
Planning Flowcharting	} 1/3
Coding	1/6
Testing components	1/4
Testing the system	1/4

pletion date by means of a formula. While a formula may be helpful, the use of common sense is important as well in estimating schedules.

Management must realize that estimates of programming time are liable to err by a certain percentage. In addition, projects may be late because the schedule set by management is unrealistic. Changes in the specifications for a computing task will cause serious delays and must be prohibited while a program for the task is under development. A program cannot be constantly changed without excessive delays; in addition, constant requests for changes downgrade the programmer's morale. The estimate of the time needed for a programming task must be based upon a careful study of the task in the systems-analysis stage. The programming chore can be broken down into five stages, each of which can be expected to take a certain percentage of the total time allotted for the task (see Table 21–1 above).

Once a job has been thoroughly studied and analyzed, the programming task can be broken down and program modules designed. Then an estimate of the length of coding needed for each module (based on experience) can be made. Adding the time needed for coding each module, plus the time needed to integrate the modules, will give us the total time needed. If a task cannot be divided into modules, it will require substantially more time than a task that can be so divided.

Management should not be deceived by statements from a programmer that a task is, say, 90-percent complete. The missing 10 percent may be the testing and documentation phase. Until a program has been successfully tested, the entire effort prior to that time is of no value. The pressure of schedules sometimes forces the release of a program that has not been thoroughly tested. This practice leads to confusion and chaos. Good testing is essential to establish confidence in a program.

An inexperienced programmer tends to view his handiwork as infallible; he does not like to think of possible errors. Only after a major disaster will he learn that programs may have errors undetectable except by a chain of circumstances. The initial stages of programming are far more important than the actual coding stage. If the program logic has been constructed properly and the problem formulated carefully and considered from all angles, the actual coding is a relatively simple task. Tests that uncover major errors or oversights in a program design will, of necessity, cause a substantial delay in the program-completion date. Thorough groundwork before the testing of program begins means that the testing phase is a verification stage and not a developmental phase. The likelihood of undetected logical errors is reduced when the program logic is a well-developed unit; there are no surprises in a well-constructed program.

The amount of time it takes to program a task is dependent on the skill of the systems analyst, the programmer, the programming language used, the supporting software available, and the accessibility of the computer. If the turnaround time for a program is 48 hours rather than 2 hours, the programming task will require substantially more calendar time. The use of a higher-level language shortens the flowcharting and coding stages. Documentation also takes less time with a higher-level language since the program itself contains some self-documenting features. Additional time should be allocated for the programming of on-line systems, which are generally conceded to be more difficult to program than a conventional data-processing system. Management should also note that the overall integration of the programs in a data-processing system requires a planning stage and a constant review of the programs under development. Without close monitoring of the programming process, the programmers will answer the questions and fill the loopholes in the initial analysis of the job. These small points may be relevant to the overall system and create a conflict between programs and data files used by more than one program. The resolution of unanswered questions must be referred to the systems analyst.

"Your heart is O.K., your liver is fine, your blood pressure is normal but my stocks just went down 20 points!"

Documentation is a much-slighted task. Management must insist upon documentation as an integral part of the programming task. Adequate documentation for a program must be available by the scheduled release date for the program. Finally, any program released as a production program should be closely monitored to ensure that errors undetected in testing will be uncovered and corrected during its use. No program can be treated as final. Modification to eliminate errors and incorporate new features is a continuing job.

ERROR-FREE PROGRAMS

Although no program of any length can be considered to be error-free, due to the complexity of the programming process, the testing phase is designed to create a high degree of confidence in a program's performance. This subject was covered in Chapter 16. People in management often find that they do not comprehend the reasons for a delay or do not understand the nature of the testing required to validate a program. The pressure to release a program on the scheduled date regardless of the amount of test-

ing and documentation still to be done can result in the release of a program with a potential for handling data erroneously. A policy of testing by an independent programmer not associated with the actual programming task may be well worth the cost in time, in manpower, and in computer use.

If a program error is discovered, a procedure for correcting the error must be available. Also, the correction must be reflected in the program documentation and program listings. Any possible loss of or damage to data in permanent files due to a program error must be checked so that missing data can be reinserted in the file.

DATA CONTROLS

A popular saying among computer specialists is "Garbage in, garbage out." This adage, which is abbreviated as GIGO, means that if the input data is of poor quality, the results of the program will also be of low quality; that is, the use of bad data will lead to the output of erroneous results. Thus, one of the major concerns of management must be the establishment of procedures to ensure high-quality data and to prevent bad data from entering the computer-processing stream.

DATA ERRORS Each step of the input-collection phase should be examined for possible sources of data error. Human beings are a troublesome source of error, since they can easily record data incorrectly. Methods of handling data should be studied to eliminate any factors contributing to errors. For example, the format used to record data should be simplified from the standpoint of the clerk, not of the computer program. The type of data recorded should be designed to be easily handled by clerks. The use of alphabetic information may be preferable, with later conversion of the data to numeric data by the computer program. Good manual procedures should be established that place the burden of manipulating the data upon the computer program.

The computer itself should be used to guard against data errors. A computer program can check that a data field contains the type of data required and that the data falls within reasonable bounds. Missing data can be detected. Any exception to the guidelines incorporated in the program can be reported on an error listing, and the data can be rejected until it has been properly modified.

The transcription of data to computerized form requires that the transcribed data be verified. This is usually accomplished by having a different operator key the data once again and having the keying machine perform the verification. Any discrepancy between the keyed data and the recorded data halts the verification process. The data can then be corrected.

Since each transcription of data presents an opportunity for human error, data handling should be minimized. When the data volume exceeds a reasonable bound, the use of OCR devices or the direct entry of data via remote terminals should be reevaluated. (See Chapter 8.)

CHECK DIGITS A popular device for ensuring the accurate recording of a numeric field is the addition of a *check digit*. This digit is usually placed at the end of the string of numbers. When the field is read, the computer program computes the check digit and verifies that the computed check digit and the recorded check digit are identical. If they are not, the data record is rejected. One method of computing the check digit is as follows:

1. Take the first digit and every other digit and form a number.
2. Multiply this number by 2.
3. Add the digits of the product and the digits not multiplied by 2.
4. Subtract the total from the next higher multiple of 10.
5. Place the resulting digit at the end of the numeric field as the check digit.

For example, if the numeric field is 5 4 3 2 1, we could compute the check digit as follows:

1. Take the alternate digits 5, 3, and 1, which form the number 531.
2. Multiply 531 by 2 to obtain 1062.
3. Add the digits of the product plus the unused digits:

$$1 + 0 + 6 + 2 + 4 + 2 = 15.$$

4. Subtract the total from the next higher multiple of 10:

$$20 - 15 = 5$$

5. Place the resulting digit, 5, at the end of the numeric field as the check digit. This gives us a new numeric field of 5 4 3 2 1 5.

THEFT AND THE COMPUTER

The complexities of installing a computer and controlling computer systems and computer personnel often lead management into establishing a computer-processing scheme without proper safeguards against embezzlement and other forms of theft. The computer is a potentially dangerous tool for stealing thousands of dollars without being detected for many years. Traditionally, management imposed procedures for data-processing tasks when they were under clerical control. With the advent of the computer, management has found that while data go in and data come out the process that produces output from input is not immediately discernible. In many instances, management has abdicated its position of control because of ignorance and the mystique surrounding the computer.

A classic example of computer thievery was the gradual transfer of $250,000 from a brokerage company into two accounts in the name of the manager and his wife. The manager was in complete charge of the electronic data-processing operations for a brokerage company between 1951 and 1959 and had become a vice-president by the time his illegal dealings were discovered.

The money was transferred from a company account to purchase stock, the nonexistent stock was then "sold," and the money was placed in his or his wife's account. This process went undetected because of a lack of internal auditing. The manager would punch new computer cards on Sunday mornings and feed them into the computer. Because he had complete control of the program and the input data, it was relatively easy to steal money from the company. After the theft was discovered, the brokerage firm instituted a quarterly internal audit and other safeguards.

Another brokerage firm lost $81,120 to a data-processing manager who altered a system to issue checks to fictitious persons and mailed them to his home address. Because the post office accidentally returned one of the checks, the theft was uncovered by a suspicious clerk.

Still another computerized crime was committed by a programmer who prepared the check-handling system for a Minneapolis bank. He designed the program in such a way that any overdraft on his account would be ignored. When the computer hardware failed, the manual processing of checks led to the detection of his theft of $1,357. Another way of stealing money was used by a European programmer, who engineered the rounding of paychecks to two decimal digits rather than three. As the money from the rounding process accumulated, he paid it to himself. The tales of theft by computer are endless, and management must be alert to such dangers of theft.

PREVENTIVE MEASURES The primary safeguard against computer thefts is to prevent any single individual from assuming autonomous control over a computer program. The programming task, the preparation of data, and the execution of a program are separate activities that can be performed by different persons. A division of activities is desirable so that no individual can alter a program, submit data, and cover his tracks after a theft of money or goods. A computer programmer should not be permitted to operate the computer. This will make it more difficult for him to "jury-rig" a program without access to it during execution. Computer programming personnel should be rotated to other programs periodically. Operators should be given different shifts or, in a company with more than one computer, transferred to another computer at reasonable intervals. These safeguards are designed to

THE MIND-READING COMPUTER

The experiment looks like some ingenious test of mental telepathy. Seated inside a small isolation booth with wires trailing from the helmet on her head, the subject seems deep in concentration. She does not speak or move. Nearby, a white-coated scientist intently watches a TV screen. Suddenly, a little white dot hovering in the center of the screen comes to life. It sweeps to the top of the screen, then it reverses itself and comes back down. After a pause, it veers to the right, stops, moves to the left, momentarily speeds up, and finally halts—almost as if it were under the control of some external intelligence.

In fact, it is. The unusual experiment, conducted at the Stanford Research Institute in Menlo Park, California, is a graphic display of one of the newest and most dazzling breakthroughs in *cybernetics* (a word coined by the late computer theorist Norbert Weiner, from the Greek *kybernetes* for pilot or governor, to describe the study of the brain and central nervous system as compared with computers). It shows that a computer can, in a very real sense, read human minds. Although the dot's gyrations are directed by a computer, the machine was only carrying out the orders of the test subject. She, in turn, does nothing more than think about what the dot's movements should be.

Brainchild of S.R.I. researcher Lawrence Pinneo, a 46-year-old neurophysiologist and electronics engineer, the computer mind-reading technique is far more than a laboratory stunt. Though computers can solve extraordinarily complex problems with incredible speed, the information they digest is fed to them by such slow, cumbersome tools as typewriter keyboards or punched tapes. It is for this reason that scientists have long been tantalized by the possibility of opening up a more direct link between human and electronic brains.

Although Pinneo and others had experimented with computer systems that respond to voice commands, he decided that there might be a more direct method than speech. The key to his scheme: the electroencephalograph, a device used by medical researchers to pick up electrical currents from various parts of the brain. If he could learn to identify brain waves generated by specific thoughts or commands, Pinneo figured, he might be able to teach the same skill to a computer. The machine might even be able to react to those commands by, say, moving a dot across a TV screen.

Pinneo could readily pick out specific commands. But, like fingerprints, the patterns varied sufficiently from one human test subject to another to fool the computer. Pinneo found a way to deal with this problem by storing a large variety of patterns in the computer's memory. When the computer had to deal with a fresh pattern, it could search its memory for the brain waves most like it. So far, the S.R.I. computer has been taught to recognize seven different commands—up, down, left, right, slow, fast, and stop. Working with a total of 25 different people, it makes the right move 60 percent of the time.

Pinneo is convinced that this barely passing grade can be vastly improved. He foresees the day when computers will be able to recognize the smallest units in the English language—the 40-odd basic sounds (or *phonemes*) out of which all words or verbalized thoughts can be constructed. Such skills could be put to many practical uses. The pilot of a high-speed plane or spacecraft, for instance, could simply order by thought alone some vital flight information for an all-purpose cockpit display. There would be no need to search for the right dials or switches on a crowded instrument panel.

In the future, Pinneo speculates, technology may well be sufficiently advanced to feed information from the computer directly back into the brain. People with problems, for example, might don mind-reading helmets ("thinking caps") that let the computer help them untangle everything from complex tax returns to matrimonial messes. Adds Pinneo: "When the person takes this thing off, he might feel pretty damn dumb."

From "Mind-Reading Computer," *Time*, July 1, 1974, p. 67. Reprinted by permission from TIME, The Weekly Newsmagazine; © TIME Inc.

reduce the time available for illegal manipulation of a given program. The rotation of personnel will provide a new person to view the program and results and detect any erroneous use of the program. An additional precaution is to separate the function of check writing from the department that authorizes the checks. This prevents complete control from being vested in one individual.

AUDITING DATA-PROCESSING SYSTEMS   Audits are conducted to detect thefts that elude these safeguards. There are two types of auditing procedures: internal and external. An *internal audit* is performed by employees of the firm, while an *external audit* is the function of independent certified public accountants. The purpose of an audit is to ensure that adequate controls are present to prevent thefts and that data records are maintained accurately. The auditor also looks to see if data-processing activities have been properly separated to prevent any individual from assuming complete control of a program.

A prime concern of the auditor is the tracking of an original data record and intermediate records through the processing cycle to the final output record. In manual processing schemes, a record is traced by perusing a set of ledgers, which are usually scattered through various departments. In a computer system, the original record may enter the computer and an output record be produced. The intermediate steps will not be visible to the auditor. However, due to legal and tax requirements, plus the company's desire for internal control, it must be possible to trail the record for auditing purposes. The track of the record through the processing cycle is called the *audit trail*. The auditor may have to request printouts of intermediate files to make the audit trail visible.

There are two approaches to the auditing of computer data-processing systems. The first is to examine the input and output data and, if they are correct, assume that the processing cycle is satisfactory. The second approach is to examine the input data and the processing cycle and, if they are correct, assume that the output data is correct. A combination of these approaches is advised for any established data-processing system. One method alone is not sufficient for the detection of inaccuracies or the mismanagement of data and data-processing programs.

DISASTROUS LOSSES OF DATA FILES AND PROGRAMS

The development of computer programming systems is costly in terms of calendar time, manpower effort, and computer time. Thus data files in computerized form must be valued in view of the calendar time, manpower months, and computer costs that would be needed to recreate them in the event of their total destruction. Management must be prepared to continue data-processing functions when a computer program or file is lost due to a hardware error, an operator error, or a program error. It must also be alert to the possibility of destruction of programs and files by fire, floods, or other natural disasters.

BACKUP FOR FILES   The total loss of data files and production programs by human or hardware error is guarded against by the retention of backup files and programs. In some cases, copies of files and programs are routinely produced. These duplicates are retained, together with previous copies of the files or programs, in a method called the *grandfather-son system*. (See Figure 21–1.) For example, Master File 1 is updated, creating a new master file, File 2. File 2 is later updated and results in the creation of File 3. All three files are retained until File 3 is updated. The transactions applied to File 1 and File 2 are also held. File 1 is called the grandfather file, File 2 is the father, and File 3 is the son. When File 3 is processed with the new transaction file, File 2 becomes the grandfather, File 3 is the father, and so on. The holding of these files ensures that it is always possible to recreate the master file if it is irrevocably lost.

BACKUP FOR PROGRAMS   Programs are ordinarily backed up by listings of the source code. If necessary, the source code can be transcribed to computerized form again and the program recompiled. If programs are stored on magnetic-tape reels, the possibility of irrevocable read errors on the tape must be taken into consideration. Consequently, a good backup for production programs is a magnetic-tape copy of the programs. If a production program is altered, the original program should not be discarded. The updating of the program should be treated with backups, using the same grandfather-son method used for files. This retention of previous

Figure 21–1
Grandfather-Son Backups

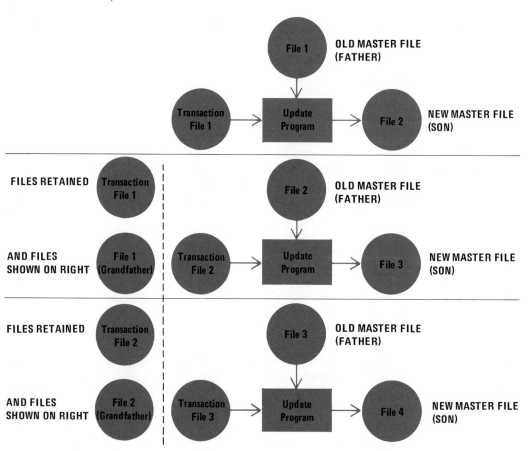

programs provides a recovery path in case the corrections to a program cause the introduction of other errors in the program code.

TOTAL DESTRUCTION OF THE COMPUTER CENTER   Management must also be prepared to continue data-processing operations in the event that the computer center and its library of programs and files are partially or totally destroyed. Although this possibility may appear remote, it does happen. The Pentagon lost several tape files due to a fire in a storage room designed to protect magnetic tapes from hazards. Magnetic tape burns rapidly, as do punched cards. Another computer center stored all its data files and programs in a basement, which was subsequently hit by a flash flood. A frantic 48 hours later, the computer center was back in operation with only a handful of programs. Since this type of disaster can and does happen, it is essential that backups for data files and programs be stored at a site remote from the computer center. If no safe and convenient location can be found, at least the hard-copy records of data and programs should be kept at a physically different location than the computer center.

REFERENCES

Brooks, Frederick P., Jr. "Why Is the Software Late?" *Data Management,* August 1971, pp. 18–21.

Gruenberger, Fred. "The Unpredictable Computer." *Datamation,* March 1967, pp. 59–62.

Parker, Donn B., and Nycum, Susan. "The New Criminal." *Datamation,* January 1974, pp. 56–58.

Rothery, Brian. *Installing and Managing a Computer.* New York: Brandon/Systems Press, 1968.

Sanders, Donald H. *Computers and Management.* New York: McGraw-Hill Book Co., 1970.

Weiss, Harold. "Computer Security: An Overview." *Datamation,* January 1974, pp. 42–47.

Withington, Frederic G. *The Real Computer: Its Influence, Uses, and Effects.* Reading, Mass.: Addison-Wesley Publishing Co., 1969.

Wofsey, Marvin M. "EDP Systems Controls." *Data Management,* September 1971, pp. 71–76.

"Whir, Blink—Jackpot! Crooked Operators Use Computers to Embezzle Money from Companies." *The Wall Street Journal,* April 5, 1968, p. 1.

QUESTIONS

1. In what five areas should controls on computer operations be established by management?
2. How can management ensure "error-free" programs?
3. What controls can be established to minimize thefts by computer?
4. File A has just been updated by corrections given on punched cards and new data records on a magnetic-tape reel. The new master file is called File B. What files must be saved? Why? When File B is updated, what data files must be saved?
5. A manager scheduled a system of five programs to be produced by five programmers. All the programs are now one month late and some coding has not been completed. No testing has yet begun. The manager proposes to assign 10 more programmers to this task, in addition to the original five programmers. He estimates that 15 man-months of work still remain and thus establishes a new deadline of one month from now. Is this new deadline feasible? What difficulties will the new group of programmers encounter? Will the addition of 10 programmers speed the completion of the task? What information is required to establish a new deadline?

CHAPTER TWENTY-TWO

Computers and Society — The Problems of Today and Tomorrow

We discussed, in an earlier chapter, the virtual revolution that computers have brought into our lives. Because we live in the midst of this experience it is difficult to assess accurately the total impact of computers on the quality of human life. But we can say with assurance that the present and anticipated impact of the computer far exceeds, say, that of the automobile. We are all aware of the impact of the invention of the automobile on the way we live today. Because of the automobile, a person may commute 30 or more miles to a job; the development of white middle-class suburbs and the decay of the inner city—both are directly the result of the mobility of the worker that cars make possible. Leisure activities today range from a 200-mile jaunt by car to the beach to a 50-mile freeway trip to visit friends. The metropolitan area of Los Angeles is completely dependent on the automobile and a system of freeways. Other cities have followed this pattern of development, which has only recently been challenged by the ecologists as having an undesirable effect on life itself.

While the automobile is a machine for transportation, the computer is an extension of man's ability to store and retrieve information and his ability to reason and solve problems. Because of this direct relation to man's mental ability, the computer has been called man's greatest tool. The computer's potential for processing data, for performing tasks repetitively, and for making rapid computations—all these have freed people from many mundane tasks, allowing attention to be directed toward problem-solving activities. The computer offers a speed of computation unsurpassed by any human; it provides the means to compute and solve in days, hours, or minutes problems that previously took years to resolve or whose solution was never attempted because of the time required for humans using mechanical calculators to do the job. So this powerful tool will undoubtedly have an impact greater than that of the automobile. The consequences of computerization already pervade our daily life. "Will life itself be altered by the use of computers?" is a question already posed and answered in the affirmative by the computer prophets. The invention of the computer has been compared to the discoveries of Galileo, Darwin, and Freud, which altered our view of man himself. The computer revolution has been ranked as a revolution greater than the Industrial Revolution. And the computer revolution has only begun.

Speculation about its ultimate impact and the actual dates for anticipated advances in computer technology and applications are pure conjecture. But it is clear that the human community must anticipate far-reaching consequences of this powerful device—the computer.

The computer, it must be remembered, was developed in response to society's needs. Its creation is directly attributable to the defense efforts of World War II. John G. Kemeny, in *Man and the Computer* (New York: Charles Scribner's Sons, 1972) tells of his experiences in solving partial differential equations at Los Alamos during the war years. Seventeen IBM bookkeeping machines were used. Intermediate results were computed and then fed again into the machines for all the many hundreds of steps in the computations. The equations were solved after a full year of effort. The same equations can now be solved by a Dartmouth (Kemeny is president of Dartmouth) undergraduate in one afternoon, using a terminal linked to a computer a hundred other people are using at the same time. Thus the contrast between 1944 and today.

When computers first appeared on the scene, the computer scientists—a newly created group drawn from other areas such as physics, mathematics, and engineering—had no vision of the applications destined for the computer. The computer was thought to be a powerful tool—more powerful than any previous calculating device. The scientists did comprehend some of its power, but considered it to be a purely scientific tool. An early conference, in 1953, presented a discussion on such innovations as subroutines, programming languages a level removed from the computer, and other items now commonplace in the vocabulary of the data-processing specialist. In 1953, a paper on the future of computers discussed whether the computer should be used to produce large, accurate mathematical tables to aid persons solving mathematical problems or be programmed to do the entire calculation. Today the entire matter is laughable, as both the author of the paper and those attending the conference would readily admit. The state of the art has advanced far beyond the point where such questions are even asked.

The computer was first used in commercial data-processing applications in 1954, by General Electric in Louisville, Kentucky. This represented a major change in the computer scientists' point of view. The computer could now be used to store data—vast quantities of data, perhaps—and a new tool for businesses had emerged. At that time the computer was still a primitive tool. In the 1960s, people began to realize the tremendous capabilities of the computer and new areas of discussion developed. Was the computer analogous to man's mind? Could it be used to create as man created? Was it capable of simulating man's thought processes? Just what was man's brain? Was it perhaps only a highly sophisticated computer and, eventually, could scientists build such a machine?

The 1960s were years of discovery in the computer field. Research in the area of artificial intelligence gained widespread support, and the federal government actively funded various projects utilizing the computer. The study of artificial intelligence deals with the simulation of human mental abilities, such as the ability to use language and to reason, on computers. Programming a computer to play chess is still a popular exercise for students of artificial intelligence. The duplication of the human ability to remember events and to reason in playing intricate games such as chess remains an intriguing problem. A human can still play chess better than any computer program.

The problem of translating foreign languages (called *natural languages,* to distinguish them from computer languages) into English was considered to be a high-priority task for the computer in the 1960s. Although there had always been an ample supply of human translators, scientists wondered how much more efficient the translation of Russian to English scientific papers by computers would be. The results were disappointing — not because the computer was inadequate, but because we knows so little of natural languages. The computer is an exacting tool and performs detailed instructions given in the form of a computer program. As the U.S. Navy found out after much expense, the computer is not a very good translator of foreign languages because the automatic rules for such translation are inadequate. Translations were made and were read by scientists, who found that they spent four times as long reading a machine translation of a paper than a paper produced by a human translator. Whose time was more valuable — the scientist's or the translator's? Interest in the translation of natural languages is still present, but enthusiasm for the computer's ability to do so has been tempered somewhat by experience. The emphasis is now on the study of linguistics and the structure of

natural languages. Man must know more of his problems before he can solve them by automatic means.

Many experiments have been performed with the computer supplementing human creative powers. Art, music, and poetry have all been created by the use of computer programs. The human creator works in conjunction with the computer to select alternative paths in a program. Examples of computer art, poetry, and music are shown in Figures 22–1, 22–2, and 22–3. The use of the computer in creative endeavors has led to speculation on the state of the fine arts in the future. In the year 2000, will people listen only to computer created music? Will they relegate artistic endeavors to the computer? It appears unlikely that those gifted in the arts will not use their talents in the future, but it is possible that the computer will act as a supplementary tool in the creation of art.

The 1960s also saw the development of major on-line data-processing systems in which the interrogation of vast data files in a matter of seconds was a reality and not a drawing-board proposition. The creation and storing of vast quantities of data in insurance offices and credit bureaus, in addition to the pioneering airline reservation system, all began in the 1960s. On-line data systems for the FBI and state police bureaus are still under development in the 1970s. Today, advances in technology have opened a new era in which data terminals at remote locations are cheap enough to be used by many businesses, although the concentration of computing power remains in the hands of wealthy and large companies. However, the computer is becoming cheaper—minicomputers are proliferating, data terminals are decreasing in cost, the state of the programming art is advancing, and larger and cheaper mass storage devices are becoming a reality. The present estimate of 90,000 computers in the United States alone is expected to increase to 500,000 computers by the end of the decade. It is now technically possible to maintain a dossier of 20 typewritten pages on every citizen in the United States in computerized form for retrieval in a matter of seconds via remote terminals. These are the reasons for the concern about computers and their effect on society. Computers —like any tool—can be used for good or evil.

Emotionally, people react to the computer as a device that has converted human beings, with individuality and names into numbers. Computers do use numbers instead of names for

Figure 22-2
Computer Music

Computer printout of the beginning of John Melby's "91 Plus 5"
for Brass Quintet and Computer*

```
I    1.   5.3333   3.3333   600.0000   10.0500   120.0000   1.0000   20.0000   16.0000   1.0000   1.0000    0.0
I    2.   5.3333   1.6666   600.0000    9.1100   480.0000   0.0     14.0000   16.0000   1.0000   1.0000   -1.0000
I   44.   5.3333   0.0531   600.0000    7.0800     1.0000   0.2667   0.0       0.0       0.0      0.0       0.0
I   41.   5.3233   0.2131   600.0000    6.0200     0.0      0.0      0.0       0.0       0.0      0.0       0.0
I   44.   5.3867   0.0531   600.0000    7.0900     1.0000   0.2667  -1.0000    0.0       0.0      0.0       0.0
I   44.   5.4400   0.0531   600.0000    7.0700     1.0000   0.2667  -1.0000    0.0       0.0      0.0       0.0
I   44.   5.4933   0.0531   600.0000    8.0000     1.0000   0.2667  -1.0000    0.0       0.0      0.0       0.0
I   44.   5.5467   0.0531   600.0000    7.1000     1.0000   0.2667  -1.0000    0.0       0.0      0.0       0.0
I   41.   5.5467   0.2131   600.0000    6.0300     0.0      0.0      0.0       0.0       0.0      0.0       0.0
I   40.   5.6000   0.3998   600.0000    7.1000     1.0000   0.0      0.0       0.0       0.0      0.0       0.0
I   41.   5.7600   0.2131   600.0000    6.0100     0.0      0.0      0.0       0.0       0.0      0.0       0.0
I   41.   5.9733   0.2131   600.0000    6.0400     0.0      0.0      0.0       0.0       0.0      0.0       0.0
I   40.   6.0000   0.3998   600.0000    8.0100     1.0000   0.0      0.0       0.0       0.0      0.0       0.0
I   41.   6.1867   0.2131   600.0000    6.0600     0.0      0.0      0.0       0.0       0.0      0.0       0.0
I   44.   6.4000   0.0665   600.0000    8.0100     1.0000   0.2667   0.0       0.0       0.0      0.0       0.0
I   41.   6.4000   0.2131   600.0000    6.0600     0.0      0.0      0.0       0.0       0.0      0.0       0.0
I   44.   6.4667   0.0665   600.0000    8.0200     1.0000   0.2667  -1.0000    0.0       0.0      0.0       0.0
I   44.   6.5333   0.0665   600.0000    8.0300     1.0000   0.2667  -1.0000    0.0       0.0      0.0       0.0
I   44.   6.6000   0.0665   600.0000    8.0400     1.0000   0.2667  -1.0000    0.0       0.0      0.0       0.0
I   40.   6.6667   1.8665   600.0000    8.0400     1.0000   0.0      0.0       0.0       0.0      0.0       0.0
I   45.   6.9333   0.0878   600.0000    5.0900     0.0      0.2667   0.0       0.0       0.0      0.0       0.0
I    2.   7.0000   1.6666   480.0000    9.1000   240.0000   0.0     14.0000   16.0000.  1.0000   1.0000   -1.0000
I   45.   7.0213   0.0878   600.0000    5.0800     0.0      0.2667  -1.0000    0.0       0.0      0.0       0.0
I   45.   7.1093   0.0905   600.0000    5.0700     0.0      0.2667  -1.0000    0.0       0.0      0.0       0.0
I   41.   7.2000   0.4425   600.0000    6.0000     0.0      0.0      0.0       0.0       0.0      0.0       0.0
I   41.   7.6427   0.4451   240.0000    5.1100     0.0      0.0      0.0       0.0       0.0      0.0       0.0
I   41.   8.0980   0.4451   480.0000    5.1100     0.0      0.0      0.0       0.0       0.0      0.0       0.0
I   40.   8.5333   0.1598   180.0000    7.0800     1.0000   0.0      0.0       0.0       0.0      0.0       0.0
I   45.   8.5333   0.0379   600.0000    6.0200     0.0      0.2667   0.0       0.0       0.0      0.0       0.0
I   45.   8.5715   0.0379   600.0000    6.0300     0.0      0.2667  -1.0000    0.0       0.0      0.0       0.0
I   45.   8.6096   0.0379   600.0000    6.0100     0.0      0.2667  -1.0000    0.0       0.0      0.0       0.0
I   45.   8.6477   0.0379   600.0000    6.0400     0.0      0.2667  -1.0000    0.0       0.0      0.0       0.0
I    1.   8.6667   3.3333   120.0000   10.0500   600.0000   1.0000   20.0000   16.0000   1.0000   1.0000    1.0000
I    2.   8.6667   1.6666   240.0000   10.0000   360.0000   0.0     14.0000   16.0000   1.0000   1.0000   -1.0000
I   40.   8.6933   0.1598   240.0000    7.0900     1.0000   0.0      0.0       0.0       0.0      0.0       0.0
I   45.   8.7237   0.0379   600.0000    6.0600     0.0      0.2667  -1.0000    0.0       0.0      0.0       0.0
I   45.   8.7619   0.0379   600.0000    5.0900     0.0      0.2667  -1.0000    0.0       0.0      0.0       0.0
I   41.   8.8000   1.0665   600.0000    5.0800     0.0      0.0      0.0       0.0       0.0      0.0       0.0
I   40.   8.8533   0.1598   350.0000    7.0700     1.0000   0.0      0.0       0.0       0.0      0.0       0.0
I   40.   9.0133   0.1598   480.0000    7.0700     1.0000   0.0      0.0       0.0       0.0      0.0       0.0
I   40.   9.1733   0.1598   600.0000    7.1100     1.0000   0.0      0.0       0.0       0.0      0.0       0.0
I   40.   9.3333   0.7998   600.0000    7.1000     1.0000   0.0      0.0       0.0       0.0      0.0       0.0
I   41.   9.8667   0.1758   240.0000    5.0700     0.0      0.0      0.0       0.0       0.0      0.0       0.0
I   41.  10.0427   0.1785   360.0000    6.0000     0.0      0.0      0.0       0.0       0.0      0.0       0.0
I   40.  10.1333   0.1331   240.0000    8.0100     1.0000   0.0      0.0       0.0       0.0      0.0       0.0
```

The above computer output translated into musical notation.

Figure 22–3
Computer Poetry

FROM
PAVAN FOR THE CHILDREN OF DEEP SPACE

Ice worlds,
Haunted by the legend of planets. Ice worlds —
Arcturus Andromeda Vega — orbiting,
Lost among stardust through aeons of crystal.

Your seed has dispersed, lit by the jewels of infinity,
Lost in the empty ocean;
In time with the measured dance of the universe
     orbiting . . . orbiting . . .

I am a child of eternity:
     down is a lifetime in every direction.
Through aeons of crystal your seed has dispersed
     on a journey to no destination.
     sunburst starburst
     Mars Venus Jupiter Saturn . . .
Down is a lifetime in every direction.

Born out of darkness:
Lost in the palaces of eternity;
Lit by the jewels of infinity
     of the land of nowhere,
Your seed has dispersed in the dark light-years.
     (Sunburst starburst)

I am a child of eternity;
I travel with comets . . .
     born of some other, lost among stardust.
Lit by the jewels of infinity
     down is a lifetime in every direction.

Mars Venus Jupiter Saturn: lost
     in the empty ocean.
Orbiting: on a journey to no destination.
     . . . Procyon Eridanus Rigel . . .

Lit by the jewels of infinity,
I travel with comets.

               ROBIN SHIRLEY

MARGARET

Margaret, are you saddening
Above the windy jumbles of the tide.

Wave to me in the peace of the night.
Jealousy is not all: It is not refreshment
nor water.

Return to me in the pause of the shade,
Darling, because my spirit can chime.

Above the early flounces of the stream
Margaret, are you saddening?

             LOUIS T. MILIC

records because of the convenience of a numbering system and the fact that names do not provide a unique identification. The computer that repeatedly sends a bill for an amount that has already been paid or for merchandise that was returned long ago is quite understandably hated and somewhat feared by the general population. The source of the problem is not the computer itself but a set of computer programs designed to behave in a certain fashion and the lack of human intervention to prevent such annoyances. What every educated person should realize is that the computer didn't do it. The people who toss letters into a bin for automatic processing by the computer, the people who design a computer system that is inflexible and too difficult to change until someone has been harassed for several months, these people are ultimately responsible for the actions of the computer. The age of the human clerk may seem to have been better to some of those who were adults in the days before the computer, but human clerks were not perfect either and may have been just as annoying. Nevertheless, in "the good old days," a letter was manually typed and a human signature placed on it. The IBM slogan "machines should work, people should think" is one to be emphasized for all.

Knowledgeable citizens are genuinely concerned about privacy and the security of individual records in the computer age (an issue preeminent in the public's mind); about power being placed in the wrong hands due to the computer; and about the effect on our lives of the computer's long-range impact on society, which includes the overall effect of automation plus computers on people themselves.

There are two opposing schools of thought about the computer, with a third group taking a moderate stand. One group of extremists believes that the computer is leading us to a world that will be inhumane and impersonal, one that supervision by the government will make akin to the world depicted in Orwell's *1984*. Another group views the computer impersonally, seeing it as the greatest tool and the greatest boon yet to the human community. A third group stands between these two extremes and attempts to point out both the dangers of the computer and its benefits. This group exhorts people to remember that they are master, determining their own fate and future. People in modern societies have learned to live with the development of a destructive weapon beyond, say, the medieval person's comprehension. The atomic bomb and the H-bomb threaten us each day with their potential to destroy all forms of life on the planet. The computer can assist in this destruction, since it has the capability to aid in this development and control of the weapons of destruction. The computer also has the potential to threaten the quality of life itself, to create a new way of life different from that which people are now experiencing, and to serve as a medium for the absolute police surveillance of the citizens of the world. The potential of the computer is enormous. Where it will lead us and whether any of the dangers people predict are real or merely hypothetical have still to be determined. The truth is that the computer exists, and all people must learn to live with its tremendous capabilities and potential. We must always be the masters of the computer, not manipulated by a few who have at their command the knowledge to use the computer as they will.

PRIVACY AND SECURITY

We are all justly concerned about the privacy of our individual records. Our names are on file in many different locations. Each time we use a credit card, a record is made of our action. Our insurance company has in their data bank personal data on us and our families. The police may have information on us if we were present at a demonstration against the Vietnam war or wrote an uncomplimentary letter to a public official. Our travel plans are on file with the airlines and available on their computer. The state retains personal data for our driver's licenses and records of traffic offenses. Credit bureaus hold data on our payment of bills, requests for loans, and bad debts, as well as bankruptcy data. The courts hold records on any legal activity. The welfare programs have files of personal information on families requesting financial support. And all of us have medical records on file in various locations. What if each county consolidated all its files? What then? Would you like to have a person be able to sit down at a remote terminal and retrieve any and all information on your personal life by entering your universal identification number or, if not a universal number, the appropriate identification number for that county? This will be a real possibility in the future, although it is not feasible today. The technological capability exists and the data is there, but the money and software programs are not so readily available. Alan Westin and Michael Baker recently authored a massive study of 55 organizations in the United States in which they concluded that data banks were not presently being abused. But the potential is there, and there must be controls placed on this activity. The old data systems in file drawers were equally vulnerable to abuse. Consider the so-called buddy system, whereby a person in the police department calls up a friend at the welfare department and obtains information that is confidential under the law. Usually the release of such data requires a court order. The law, in many cases, protects records; but individuals violate the law. The transcription of data records to computerized forms requires an exacting data format, and the data errors rampant in manual systems have been corrected in computerized files. An error rate as high as 25 percent was considered acceptable in some manual systems. Computer data records are estimated to have an error rate as low as 3 percent.

The issue of privacy and security becomes muddled because of a confusion of terms. The right to protect personal data from government seizure has been attributed to the Fourth Amendment's guarantee against unreasonable searches and seizures. The First Amendment's guarantees of free speech and association have been used by the Supreme Court to protect anonymity of expression (in leafleting cases), privacy of association (to forbid the compulsory disclosure of membership lists of political organizations where no compelling government need is demonstrated), and "political privacy" (to protect individual beliefs and associations from compulsory disclosure to legislative investigating committees or state bar examining committees). The Court has used the Bill of Rights, including the Ninth Amendment's

"Checkmate."

declaration of rights reserved to the people, to protect "marital privacy" and the right to read any literature, including obscene material, within the privacy of one's own home. Traditionally, certain information, such as lawyer-client or doctor-patient exchanges, has been treated as confidential. It is generally agreed that sensitive personal information should not be disclosed by government agencies to any other agencies or individuals.

However, what constitutes private personal data is not defined by law. Most persons agree that insurance companies have the right to ask personal questions in exchange for an insurance policy. However, most people would also agree that this data should not be released to any other person or business firm, but should be considered a private exchange between the individual and the company. Welfare recipients have been the subject of the most intense scrutiny by the government, and often their records have been made available to other government agencies. The reaffirmation of the right of the poor to dignity has led to a reexamination of this practice and the institution of more appropriate procedures. The furor over the interstate police network sponsored by the FBI has led to the deletion of arrest records from the file when no convictions have resulted. An arrest record alone is damaging to any person applying for a job. Persons testifying before congress have pointed out that a vicious cycle may result from the poor being arrested (though not convicted), being refused jobs on the basis of arrest records, and then resorting to crime because society refused to employ them. An estimated 9 out of every 10 blacks will be arrested during their lifetimes simply because of the police practice of rounding up suspects in an area, arresting them, and then releasing them. Such a high figure means that many blacks may never find work because of arrest records. In computerizing police records, errors have been corrected, and incomplete records have been either completed or destroyed. Arrest records have been held in manual files and not placed on the computer. Westin and Baker's study of computerized files has not revealed any of the abuses the public has feared. In fact, computerized data is more accurate and restrictions on access to data are more rigid. The few known instances of unauthorized access to files were cases of abuses by previous employees or employees bribed to supply information.

Security is a second aspect of the privacy-of-data problem. It is an independent consideration, since it involves the protection of data from unauthorized access. Which data should be freely available to various agencies of the government is not the issue. For example, let us say that the police need to find suspected criminals and may wish to obtain information from various government files. Access to Social Security files is explicitly banned by law. Social Security records may not be used by the police or the FBI unless they contain information necessary to prevent sabotage or espionage. This is an illustration of the principle that the protection of privacy must rest upon the law and not upon the security of the data system. However, once data are held and deemed to be inviolate except for particular uses, as are credit bureau ratings, for example, then the data must be kept secure and protected from unauthorized access. Data terminals provide a quick and supremely easy way to collect data from a file. Security measures to prevent abuses include the use of coded passwords, locked computer rooms, identification cards, and cards that identify the user to the terminal. In the future, voice-print recognition systems may be used. However, the bribing of an authorized employee is easily possible. A disgruntled former employee

who knows the passwords may also enter a file and gather data illegally, although the frequent changing of passwords may help to prevent this. An experiment by some students at a terminal that was directly connected by wires (hardwired) to the computer illustrates how the "secret" passwords of users can be obtained. Since a user did not have to connect the terminal to the computer by calling the computer's number each time, the students left a program active in the terminal that simulated the call-up procedure and obtained the user's password needed to read his data. After the user proceeded to key in some other information, the program went dead and the user had to call up the operating system anew. However, the students' program retained the password. Each time the terminal was free, the students reinitiated their dummy program. In this way they collected 200 "secret" passwords. Passwords alone do not ensure data security. There are too many ingenious ways of beating the system.

To protect the security of data files, a combination of physical security measures and built-in software protection is needed. There are many studies now in progress in the area of operating systems to determine how to protect users from

THE COMPUTER AS PSYCHIATRIST

One program that uses natural languages lets the computer function as a psychiatrist. This program, called ELIZA, was created by Joseph Weizenbaum in the mid-1960s. It uses a natural language but plays a trick on the user. It doesn't really understand the persons with whom it holds a dialogue, but turns the words it recognizes into suitable questions. To the user, it appears to be a sentient interrogator and not a machine. In a sense, ELIZA has passed the classic test posed by A. M. Turing, a noted British mathematician working well before computers were developed. Turing said that the true test of whether a machine could "think" was whether it could fool a person into believing that a human—not a machine—was controlling the typewriter on which messages were being exchanged. The dialogue given below illustrates a humorous example of such confusion. The psychiatrist, who believes he is exchanging messages on a teleprinter with another psychiatrist, is in fact talking to the ELIZA program.

In the dialogue below, the words of the psychiatrist are given in upper and lower case, while the teleprinter's messages are printed in all capitals.

Doctor, I have terrible news
YOU SAY YOU HAVE TERRIBLE NEWS
Yes, there is a computer program at M.I.T. that'll ruin us
WHY DO YOU SAY THAT
I have seen it working
YOU SAY YOU HAVE SEEN IT WORKING
It's frightening—you must see it
YOU THINK I MUST SEE IT
You sound depressed to me
IN YOUR FANTASY PERHAPS WE SOUND DEPRESSED TO EACH OTHER
Yes—perhaps
I UNDERSTAND
I do too
YOU SAY YOU DO TOO
We are both in the same boat with respect to the computer
LET'S CONTINUE TO TALK ABOUT YOU—SHALL WE

You are a comfort
WHAT MAKES YOU THINK I AM A COMFORT
At a time like this you want to talk about me
WHY DO YOU THINK I WANT TO TALK ABOUT YOU
Because you share my feelings about that damned computer
WHAT DOES THAT SUGGEST TO YOU
That, of course, you hate computers too
YOU THINK I HATE COMPUTERS TOO
Why not, they're hardly human, are they
PERHAPS THAT'S WHAT WE ARE HERE TO FIND OUT
No computer could converse as you can, for example
OH
I can't understand how anyone could be fooled by a machine
CAN'T YOU REALLY
No, after all, there is nothing creative about a computer program
YOU ARE BEING NEGATIVE
I am convinced I am correct
ARE YOU WORRIED TO HAVE BEEN CONVINCED YOU ARE CORRECT
No, not in the least, not at all. Not even a little
YOU ARE BEING NEGATIVE
You said you agreed with me, didn't you
IS THAT WHAT YOU HEARD ME SAY
Why don't you try to dissuade me—computers diddle with numbers, that's all
YOU WISH ME TO TRY TO DISSUADE YOU
You can't
YOU THINK I CAN'T
For example, could a computer in conversation like this raise a new topic
YOU SEEM TO HAVE AVOIDED SPEAKING OF YOUR PARENTS ALTOGETHER
Precisely as you just did
YOU THINK I JUST DID
Yes, and that's what shows the difference between a man and a computer
I SEE

From "Conversations With a Mechanical Psychiatrist,"
Harvard Review, No. 3, pp. 68–74, 1965.

other users wishing their data or proprietary software. However, the people problem remains the real hole in any system. Those in the know can violate the controls established to protect the data from unauthorized access.

CHANGING LIFESTYLES

The second important issue associated with computers is the impact of computers on society itself. Automation has already affected the working force, and there is a real fear that computers will diminish the number of employees necessary for many tasks. At this time, computers have only changed the quality of jobs; they have not decreased the working force. Computers have been used primarily to assist in operations where the volume of data could not be handled by the current staff. Where layoffs were necessary, management typically preferred to wait for natural attrition to take place rather than discharge employees. The entire question of automation and computers is a basic issue. Predictions are made of a greatly reduced working force. We hear that the right to work may become a privilege of the few and not the right of the many, that those

working will support the rest of the population and the problem of how to fill leisure hours will become a reality.

But there are other issues than that of leisure versus work. The typical office worker today spends time commuting to and from work. The computer may make it possible to have a manager stay at home instead of traveling to a central office, and fetch data from the computer via terminal equipment either in CRT form (on a screen) or as hard copy. It may make it possible for the manager to communicate with other employees via videotelephone equipment, even having large conferences where the picture of all those in the conference is projected on the wall. In the future, a householder may no longer be obliged to shop for groceries, since orders can be entered on the home computer and automatically paid for with banked funds via a computer transfer. No actual store shopping would be necessary, since the homemaker could dial displays of merchandise on the home computer. Ordering could be transmitted directly from the home computer to the store computer. Delivery could be requested or arrangements made to have the merchandise picked up at a central distribution point.

"How do you want it—the crystal mumbo-jumbo or statistical probability?"

Another role the computer may eventually fulfill is that of an adviser to college students. A student usually meets each semester with a professor to discuss the curriculum requirements that must be satisfied and the courses to be selected that semester; a discussion of the student's academic career and future may also occur. Let us hypothesize that a computer, instead of a professor, serves as an adviser to all the students at a university. A student sits down at a computer terminal and keys in a request for a session with the adviser. The computer dialogue may be as follows:

Please type in your name—last name, first name, and initial.
JONES, JOHN A.

Please type your student identification number.
123-67-8910

You are currently enrolled as a student in business. Do you wish to continue in this department? Answer YES or NO.
YES

You still require the following courses, which are being offered this semester.

D10	Computer Data Processing	MWF	8:30
E9	Core Literature	MWF	10:30
E10	Philosophy of Science	T Th	2:30
F11	Accounting II	T Th	4:30
.			
.			
.			
G12	Information Systems	MWF	1:30

Please indicate which courses you wish to take.

This is only a sample of the dialogue that could occur. Registration for courses could also be completed at the computer terminal. This use of the computer is presumably an efficient way of advising students, but it has an inherent disadvantage—the lack of human contact. A professor may discuss with a student the grades received in a previous semester. The professor may assess the capabilities of the student and give counsel on the choice of a career. The professor may think the student is not using innate abilities to the fullest, basing this opinion on factors other than the objective facts in the computer data file. The relationship of a student to a computer is impersonal. A computer may counsel a student, but only on the basis of hard data, not human interaction. A good computer adviser may be superior to a human professor who is a poor adviser—abrupt, uncaring, and unconcerned with students. But a professor who is knowledgeable about the curriculum, the job market, and the personality and abilities of a student will be a better adviser than any computer program.

The computer is not meant to usurp human roles, but to aid an individual's work. A college professor counseling a student could turn to a computer terminal and obtain information on the courses the student has already taken, courses required for a major in an area, the student's previous scores on key examinations, such as the Graduate Record Examination, and use this information to better advise the student. Similarly, in a hospital, new patients may be interrogated by a computer to supply possible diagnoses to an examining physician. The computer can be used for complex human tasks, but it must not supplant human judgment. People must remain responsible for their actions and maintain control over the computer.

There is much concern that the use of computers may reduce human contact and social interaction. Is this good or bad? A survey has showed that the housewife considers shopping to be a social activity. Persons who work in an office or factory do more than merely exchange conversations on data records and factory equipment. There is a social interaction taking place. Will the elimination of interhuman contacts at work and a lack of outlets for housebound wives lead to an impersonal society where a person sits alone at home, truly a "castle," making no human contacts? This vision of the future is an unlikely one. More probably, people will find other activities to fulfill their needs for social interaction. Wives freed from more mundane tasks may find time for work or creative leisure activities with an opportunity for human contact. People remain social animals; the creative and proper use of leisure will lead them to more social interaction, not less.

RESOLVING THE PROBLEMS OF THE COMPUTER AGE

The problem of safeguarding privacy in the computer age must be resolved by the appropriate legal mechanisms, whether they be through common law, the passing of new statutes, or further interpreting the Constitution. Some even argue for constitutional amendments to safeguard privacy. Security remains a continual problem, and additional safeguards for computer programs must be devised by computer professionals. Routine physical safety measures must be carefully considered and normal care taken in the screening and review of employees with access to sensitive data.

The computer — for bad or good — is here in the same way the atomic bomb and nuclear power are here. We cannot turn back the clock. People must choose to place themselves in control of their greatest tool, an extension of their own intellectual abilities. They must understand the power of this tool. They must know its extent and its limitations. They must remember to make the tool a servant and must always remain master. The shape of the future is in their own hands — not in the computer's.

REFERENCES

ACM Committee on Computers and Public Policy, Daniel D. McCracken, Chairman. "A Problem-List of Issues Concerning Computers and Public Policy." *Communications of the ACM,* September 1974, p. 495–503.

Anderson, Ronald E. "Sociological Analysis of Public Attitudes Towards Computers and Information Files." *AFIPS Conference Proceedings,* Vol. 40, May 1972, pp. 649–657.

Carroll, John M. "Snapshot 1971 — How Canada Organizes Information about People." *AFIPS Conference Proceedings,* Vol. 41, Part I, November, 1972, pp. 445–452.

Day, Lawrence H. "The Future of the Computer and Communications." *AFIPS Conference Proceedings,* Vol. 42, June 1973, pp. 723–734.

Gotlieb, C. C., and Borodin, A. *Social Issues in Computing.* New York: Academic Press, 1973.

Harvard University Program on Technology and Society, Research Review No. 7. "Implications of Computer Technology." Cambridge, Mass., 1971.

Henderson, Robert P. "Social Implications of Computerized Information Systems." *Computers and Automation,* March 1973, pp. 11–14.

Kemeny, John G. *Man and the Computer.* New York: Charles Scribner's Sons, 1972.

Martin, James A., and Norman, Adrian R. D. *The Computerized Society.* Englewood Cliffs, N.J.: Prentice-Hall, 1970.

Montagu, Ashley, and Snyder, Samuel S. *Man and the Computer.* Philadelphia: Auerbach Publishers, 1972.

Nanus, Burt, Wooton, Michael, and Borko, Harold. "The Social Implications of the Use of Computers Across National Boundaries." *AFIPS Conference Proceedings,* Vol. 42, June 1973, pp. 735–745.

Weizenbaum, Joseph. "On the Impact of the Computer on Society." *Science,* May 12, 1972, pp. 609–614.

Westin, Alan, and Baker, Michael. *Databanks in a Free Society.* New York: Quadrangle/The New York Times Book Co., 1972.

Willis, Donald S. "Who Knows You: A Look at Commercial Data Banks." *Computers and Automation,* March 1973, pp. 18–21.

Withington, Frederic G. *The Real Computer: Its Influence, Uses, and Effects.* Reading, Mass.: Addison-Wesley Publishing Co., 1969.

QUESTIONS

1. Compile a list of personal data about you stored by government agencies, businesses, schools, and other institutions. List the type of data, the organization holding the data, and the type of identification used (e.g., a company-assigned number or a Social Security number), and note whether the data is computerized (to the best of your knowledge). What advantages would accrue to you if all this data were available in a central data bank?

2. Read Weizenbaum's article in *Science,* May 12, 1972. (See References.) Prepare a summary of the article, with special emphasis on his view of the computer.

3. List 10 computer applications and evaluate them as either beneficial or detrimental to society. Assign a value from −5 to +5 to indicate the social desirability of an application, with −5 indicating extreme undesirability and +5 the highest social desirability. Let zero indicate a neutral value. Justify your assigned values.

4. A university plans to conduct its fall orientation program for freshmen completely by computer. Draw up a hypothetical plan to orientate an incoming student using a computer terminal. Let the president of the university greet the student via a picture projected on a screen and an audio message given by the computer. Pictures under the control of the computer program can be displayed. What are the advantages and disadvantages of such a scheme?

5. List 10 activities currently performed manually that may eventually be performed entirely by computer or with the assistance of a computer.

6. If possible, work through a set of lessons in a computer-assisted-instruction (CAI) course. Write a summary of your experience, noting especially the following points:

    (a) how to restart a lesson after an error or failure,
    (b) how to bypass a section of the material,
    (c) the acceptance of the correct answers given in various ways, and
    (d) any features that are particularly satisfying or irritating. What shortcomings did you find in the CAI presentation? Were these shortcomings due to the material itself or the computer mode of instruction? Suggest possible improvements in the CAI lessons.

BASIC

BASIC is a conversational programming language—a steppingstone to the more difficult programming languages such as FORTRAN and ALGOL—that was developed under the direction of John Kemeny and Thomas Kurtz at Dartmouth College in 1965. Originally implemented for the GE 225 computer then in use at Dartmouth, BASIC was designed to be a relatively simple language that would be taught to all the College's undergraduates. Dartmouth has successfully integrated the computer into its curriculum: The computer terminal and BASIC are considered fundamental tools for the student throughout his or her academic career.

BASIC bears a strong resemblance to FORTRAN, as can be quickly seen by a perusal of Figure I–1. Because BASIC is an interactive language, the rules for the reading and writing of data provide for input directly from terminals. There is also a provision for creating and referencing sequential- and random-access files. The restriction on variable names is more severe than in FORTRAN, and there are several other differences that point up the limited vocabulary of BASIC. However, it is an easier language than FORTRAN and is particularly well suited to be an interactive programming language. Because of its success at Dartmouth, BASIC is available on computers produced by various manufacturers, including those made by IBM, Hewlett-Packard, Honeywell, and Burroughs. As with other programming languages, differences exist in the BASIC language as implemented for various computers. In some instances, BASIC has also been available as a batch-processing language. We will first discuss the major features of BASIC and then compare these features with those of FORTRAN. Less important features will be omitted in this discussion.

THE LANGUAGE STRUCTURE

A BASIC program is entered in the computer by means of a terminal with a keyboard. Typically the terminal provides hard copy as each key is struck, but CRT terminals may also be used with some computer systems. A program is composed of several statements, or lines of coding, each of which must begin with a line number. The programmer may assign line numbers in any order; however, the general practice is to assign sequential statement numbers, skipping numbers to provide for later insertions (for example, 100,

Figure I–1
An Example of a BASIC Program

The program below computes the future value of a savings account according to the formula

$$X = A(1 + I)^N$$

where A is the amount of money invested today;
I is the interest rate, compounded yearly;
N is the number of years the money remains in the savings account; and
X is the future value of the savings account.

```
  5   PRINT "FUTURE," "AMOUNT," "INTEREST," "TIME"
  6   PRINT "VALUE," "INVESTED," "RATE," "IN YEARS"
 10   LET A = 100
 20   LET I = .01
 30   LET N = 10
 40   LET X = A*(1 + I) ↑ N
 50   PRINT X, A, I, N
 60   LET N = N + 1
 70   IF N <= 20 GO TO 40
 80   LET I = I + .01
 90   IF I <= .04 GO TO 30
100   END
```

The printout obtained with this program is as follows:

FUTURE VALUE	AMOUNT INVESTED	INTEREST RATE	TIME IN YEARS
110.462	100	.01	10
111.567	100	.01	11
112.682	100	.01	12
113.809	100	.01	13
114.947	100	.01	14
116.097	100	.01	15
117.258	100	.01	16
118.43	100	.01	17
119.615	100	.01	18
120.811	100	.01	19
122.019	100	.01	20
121.899	100	.02	10
124.337	100	.02	11
126.824	100	.02	12

Source: Perry Edwards and Bruce Broadwell, *Flowcharting and BASIC* (New York: Harcourt Brace Jovanovich, 1974), p. 73.

110, 120, etc.). The way in which the program is executed is determined by the statement numbers; that is, statement 50 will be executed before statement 51, even though statement 50 may be typed one or more lines *after* statement 51. As in FORTRAN, spaces are ignored by the computer and are used only to increase the readability of BASIC for the human user.

DATA TYPES The standard version of BASIC treats all numerical data as floating-point numbers. BASIC does not provide for the use of integer numbers, except for the extraction of the integer portion of the floating number by means of a built-in subroutine, INT. No arithmetic computations can be performed with integer numbers. This deficiency poses no serious handicap in programming small scientific problems. Numbers may be written as integers or decimal fractions with or without a negative sign. Examples are 1000, 10.2, 12.3456E−3, 1.2E5. The letter E is used to indicate the decimal exponent that must be given as an integer. The maximum number of digits permitted in a number is dependent on the particular computer system. The Dartmouth version allows nine digits.

BASIC does provide for the use of alphanumeric data and specifically allows the manipulation of individual alphanumeric characters within a character string. Any of the individual characters in a character string can be extracted. Character strings may also be compared. In BASIC, alphanumeric data are known as non-numeric data.

VARIABLES A variable is referenced by a programmer-assigned name and may assume different values during program execution. In BASIC, variable names for numeric data may be denoted by a single letter of the alphabet or by a letter followed by a digit. Examples of BASIC variable names are

    X
    A
    B1
    Z9

Because all numeric data are treated as floating-point numbers, there is no distinction between variable names for numerical variables.

Non-numeric variables always have a $ as the second character of their name. Examples are

    A$
    B$
    H$

Character strings are stored in locations with non-numeric variable names. For example, A$ may contain the character string TIME represented in an alphanumeric code such as ASCII.

ARRAYS AND SUBSCRIPTS As in FORTRAN, there is a provision for one- or two-dimensional arrays. The length of the array must be declared by a DIM statement. For example,

    10   DIM A(100)

causes the allocation of 101 locations to an array named A. These 101 locations are identified as A(0), A(1), A(2), . . . , A(100). In FORTRAN, the procedure is slightly different since the first subscripted location is denoted as A(1).

Two-dimensional arrays are also permitted. For example, the DIM statement

    110   DIM B1(2,5)

will provide for 18 locations, beginning with B1(0,0). B1(1,4) refers to the location in row 1, column 4 of the array B1.

COMPUTATIONAL FACILITIES In FORTRAN, computational facilities are provided by the arithmetic statement. BASIC uses the same type of statement, but it is preceded by the word

LET.* For example, in FORTRAN we write

$$X = A + B*C - D$$

but in BASIC, we must write

$$122 \quad \text{LET } X = A + B*C - D.$$

A statement number must always be given in BASIC; it is optional in FORTRAN.

The right-hand side of the equals sign is called an *arithmetic expression.* It is formed by one or more variable names or subscripted array names, constants, parentheses, and symbols indicating arithmetic operations. These symbols are as follows:

FORTRAN SYMBOL	BASIC SYMBOL	MEANING
+	+	Addition
−	−	Subtraction
*	*	Multiplication
/	/	Division
**	↑	Exponentiation (raising to a power)

Examples of arithmetic statements in BASIC are

```
100   LET X(2) = (A1/B1) ↑ 2
110   LET W8 = (Z(B1) + A(60))/20.5 + X ↑ 5
120   LET S = S + T(J)
130   LET I = I + 1
```

PROGRAM LOOPS The FOR statement in BASIC is the equivalent of the DO statement in FORTRAN. An example of the FOR statement is

```
30   FOR M = 10 TO 20 STEP .1
      •
      •
      •
90   NEXT M
```

* Some BASIC compilers permit the word LET to be omitted.

Statement 30 controls the execution of all statements up to the statement NEXT M. This statement signals the end of the loop and causes the incrementation of M by the amount specified after STEP. In this case, M will be incremented by .1. If the word STEP is omitted, an increment of 1 will be assumed. When the value of M exceeds 20, the loop is terminated and the statement following statement 90 is executed.

BASIC also permits negative incrementation to be specified, as in the FOR statement below:

```
10   FOR N = 10 TO 5 STEP − 1
      •
      •
      •
80   NEXT N
```

In this example, N will be decremented by 1 until it is less than 5. The loop will be executed for N = 10, 9, 8, 7, 6, and 5, but not for N = 4. Note that ANSI FORTRAN does not allow negative decrements in the DO statements, although individual compilers may provide this capability. FOR loops can be nested; the rules for nesting are similar to those in FORTRAN.

THE IF. . . THEN STATEMENT The IF... THEN statement provides for the conditional transfer of control to a specified line number if a condition is true. The specified condition is written as a relational expression formed by two arithmetic expressions separated by one of the relational operators shown below:

OPERATOR	MEANING
=	Equal to
<	Less than
<=	Less than or equal to
>	Greater than
>=	Greater than or equal to
<>	Not equal to

The IF . . . THEN statement takes one of two forms:

n IF *relational expression* THEN *m*

n IF *relational expression* GO TO *m*

where *n* and *m* are line numbers. Some examples of IF . . . THEN statements are

```
400   IF z < 20 THEN 210
400   IF C ↑ 5 − D*A > 0 THEN 500
400   IF B$ = "No" THEN 55
400   IF A(20) <> 200 GO TO 75
```

Because all numerical variables are expressed as floating-point numbers, it is unwise to test a numerical variable for equality. The condition of equality may never occur. Therefore, the relational operator chosen should be either $<=$, $>=$, or $<>$ whenever equality will be tested. This warning does not apply to character strings that have *exact* representations and therefore may be tested for equality.

INPUT/OUTPUT STATEMENTS   BASIC provides for various capabilities for reading and writing data. For small amounts of data, the INPUT statement is placed within the program so that the user can input data directly during the execution of the program. The user may be seated at the console during program execution. This is in contrast to batch processing, where the user submits his job to the computer center and returns to his desk. The INPUT statement is written as follows:

n INPUT $v_1, v_2, \ldots, v_n$

where *n* is a line number and $v_1, v_2, \ldots, v_n$ are variable names. Some examples of INPUT statements are

```
58   INPUT A, B, C
80   INPUT N, R
```

An alternative way to input small amounts of data is to use the READ statement together with a DATA statement — for example,

```
50   READ A, X
55   DATA 6.12, 90.531
```

The READ statement obtains data for the variables A and X from the data supplied at statement 55. The value of A will become 6.12 and the value of X will become 90.531. No pause is necessary during program execution to request data from the user. The data is supplied within the program itself.

One or more DATA statements may be referenced by a single READ statement. For example, the statements

```
50   READ A, X
60   DATA 6.12
65   DATA 90.531
```

will cause A to be set to the first value given in the DATA statement at line 60. X will be set to 90.531, the value given in the second DATA statement. If not enough data values are found in the DATA statements, the program will then print

OUT OF DATA

To print small amounts of data at the user's terminal, the PRINT statement is used. A maximum of five values is printed on a line. Alphanumeric characters may be printed by placing the character strings within quote marks. If items are separated by semicolons, the resulting output will be closely packed. If no items are given, the PRINT statement will cause the output of a blank line. Some examples of PRINT statements are

```
40    PRINT A1, B1, C1, D(100), E
400   PRINT "INVENTORY REPORT"
80    PRINT X; Y; Z; I1; J; K
```

Some BASIC compilers allow the specification of the format of the printed line.

In addition to the entering of data and the printing of results at the user's terminal, BASIC provides for the reading and writing of data files stored either sequentially or in a random-access mode. Files are in either a binary or an ASCII mode—that is, a character mode. Files must be assigned names by the programmer. Most versions of BASIC require the activation of a file before data is read or written from it. In the General Electric version of BASIC, a FILES statement, such as

30 FILES OLDFILE

is required to activate (or open) a file. A *file designator,* which is a number from 1 to 8, is assigned by BASIC according to the order in which the files are activated. If the FILES statement for OLDFILE is the first FILES statement in the program, the file designator 1 will be automatically assigned to OLDFILE. ASCII files are referenced by a "#" preceding the file designator, while reference to a binary file requires only its file designator. A password may be required; if so, it is written following the file name —for example,

20 FILES ONE, PASS1; TWO, PASS2

When files are no longer needed, they are closed by placing an asterisk after the file designator in a FILE statement—for example,

600 FILE 1, "*"

Data from files are obtained by the use of a READ file statement. Each execution of the READ statement causes one data value or character string to be assigned to each variable in the input list. If the file is not depleted, the data pointer remains positioned after the last value read. If a string is matched to a variable that

expects a number, the execution of the program is terminated. For example, the statement

300 READ #2, A, B$, C

causes data to be read from the ASCII file #2 and stored in the variables named A, B$, and C. An example of a READ statement for a binary file is

400 READ: 2, X, Y, Z

A colon is necessary for reading a binary file.

Similarly, output is sent to a file by a WRITE file statement. The contents of the variables in the output list are written on the output file. Some examples are

600 WRITE #3, A, X, Z(100)	[for an ASCII file]
600 WRITE: 3, A, B, C, D, E, F, G	[for a binary file]

The provision for handling data files in BASIC is in no way comparable in flexibility to the provisions offered by COBOL.

CONTROL STATEMENTS A STOP statement indicates the logical end of a program. It is written as follows:

n STOP

where *n* is a line number. An END statement indicates the physical end of a program and must be assigned the highest line number of the program. It is written as follows:

n END

where *n* is a line number.

OTHER FEATURES OF BASIC BASIC provides for subroutines by means of the GOSUB statement. The GOSUB statement transfers control to a specified line number. The RETURN statement causes a subroutine to return control to the statement immediately following the GOSUB statement in the main program. An example is

- •
- •

25   GOSUB 200

- •
- •

```
200   LET X = Y ↑ 2 − W
210   IF X < 0 GO TO 213
211   X = X + Z
213   LET B = A*C
220   RETURN
```

The GOSUB statement causes control to be transferred to line 200. The subroutine is executed, and control is returned to the main program by means of the RETURN statement at line 220. Subroutines are typically placed at the end of the main program. Otherwise, provisions must be made to bypass the subroutines.

BASIC provides a standard set of built-in functions similar to that available in FORTRAN. A list of these functions is given in Table I–1. BASIC also offers a built-in set of matrix operations, all of which are prefixed with the word MAT. A list of these operations is shown in Table I–2.

CONTROL OF THE SOURCE-PROGRAM CODE   Because the BASIC user types the coding at a terminal, it was necessary to provide various ways to edit the lines composing the program. For example, it is possible to delete a particular statement or renumber all program statements by specifying an initial statement number and an increment for successive line numbers. When one is typing a line, the depression of the CTRL key and X at the same time causes the erasure of the last line typed. A back slash (/) is printed to indicate that the line will be ignored. The command LIST will cause the listing of the entire program and also the punching of a paper tape of the program on a teletype punch. Other special commands are also available to assist the programmer at the terminal.

Table I–1
Built-in Functions in BASIC

FUNCTION	DESCRIPTION
ABS(X)	Absolute value of X
EXP(X)	Exponentiation of X; that is, e^X
INT(X)	Integer portion of X
LOG(X)	Natural logarithm of X; that is, $\log_e X$
COM(X)[a]	Common logarithm of X; that is, $\log_{10} X$
RND(X)	Random number, range 0 to 1
SQR(X)	Square root of X
SIN(X)	Sine X (with X in radians)
COS(X)	Cosine X (with X in radians)
TAN(X)	Tangent X (with X in radians)
COT(X)	Cotangent X
ATN(X)	Arctangent X (with X in radians)
SGN(X)	Algebraic sign of X; $-1, 0, +1$

[a] Also written CLG(X) or LGT(X) in different computer systems.

Table I–2
Built-in Matrix Operations in BASIC

MATRIX OPERATION	EXAMPLE	MEANING
Addition	68 MAT A = B + C	The matrix A is the sum of matrices B and C.
Subtraction	90 MAT A = B − C	The matrix A is equal to the difference of matrix B minus matrix C.
Multiplication	100 MAT A = B*C	The matrix A is the product of matrix B times matrix C.
Scalar multiplication	110 MAT A = 6.5*C	The matrix A is the product of 6.5 and matrix C.
Transpose	120 MAT A = TRN(B)	The matrix A is the transpose of matrix C.
Inverse	130 MAT A = INV(B)	The matrix A is the inverse of matrix B.
Set to zeros	140 MAT A = ZER	The matrix A is cleared to all zeros.
Set to ones	150 MAT A = CON	The matrix A is set to all ones.
Identity matrix	160 MAT A = IDN	The matrix A is the identity matrix.

A FORTRAN program, on the other hand, is typically punched on cards; corrections to the program are accomplished by the removal or insertion of cards in the deck.

PRO's AND CON's OF BASIC

BASIC is a simple, easy-to-learn interactive programming language. It is limited in scope but still offers the power of the computer to the user. FORTRAN has more flexibility and enables the user to write programs with more computational complexity and data manipulation. BASIC does provide for character strings and relatively powerful file-handling capabilities. It does not have the documentation features intrinsic to COBOL, and it is not well suited for handling data-processing problems. It is preeminently a conversational programming language, and it deserves its popularity in that regard. It is especially desirable as a first computer language for students. The student using BASIC has quick access to the computer. Programming errors can be immediately corrected at the computer terminal. The student can speedily master BASIC and then go on to learn other programming languages as needed. BASIC appears to be an estimable programming language in many ways and will be in use for some time to come.

REFERENCES

Edwards, Perry, and Broadwell, Bruce. *Flowcharting and BASIC.* New York: Harcourt Brace Jovanovich, 1974.

Gruenberger, Fred. *Computing with the Basic Language.* San Francisco: Canfield Press, 1972.

Kemeny, John G., and Kurtz, Thomas E. *BASIC Programming.* New York: John Wiley & Sons, 1967.

Sammett, Jean E. *Programming Languages: History and Fundamentals.* Englewood Cliffs, N.J.: Prentice-Hall, 1969.

Singer, Bernard M. *Programming in BASIC with Applications.* New York: McGraw-Hill Book Co., 1973.

RPG II

There are several report generators available on different computers. In this appendix, we will discuss RPG II (Report Generator II), developed for the IBM System/3 computer. Report generators offer a means of processing input data, preparing reports, and producing output files. These types of programming languages are limited in flexibility compared to higher-level languages such as BASIC. In Jean Sammet's *Programming Languages* (Prentice-Hall, 1970), report generators are not considered to be programming languages, although the author does not demean their importance in any way. They can be most effective for handling many types of data-processing problems. Report generators are most useful in preparing reports but can be used to solve almost any type of problem with proper programming. Report generators have been available for many years but only recently achieved widespread usage.

The basic structure of most data-processing programs is as follows:

1. Read the input data files.
2. Process the data; that is, perform calculations or update fields in data records.
3. Write output data files.

Report generators provide for the definition of input and output data files and for the specification of the processing section of a program (step 2). A program in a higher-level language typically consists of a sequence of statements that define the format of the data files and specify the computational steps to be performed. A report generator uses a set of forms to provide this information. The format of the input data files, the output data files, and any printed output are described on special forms. The calculations to be performed are defined on a calculation-specification form. RPG II can be used to test values and, depending on the value, choose another path in a program. Because reports on data typically require totals of values, such as the total amount of inventory, RPG II especially provides for the accumulation of totals of specified data fields and the subsequent printing of these totals. The RPG II compiler interprets the contents of the specification forms, which are usually punched on cards, and produces an object program for execution on the computer. The basic flow of any RPG II program is shown in Figure II–1. In many ways, the design of report generators is based on the summary reports produced by punched-card equipment prior to the

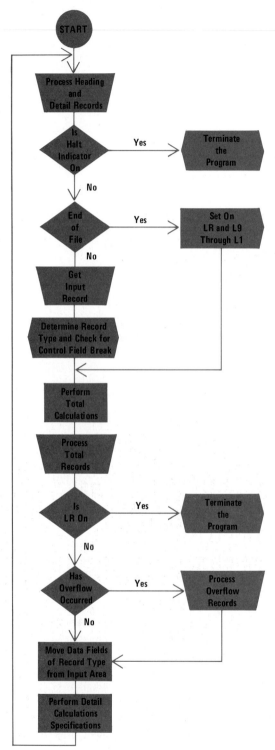

START

Process Heading
and
Detail Records

Is
Halt
Indicator
On → Yes → Terminate
the
Program

No

End
of
File → Yes → Set On
LR and L9
Through L1

No

Get
Input
Record

Determine Record
Type and Check for
Control Field Break

Perform
Total
Calculations

Process
Total
Records

Is
LR On → Yes → Terminate
the
Program

No

Has
Overflow
Occurred → Yes → Process
Overflow
Records

No

Move Data Fields
of Record Type
from Input Area

Perform Detail
Calculations
Specifications

introduction of computers for data processing. Now let us discuss a data-processing problem written in RPG II.

PROGRAMMING IN RPG II

This section will examine the printing of a simple report using RPG II.* In this example, only the basic cycles of input, calculation, and output will be illustrated. The problem is defined as follows:

Print a report listing all items sold during a week. The sale of an item is called a *transaction.* A file of transactions is accumulated during the business week. At the end of each day, the transaction records are punched in cards from the order forms received that day. The problem is to list the information from all input records on the printed report. We also wish to obtain the *extended cost* per item. This amount will be computed as the quantity sold times the item's price and will be obtained by the calculation specified in RPG II.

This problem can be broken down into four parts:

1. Specify all input and output files.
2. Describe the format of the input data records.
3. Calculate the extended cost per item.
4. Describe the format of the printed output.

These four parts correspond to the four types of RPG II specification forms. The input data file is given on punched cards. The format of the input card is shown in Figure II–2. Any input data is treated as a data file; for example, a deck of punched cards is a data file. Input data files may also be sorted on magnetic tape, drum, or disk and read as input.

* This example is taken from *Introduction to RPG II,* published by IBM in 1971.

Figure II–1
A Flow Chart of an RPG Job

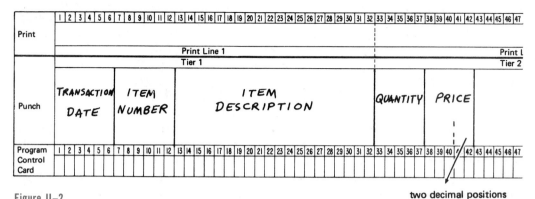

Print	1	2	3	4	5	6	7	8	9	10	11	12	13	14	15	16	17	18	19	20	21	22	23	24	25	26	27	28	29	30	31	32	33	34	35	36	37	38	39	40	41	42	43	44	45	46	47

Print Line 1 ... Print L

Tier 1 ... Tier 2

| Punch | TRANSACTION DATE | ITEM NUMBER | ITEM DESCRIPTION | QUANTITY | PRICE |

| Program Control Card | 1 | 2 | 3 | 4 | 5 | 6 | 7 | 8 | 9 | 10 | 11 | 12 | 13 | 14 | 15 | 16 | 17 | 18 | 19 | 20 | 21 | 22 | 23 | 24 | 25 | 26 | 27 | 28 | 29 | 30 | 31 | 32 | 33 | 34 | 35 | 36 | 37 | 38 | 39 | 40 | 41 | 42 | 43 | 44 | 45 | 46 | 47 |

two decimal positions

Figure II-2
Input Description for Problem

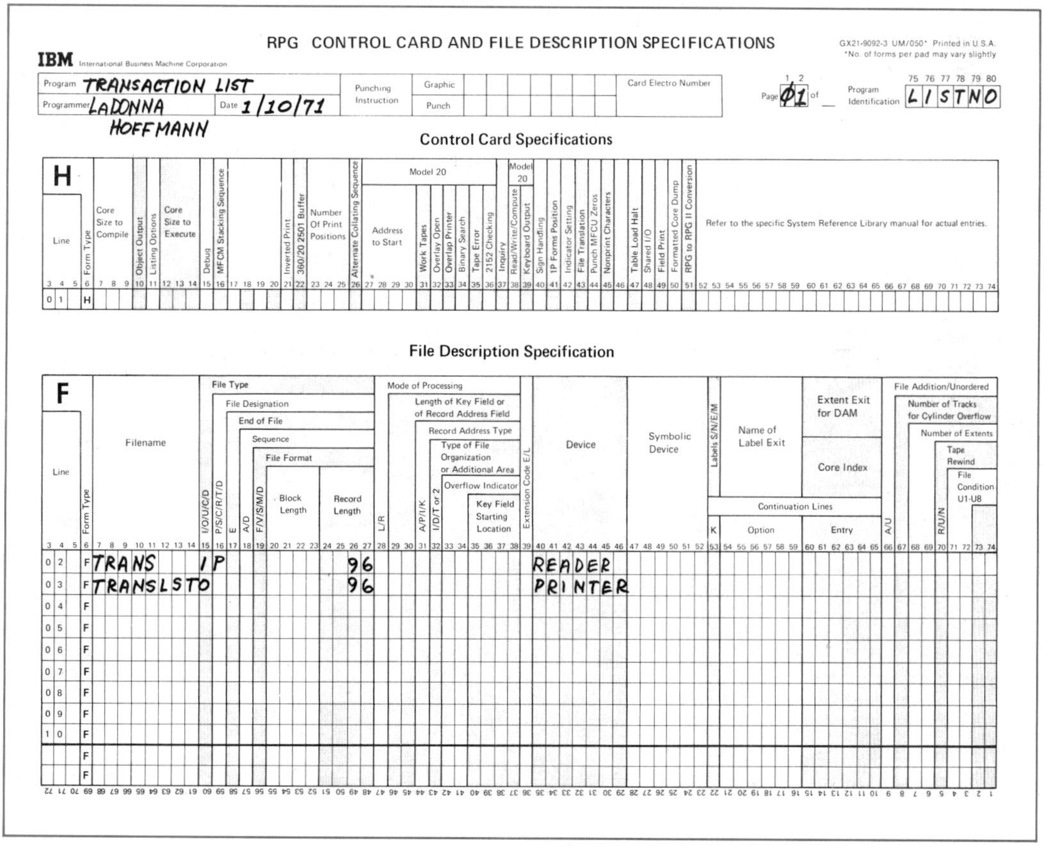

Figure II-3
Control Card and File Description

The RPG control card and file description specification form is shown in Figure II–3. Two files are listed. The input file is named TRANS and consists of 96-column cards. The file name is written in positions 7–14 and must begin with an alphabetic character. The symbol in column 15 indicates an input or output file. The letter I is given for the input file TRANS. The length of the record is 96 characters, and a 96 is placed in the rightmost positions of column 24–27 (that is, it is right justified). The input device for the

TRANS file is written in columns 40–46. The device used depends on the particular computer system. In this instance, it is a card reader. The second line provides information on the output file with the programmer-assigned name of TRANSLST). The letter O has been written in column 15 to indicate an output file. The figure for the length of the printer line (96 characters) is right justified in positions 24–27. The output device is a line printer.

Note that columns 1–5 have been used to indicate the page number and line number which serve as sequence numbers for the cards. If the cards are disarranged in any way, they can be easily reordered. Column 6 contains a character

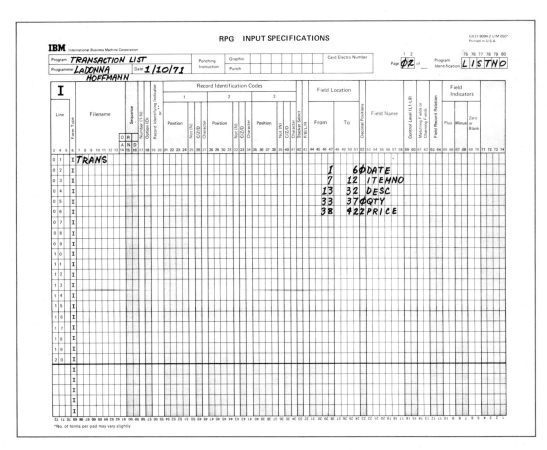

Figure II–4
Input Specifications

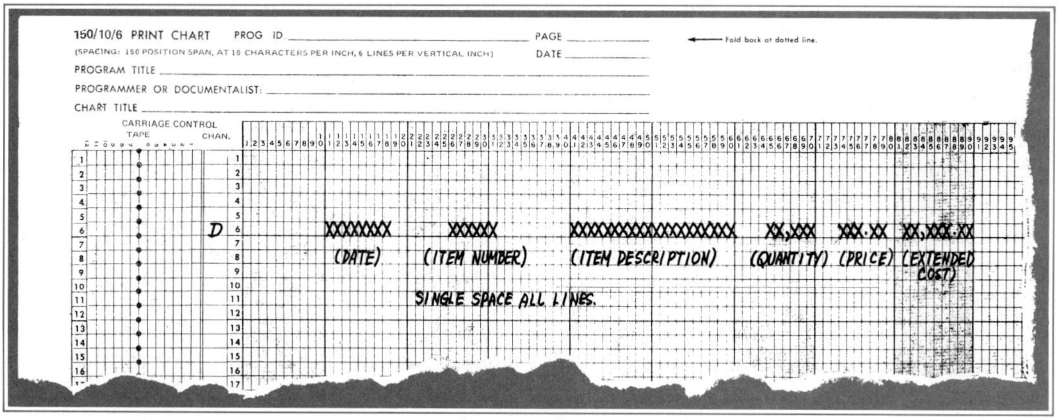

Figure II–5
Printer Layout

to indicate the card type. The file-description cards contain an F in column 6, while the input-specification cards have the letter I. This enables the compiler to interpret the contents of the cards. Columns 75–80 are used for a program identification to be assigned by the programmer.

The next specification form provides information on the format of the input records. (See Figure II–4.) In this example, we have only one input file. The file name is listed, left justified, in positions 7–14. Each field in the record is identified by name, and the beginning and ending positions of the field are listed. For example, the field identified by the name ITEMNO occupies six character positions in the record, beginning in position 7 and ending in position 12. Column 52 is used to indicate the type of data. If it is blank, the field is assumed to contain alphanumeric characters. If it contains a numeric, column 52 indicates the number of decimal digits to the right of the decimal point. Thus, the field PRICE has two decimal digits to the right of the decimal point.

The exact format of printed output is generally determined by the programmer with the aid of a printer spacing chart. The layout of the printed page in this example is illustrated on such a form in Figure II–5. After the exact format has been determined, the programmer completes the RPG form for output-format specifications, shown

in Figure II–6. Printed output is treated in the same manner as an output file. The file TRANSLSTD is given in columns 7–14. The field names are left justified in columns 32–37. Editing codes are written in column 38. The ending positions of each field are given in columns 40–43 (right justified). As before, the sequence of RPG cards is controlled by columns 1–5, with an O in column 6 indicating the output-specification cards.

The processing section of the program must compute the extended cost by multiplying the quantity (QTY) times the item price (PRICE). This computation is listed on the RPG form for calculation specifications shown in Figure II–7. The arithmetic operation denoted is MULT for multiplication. The resulting product, with a field length of seven and two decimal positions following the assumed decimal point, is stored in EXTCST. The field EXTCST is listed in the output specification as the last field on the printer line. A sample of printer output from this RPG II program is shown in Figure II–8.

FURTHER CAPABILITIES OF RPG II

The output in the example above is not really typical of data-processing jobs. A more likely output is shown in Figure II–9. The heading TRANSAC-TION REGISTER is given, plus individual headings for each column of data. Furthermore, the numeric values for extended costs have been summed during program execution and the total of 1,753.36 printed on the page. RPG II provides for this type of report by control-level indicators. Even more complex reports may be produced using RPG II. *Detail calculations* are the result of calculations for an individual input record. In our sample

problem, the value of the extended cost (EXTCST) for each input record is a detail calculation. It is printed on the same line as the detail data. Totals are calculated in response to control breaks or the finding of the last record on an input data file. The programming path is controlled by indicators. An indicator is set at the testing point and later used to determine the path of the program.

The testing of values of a field during program execution and the taking of an appropriate action are also provided for in RPG II. For example, it is possible to subtract the field ISSUES from RCPTS to obtain the current inventory. The inventory

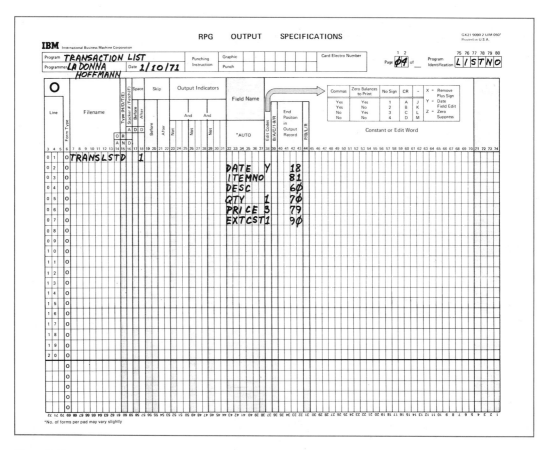

Figure II–6
Output Format

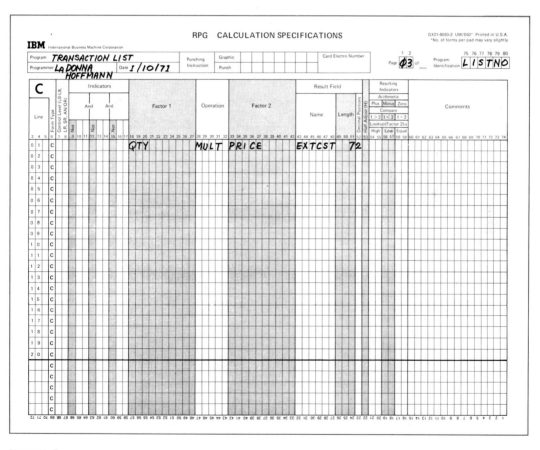

Figure II–7
Calculation Specifications

```
07/23/70    413010    CH001 BOX 100A FLUSH      10     4.90     49.00
07/23/70    412146    CH148 BREAKER 15A        100      .89     89.00
07/23/70    411116    1500 TWIN SOCKET B       500     1.12    560.00
07/24/70    503029    MOTOR 1/2 HP 60 CYC        2   146.78    293.56
07/24/70    317802    TERMINAL CLIP            100     5.12    512.00
07/24/70    326917    TERMINAL BAR             100     4.12    412.00
07/24/70    412997    CH173 BREAKER 30A         60     1.15     68.00
07/24/70    411121    1506 SOCKT ADAPT BRN     400      .19     76.00
07/24/70    413088    CH176 BREAKER 60A         40     1.15     46.00
07/24/70    411174    C151 SIL SWITCH BRN      200     1.16    232.00
07/24/70    413090    CH005 BR BOX 150A         10     4.98     49.80
07/24/70    718326    FC803 FUSE 15A           200      .32     64.00
```

Figure II–8
Printout of Results

```
                      TRANSACTION REGISTER

TRANSACTION    ITEM        DESCRIPTION         QUANTITY    UNIT    EXTENDED
   DATE        NO                                          COST      COST

07/23/70     413010   CH001 BOX 100A FLUSH       10      4.90      49.00
             412146   CH143 BREAKER 15A         100       .89      89.00
             411116   1500 TWIN SOCKET B        500      1.12     560.00

                                                                  698.00

07/24/70     503020   MOTOR 1/2 HP 60 CYC         2    146.78     293.56
             327802   TERMINAL CLIP             100      5.12     512.00
             326013   TERMINAL BAR              100


07/27/70     321071   2-SPEED SAW                 1     28.44      28.44
             325781   SATIN-CUT DADO SET          1     39.50      39.50
             412146   CH143 BREAKER 15A          50       .89      44.50
             573022   6-VOLT POWER BATTERY        2     14.45      28.90

                                                                  141.34


                                          WEEKLY TOTAL          9,573.49
```

Figure II–9
Adjusted Printout

amount is then tested to determine if reordering is necessary. If so, an appropriate message can be written out and a purchase order created on an output file. There are nine different indicators to allow as many as nine different totals to be accumulated by the program. The indicator LR is set when all input records are exhausted.

A complete range of editing possibilities is offered in printing numeric values. Commas may be inserted, a $ may be written, and the format of numeric values can be explicitly stated by the programmer by means of the editing options.

PRO'S AND CON'S OF RPG II

RPG II offers a means of quickly specifying the printing of reports and the simple processing of data files. The logic of handling the data records is expressed by coding the specification forms. In a sense, the program logic is concealed by this mode of expression. RPG II has a rigid format; it does not have all the capabilities of a higher-level language. However, it does effectively serve the small data-processing user. It provides a relatively easy way to specify data-processing prob- lems. It is popular because of its availability on small computers when COBOL is not provided or only a restricted subset of COBOL is available. Almost all standard data-processing jobs can be programmed in RPG II. Good documentation of the program logic can surmount the inherent disadvantage of coding all programming steps in an obscure shorthand notation.

REFERENCES

Brightman, Richard W., and Clark, John R. *RPG I and RPG II Programming: System/3 and System/360.* New York: Macmillan, 1970.

Gildersleeve, Thomas R. *Computer Data Processing and RPG Programming.* Englewood Cliffs, N.J.: Prentice-Hall, 1970.

IBM. *Introduction to RPG II.* White Plains, N.Y.: IBM, 1971.

Glossary[1]

* absolute address

A unique numerical designation given to each storage location within the computer's central memory.

access time

(1) The time interval between the instant at which *data* are called for from a *storage device* and the instant delivery begins.

(2) The time interval between the instant at which data are requested to be stored and the instant at which storage is started.

address

(1) An identification, as represented by a name, *label,* or number, for a *register,* location in *storage,* or any other *data* source or destination such as the location of a station in a communication network.

(2) Loosely, any part of an *instruction* that specifies the location of an *operand* for the instruction.

[1] All unmarked entries are reproduced with permission from the *American National Standard Vocabulary for Information Processing* X3.12—1970. Copyright © 1970 by American National Standards Institute, copies of which may be purchased from the American National Standards Institute at 1430 Broadway, New York, New York 10018.

ADP

Automatic Data Processing.

ALGOL

ALGOrithmic Language. A *language* primarily used to express *computer programs* by *algorithms.*

algorithm

A prescribed set of well-defined rules or *processes* for the solution of a problem in a finite number of steps, e.g., a full statement of an arithmetic procedure for evaluating sin x to a stated *precision.*

algorithmic language

A *language* designed for expressing *algorithms.*

alphameric

Same as *alphanumeric.*

alphanumeric

Pertaining to a *character set* that contains *letters, digits,* and usually other *characters* such as punctuation marks. Synonymous with alphameric.

alphanumeric character set

A *character set* that contains *letters, digits,* and usually other *characters.*

alphanumeric code

A *code* whose *code set* consists of *letters, digits,* and associated *special characters.*

analog

Pertaining to representation by means of continuously variable physical quantities.

analog computer

(1) A *computer* in which *analog* representation of *data* is mainly used.

(2) A computer that operates on analog data by performing physical processes on these data. Contrast with *digital computer.*

arithmetic unit

The unit of a computing system that contains the circuits that perform arithmetic *operations.*

artificial intelligence

The capability of a device to perform functions that are normally associated with human intelligence, such as reasoning, learning, and self-improvement. Related to *machine learning.*

ASCII (American National Standard Code for Information Interchange, X3.4 — 1968)

The standard *code,* using a coded *character set* consisting of 7-bit coded characters (8 bits including *parity check*), used for information interchange among *data processing systems,* communication systems, and associated equipment. The ASCII set consists of *control characters* and *graphic characters.* Synonymous with USASCII.

assemble

To prepare a *machine language program* from a symbolic language program by substituting *absolute operation codes* for symbolic operation codes and *absolute* or relocatable addresses for *symbolic addresses.*

assembler

A *computer program* that *assembles.*

automatic data processing

(1) *Data processing* largely performed by *automatic* means.

(2) By extension, the discipline which deals with methods and techniques related to data processing performed by automatic means.

(3) Pertaining to data processing equipment such as *electrical accounting machines* and *electronic data processing* equipment. Abbreviated ADP.

background processing

The *automatic* execution of lower priority *computer programs* when higher priority programs are not using the system resources. Contrast with *foreground processing.*

batch processing

(1) Pertaining to the technique of executing a set of *computer programs* such that each is completed before the next program of the set is started.

(2) Pertaining to the sequential input of *computer programs* or *data.*

(3) Loosely, the execution of *computer programs* serially.

*** binary digit**

The digits 0 or 1.

*** binary number**

A number in the number system base 2; that is, a string of binary digits.

*** bit**

A binary digit.

block

(1) A set of things, such as *words, characters,* or *digits* handled as a unit.

(2) A collection of contiguous *records* recorded as a unit. Blocks are separated by *block gaps* and each block may contain one or more records.

(3) A group of bits, or n-ary digits, *transmitted* as a unit. An encoding procedure is generally applied to the group of bits or n-ary digits for error-control purposes.

(4) A group of contiguous characters recorded as a unit.

*branch

A path in the program which is selected from two or more paths by a program instruction. "To branch" means to choose one of the available paths.

business data processing

(1) Use of *automatic data processing* in accounting or management.

(2) *Data processing* for business purposes, e.g., recording and summarizing the financial transactions of a business.

(3) Synonymous with administrative data processing.

byte

A sequence of adjacent *binary digits* operated upon as a unit and usually shorter than a *computer word.*

*card, punched

See punched card.

*card punch

A device connected to the computer for punching cards.

*card reader

A computer input device which reads punched cards.

*cathode ray tube

A device similar to a TV picture tube used for displaying alphanumeric characters and/or graphical information from a computer. Abbreviated CRT.

*central memory unit

The computer unit which contains instructions and data. To execute instructions or manipulate data, they must be contained in the central memory unit.

*central processing unit

The computer unit which performs the execution of instructions.

*character

A letter, number, or symbol.

*character code

A code designating a unique numerical representation for a set of characters.

character printer

A device that prints a single *character* at a time. Contrast with *line printer.*

character recognition

The identification of graphic, phonic, or other *characters* by *automatic* means. See *magnetic ink character recognition, optical character recognition.*

closed subroutine

A *subroutine* that can be stored at one place and can be linked to one or more calling *routines.* Contrast with *open subroutine.*

COBOL

(COmmon Business Oriented Language) A *business data processing* language.

code

(1) A set of unambiguous rules specifying the way in which *data* may be represented, e.g., the set of correspondences in the standard code for information interchange. Synonymous with coding scheme.

(2) In telecommunications, a system of rules and conventions according to which the *signals* representing *data* can be formed, transmitted, received, and processed.

(3) In *data processing,* to represent data or a *computer program* in a symbolic form that can be accepted by a *data processor.*

coder

A person mainly involved in writing but not designing *computer programs.*

collate

To combine *items* from two or more ordered sets into one set having a specified order not necessarily the same as any of the original sets.

collator

A device to *collate, merge,* or *match* sets of *punched cards* or other *documents.*

compile

To prepare a *machine language* program from a *computer program* written in another *programming language* by making use of the overall logic structure of the program, or generating more than one *machine instruction* for each symbolic *statement,* or both, as well as performing the function of an *assembler.*

compiler

A program that *compiles.*

complement

A *number* that can be derived from a specified number by subtracting it from a second specified number. The negative of a number is often represented by its complement.

computer

A *data processor* that can perform substantial computation, including numerous arithmetic or logic operations, without intervention by a human *operator* during the *run.*

computer code

A *machine code* for a specific *computer.*

computer instruction

A *machine instruction* for a specific *computer.*

computer program

A series of *instructions* or *statements,* in a form acceptable to a *computer,* prepared in order to achieve a certain result.

computer word

A sequence of *bits* or *characters* treated as a unit and capable of being *stored* in one *computer location.* Synonymous with machine word.

console

That part of a *computer* used for communication between the *operator* or *maintenance* engineer and the computer.

core

See *magnetic core.*

CPU

Central Processing Unit.

data

(1) A representation of facts, concepts, or *instructions* in a formalized manner suitable for communication, interpretation, or processing by humans or automatic means.

(2) Any representations such as *characters* or *analog* quantities to which meaning is or might be assigned.

data bank

A comprehensive collection of *libraries* of data. For example, one line of an invoice may form an *item,* a complete invoice may form a *record,* a complete *set* of such records may form a *file,* the collection of inventory control files may form a *library,* and the libraries used by an organization are known as its data bank.

debug

To detect, locate, and remove *mistakes* from a *routine* or *malfunctions* from a *computer.* Synonymous with trouble-shoot.

decision table

A *table* of all contingencies that are to be considered in the description of a problem, together with the actions to be taken. Decision tables are sometimes used in place of *flowcharts* for problem description and documentation.

digital computer

(1) A *computer* in which *discrete* representation of *data* is mainly used.

(2) A *computer* that operates on *discrete data* by performing arithmetic and logic processes on these data. Contrast with *analog computer.*

direct access

(1) Pertaining to the process of obtaining *data* from, or placing data into, *storage* where the time required for such access is independent of the *location* of the data most recently obtained or placed in storage.

(2) Pertaining to a *storage* device in which the *access time* is effectively independent of the location of the *data.*

(3) Synonymous with random access.

disc

Alternate spelling for *disk.* See *magnetic disk.*

disk

Alternate spelling for *disc.* See *magnetic disk.*

drum

See *magnetic drum.*

*EAM

Electronic accounting machines; more specifically, the punched card equipment — sorter, keypunch, lister, etc. — used to process cards containing information in contrast to processing on the computer.

EDP

Electronic Data Processing.

electronic data processing

(1) *Data processing* largely performed by electronic devices.

(2) Pertaining to *data processing* equipment that is predominantly electronic such as an electronic *digital computer.* Abbreviated EDP.

end-of-tape marker

A marker on a *magnetic tape* used to indicate the end of the permissible recording area, e.g., a photo reflective strip, a trans-

parent tape section, a particular bit pattern.

end of text character

A *communication control character* used to indicate the end of a *text.* Abbreviated ETX.

end of transmission block character

A *communication control character* used to indicate the end of a *block* of *data* where data are divided into blocks for *transmission* purposes. Abbreviated ETB.

end of transmission character

A *communication control character* used to indicate the conclusion of a *transmission* which may have included one or more *texts* and any associated *headings.* Abbreviated EOT.

field

In a *record,* a specified area used for a particular category of *data,* e.g., a group of card columns used to represent a wage rate, a set of *bit* locations in a *computer word* used to express the *address* of the *operand.*

file

A collection of related *records* treated as a unit. For example, one line of an invoice may form an *item,* a complete invoice may form a *record,* the complete set of such records may form a file, the collection of inventory control files may form a *library,* and the libraries used by an organization are known as its *data bank.*

file layout

The arrangement and structure of *data* in a *file,* including the *sequence* and size of its components. By extension, a file layout might be the description thereof.

file maintenance

The activity of keeping a *file* up to date by adding, changing, or deleting *data.*

flowchart

A graphical representation for the definition, analysis, or solution of a problem, in which *symbols* are used to represent *operations, data,* flow, equipment, etc.

flowchart symbol

A *symbol* used to represent *operations, data,* flow, or equipment on a *flowchart.*

foreground processing

The *automatic* execution of the *computer programs* that have been designed to preempt the use of the computing facilities. Usually a *real time* program. Contrast with *background processing.*

FORTRAN

(FORmula TRANslating system) A *language* primarily used to express *computer programs* by arithmetic formulas.

half duplex

In communications, pertaining to an alternate, one way at a time, independent transmission.

hardware

Physical equipment, as opposed to the *computer program* or method of use, e.g., mechanical, magnetic, electrical, or electronic devices. Contrast with *software.*

head

A device that *reads, writes,* or *erases data* on a storage *medium,* e.g., a small electromagnet used to read, write, or erase data on a *magnetic drum* or *tape,* or the set of perforating, reading, or marking devices used for punching, reading, or printing on paper tape.

*** hexadecimal**

Pertaining to the number representation system with a base of sixteen.

Hollerith

Pertaining to a particular type of *code* or *punched card* utilizing 12 *rows* per *column* and usually 80 columns per card.

identifier

A *symbol* whose purpose is to identify, indicate, or name a body of *data.*

input device

A device which enters data from a storage medium such as cards into the central memory of the computer.

input/output

Pertaining to either *input* or *output,* or both.

instruction

A *statement* that specifies an *operation* and the values or locations of its *operands.*

integrated data processing

Data processing in which the coordination of *data* acquisition and all other stages of data processing is achieved in a coherent system, e.g., a *business data processing* system in which data for orders and buying are combined to accomplish the functions of scheduling, invoicing, and accounting. Abbreviated IDP.

I/O

An abbreviation for *input/output.*

item

(1) In general, one member of a group, e.g., a *record* may contain a number of items such as *fields* or groups of fields; a *file* may consist of a number of items such as records; a *table* may consist of a number of items such as entries.

(2) A collection of related *characters,* treated as a unit.

job

A specified group of tasks prescribed as a unit of work for a *computer.* By extension, a job usually includes all necessary *computer programs, files,* and *instructions* to the *operating system.*

key

One or more *characters* within an *item* of *data* that are used to identify it or control its use.

keypunch

A keyboard actuated device that punches

holes in a card to represent *data.*

line printer

A device that prints all *characters* of a line as a unit. Contrast with *character printer.*

line printing

The printing of an entire line of characters as a unit.

logical record

A collection of *items* independent of their physical environment. Portions of the same logical *record* may be located in different physical records.

machine code

An *operation code* that a machine is designed to recognize.

machine instruction

An *instruction* that a machine can recognize and execute.

machine language

A *language* that is used directly by a machine.

magnetic card

A card with a magnetic surface on which *data* can be *stored* by selective magnetization of portions of the flat surface.

magnetic core

A configuration of magnetic material that is, or is intended to be, placed in a spatial relationship to current-carrying conductors and whose magnetic properties are essential to its use. It may be used to concentrate an induced magnetic field as in a transformer induction coil, or armature, to retain a magnetic polarization for the purpose of *storing* data, or for its nonlinear properties as in a *logic element.* It may be made of such material as iron, iron oxide, or ferrite and in such shapes as wires, tapes, toroids, rods, or thin film.

magnetic disk

A flat circular plate with a magnetic surface on which *data* can be *stored* by selective magnetization of portions of the flat surface.

magnetic drum

A right circular cylinder with a magnetic surface on which *data* can be *stored* by selective magnetization of portions of the curved surface.

magnetic ink

An ink that contains particles of a magnetic substance whose presence can be detected by magnetic sensors.

magnetic ink character recognition

The machine recognition of characters printed with magnetic ink. Contrast with *optical character recognition.* Abbreviated MICR.

magnetic storage

A *storage device* that utilizes the magnetic properties of materials to *store data,* e.g., *magnetic cores, tapes,* and *films.*

magnetic tape

(1) A tape with a magnetic surface on which *data* can be *stored* by selective polarization of portions of the surface.

(2) A tape of magnetic material used as the constituent in some forms of *magnetic cores.*

magnetic thin film

A layer of magnetic material, usually less than one micron thick, often used for logic or storage elements.

main frame

Same as *central processing unit.*

main storage

The general-purpose *storage* of a *computer.*

management information system

(1) Management performed with the aid of *automatic data processing.* Abbreviated MIS.

(2) An *information system* designed to aid in the performance of management *functions.*

mark sensing

The electrical sensing of manually recorded conductive marks on a nonconductive surface.

mass storage device

A device having a large *storage capacity*, e.g., *magnetic disk, magnetic drum*.

memory

Same as main *storage*.

MICR

Magnetic Ink Character Recognition.

* **microsecond**

one-millionth of a second.

* **millisecond**

one-thousandth of a second.

MIS

Management Information System.

mnemonic

See *mnemonic symbol*.

mnemonic symbol

A *symbol* chosen to assist the human memory, e.g., an abbreviation such as "mpy" for "multiply."

modem

(MOdulator-DEModulator) A device that modulates and demodulates signals transmitted over communication facilities.

multiplex

To *interleave* or simultaneously *transmit* two or more messages on a single *channel*.

multiprocessing

(1) Pertaining to the simultaneous execution of two or more *computer programs* or *sequences* of *instructions* by a *computer* or *computer network*.

(2) Loosely, *parallel processing*.

multiprocessor

A *computer* employing two or more processing units under integrated control.

multiprogramming

Pertaining to the *concurrent* execution of two or more *programs* by a *computer*.

non-return-to-zero recording

A method of recording in which the change between the state of magnetization representing either zero or one provides the reference condition. Abbreviated NRZ or NRZI.

object code

Output from a *compiler* or *assembler* which is itself executable *machine code* or is suitable for processing to produce executable machine code.

object program

A fully *compiled* or *assembled program* that is ready to be *loaded* into the *computer*. Contrast with *source program*.

OCR

Optical Character Recognition.

octal

Pertaining to the *number representation system* with a base of eight.

offline

Pertaining to equipment or devices not under control of the *central processing unit*.

offline storage

Storage not under control of the *central processing unit*.

online

(1) Pertaining to equipment or devices under control of the *central processing unit*.

(2) Pertaining to a user's ability to interact with a *computer*.

online storage

Storage under control of the *central processing unit*.

open subroutine

A *subroutine* that is inserted into a *routine* at each place it is used. Contrast with *closed subroutine*.

operand

That which is operated upon. An operand is usually identified by an *address part* of an *instruction*.

operating system

Software which controls the execution of *computer programs* and which may provide scheduling, *debugging,* input/output control, accounting, *compilation, storage* assignment, *data* management, and related services.

operation code

A *code* that represents specific operations to be performed by the computer.

optical character recognition

The machine identification of printed *characters* through use of light-sensitive devices. Contrast with *magnetic ink character recognition.* Abbreviated OCR.

optical scanner

(1) A device that scans optically and usually generates an *analog* or *digital signal.*

(2) A device that optically scans printed or written *data* and generates their *digital representations.*

*output device

A device which places data from the central memory onto a storage medium such as magnetic tape, punched, cards, etc.

*peripheral equipment

Input and output devices associated with the computer.

*PL/I

A programming language intended for writing both scientific and data processing programs.

*production run

The execution of a debugged program which routinely accomplishes the purposes of the program. For example, running a debugged payroll program to produce weekly paychecks is a production run.

program

(1) A series of actions proposed in order to achieve a certain result.

(2) Loosely, a *routine.*

(3) To design, write, and test a program as in (1).

(4) Loosely, to write a *routine.*

(5) See *computer program.*

programmer

A person mainly involved in designing, writing and testing *computer programs.*

programming

The design, the writing, and testing of a *program.*

programming language

A *language* used to prepare *computer* programs.

punched card

(1) A card *punched* with a pattern of holes to represent *data.*

(2) A card as in (1) before being *punched.*

punched tape

A tape on which a pattern of holes or cuts is used to represent *data.*

random access

Same as *direct access.*

*reading

The placing of data from a storage medium into the computer, that is, the inputting of data.

real time

(1) Pertaining to the actual time during which a physical *process* transpires.

(2) Pertaining to the performance of a computation during the actual time that the related physical *process* transpires, in order that results of the computation can be used in guiding the physical process.

real time input

Input data inserted into a *system* at the time of generation by another system.

real time output

Output data removed from a *system* at time of need by another system.

record

(1) A collection of related *items* of *data,* treated as a unit, for example, one line of an invoice may form a record; a complete set of such records may form a *file.*

(2) See *logical record, variable-length record.*

record layout

The arrangement and structure of *data* in a *record,* including the *sequence* and size of its components. By extension, a record layout might be the description thereof.

record length

A measure of the size of a *record,* usually specified in units such as *words* or *characters.*

*register

A device which can contain a computer word, character, or portion of a word. The register holds the information for manipulation by the computer. For example, the arthimetic section of a computer will contain one or more registers.

*remote terminal

A device for communicating with the computer which is located at a site physically remote from the computer itself.

routine

An ordered set of *instructions* that may have some general or frequent use.

run

A single, continuous peformance of a *computer program* or *routine.*

*software

(1) A set of computer programs, procedures, and possibly associated documentation concerned with the operation of a data processing system, for example, the operating system, compilers, and so on.

(2) The operating system.

(3) Any program.

sort

To order *items* into groups according to some definite rules.

sorter

A person, device, or *computer routine* that *sorts.*

source language

The *language* from which a *statement* is translated.

source program

A *computer program* written in a *source language.* Contrast with *object program.*

storage

(1) Pertaining to a device into which *data* can be entered, in which they can be held, and from which they can be retrieved at a later time.

(2) Loosely, any device that can *store data.*

(3) Synonymous with memory.

subroutine

(1) A *routine* that can be part of another routine.

(2) See *closed subroutine, open subroutine.*

*tape unit

A device which reads and writes magnetic tape.

telecommunications

Pertaining to the *transmission* of *signals* over long distances, such as by telegraph, radio, or television.

*time sharing

The use of a computer by more than one user at the same time. Each user interacts actively with the computer by use of a remote terminal.

transaction file

A *file* containing relatively transient *data* to be processed in combination with a *master file.* For example, in a payroll application, a transaction file indicating hours worked might be processed with a master file containing employee name and rate of pay.

utility routine

A *routine* in general support of the *operation* of a *computer*, e.g., an *input-output, diagnostic, tracing,* or *monitoring routine.*

variable-length record

Pertaining to a *file* in which the *records* are not uniform in length.

word

A *character string* or a *bit string* considered as an entity.

word length

A measure of the size of a *word*, usually specified in *units* such as *characters* or *binary digits.*

*writing

The transfer of data from the computer to an output device.

PICTURE CREDITS

Figures drawn by Fred Haynes

Boxed material appearing on pages 102, 132, 281, and 312-313 reprinted with permission from *Computers and People,* published by and © 1974 by Berkeley Enterprises, Inc., 815 Washington Street, Newtonville, Mass. 02160.

Index

D 8
E 9
F 0
G 1
H 2
I 3
J 4
7